Creative Imagination in the Ṣūfism of Ibn ʻArabī

The Image of the Kaʿaba

Miniature from Bibliothèque nationale, Paris, MS supplément persan 1389, sixteenth century

HENRY CORBIN

Creative Imagination in the Ṣūfism of Ibn ʻArabī

Translated from the French by
RALPH MANHEIM

ROUTLEDGE & KEGAN PAUL
LONDON

FIRST PUBLISHED IN ENGLAND
BY ROUTLEDGE & KEGAN PAUL LTD.
BROADWAY HOUSE, 68–74 CARTER LANE,
LONDON E.C. 4
1969

Published in French as
L'Imagination créatrice dans le Soufisme d'Ibn 'Arabî
Flammarion, Paris, 1958
Parts One and Two were originally published in French
(in slightly different form) in *Eranos-Jahrbücher*
XXIV (1955) and XXV (1956) by Rhein-Verlag, Zurich.

SBN 7100 2956 X
Printed in the United States of America
by Kingsport Press, Inc., Kingsport, Tennessee

Plates Printed by Meriden Gravure Co.,
Meriden, Connecticut

CONTENTS

Owing to production delays this book was published in 1970

CONTENTS

LIST OF PLATES

INTRODUCTION

1. *Between Andalusia and Iran: A Brief Spiritual Topography*

A more complete title for the present book would have been "Creative Imagination and Mystical Experience in the Ṣūfism of Ibn ʿArabī." An abbreviation, however, is permissible, since the mere word "Ṣūfism" suffices to place "Imagination" in our specific context. Here we shall not be dealing with imagination in the usual sense of the word: neither with fantasy, profane or otherwise, nor with the organ which produces imaginings identified with the unreal; nor shall we even be dealing exactly with what we look upon as the organ of esthetic creation. We shall be speaking of an absolutely basic function, correlated with a universe peculiar to it, a universe endowed with a perfectly "objective" existence and perceived precisely through the Imagination.

Today, with the help of phenomenology, we are able to examine the way in which man experiences his relationship to the world without reducing the objective data of this experience to data of sense perception or limiting the field of true and meaningful knowledge to the mere operations of the rational understanding. Freed from an old impasse, we have learned to register and to make use of the intentions implicit in all the acts of consciousness or transconsciousness. To say that the Imagination (or love, or sympathy, or any other sentiment) *induces knowledge,* and knowledge of an "object" which is proper to it, no longer smacks of paradox. Still, once the full noetic value of the Imagination is admitted, it may be advisable to free the intentions of the Imagination from the parentheses in which a purely phenomenological interpretation encloses them, if we wish, without fear or misunderstanding, to relate the imaginative function to the view of the world proposed by the Spiritualists to whose company the present book invites us.

For them the world is "objectively" and actually threefold:

between the universe that can be apprehended by pure intellectual perception (the universe of the Cherubic Intelligences) and the universe perceptible to the senses, there is an intermediate world, the world of Idea-Images, of archetypal figures, of subtile substances, of "immaterial matter." This world is as real and objective, as consistent and subsistent as the intelligible and sensible worlds; it is an intermediate universe "where the spiritual takes body and the body becomes spiritual," a world consisting of real matter and real extension, though by comparison to sensible, corruptible matter these are subtile and immaterial. The organ of this universe is the active Imagination; it is the *place* of theophanic visions, the scene on which visionary events and symbolic histories *appear* in their true reality. Here we shall have a good deal to say of this universe, but the word *imaginary* will never be used, because with its present ambiguity this word, by prejudging the reality attained or to be attained, betrays an inability to deal with this at once intermediate and intermediary world.

The two essays that make up the greater part of this book were originally given as lectures at two sessions (1955 and 1956) of the Eranos conference, at Ascona, Switzerland. They are complementary and pursue the same design. They do not claim to provide a monograph on Ibn ʿArabī. The time for an over-all interpretation is far off; countless preliminary studies will still be needed before we can hope to orient ourselves amid all the aspects of so colossal an opus, the work of a spiritual genius who was not only one of the greatest masters of Ṣūfism in Islam, but also one of the great mystics of all time.[1] It is not even our ambition to make a "contribution to the history of ideas." A thematization of this kind often tends to "explain" an author by tracing him back to his sources, by listing influences,

1. Such an orientation is indispensable to the progress of our knowledge concerning Ibn ʿArabī. See, in this connection, the comprehensive work by ʿOsmān Yaḥià, *L'Histoire et la classification des œuvres d'Ibn ʿArabī*. (For full bibliographical data on references, see the List of Works Cited.)

and demonstrating the "causes" of which he is supposedly the mere effect. In speaking of a genius as complex as Ibn ʿArabī, so radically alien to literal, dogmatic religion and to the schematizations such religion encourages, some writers have employed the word "syncretism." This is the summary, insidious, and facile kind of explanation that appeals to a dogmatic mind alarmed at the operations of a thinking which obeys only the imperatives of its internal norm but whose personal character does not impair its rigor. To content oneself with such an explanation is to confess one's failure, one's inability to gain so much as an intimation of this norm which cannot be reduced to a school or other collective conformism.

Ibn ʿArabī is one of those powerful and rare spiritual individuals who are the norm of their own orthodoxy and of their own time, because they belong neither to what is commonly called "their" time nor to the orthodoxy of "their" time. What by a historical convention is termed "their" time is not really *their* time. Accordingly, to affect to believe that such masters are nothing more than representatives of a certain "tradition" is to forget their considerable personal contribution, is to neglect the perfect assurance with which an Arab of Andalusia like Ibn ʿArabī, or Iranians like Abū Yaʿqūb Sejestānī (tenth century), Suhrawardī (twelfth century), Semnānī (fourteenth century), Mullā Ṣadrā of Shīrāz (seventeenth century) proclaim that such and such an idea, developed on such and such a page of their books, can be found nowhere else, because it is their discovery of their personal experience.

Our design is limited to meditating in depth, with the help of the texts themselves, on certain themes which run through the work as a whole. To our mind the best explanation of Ibn ʿArabī remains Ibn ʿArabī himself. The only means of understanding him is to become for a moment his disciple, to approach him as he himself approached many masters of Ṣūfism. What we have tried to do is to live his *spirituality* for a moment with him. And now we should like to communicate something of this spirituality as we have experienced it to those who are seeking along the same path. We have used the word *spirituality* by design, fully aware of how misplaced it may seem. It concerns the most secret and most profound life of the soul; but more often than not age-old habits make it impossible for us to dissociate this personal life from its social frame, lead us to regard it as dependent on the mediation of an "ecclesiastical reality"—so much so that detachment from this reality appears equivalent to the irrevocable loss of spirituality itself. To those who are unable to effect this dissociation, the spirituality of an Ibn ʿArabī will have little to say. To those who seek an encounter "alone with the Alone," those who are capable of being like him the "disciples of Khiḍr" and for whom no conformism prevails over the personal imperative—to those Ibn ʿArabī and his school will unquestionably have much to say.

It may also seem misplaced to speak of spirituality in a study of the Imagination. We shall try to show in what sense this Imagination is creative: because it is essentially the *active* Imagination and because its activity defines it essentially as a theophanic Imagination. It assumes an unparalleled function, so out of keeping with the inoffensive or pejorative view commonly taken of the "imagination," that we might have preferred to designate this Imagination by a neologism and have occasionally employed the term *Imaginatrix*. Here perhaps we should anticipate a question: Does not spirituality, does not mystical experience tend to cast off images, to forgo all representation of forms and figures? Yes indeed, some masters have sternly and implacably rejected all imaginative representation, all use of images. Here, however, we shall be dealing with an effort to utilize the image and the Imagination for spiritual experience. The inner, structural reasons for this will become apparent when we consider the themes themselves; they are already foreshadowed by the belief in the existence and ontological consistency of an intermediate world. But this belief in turn is embedded in other themes, which it has not been possible to analyze in the main body of this book, but some knowledge of which must be presupposed.

Such a presupposition is far from lightening our task. For it implies in the reader a knowledge of the context embracing not only the work of Ibn ʿArabī, but also his life, a life so intimately mingled with his work that the events of his inner experience are projected upon his work and in it raised to the level of symbols. The bibliography concerning Ibn ʿArabī in French and other European languages takes up no more than a few lines. Thus there is little reason to suppose that a reader unfamiliar with Arabic will possess the requisite minimum of information. Moreover, both the man and his doctrine have suffered numerous misunderstandings. The Ṣūfism of Ibn ʿArabī aroused alarm and indignation—and not only in Islam. If we set out to develop the idea, or to demonstrate the existence of an "orthodox Ṣūfism," we are in danger of being refuted and overwhelmed by the scope, the audacity, and the wide distribution of this incomparable mystical theosophy. If we try to reduce his doctrine to the categories of our Western philosophies (monism, pantheism, etc.), we run the risk of distorting its perspectives. As to whether a conciliation between mystical religion and legalist religion is thinkable, we shall have occasion to discuss later on. To raise the question is at the same time to inquire into the significance of Ṣūfism in Islam and consequently into the significance of its affinity with the other forms of mystical religion known elsewhere. But to do so it will be necessary to touch at least on certain things that happened in Islam in the medieval period when Islam and Christianity communicated their philosophies to one another. If we are to avoid an over-hasty use of the categories by which we characterize our own philosophical systems, if we are to grasp the unique conjunction between prophetic religion and mystical religion presented by Ṣūfism, we must briefly consider the thinkers and the ideas which provide Ibn ʿArabī and his school with their context.

But in the present state of our knowledge it is no simple

matter to give a clear account of them. In any event we must start by breaking with two old habits: we must cease to draw a dividing line between the history of philosophy and the history of spirituality, and we must discard the picture so long presented by our handbooks on the history of philosophy, which persist in confounding philosophy in Islam with "Arab philosophy" pure and simple and reduce the latter to five or six great names, those known to our Latin scholastics. The context we are trying to delimit is infinitely larger and has nothing in common with this threadbare simplification. It was long a commonplace to suppose that the critique of the theologian al-Ghazālī was the death blow to "Arab philosophy," and that with Averroes, the great philosopher of Cordova, the same Averroes who expressed his eagerness to meet the young Ibn ʿArabī, it attained at once its apogee and its end. This may have been the case if we consider only the destinies of philosophy in Western, if not in all Sunnite Islam, but it would be absurd to identify the entire fate of philosophical thought in Islam with this struggle, however moving, between Ghazālī the theologian and the Andalusian philosopher who claimed, with perfect sincerity, to be nothing more than the pure interpreter of Aristotle. Or rather we should say that this is the view taken in the West, because the Occidentals who had witnessed the disappearance of Avicennism beneath the rising tide of Averroism failed even to suspect that Avicennism had continued to thrive at the other end of the Islamic world, in Iran. Seen from Iran, the situation takes on an entirely different aspect. Here no trace remained either of al-Ghazālī's "destruction of the philosophers," of Averroes' restoration of Aristotelianism, or even of the rearguard action in which the philosopher of Cordova disclosed his readiness to sacrifice Avicenna to the theologian of Islam in order to save at least the peripatetic philosophy. The event which followed the system of Avicenna was not the destruction of his Neoplatonism by the Aristotelian Averroes but the inauguration by Suhrawardī (d. 587/1191) of the theosophy of Light (*ḥikmat al-Ishrāq*) as

"Oriental wisdom." The determining influence on Ṣūfism and spirituality was not Ghazālī's pious agnostic critique, but the esoteric doctrine of Ibn ʿArabī and his school.

Furthermore, the spiritual ferment arising from the coalescence of these two schools, that of Suhrawardī's *Ishrāq* and that of Ibn ʿArabī, created a situation which lent crucial importance to the relations between Ṣūfism and Shīʿism. The significance of both these currents in Islam was clarified, the one throwing light on the other. We shall see that the genealogies of the various branches of Ṣūfism lead back to one or the other of the Holy Imāms of Shīʿism, principally to the Sixth Imām, Jaʿfar al-Ṣādiq (d. 148/765) or the Eighth Imām ʿAlī Riḍā (d. 203/819). This return of Shīʿism to the spiritual horizon prepared the way for a new answer to the question raised by the presence of Ṣūfism in Islam, by the Ṣūfī interpretation of Islam; it led to a situation which, though almost entirely disregarded in the West today, might radically change the conditions of dialogue between Islam and Christianity, provided the interlocutors were Spirituals. Related to this context, the triumph of Averroism in the West and Ibn ʿArabī's removal to the Orient are two events to which we shall here attach a symbolic significance.

Can this brief sketch stand by itself, or does it not call for a minimum of detail showing why the events of Ibn ʿArabī's biography can be taken as exemplary events? Without such an explanation this book as a whole might seem obscure.

We have just referred to a phenomenon of coalescence between the esoteric doctrine of Ibn ʿArabī and Suhrawardī's theosophy of Light; a similar coalescence occurred between the latter and Avicennism. The whole gives its coloration to the Shīʿite Ishrāqī Avicennism professed by the school of Ispahān at the time of the Ṣafavid renaissance. And it is this totality that we must bear in mind if we are either to appreciate the original consonances of Ibn ʿArabī's work with Shīʿism in general or with Ismailian Shīʿism in particular or to understand the determining influence of Ibn ʿArabī on the subsequent development of Duodeciman Shīʿite gnosis in Iran. It must also be borne in mind if we are to appreciate, by contrast, these two concomitant facts: the collapse of Latin Avicennism under the violent criticism of the orthodox Scholastics and the rise of Latin Averroism, an ambiguous body of thought, from which both the currents of late theological Scholasticism down to the seventeenth century and the "impiety" of the philosophers hostile to Scholasticism and the Church were to draw nourishment.

Very briefly we may say that it was the Neoplatonic angelology of Avicenna, with the cosmology attaching to it and above all the anthropology it implies, which provoked alarm among the doctors of medieval Scholasticism and prevented them from assimilating Avicennism. In the present context of course it will not be possible to describe the Avicennan system as a whole.[2] We shall speak chiefly of the Figure which dominates its noetics, that of the "Active (or agent) Intelligence," that "Angel of humanity," as Suhrawardī was to call it, whose importance resides in its determining function for the Avicennan anthropology, the Avicennan conception of the human individual. Avicennism identifies it with the Holy Spirit, that is, with the Angel Gabriel as the Angel of Knowledge and of Revelation. Far from regarding this Figure, as has sometimes been done, as a rationalization, a reduction of the Spirit to the intellect, we, quite on the contrary, look upon it as the very foundation of the *prophetic philosophy* which plays so important a role among the followers of Avicenna, and which is intimately related to the spiritual existence on which we shall here be meditating.

This Intelligence is the tenth in the hierarchy of the Cherubim or pure separate Intelligences (*Angeli intellectuales*), and this hierarchy is paralleled by the secondary hierarchy of the Angels

2. We shall content ourselves with referring the reader to our *Avicenna and the Visionary Recital* and our *Histoire de la philosophie islamique*, pp. 235 ff. and 334 ff.

who are the Souls which move the celestial Spheres; at every degree of these hierarchies, at every resting place in the descent of being, couples or *syzygiai* are formed between them. Since these Angel-Souls (*Animae coelestes*) communicate to the Heavens the movement of their desire, the orbits of the heavenly bodies are characterized by an aspiration of love forever renewed and forever unstilled. At the same time these "celestial Souls," exempt from sense perception and its deficiencies, possess Imagination; they are indeed Imagination in its pure state since they are freed from the infirmities of sense perception. They are par excellence the Angels of this intermediate world where prophetic inspiration and theophanic visions have their place; their world is the world of symbols and of symbolic knowledge, the world to which Ibn 'Arabī penetrated with ease from his earliest years. Thus we can easily surmise the grave consequences that would result from their elimination in the cosmology of Averroes. As to the Intelligence, or Holy Spirit, it is the source from which our souls emanate, the source at once of their existence and of their light. All knowledge and all reminiscence are a light projected by the Intelligence upon the soul. Through the Intelligence the human individual is attached directly to the celestial pleroma without the mediation of any magistery or ecclesiastical reality. This no doubt is what inspired the anti-Avicennan Scholastics with their "fear of the Angel." This fear had the effect of utterly obscuring the symbolic significance of such recitals of initiation as those of Avicenna or of Suhrawardī or of the mystical romances which are so plentiful in Persian literature. For fear of the Angel the anti-Avicennans saw nothing more than inoffensive allegories in these recitals. The human soul, whose initiation the recitals "image," has itself the structure of a pair, formed of the practical intellect and the contemplative intellect. In its superior state, the state of intimacy with the Angel of Knowledge and Revelation, the second of these "terrestrial angels," the contemplative intellect, is qualified as *intellectus sanctus* and prophetic spirit.

Thus taken as a whole, the Avicennan angelology provides the foundation of the intermediate world of pure Imagination; it made possible the prophetic psychology on which rested the spirit of symbolic exegesis, the spiritual understanding of Revelations, in short, the *ta'wīl* which was equally fundamental to Ṣūfism and to Shīʿism (etymologically the "carrying back" of a thing to its principle, of a symbol to what it symbolizes). This Avicennan angelology provides a secure foundation for the radical autonomy of the individual, not in what we should simply call a philosophy of the Spirit but in a theosophy of the Holy Spirit. It is not in the least surprising that all this should have alarmed the orthodox; what Etienne Gilson brilliantly analyzed as an "Augustinism tinged with Avicennism" bears only the remotest resemblance to pure Avicennism.

With Averroes the situation and doctrine change completely. Averroes wished to restore authentic Aristotelianism and severely criticized the Neoplatonism of Avicenna. He rejected Emanation because he regarded Emanationism as crypto-creationism and as a Peripatetic had no use for the idea of creation. In addition to the active Intelligence, which is separate and unique, he (unlike Alexander of Aphrodisias) accepts the existence of a human intelligence independent of the organic world, but this intelligence is not the individual. The individual is identified with the perishable; what can become eternal in the individual pertains exclusively to the separate and unique active Intelligence. It will be worthwhile, at some future date, to reconsider the doctrine of the *intellectus materialis* on the strength of what we have learned from recently published Ismailian texts, which throw an entirely new light on it. But even now it can be stated that this doctrine is far removed from the sense of imperishable individuality which the Avicennan philosopher or Spiritual derives from the mere fact of his conjunction with the active Intelligence; and still farther perhaps from the eternal hexeity, the absolute individual, of Ibn ʿArabī. And no less important: in his striving to be strictly faithful to peripateticism, Averroes excludes from his cosmology the entire second angelic hierarchy, that of the celestial Angel-Souls, governing the world of the active Imagination or Imagination of desire, the world which is the scene of visionary events, of symbolic visions, and of the archetypal persons to whom the esoteric meaning of Revelation refers. The magnitude of the loss becomes apparent when we consider that this intermediate world is the realm where the conflict which split the Occident, the conflict between theology and philosophy, between faith and knowledge, between symbol and history, is resolved. The development of Averroism with its inherent ambiguity was to exacerbate this conflict.

This ambiguity extends to our own time. Renan looked upon Averroes as a hero of free thought, the source of every kind of impiety. By reaction other interpretations tend to make him a theologian, to bring him back into the bosom of orthodox Islam. Perhaps both parties have neglected to consider an essential point of his doctrine in the context with which we shall here be concerned. True, Averroes was inspired by the idea that all minds have not the same degree of discernment: to some men the literal aspect, the *ẓāhir*, is addressed, while others are capable of understanding the hidden meaning, the *bāṭin*. He knew that if what only the latter can understand were revealed to the former, the result would be psychoses and social disasters. All this is close to the "discipline of the arcanum" practiced in Ismailian Gnosis, and to the idea of the *ta'wīl* professed in Ṣūfism. What is forgotten is that the *ta'wīl* was not the invention of Averroes, and that to understand the way he makes use of it we must understand the way in which it is handled by the true Esoterics. The *ta'wīl* is essential symbolic understanding, the transmutation of everything visible into symbols, the intuition of an essence or person in an Image which partakes neither of universal logic nor of sense perception, and which is the only means of signifying what is to be signified. And we have just called attention to the metaphysical tragedy involved, from this point of view, in the disappearance of the world of the celestial Souls, the world of correspondences and substantive Images, whose specific organ of knowledge was the active Imagination. How, in the absence of this world, are we to apprehend symbols and carry out a symbolic exegesis?

At this point we must recapitulate the distinction, fundamental for us, between allegory and symbol; allegory is a rational operation, implying no transition either to a new plane of being or to a new depth of consciousness; it is a figuration, at an identical level of consciousness, of what might very well be known in a different way. The symbol announces a plane of consciousness distinct from that of rational evidence; it is the "cipher" of a mystery, the only means of saying something that cannot be apprehended in any other way; a symbol is never "explained" once and for all, but must be deciphered over and over again, just as a musical score is never deciphered once and for all, but calls for ever new execution. For this reason it will be necessary to undertake a comparative study of the *ta'wīl*, to measure the difference between the way in which it is conceived and practiced by Averroes and the way in which Shī ʻism and all spiritual movements deriving from it, ground their attitude toward prophetic Revelation, which is to say their striving to accomplish it, in the *ta'wīl*. Beneath figures and events, for example, the Shīʻite *ta'wīl* distinguishes references to earthly persons who exemplify celestial archetypes. It will be necessary to ascertain whether an Averroist *ta'wīl* still perceives symbols, or merely elaborates a rational, metaphysically inoffensive allegory.

At this very point an analysis discloses the most significant contrasts. The *ta'wīl* presupposes a flowering of symbols and hence the active Imagination, the organ which at once produces symbols and apprehends them; it presupposes the angelic world intermediate between the pure Cherubic intelligences and the universe of sensory, historical, and juridical facts. By its very essence the *ta'wīl* cannot inhabit the realm of everyday fact; it postulates an esoterism. Either the human community must offer a structure in which esoterism is an organic component; or else it must suffer all the consequences implied by a rejection of esoterism. There is a common ground between the ancient mystery religions, whose adepts are initiated into a mystery, and the initiatory brotherhoods within the revealed religions, whose adepts are initiated into a gnosis. But these adepts differ in status. In its official historical form neither Christianity nor Islam is an initiatory religion. But there is an initiatory version of these religions, a Christian as well as an Islamic gnosis. Nevertheless the questions remains: whether and to what extent do the fundamental dogmas of these religions justify or negate, necessitate or contradict the function of gnosis? Does the official doctrine of the Incarnation, for example, tie in with the historical consciousness of Christianity, or does it derive its true meaning from gnosis; does the prophetism essential to Islam call for a gnosis, because the truth of the Book postulates a prophetic hermeneutics, or does it exclude gnosis? There is also a question of fact which merits close investigation, namely, the comparative destinies of gnosis in Islam and in Christianity. We can perfectly well conceive of a metahistorical dialogue between the Basra "Brethren of Purity," an association with Ismailian connections, and the Rosicrucians of Johann Valentin Andreae; they would have understood each other perfectly. But the question remains: Was there in Christianity a phenomenon comparable to Ismailian Gnosis in Islam? Or at what date did such a phenomenon become impossible? There were in the Christian world Spirituals comparable to Ibn 'Arabī: did they exert a comparable influence? Is there in the Christian world a phenomenon comparable in scope and depth to Ṣūfism?—and here I am thinking first and foremost of Iranian Ṣūfism. Christian monasticism has been mentioned, but such facile comparisons must be approached with caution; the phenomena are profoundly different. One may think of a Third Order or of a Lodge. But Ṣūfism is neither one nor the other.

An excellent introduction to these questions will assuredly be provided by comparison of two trends: that typefied in the West by the rejection of Avicennism and the triumph of Averroism; and the contrasting trend represented in the Orient by the spread of the gnoses of the *Ishrāq*, of Shīʿism and of Ibn ʿArabī. The phenomenon of the "Church" as established in the West, with its Magistery, its dogmas, and its Councils, is incompatible with the recognition of initiatory brotherhoods. This phenomenon has no equivalent in Islam. Nevertheless there was a clash between official Islam and the initiatory movements. It would be worth while to study in both spheres how the refusal of all the spiritual forms that can be designated by the term initiationism or esoterism marks the starting point of laicization and socialization. Like that of Christianity, the situation of Islam today cannot be understood in depth if this essential fact is disregarded.

This laicization or secularization goes far deeper than the separation or non-separation of the "temporal power" and the "spiritual power"; rather, it is the secularization which causes the question to be raised and to persist regardless of the solution adopted, for the very idea of associating such concepts as "power" and the "spiritual" implies an initial secularization. From this point of view the passing triumph of Ismailism under the Fātimids was unquestionably a success from the standpoint of political history; from the standpoint of initiatory religion it could only be a paradox. Shīʿite esoterism implies an invisible mystical hierarchy; its most profoundly characteristic idea is that of the occultation (*ghayba*) or absence of the Imām. And perhaps the idea of this pure mystical hierarchy in the doctrine of Ibn ʿArabī and in Ṣūfism in general bears the original imprint of Shīʿism. It is still very much alive in the Shaikhism of Iran. A comparison of this development with the development of

Averroism into political Averroism as represented for example by Marsilius of Padua (fourteenth century) suffices to show the differences. But the radical secularization disclosed in the work of Marsilius was possible only because Marsilius had before his eyes something capable of being laicized, namely, the reality of power to which the priesthood lays claim but ultimately fails to obtain, whereupon it projects a fiction of that same power into the realm of the supernatural. Another striking aspect of the ambiguity to which we have already referred is to be found in the fact that in the school of Padua Averroism became, and remained until the seventeenth century, at once a refuge of rationalistic thinkers and a fountainhead of late Scholasticism. And yet the exponents of both these currents would have been unable to understand either the spirituality of an Ibn ʿArabī or Imāmology, that is, the *walāya* or spiritual ministry of the Imām and his followers, the source of initiation into the esoteric meaning, the gnosis of the Revelations.

To say that laicization begins with the elimination of gnosis is to consider the phenomenon of essential *desecration*, a metaphysical decline of the *sacred,* which no canon law either codifies or compensates. This process of desecration begins with the individual, whom it strikes in his innermost depths. Averroism denies the human individual as such any possibility of becoming eternal. In his radical answer to the problem of the intellects, St. Thomas grants the individual an "active intellect," but not a separate intellect; the intellect of the individual is no longer a transcendent or celestial Intelligence. This seemingly technical solution implies a fundamental decision, the decision to do away with the transcendent dimension of the individual as such, that is, his immediate and personal relationship with the Angel of Knowledge and of Revelation. Or rather, if such a decision was inevitable, it is because the individual's relationship with the divine world depends on the Magistery, that is, on the Church as mediatrix of Revelation. The paradox is only apparent if what appears to insure the noetic autonomy of the individual goes hand in hand with a socialization. This alienation of the individual's transcendent dimension was ineluctable, because the problem raised by the symptomatic problem of the intellects (beneath its seeming technical barrenness), namely, the problem of the intellectual autonomy of the individual, called for a solution which was neither the unique Intelligence of Averroism nor an active intellect which is merely immanent in the individual, but something of which the *Fedeli d'amore* were clearly aware when in their sophiology they designated the Active Intelligence as *Madonna Intelligenza.* Madonna Intelligenza was the separate active Intelligence of every spiritual individual, his Holy Spirit, his personal Lord and direct bond with the pleroma. This same figure can be identified under various names and our Spirituals searched for it by itineraries that are no less various. In the following we shall indicate its recurrences in Abu'l-Barakāt, in Suhrawardī, and in Ibn ʿArabī. Unfortunately, once the religious norm is socialized, "incarnated" in an ecclesiastical reality, rebellions of the spirit and the soul will inevitably be directed against it. But, preserved as an inner personal norm, it becomes identified with free flight of the individual. In the opposition which led to the failure of Latin Avicennism and concomitantly of other religious movements in the twelfth and thirteenth centuries, it is possible to discern the same causes as those which motivated the efforts of the Great Church in the first centuries of our era to do away with gnosis. But this elimination of gnosis foreshadowed the victory of Averroism with all its implications.

Very different is the situation in the Orient, resulting in particular from the influence of the two masters whose names have here been associated, not because they make it unnecessary to mention others, but because they are the most typical: the young Iranian master Shihābuddīn Yaḥyā Suhrawardī (1155–1191) and the Andalusian master Ibn ʿArabī (1165–1240), the compatriot of Averroes, who at the age of thirty-six (the same age at which Suhrawardī attained to the "Orient of the soul") resolved to set out for the Orient, never to return. The situation is so completely different that it inevitably goes beyond the schematic notion of "Arab philosophy" with which Western thinkers have too long contented themselves. Of course one can justifiably speak of "Arab" philosophy just as one can speak of "Latin" Scholasticism. But what justification has the term when our history of philosophy and spirituality comes to include Iranian authors who left essential works and wrote only in Persian?—such men as Nāṣir-e Khusraw (eleventh century), ʿAzīzuddīn Nasafī (twelfth-thirteenth centuries), Afzāluddīn Kāshānī, a contemporary of the great Shīʿite philosopher Naṣīruddīn Ṭūsī (thirteenth century), quite apart from the fact that Avicenna himself was an Iranian who wrote Persian as well as Arabic. Then it becomes not only inadequate, but positively misleading to speak of "Arab philosophy." These men exerted an influence chiefly on non-Arabic Islam and moreover their thinking, associated in one way or another with Shīʿism, throws an entirely new light on the significance of Ṣūfism in Islam. Here I am not questioning the pre-eminence of Koranic Arabic in liturgy and theology; on the contrary, there is every reason to stress the grandeur of the term "Arab" when it is associated with investiture with the prophetic mission. But it must be acknowledged that today the concept of the prophetic mission is undergoing a laicization with predictable effects. To continue to employ the term employed by the Scholastics because they were unable to draw the ethnic distinctions that are inescapable today would be to encourage disastrous confusion.

Suhrawardī died a martyr at the age of thirty-eight in Aleppo, whither he had rashly journeyed (1191), a victim of the rabid intolerance of the doctors of the Law and of Ṣalāḥaddīn, the fanatic known to the Crusaders as Saladin. Though his life was cut off too soon, he succeeded in carrying out a great design: in reviving in Iran the wisdom of the ancient Persians, their doctrine of Light and Darkness. The result was the philosophy, or rather, to take the Arabic term in its etymological sense, the "theosophy of Light" (*ḥikmat al-Ishrāq*) to which we find parallels in many pages of the work of Ibn ʿArabī. In accomplishing this great design, Suhrawardī was conscious of establishing the "Oriental wisdom" to which Avicenna too had aspired and knowledge of which reached Roger Bacon in the thirteenth century. But of this work of Avicenna only fragments remain, and Suhrawardī was of the opinion that because Avicenna was without knowledge of the sources of ancient Iranian wisdom, he had been unable to complete his project. The effects of Suhrawardī's theosophy of Light have been felt in Iran down to our own time. One of its essential features is that it makes philosophy and mystical experience inseparable: a philosophy that does not culminate in a metaphysic of ecstasy is vain speculation; a mystical experience that is not grounded on a sound philosophical education is in danger of degenerating and going astray.

This element in itself would suffice to place Suhrawardī and Ibn ʿArabī in the same spiritual family. It situates this theosophy on a spiritual plane higher than the rational plane on which the relations between theology and philosophy, belief and knowledge, are ordinarily discussed. The controversy concerning these relations, so characteristic of postmedieval Western philosophy, has its sources in the situation briefly analyzed above. Actually, Suhrawardī deals not with a problem but with an imperative of the soul: the fusion of philosophy and spirituality. The ecstatic heroes of this "Oriental theosophy" of Light are Plato, Hermes, Kay-Khusraw, Zarathustra, Muḥammad: the Iranian prophet and the Arab prophet. By the conjunction of Plato and Zarathustra (Zoroaster) Suhrawardī expresses a characteristic intention of the Iranian philosophy of the twelfth century, which thus anticipates by some three centuries the thinking of the famous Byzantine philosopher Gemistos Pletho. In contradistinction to the Peripatetics, the Ishrāqīyūn, the disciples of Suhrawardī, are designated as "Platonists" (*Aṣḥāb*

Aflaṭūn). Ibn ʿArabī was to be surnamed the Platonist, the "son of Plato" (*Ibn Aflaṭūn*). This clarifies certain co-ordinates of the spiritual topography which we are here trying to establish. Anticipating the projects of Gemistos Pletho and Marsilio Ficino, this oriental Platonism, this Zoroastrian Neoplatonism of Iran escaped the rising tide of Aristotelianism which invaded the Latin Middle Ages and for several centuries determined not only their philosophy but also their world feeling. Accordingly, when in Cordova the young Ibn ʿArabī attended the funeral of Averroes, the great master of medieval Aristotelianism, the melancholy scene becomes transfigured into a symbol which we shall do well to consider attentively.

Such resurgences of Platonism point up the contrast: in the West, the defeat of Latin Avicennism, overwhelmed first by the attacks of the pious Guillaume d'Auvergne, bishop of Paris, then by the rising tide of Averroism; in Iran, drawing fresh vigor from Suhrawardī's Zoroastrian Neoplatonism, Avicennism entered on a new life that has endured down to our own time. Iran moreover, knows no development corresponding to the disappearance, with all it implied, of the *Animae coelestes*, the hierarchy of the Angelic Souls rejected by Averroism. Along with the *Animae coelestes* Iranian Islam preserved the objective existence of the intermediate world, the world of subsistent Images (*ʿālam al-mithāl*) or immaterial bodies, which Suhrawardī calls the cosmic "Intermediate Orient." Concomitantly it preserved the prerogative of the Imagination which is the organ of this intermediate world, and with it the specific reality of the events, the theophanies, enacted in it, a reality in the fullest sense, though it is not the physical, sensory, historical reality of our material being. This world is the scene of Suhrawardī's symbolic dramaturgy. His work includes a complete cycle of Recitals of Initiation in Persian, which are a continuation of the Avicennan Recitals. Their titles are suggestive: the "Recital of Occidental Exile"; the "Vademecum of the *Fedeli d'amore*"; "The Purple Archangel," etc. The theme is always the Quest of, and encounter with, the Angel who is the Holy Spirit and the Active Intelligence, the Angel of Knowledge and Revelation. In the "Recital of Exile" the symbolic narrative is taken up where it was left off by the Avicennan recital of Ḥayy ibn Yaqẓān, an episode which Avicenna himself transcended in the "Recital of the Bird," later translated into Persian by Suhrawardī. How irremediable was the defeat of Avicennism in the Occident is demonstrated by the fact that Westerners in our time still refuse to perceive the mystical implications of Avicenna's noetics as illustrated in his symbolic recitals.

In the Suhrawardian theosophy of Light, the entire Platonic theory of Ideas is interpreted in terms of Zoroastrian angelology. Expressing itself as a metaphysic of essences, the Suhrawardian dualism of Light and Darkness precludes the possibility of a physics in the Aristotelian sense of the word. A physics of Light can only be an angelology, because Light is life, and Life is essentially Light. What is known as the material body is in essence night and death; it is a corpse. Through the varying intensity of their luminescence, the Angels, the "lords of the species" (the Fravashis of Mazdaism), give rise to the different species, which the natural body can never account for. What Aristotelianism considers as the concept of a species, the logical universal, ceases to be anything more than the dead body of an Angel.

The Sage in whose person this sense of the universe culminates in a metaphysic of ecstasy, who combines the fullness of philosophical knowledge with that of mystical experience, is the perfect Sage, the "Pole" (*Quṭb*); he is the summit of the invisible mystical hierarchy without which the universe could not continue to subsist. Through this idea of the Perfect Man (cf. the *anthropos teleios* of Hermetism), the theosophy of Ishrāq was spontaneously oriented toward an encounter with Shīʿism and its Imāmology; it was eminently equipped to provide a philosophical foundation for the concept of the eternal Imām and for its exemplifications in the pleroma of the Holy Imāms (the "spiritual Guides"). In the sixteenth and seventeenth centuries, with the masters of the school of Ispahān (Mīr Dāmād, Mullā Ṣadrā Shīrāzī, Qāḍī Saʿid Qummī, etc.), *Ishrāqī* Avicennism became *the* Shīʿite philosophy, and the consequences of this development may be felt even in the most recent form of Imāmist philosophy, the school of Shaikh Ahmad Aḥsā'ī and his successors, or Shaikhism. Mullā Ṣadrā might be called the "St. Thomas of Iran," if we had in mind a St. Thomas combined with a Jacob Boehme and a Swedenborg, a possibility which is perhaps conceivable only in Iran. But the way to Mullā Ṣadrā's work was paved by a long line of masters who integrated the doctrines of Ibn ʿArabī into the Shīʿism of the twelve Imāms (or perhaps we should speak of a re-integration, for a study of the origins of these doctrines suggests a return to their source). This work was carried on between the fourteenth and sixteenth centuries by such men as Ibn Abī Jumhūr, Ḥaydar Amulī, ʿAlī Turka Ispāhānī, etc. Moreover an entire philosophy of Light is at work in the doctrines of Ibn ʿArabī; it remains to be established to what extent Mullā Ṣadrā is indebted to Ibn ʿArabī for his own existential interpretation of the theosophy of *Ishrāq*, which Suhrawardī had conceived in terms of a metaphysics of essence.

All this, we are well aware, has been recalled in broad strokes and too quickly. Nevertheless, it has to be recalled, for in the present state of Islamic studies it is to be feared that these figures would not spontaneously group themselves in the reader's mind. And only through such a grouping can the reader gain an intimation of the perspectives we have set out to explore. The little we have said suffices to prove that the development of philosophical thought in Islam reached neither its conclusion nor its apogee with Averroes. We shall have occasion to analyze elsewhere the reasons why it was to reach its full flowering principally in Iran and to investigate the profound meaning of this fact. In this flowering the names of Suhrawardī and of Ibn ʿArabī, with what they imply, are profoundly intermingled. But we are still far from having exhausted the benchmarks and co-ordinates of our spiritual topography. The biography of Ibn ʿArabī will itself provide us with an opportunity to group certain necessary complements, because the events that occupy it never reduce themselves to the simple material facts of a biography, but always seem to express, to symbolize, some inner happening. Even the dates to which they attach are only outward references; their true reference is "transhistorical"; most frequently it is situated in that intermediate world of subsistent Images, without which there would be no theophanies. We shall consider these events later on, grouped according to the sequence of three privileged symbols which orient the inner life curve of our *shaikh*. We should first like to consider them, as it were, in their polarizing function.

We have already gained a glimpse of the first event in evoking Ibn ʿArabī looking on as the body of Averroes was brought back to Cordova; in his mind there arises a question whose sadness falls back upon the person of the great dead philosopher. As though in standing there Ibn ʿArabī had felt himself in advance to be the silent victor in the conflict between theology and philosophy in the West, that conflict in which they were both to exhaust themselves, unaware that their very antagonism had its origin in common premises which are absent in esoteric gnosis, whether it be that of Ismailism, of the *Ishrāqīyūn*, or of an Ibn ʿArabī. The scene occurred only a few years before the moment when Ibn ʿArabī, becoming aware that his spiritual situation was without issue in the West, that is, in the Islam of Andalusia and North Africa, set out for the Orient, as though miming in his own life and on the stage of visible geography, the mystical drama of Suhrawardī's "Recital of Occidental Exile."

When Ibn ʿArabī was born (560/1165), Suhrawardī, who was to be in Iran the resurrector of the wisdom of the ancient Persians, was still a boy of ten; he was at school in Marāgha in Azerbaijan. The date of Ibn ʿArabī's birth (17 Ramaḍān, 560) coincides in the lunar calendar with the first anniversary of what is perhaps the most crucial event in the history of Iranian Ismailism: the proclamation of the Grand Resurrection at Alamūt. This unusual synchronism may be imputed to chance. But is this a truly satisfactory answer? To mention the synchronism, in any event, is to introduce, if only in passing, the questions it will be possible to study as we pursue our parallel studies of Ibn ʿArabī and of Shīʿite theology. It seems paradoxical that the proponents of the Western movement that has been called "Neotraditionalism" should have taken so little interest in Shīʿism, which represents par excellence the esoteric tradition of Islam, whether we have in mind Ismailian Gnosis or the theosophy of Imāmism, that is, of Duodeciman Shīʿism down to its traditional modern elaborations, such as the Iranian Shaikhism to which we have already referred. It is evident, however, that the conditions for a *spiritual* dialogue between Islam and Christianity change radically accordingly as Christianity addresses itself to Shīʿite Islam or to another branch of Islam.

The first question we shall ask about Ibn ʿArabī is: Exactly how much of Ismailian esoterism, or of a related esoterism, can he have assimilated before leaving the Maghrib forever? We find indications in his familiarity with the school of Almería and in the fact that he composed a commentary to the only surviving work of Ibn Qasī, initiator of the movement of the Murīdīn in southern Portugal, where many characteristic traits of Ismailian-Shīʿite inspiration are discernible. We shall take account of a remarkable phenomenon which occurred simultaneously at both geographic limits of Islamic esoterism: the part played by the teachings of Empedocles, transfigured as a hero of prophetic theosophy. Asín Palacios carefully noted the importance of this Neoempedoclism in the school of Almería in Andalusia, while at the same time he saw fit to regard the disciples of Ibn Masarra (d. 319/931) as the heirs to Priscillian's gnosis. Simultaneously in Iran, the influence of this same Empedocles made itself felt in a philosopher who corresponded with Avicenna, namely, Abu'l-Ḥasan al-ʿĀmirī and in the cosmogonies of Suhrawardī and of Ismailism.

The second question will concern the immense opus of Ibn ʿArabī's maturity. Certain chapters of the great book of the *Futūḥāt* might have been written by a pure Shīʿite. Such is the case for example with Chapter XXXIX[3], dealing with the secret of Salmān (Salmān Pārsī, Salmān the Persian, or Salmān Pāk, "Salmān the Pure"). This is the secret which gained admittance to the "members of the Prophetic House" (*Ahl al-Bayt*), that is, to the Holy Imāms, for this son of a Mazdean knight of Fārs (Persis), turned Christian, who set out in quest of the True Prophet, whom he found in Arabia, and in whose house he assumed the angelic ministry of an initiator into the secret meaning of past Revelations. The indications become more precise. Ibn ʿArabī regards as his heirs—along with Salmān—those whom the Ṣūfīs called the "poles"; in terms to which any Shīʿite might subscribe, he interprets the Koranic verse (XXXIII: 33), which is one of the scriptural foundations of Shīʿism (a verse sanctifying the persons of the Fourteen Most-Pure: the Prophet, his daughter Fāṭima, and the twelve Imāms). These indications, and they are not alone of their kind, are worthy of meditation. They explain in any case the reception given his work by those Shīʿites who were preparing the way for the Ṣafavid renaissance to which we have referred above. We shall have to determine in what measure the influence of Ibn ʿArabī was responsible for the feeling which may have enabled Ṣūfism to find the secret of its origins, witness for example Ḥaydar Amulī (fourteenth century), himself a Shīʿite commentator of Ibn ʿArabī, who proclaimed that the true Shīʿism was Ṣūfism and that reciprocally the true Ṣūfism was Shīʿism.

This chain of thinkers in itself gives us an idea of the development of a philosophy and of a spirituality incommensurably

3. *Kitāb al-Futūḥāt al-Makkīya,* I, 195 ff.

broader and deeper than the schema to which our handbooks on the history of philosophy have accustomed us. They already lead us to ask the question: How is it that the philosophical ferment remained alive in the Shīʿite world and nowhere else in Islam, and that in the sixteenth century school of Ispahān a renaissance occurred whose effects have been felt down to our own time? Shīʿite sentiment must in itself imply or provoke a certain number of speculative and spiritual possibilities to which thus far the philosophers and theologians of the West have accorded very little interest. And yet they would find in this body of ideas a number of themes at once familiar and strange. Shīʿite Imāmology indeed arouses reminiscences of a Christology, but of a Christology which knows nothing of Paulinism. Many chapters of the history of dogmas considered as closed and "superseded" would then have to be reopened, revealing unsuspected possibilities that have burgeoned elsewhere.

All the great themes constitutive of Shīʿite thought provide the theological reflection they arouse with material incomparably richer than the contribution of Sunnite Islam. Their dominant is the idea of the Theophany in Human form, the divine anthropomorphosis which fills the gulf left open by abstract monotheism. Here I am not speaking of the Christian dogma of the Incarnation, of the hypostatic union defined by the Councils, but of the manifestation of the unknowable God in the angelic form of the celestial Anthropos, of which the Holy Imāms were the exemplifications on earth, the "theophanic forms" (*maẓāhir*). Whereas the idea of the Incarnation postulates a unique material fact situated among the chronological facts of history, and upon that fact builds the ecclesiastical reality which sociological monism would laicize as a "social Incarnation," the theophanic idea, as we shall see in the course of this book, will call for a celestial assumption of man, the return to a time that is not the time of history and its chronology.

The recurrence of the theophanies, the perpetuation of their their mystery, postulate neither an ecclesiastical reality nor a dogmatic magistery, but the virtue of the revealed Book as the "cipher" of an eternal Word, forever capable of producing new creations (cf. in the second part of this book, the idea of "recurrent creation" in Ibn ʿArabī). This precisely is the Shīʿite idea of the *ta'wīl*, the esoteric spiritual exegesis which apprehends all material data, things and facts as symbols, transmutes them, and "carries them back" to symbolized Persons. All appearance, every exoteric meaning (*ẓāhir*) has an esoteric meaning (*bāṭin*); the book "descended from Heaven," the Koran, limited to the apparent letter, perishes in the opacity and servitude of legalist religion. It is necessary to bring out the transparency of its depths, the esoteric meaning. And that is the mission of the Imām, the "spiritual Guide," even if as in the present period of the world he is in "great Occultation"— or rather, this meaning is himself, not to be sure his empirical individuality, but his theophanic Person. His "magistery" is an initiatory "magistery"; the initiation to the *ta'wīl* is a spiritual birth (*wilādat rūḥānīya*). Because here, as among all those who have practiced it in Christianity, that is, those who have not confused spiritual meaning with allegory, the *ta'wīl* enables men to enter a new world, to accede to a higher plane of being.

Although it may seem arbitrary to a philologist reduced to the plane of the *ẓāhir* (the exoteric), to a phenomenologist attentive to structures, *ta'wīl* (spiritual hermeneutics) reveals the rigorous laws of its objectivity. And it is the philosophy of Light, represented by Suhrawardī as well as Ibn ʿArabī, which provides the foundations for this objectivity of the *ta'wīl* and regulates the "science of the Scales," the "symbolism of the worlds" practiced by Shīʿite theosophy. Indeed the numerous esoteric meanings merely corroborate, by spiritual experience, the geometric laws of the science of *perspective* as it is known to our philosophers.[4]

4. For further details, see our study, "L'Intériorisation du sens en herméneutique soufie iranienne" (ʿAlī Turka Ispāhānī and ʿAlā'uddawla Semnānī).

§ 1. *Between Andalusia and Iran*

The *ta'wīl*, Shī'ite hermeneutics, does not deny that prophetic Revelation was concluded with the prophet Muḥammad, the "seal of prophecy." It postulates, however, that prophetic hermeneutics is not concluded and will continue to bring forth secret meanings until the "return," the *parousia*, of the awaited Imām, of him who will be the "seal of the Imāmate" and the signal for the resurrection of Resurrections. All this, it is true, alarmed official Sunnite Islam, which felt the Law shaking on its foundations and reacted accordingly, as the tragic history of Shī'ism bears witness.

Thus, because Averroes the great Aristotelian also practiced a *ta'wīl*, whose foundations and the questions it led him to ask have been evoked above, the scene of Ibn 'Arabī attending the funeral of Averroes, appears as a symbol, polarizing the themes we have just recapitulated. For Ibn 'Arabī was himself a great master of *ta'wīl*—we shall see him at work in the course of this book—and it is impossible to speak of *ta'wīl* without speaking of Shī'ism, for *ta'wīl* is basic to its attitude toward Scripture. Thus we are introduced to an Oriental spirituality which, unlike that of the Occident, was unaware of the problems raised by Averroism, or rather an environment whose spiritual situation was alien to the problems of which Averroism and Thomism are symptoms.

Three years after this funeral another event was to assume a symbolic significance in the life of Ibn 'Arabī. Resolved to leave his native Andalusia, Ibn 'Arabī set out for the Orient without hope of return. Concurrently, at the extreme eastern limits of the Islamic world, tragic events had led to an exodus in the opposite direction. For us this movement derives symbolic significance from the fact that it came, as it were, to meet Ibn 'Arabī, himself returning to the land of his origins. The meeting place was the Middle East. Ibn 'Arabī was to die in Damascus in 1240, exactly sixteen years before the capture of Baghdād by the Mongols announced the end of a world. But for years the ravages of the Mongol onslaught had induced a reflux of Islam from Central Asia across Iran toward the Middle East. (Among the famous refugees: Najmuddīn Dāya Rāzī, Mawlānā Jalāluddīn Rūmī and his father, etc.) One of the greatest masters of Central Asian Ṣūfism, Najm Kubrà, met a martyr's death resisting the Mongols at Khwārezm (Khiva) in 618/1220. It was this same Najm Kubrà who imprinted upon Ṣūfism a speculative, visionary tendency which clearly distinguishes it from the way of life of the pious ascetics of Mesopotamia who had taken the name of Ṣūfīs in the first centuries of Islam.[5]

Among the first generation of the disciples of Najm Kubrà there occurred an event of great importance for the question which concerns us here and which has never been adequately dealt with—the question, namely, of the affinity and reunion between the theosophy of Ibn ʿArabī and the theosophy of the Ṣūfism originating in Central Asia, and consequently of Shīʿite Ṣūfism. One of the greatest disciples of Najm Kubrà, the *shaikh* Saʿduddīn Hammūʾī (d. 650/1252) wrote a long letter to Ibn ʿArabī, in which he questions him on matters of high theosophy

5. The etymology of the word "Ṣūfī" employed to designate the Spirituals of Islam has been a subject of research and controversy. Most students of the matter have accepted the explanation given by several masters of Ṣūfism, who derive the word from *ṣūf*, the Arabic word for wool. According to this theory, a woolen garment was the distinguishing mark of the Ṣūfīs; hence, the word *taṣawwuf*, to profess Ṣūfism. But is this explanation truly satisfactory? We know that there have always been ingenious grammarians prepared to trace foreign words in Arabic back to Semitic roots. Certain Western orientalists have simply regarded the word "Ṣūfī" as a transliteration of the Greek *sophos*, sage (*ṣūfīya*, Ṣūfism, is indeed the Arabic spelling of Hagia Sophia). That was too good to be true. And yet Bīrūnī, the great tenth-century scholar, as he made clear in his book about India, was still well aware that the word was not of Arabic origin. He, too, regarded it as a transcription of the Greek *sophos*. The conclusion was all the more inescapable in that the idea of the sage embodied in Ṣūfism corresponded, if not to our idea of the sage, at least to that set forth by Empedocles of Agrigentum, namely, the sage-prophet, whose importance has been stressed in the present book; cf. ʿIzzuddīn Kāshānī, *Misbāḥ al-Hidāya*, pp. 65–66.

and *ta'wīl* and refers expressly to one of Ibn ʿArabī's works.[6] In turn his most noted disciple, ʿAzīzuddīn Nasafī, left a considerable opus all in Persian, in which Hammūʾī recognized the quintessence of his own doctrine and of his own works, which have today been largely lost. The work of ʿAzīz Nasafī is perhaps eminently suited to illustrate our vision of an Orient coming to meet the eastbound pilgrim.

Finally, there is a high place of the spirit in Iran, which cannot remain absent from our topography: Shīrāz, the capital of Fārs (Persis) in the southwest of Iran. There another contemporary, Rūzbehān Baqlī Shīrāzī (d. 606/1209), produced in Persian and in Arabic an opus of the utmost importance for the orientation of Iranian Ṣūfism; his religion, which, as we shall see below, was that of a true *Fedele d'amore*, made him not only a precursor of Ḥāfiẓ, another famous Shīrāzī poet, whose *Dīwān* is still treated as a Bible by the Iranian Ṣūfīs; moreover, the religion of Rūzbehān is in perfect and striking consonance with the passages of Ibn ʿArabī's "dialectic of love" that will be quoted here.[7]

We have established a certain number of co-ordinates, indicated a few benchmarks in our spiritual topography. These indications are far from complete, but they suffice to provide the reader with a preliminary orientation. The two events of Ibn ʿArabī's life chosen thus far as polarizing symbols will assume their deepest significance if we associate them with a dominant and permanent trait of our *shaikh*'s personality. In

6. We owe our knowledge of this letter (so important for the history of Iranian Ṣūfism) to M. Marian Molé, who found it in the private library of Dr. Minossian in Ispahān (MS 1181). In this Arabic letter (eight pages of seventeen lines each), Saʿduddīn refers expressly to the "Book of Theophanies" (*tajalliyāt*); unfortunately, to judge by an appended note, Ibn ʿArabī does not seem to have ever sent an answer.

7. See Rūzbehān Baqlī Shīrāzī, *Le Jasmin des Fidèles d'amour* (*K. ʿAbhar al-ʿĀshiqīn*), *Traité de soufisme en persan* and *Commentaire sur les paradoxes des Soufis* (*Sharḥ-i Shaṭḥīyāt*).

the presence of a Spiritual, one asks almost automatically: who were his masters? Ibn ʿArabī had many and met many; his numerous journeys and peregrinations brought him into contact with almost all the Ṣūfī masters of his day. Yet essentially he never had more than one, and that one was none of the usual visible masters; we find his name in no archives; we cannot establish his historical co-ordinates or situate him at any particular moment in the succession of the human generations. Ibn ʿArabī was, and never ceased to be, the disciple of an invisible master, a mysterious prophet figure to whom a number of traditions, both significant and obscure, lend features which relate him, or tend to identify him, with Elijah, with St. George, and still others. Ibn ʿArabī was above all the disciple of Khiḍr (Khāḍir). We shall attempt further on to indicate what it signifies and implies to be "the disciple of Khiḍr." In any event such a relationship with a hidden spiritual master lends the disciple an essentially "transhistorical" dimension and presupposes an ability to experience events which are enacted in a reality other than the physical reality of daily life, events which spontaneously transmute themselves into symbols.

Ibn ʿArabī, the disciple of Khiḍr, presents a kinship with those Ṣūfīs who called themselves Uwaysīs. They owed this name to a pious ascetic of Yemen, Uways al-Qaranī, a contemporary of the Prophet, who knew the Prophet without ever having seen him in his lifetime; the Prophet in turn knew him without ever having laid eyes on him, and it was to him that he referred in this saying preserved in a *ḥadīth:* "I feel the breath of the Compassionate coming from the direction of Yemen." Thus Uways had no visible human guide; it was only after the Prophet's death that he went to the Ḥijāz, where he became one of the first martyrs of Shīʿism dying in the battle of Ṣiffīn (36/657) for the cause of the first Imām. All those among the Ṣūfīs who had no visible *murshīd* (guide), that is, an earthly man like themselves and a contemporary, called themselves Uwaysīs. One of the most famous was Abu'l-Ḥasan

Kharraqānī (d. 425/1034), an Iranian Ṣūfī, who left us the following saying: "I am amazed at those disciples who declare that they require this or that master. You are perfectly well aware that I have never been taught by any man. God was my guide, though I have the greatest respect for all the masters." More specifically, according to a tradition reported by Jāmī, it was the "Angel" (*rūhānīya*) of an other great Iranian Ṣūfī, Abū Yazīd Basṭāmī (d. 261/875) who guided Abu'l-Ḥasan along the spiritual Path. Such was also the case with the great mystical poet Farīduddīn ʿAṭṭār of Nīshāpūr (d. 617/1220) who, again according to Jāmī, had for master and guide the "being-of-light" of Manṣūr Ḥallāj (d. 309/922).[8]

If we carry our analysis a little deeper, we shall see once again how, beneath its various technical solutions, the problem of the Intellects and of their relation to the active Intelligence conceals a crucial existential decision. The solution—the decision, rather—prefigures and conditions a whole chain of spiritual development with far-reaching consequences. For it announces either that each human being is *oriented* toward a quest for his personal invisible guide, or that he entrusts himself to the collective, magisterial authority as the intermediary between himself and Revelation. The spiritual autonomy of an Ibn ʿArabī goes hand in hand with the characteristic trait of the *Fedeli d'amore*, referred to above. Thus we shall not be surprised to find that his doctrine of love is similar to theirs. In other words, the figure of the Angel-Intelligence—as Holy Spirit, Angel of Knowledge and of Revelation—commands all orientations, all the approaches and withdrawals which occur in the spiritual topography here outlined, accordingly as we accept or as we sidestep the personal relation it suggests, the co-responsibility for personal destiny assumed by "the alone with the Alone."

8. See *Nafaḥāt al-Uns*, p. 540, in which Jāmī relates that the Light (*nūr*) of Ḥallāj was manifested, "epiphanized" (*tajallī kard*) to the spirit (*rūḥ*) of ʿAṭṭār and was his preceptor (*murabbī*).

One of those who gained the best insight into the scope and resonance of the problem of the Intelligence raised in medieval philosophy was perhaps Abu'l-Barakāt, a profound and original Jewish thinker who was converted to Islam toward the end of his life (d. 560/1165). He envisaged an answer which is neither the separate Active Intelligence, one for all, nor an active Intelligence immanent in each individual, but a plurality of separate and transcendent active Intelligences, corresponding to the specific divergencies among the multitude of souls. "Some souls . . . have learned everything from invisible guides, known only to themselves. . . . The ancient Sages . . . taught that for each individual soul, or perhaps for a number of souls with the same nature and affinity, there is a being of the spiritual world who, throughout their existence, adopts a special solicitude and tenderness toward that soul or group of souls; it is he who initiates them into knowledge, protects, guides, defends, comforts them, brings them to final victory, and it is this being whom these Sages called the *Perfect Nature.* And it is this friend, this defender and protector, who in religious language is called the *Angel.*"[9]

Suhrawardī referred on several occasions to the vision of this Perfect Nature by a Hermes in ecstasy, who was perhaps his own pseudonym. Just as we can recognize in this mysterious figure the features of the Mazdean Daēnā-Fravashi, the commentators identify it with the Angel Gabriel, denoting the Holy Spirit of each individual; in the pages that follow we shall observe, through the experience of Ibn ʿArabī, the recurrence of this Figure, which imposes itself with the insistence of an archetype. A great Iranian mystic of the fourteenth century, ʿAlā'uddawla Semnānī, was to speak in similar terms of the "invisible master," the "Gabriel of your being." His esoteric exegesis, his *ta'wīl,* carries the figures of Koranic revelation to a sevenfold depth; to attain to the "Gabriel of your being"

9. See our *Avicenna,* pp. 89–90.

is to pass successively through the seven esoteric levels and to be reunited with the Spirit which guides and initiates the "seven prophets of your being." This striving is also designated as Jacob's contest with the Angel, which was so interpreted in the symbolic exegesis of the Jewish mystic Joseph ben Judah: the intellective soul struggling to be united with the Angel, with the active Intelligence, until the rising of the light (*ishrāq*), at which time the soul emerges, delivered, from the darkness that imprisoned it.[10] Thus no doubt we should speak not of a combat with, that is against, the Angel, but of a combat *for* the Angel, for the Angel in turn needs the response of a soul if his being is to become what it has to be. A whole series of Jewish speculative mystics found the same symbolism in the *Song of Songs*, where the Beloved plays the role of the active Intelligence, while the heroine is the thinking human soul.[11]

Here let us pause, for it seems to us that with the symbol of Ibn ʿArabī as disciple of Khiḍr we have reached the center which dominates the co-ordinates of our spiritual topography. Whatever name we may give to the disciple's relationship with his personal invisible guide, the events it determines do not fall within quantitative physical time; they cannot be measured according to homogeneous, uniform units of time and chronology regulated by the movements of the stars; they find no place in the continuous chain of irreversible events. These events, to be sure, are enacted in time, but in a time that is peculiar to them, a discontinuous, qualitative, pure, psychic time, whose moments can be evaluated only according to their own measure, a measure which in every instance varies with their intensity. And this intensity measures a time in which the past remains present to the future, in which the future is already present to

10. According to Salomon Munk, quoted in E. Renan, *Averroës et l'Averroïsme*, p. 181.

11. See the fine comprehensive study by Georges Vajda, *L'Amour de Dieu dans la théologie juive du Moyen Age*, esp. pp. 142–45.

the past, just as the notes of a musical phrase, though played successively, nevertheless persist all together in the present and thus form a phrase. Hence the recurrences, the possible inversions, the synchronisms, incomprehensible in rational terms, beyond the reach of historical realism, but accessible to another "realism," that of the subtile world, *'ālam al-mithāl,* which Suhrawardī called the "Middle Orient" of celestial Souls and whose organ is the "theophanic Imagination" that will concern us here.

Once he has recognized his invisible guide, a mystic sometimes decides to trace his own *isnād,* to reveal his spiritual genealogy, that is, to disclose the "chain of transmission" culminating in his person and bear witness to the spiritual ascendancy which he invokes across the generations of mankind. He does neither more nor less than to designate by name the minds to whose family he is conscious of belonging. Read in the opposite order from their phenomenological emergence, these genealogies take on the appearance of true genealogies. Judged by the rules of our historical criticism, the claim of these genealogies to truth seems highly precarious. Their relevance is to another "transhistoric truth," which cannot be regarded as inferior (because it is of a different order) to the material historic truth whose claim to truth, with the documentation at our disposal, is no less precarious. Suhrawardī traces the family tree of the Ishrāqīyūn back to Hermes, ancestor of the Sages, (that Idrīs-Enoch of Islamic prophetology, whom Ibn 'Arabī calls the prophet of the Philosophers); from him are descended the Sages of Greece and Persia, who are followed by certain Ṣūfīs (Abū Yazīd Basṭāmī, Kharraqānī, Ḥallāj, and the choice seems particularly significant in view of what has been said above about the Uwaysīs), and all these branches converge in his own doctrine and school. This is not a history of philosophy in our sense of the term; but still less is it a mere fantasy.

Here it has been necessary to provide a minimum of information. We can only hope for the coming of an integral humanism which will make it possible to depart from the horizons of our classical programs without being taken for a "specialist" who shocks and wearies the "average enlightened reader" with his incomprehensible allusions. We all have a general idea of the Middle Ages; everybody knows that there is an "Arab" philosophy and an "Arab" science but fails to suspect that there *was* much more, and that in this "much more" there *is* a sum of human experience, ignorance of which is not without its bearing on the desperate difficulties besetting our times. For no dialogue is possible without common problems and a common vocabulary; and such a community of problems and vocabulary does not arise suddenly under the pressure of material events, but ripens slowly through a common participation in the questions that mankind has asked itself. Perhaps it will be argued that Ibn ʿArabī and his disciples, or even Shīʿism as a whole, represent only a small minority within the great masses of Islam. That is true, but have we come to the point where we can appreciate "spiritual energy" only in statistical terms?

We have tried to bring out some of the reasons that impose on us a vision more complex than that with which people ordinarily content themselves in speaking of Islam or of "Oriental philosophies." These are usually taken to comprise Arab, Indian, Chinese, and Japanese philosophy. It has become imperative—we shall have more to say on the subject further on—that Iranian philosophy be included in this list. Ancient Iran is characterized by a prophetic religion, the religion of Zoroaster, from which the religion of Mānī cannot be dissociated. Islamic Iran is marked by a philosophy and a spirituality which polarized elements that are elsewhere not assimilable. This is more than sufficient reason why our topography cannot dispense with this intermediary between Arab Islam and the spiritual universe of India. Having made this point, we shall gladly agree that such a philosophical geography is not yet enough. We must advance still further to the point where Ibn ʿArabī will lead us at the end of the present book, at least to the threshold of the mystical Kaʿaba, when we shall see what we enter in entering it, and shall also see with whom we enter it. But this mystical Kaʿaba is in the "center of the world," a center which cannot be situated by the methods of common cartography, any more than the mission of the invisible guide depends on historical co-ordinates.

It has seemed to us that three exemplary elements or traits assume the character of symbols for the characterology of Ibn ʿArabī. They seem most eminently to attract and to constellate the very themes which it is necessary to interrelate. These three motifs, the witness of Averroes' funeral, the pilgrim to the Orient, the disciple of Khiḍr, will now enable us to follow the curve of our *shaikh*'s life while becoming more intimately acquainted with him. Insofar as the events of his life take on the appearance of autobiographical data, charged with a trans-historic meaning, it will be their function to throw an anticipatory light on that twofold dimension of the human person, of which the active Imagination, investing the human person with his "theophanic function," will subsequently give us a glimpse. Ibn ʿArabī himself teaches us to meditate the facts of his autobiography in this way: in his *Kitāb al-Isrā'*, an imitation and amplification of the nocturnal assumption of the Prophet from Heaven to Heaven, he sees himself as a "pilgrim to the Orient," starting for Jerusalem from Andalusia.

2. *The Curve and Symbols of Ibn ʿArabī's Life*

At Averroes' Funeral

The earthly existence of Abū Bakr Muḥammad ibn al-ʿArabī (abridged as Ibn ʿArabī) began in Murcia, in the southeast of Spain, where he was born on 17 Ramaḍān, A.H. 560 (July 28, A.D. 1165). The synchronism has been noted above: According to the lunar calendar, this date marks the first anniversary of the proclamation of the "Great Resurrection" at Alamūt in Iran by the Imām Ḥasan (*ʿalā dhikrihi's-salām*, peace be upon his memory), instituting the pure spiritual Islam of reformed Iranian Ismailism, 17 Ramaḍān, A.H. 559 (August 8, A.D. 1164). Our *shaikh*'s surnames are well known: Muḥyi'd-Dīn, "Animator of the Religion"; al-Shaikh al-Akbar, "Doctor Maximus"; Ibn Aflaṭūn, "The Son of Plato" or "The Platonist." At the age of eight he went to Seville where he studied and grew to adolescence, leading the happy life made possible by his noble, well-to-do family, entered into a first marriage with a girl of whom he speaks in terms of respectful devotion, and who seems indeed to have influenced him in his orientation toward Ṣūfism.[12]

It was at this time that Ibn 'Arabī's visionary aptitudes became apparent. He fell gravely ill; his fever brought on a state of profound lethargy. While those about him thought him dead, he in his inward universe was besieged by a troop of menacing, diabolical figures. But then there arose a marvelously beautiful being, exhaling a sweet perfume, who with invincible force repulsed the demonic figures. "Who are you?" Ibn 'Arabī asked him. "I am the Sūra Yasīn." His anguished father at his bedside was indeed reciting that sūra (the thirty-sixth of the Koran), which is intoned specifically for the dying. Such was the energy released by the spoken Word that the person corresponding to it took form in the subtile intermediate world—a phenomenon not at all rare in religious experience. This was one of Ibn 'Arabī's first entrances into the *'ālam al-mithāl*, the world of real and subsistent Images, to which we have referred at the beginning of this book.

The experience was soon repeated. Ibn 'Arabī's memory of

12. For the whole, see the material gathered by Miguel Asín Palacios in his great work *El Islam cristianizado, estudio del sufismo a través de las obras de Abenarabi de Murcia.* The pious sentiment which inspired the great Spanish Arabic scholar with this strange title is perceptible throughout the work, which is still of the utmost value. But it is regrettable that he should have applied language and ideas befitting a Christian monk to a Ṣūfī like Ibn 'Arabī; their vocations are different, and in employing such a method one runs the risk of blurring the originality of both types.

his youth seems to have been especially marked by his friendship with two venerable Ṣūfī women, two *shaikha*, Yasmin of Marchena and Fāṭima of Cordova. The latter was a spiritual mother to him; he speaks with devotion of her teaching, oriented toward a life of intimacy with God. An extraordinary aura surrounds their relations. Despite her advanced age, the venerable *shaikha* still possessed such beauty and grace that she might have been taken for a girl of fourteen (*sic*), and the young Ibn ʿArabī could not help blushing when he looked at her face to face. She had many disciples, and for two years Ibn ʿArabī was one of them. Among other charismas that divine favor had conferred on her, she had "in her service" the Sūrat al-*Fātiḥa* (the opening sūra of the Koran). On one occasion, when it was necessary to help a woman in distress, they recited the *Fātiḥa* together, so giving it its consistent, personal and corporeal, though subtile and ethereal form.[13] The sūra fulfilled its mission, after which the saintly woman Fāṭima recited a profoundly humble prayer. Ibn ʿArabī himself gives an explanation of these events in the pages that will here be analyzed, describing the effects of the creative energy produced by the concentration of the heart (*himma*). We shall also recall this episode in studying Ibn ʿArabī's "method of theophanic prayer," the creative prayer that becomes dialogue, creative because it is at once God's prayer and man's prayer. Often the venerable *shaikha* said to her young disciple: "I am your divine mother and the light of your earthly mother." And indeed, he goes on to relate, "Once when my mother paid her a visit, the *shaikha* said to her: 'O light! this is my son, and he is your father. Treat him with filial piety, never turn away from him.' " We shall hear these same words again (Part One, *in fine*), applied to the description of the state of the mystic soul, at once mother and daughter of the God of his ecstasy. This was the exact term, "mother of her father" (*umm abīha*), which the Prophet gave to his daughter

13. *Futūḥāt*, II, 348.

Fāṭimat al-Zahrā, Fāṭima the Radiant. If the venerable *shaikha* of Cordova, homonym of the Prophet's daughter, saluted Ibn ʿArabī's mother in this way, she must have had a premonition of the unique spiritual destiny in store for her young disciple.

Ibn ʿArabī was approaching the age of twenty when he became aware of his definitive entrance upon the spiritual path and of his initiation into the secrets of mystical life. This brings us to the episode which seemed to us so eminently symbolic in the context developed above. Actually the episode consists of two scenes, separated by an interval of several years. Between his encounter as a young man with Averroes and the day of the funeral, Ibn ʿArabī did not see the great Peripatetic of Cordova, not at least in the sensible, physical world. He himself tells us that his own father, who was still living, was a close friend of the philosopher. This facilitated the interview desired by Averroes, an interview which ought to have figured prominently in our history of philosophy and spirituality. On some pretext, Ibn ʿArabī's father sent him to the house of the philosopher, who had heard a good deal about the young man and was curious to meet him. We shall let Ibn ʿArabī describe the encounter between the integrist Aristotelian master and the young man who was to be surnamed the "son of Plato."

"And so, one fine day, I went to Cordova, to the house of Abu'l Walīd Ibn Rushd (Averroes). He had expressed the desire to meet me personally, because he had heard of the revelations that God had accorded me in the course of my spiritual retirement, and he had made no secret of his astonishment at what he had been told. For this reason my father, who was one of his intimate friends, sent me to his house one day, pretexting some sort of errand, in reality to enable Averroes to have a talk with me. At that time I was still a beardless youth. When I entered, the master arose from his place, received me with signal marks of friendship and consideration, and finally embraced me. Then he said: 'Yes.' and I in turn said: 'Yes.' His joy was great at noting that I had understood. But then taking cognizance of what had called forth his joy, I added: 'No.' Immediately Averroes winced, the color went out of his cheeks, he seemed to doubt his own thought. He asked me this question: 'What manner of solution have you found through divine illumination and inspiration? Is it identical with that which we obtain from speculative reflection?' I replied: 'Yes and no. Between the yes and the no, spirits take their flight from their matter, and heads are separated from their bodies.' Averroes turned pale, I saw him tremble; he murmured the ritual phrase 'There is no power save in God'—for he had understood my allusion.

"Later, after our interview, he questioned my father about me, in order to compare the opinion he had formed of me with my father's and to ascertain whether they coincided or differed. For Averroes was a great master of reflection and philosophical meditation. He gave thanks to God, I was told, for having allowed him to live at such a time and permitted him to see a man who had gone into spiritual retirement and emerged as I had emerged. 'I myself,' he declared, 'had said that such a thing was possible, but never met anyone who had actually experienced it. Glory be to God who has let me live at a time distinguished by one of the masters of this experience, one of those who open the locks of His gates. Glory be to God who has accorded me the personal favor of seeing one of them with my own eyes.'

"I wished to have another interview with Averroes. God in His Mercy caused him to appear to me in an ecstasy (*wāqiʿa*) in such a form that between his person and myself there was a light veil. I saw him through this veil, but he did not see me or know that I was present. He was indeed too absorbed in his meditation to take notice of me. I said to myself: His thought does not guide him to the place where I myself am.

"I had no further occasion to meet him until his death, which occurred in the year 595 of the Hegira [1198] in Marakesh. His remains were taken to Cordova, where his tomb is. When the coffin containing his ashes was loaded on the flank of a beast of burden, his works were placed on the other side to counterbalance it. I was standing there motionless; with me was the jurist and man of letters Abu'l Ḥusayn Muḥammad ibn Jubayr, secretary of the *sayyid* Abū Saʿīd [an Almuhad prince] and my friend Abu'l-Ḥakam ʿAmr ibn al-Sarrāj, the copyist. Abu'l-Ḥakam turned toward us and said: 'Have you not observed what serves as a counterweight to the master Averroes on his mount? On one side the master [*imām*], on the other his works, the books he wrote.' And Ibn Jubayr answered him: 'You say I do not observe, O my child? I assuredly do. And blessed be your tongue!' Then I stored up within me [Abu'l-Ḥakam's words] as a theme of meditation and recollection. I am now the sole survivor among that little group of friends—may God have mercy on them—and then I said: 'On one side the master, on the other his works. Ah! how I wish I knew whether his hopes have been fulfilled.' "[14]

Is not all of Ibn ʿArabī in this extraordinary episode, this threefold meeting with Averroes? On the first occasion it is "the disciple of Khiḍr," he who does not owe his knowledge of spiritual experience to human teaching, who bears witness. On the second, it is the author of the "Book of Theophanies" who speaks, he who has full access to the intermediate suprasensory world, *ʿālam al-mithāl,* where the Active Imagination perceives events, figures, presences directly, unaided by the senses. Finally, overwhelming in its simplicity, fraught with the mute eloquence of symbols, the return of the mortal remains to Cordova. A last homage is rendered to the master, whose essential work has been to restore integral Aristotelianism in all its purity, by the "son of Plato," contemporary of the Platonists of Persia (Suhrawardī's Ishrāqīyūn) who, unbeknownst to the Occident, inaugurated a development which anticipated and surpassed the projects of a Gemistos Pletho or

14. Cf. Asín Palacios, *El Islam cristianizado,* pp. 39–40; *Futūḥāt,* I, 153–54.

of a Marsilio Ficino. And in the presence of this scene with its unpremeditated symbolism, of the books counterbalancing the corpse, the melancholy question: "Ah! how I wish I knew whether his hopes have been fulfilled."

The same desire—"how I wish I knew"—rose to the lips of the "interpreter of ardent desires" some years later when on a night of pensive melancholy he circumambulated the Kaʿaba. It is of no importance whether he actually performed the rite or whether it was only an inner vision. That night in any case he heard the answer—from the lips of Her who as long as he lived would remain for him the theophanic figure of *Sophia aeterna.* We shall have occasion to meditate the answer below (Ch. II). It contains the secret on which depended the fulfilment of the desires of the man of desire, because as soon as he consents to his God, he himself becomes a pledge *for* this God who shares his destiny; and it is a secret which also determines that the dawn of resurrection risen over the mystic soul will not be reversed to become the dismal twilight of doubt, the cynical rejoicing of the Ignorant at the thought that transcendence has at last been overcome. If that should happen, yes indeed, the momentary survivors would behold nothing more than the mocking spectacle of a bundle of books counterbalancing a corpse.

But Ibn ʿArabī knew that this triumph is obtained neither by the effort of rational philosophy, nor by conversion to what he was later to term a "God created in dogmas." It depends on a certain decisive encounter, which is entirely personal, irreplaceable, barely communicable to the most fraternal soul, still less translatable in terms of any change of external allegiance or social quality. It is the fruit of a long quest, the work of an entire lifetime; Ibn ʿArabī's whole life was this long Quest. The decisive encounter took place and was renewed for him through Figures whose variants never ceased to refer to the same Person. As we know, he read many books. For this very reason an inventory of his "sources" is perhaps a hopeless undertaking, especially if we persist in speaking of syncretism instead of applying ourselves to the true measure of this spiritual genius who accepted only what was consonant with his "inner Heaven" and who is above all his own "explanation." Moreover, far more is involved than a question of literary sources. There is the secret of a structure whereby the edifice was closely related in style to the edifice which sprang up in eastern Islam, where Shīʿism observed the precept "Do not strike at the face"—that is, preserve the outer face of literal Islam, not only because it is the indispensable support of the symbols, but also because it is a safeguard against the tyranny of the ignorant.

In addition there are all the invisible, inaudible factors, all that which rests on no other proof than personal testimony to the existence of the subtile world. There are, for example, the visitations of persons belonging to the esoteric, invisible hierarchy, to the confraternities of spiritual beings who form a bond between our world, or rather between each existence, and other universes. They dominate the parallelism of the cosmic hierarchies in Ismailism and live on in the Shaikhism of our time. Undoubtedly they were present to mystic consciousness long before Islam, but is it possible that they should have deserted the place of Koranic Revelation?[15] These are elements of the Spiritual Diary dispersed through the work of Ibn ʿArabī (as of Swedenborg). And all this is beyond the domain of philology or even of psychology, especially a psychology that has already

15. The idea of this mystic hierarchy recurs in variants throughout the esoterism of Islam. In Ibn ʿArabī the degrees of esoteric dignity or perfection are the following: (1) the *Quṭb* (Pole) around which the sphere of the world's spiritual life revolves; (2) two *Imāms* (Guides), who are the vicars of the "Pole" and succeed him at his death; (3) four *Awtād* (Pillars), who perform their mission at each of the four cardinal points; (4) seven *Abdāl* (Substitutes), who perform their mission in each of the seven climates; (5) twelve *Naqīb* (Chiefs) for the twelve signs of the Zodiac; (6) eight *Najīb* (Nobles) for the eight celestial spheres (Asín, *El Islam cristianizado*, p. 41, n. 2). In addition, for each of the degrees or "abodes" along the spiritual path, there is in each epoch a mystic who is the pole around which revolve the acts, specific to that "abode," of all those who occupy it in this world (ibid., p. 56).

formed an idea of the limits of man and of the negative character of mystic experience. But it is eminently the subject matter of the prophetic psychology which held the attention of every philosopher in Islam.

Finally, there are the innumerable spiritual masters, the Ṣūfī *shaikhs*, his contemporaries on earth, whom Ibn ʿArabī met and whose teaching he wished to know. He himself left a journal of these encounters in his *Risālat al-Quds*. Moreover, though he read books, though he had visible and invisible masters, the earnestness of his Quest forbade him to rely on second-hand reports; further, his complete inner freedom left him indifferent to the fear of so-called "dangerous" associations. Consequently, we can trust him and rely on the authenticity of what he relates: "I know," he says, "of no degree of mystic life, no religion or sect, but I myself have met someone who professed it, who believed in it and practiced it as his personal religion. I have never spoken of an opinion or doctrine without building on the direct statements of persons who were its adepts." This visionary master provides an example of perfect scientific probity; every student of religions, every theologian, might well adopt his maxim, even when their aim is not the specific aim of Ibn ʿArabī's quest.

The Pilgrim to the Orient

Bearing all this in mind, we shall now follow our *shaikh* in the life of wandering which was one form of his earthly calling and which began at the approach of his thirtieth year. Between 1193 and 1200 he visited different parts of Andalusia and made several journeys of varying duration to North Africa. But these restless wanderings were only a prelude to the inner call, or rather the imperious vision, which would lead him to leave Andalusia and the Maghrib forever, and make of him a symbolic pilgrim to the Orient.

Encounters with holy men, mystic conferences, sessions of instruction and discussion mark the stages of his successive or repeated itineraries: Fez, Tlemcen, Bougie, Tunis, etc. It would be of the utmost interest to co-ordinate the pages of his Spiritual Diary noting personal events occurring in the invisible dimension with the physical happenings of this period in his life. Ibn ʿArabī was actually in Cordova when the vision came to him, but it was not "in Cordova" that he contemplated the persons who were the spiritual poles of all the peoples who had succeeded one another before the coming of Islam; he even learned their names in the course of this inner vision which accorded with his secret and fundamental preoccupation with an eternal religion, extending from the origin of origins down through the history of the human race, whose Spirituals it gathers together, at all times, in a single *corpus mysticum*. Visionary event, ecstatic initiation, whose time and place are the *ʿālam al-mithāl*, the world intermediate between the corporeal and the spiritual state and whose organ of perception is the active Imagination.

It was actually in Tunis that one evening, withdrawn in a prayer niche of the Great Mosque, he composed a poem which he communicated to no one. He did not even commit it to writing, but registered the day and the hour of his inspiration in his memory. A few months later, in Seville, a young man unknown to him, approached him and recited the verses. Overwhelmed, Ibn ʿArabī asked him: "Who is their author?" And the other replied: "Muḥammad Ibn ʿArabī." The young man had never seen Ibn ʿArabī and did not know who was standing before him. Then how did he know the verses? A few months before (the very day and hour when the inspiration had come to Ibn ʿArabī in Tunis) a stranger, an unknown pilgrim, had mingled, here in Seville, with a group of young men, and had recited a poem which they, delighted, had begged him to repeat in order that they might learn it by heart. Having done so the stranger had disappeared without making himself known or leaving any trace. Similar events were well known to the masters of Ṣūfism; the experience was frequent, for example, with the great Iranian *shaikh* ʿAlā'uddawla Semnānī (fourteenth century). The parapsychology of our days registers them with care, but neither dares nor is able to draw any conclusions from this suspension, or rather transcending, of the spatiotemporal conditions of sense perception. The cosmology of Ṣūfism possesses a dimension—lacking in our view of the world—which takes account of such experience. It guarantees the "objective" reality of the supersensory world in which are manifested the effects of a spiritual energy whose source is the *heart* and whose organ is the active Imagination.

It is "on earth," however, in the vicinity of Ronda, that Ibn ʿArabī had a long discussion with a self-assured Muʿtazilite scholastic. They argued, disagreeing about the doctrine of Names which, as we shall see, is the central pillar of our *shaikh*'s theophanic edifice. In the end the Muʿtazilite capitulated. And it was "actually" in Tunis that Ibn ʿArabī began to study an exceptionally important work of mystic theosophy: the *Khalʿ al-naʿlayn* (Removal of the sandals), the title being an allusion to Koran verse xx:12, to the command heard by Moses on approaching the burning bush: "Remove thy sandals." It is the sole surviving work of Ibn Qasī, whom we have already mentioned as the founder in the first half of the twelfth century in southern Portugal (Algarbes) of the Murīdīn, an insurrectional movement directed against the Almoravides. The movement, or at least the foundations of its esoteric doctrine, was of Ismailian Shīʿite inspiration. Ibn ʿArabī himself wrote a commentary on the book; a study of it will assuredly help to throw light on the affinities that have been noted between the doctrine of Ibn ʿArabī and Shīʿite theosophy, affinities which account for his rapid assimilation by the Shīʿite Ṣūfism of Iran.

Ibn Qasī's movement of the Murīdīn (the adepts) had as its original source the school of Almería to which Asín Palacios inclined to relate Ibn ʿArabī's esoteric initiation. The teachings of the school of Almeria, in turn, can probably be traced back, through the Ṣūfī master Ibn al-ʿArīf, to Ibn Masarra (d.

319/931), and his Neoempedoclean doctrines, certain aspects of which have obvious traits in common with the Ismailian cosmology and that of Suhrawardī's *Ishrāq*. Of course we should not look to this notion of Ibn Masarra as precursor for a complete explanation of Ibn 'Arabī. The fact remains, however, that it was the ample quotations provided by Ibn 'Arabī which enabled Asín Palacios to reconstitute in its broad outlines the lost work of Ibn Masarra; and Ibn 'Arabī's friendship with Abū 'Abdallah al-Ghazzāl, who was Ibn al-'Arīf's disciple and continued his teaching, also suggests a profound tie.[16]

Be that as it may, it is in Almería that we find our *shaikh* in 1198—the year of Averroes' funeral—after the above-mentioned peregrinations and a brief return to his native Murcia. The month of Ramaḍān, unpropitious for traveling, was beginning. Ibn 'Arabī took advantage of his stay in Almería to write an opusculum whose content announces the great works to follow. This little book, which he entitled *Mawāqi' al-nujūm* (the orbits of the stars), was written in eleven days under stress of an inspiration confirmed in a dream, which commanded him to write an introduction to spiritual life. "It is a book," he writes elsewhere, "which enables a beginner to dispense with a master, or rather: it is indispensable to the master. For there are eminent, exceedingly eminent masters, and this book will help them to attain the highest mystic degree to which a master can aspire." In it, under the veil of the astronomical symbols, our *shaikh* describes the Light that God bestows on the Ṣūfi in the course of the three stages of the Way. The first stage, purely exoteric, consists in the outward practice of the *sharī'a*, or literal religion. Ibn 'Arabī symbolizes it by the stars whose brilliance darkens as soon as the full moon of the other two

16. Cf. Asín Palacios, "Ibn Masarra y su escuela: origines de la filosofía hispano-musulmana," in *Obras escogidas*, I, 144–45, and "El Místico Abu'l-'Abbās ibn al-'Arīf de Almería," ibid., I, 222–23. We have referred above to the links established by Asín between the school of Almería and Neoempedoclism as well as the gnosis of Priscillian; cf. Asín, "Ibn Masarra," I, 38 ff.

stages rises, the stages in the course of which the Ṣūfi is initiated into the *ta'wīl*, the symbolic exegesis which "carries back" the literal statements to that which they symbolize and of which they are the "cipher,"—taught, in other words, how to interpret the external rites in their mystic, esoteric sense. Now, as we have said, it is not possible to utter the word *ta'wīl* without suggesting Shī'ism, whose fundamental scriptural principle it is that every exoteric meaning (*ẓāhir*) has an esoteric counterpart (*bāṭin*). And throughout Western Islam this sufficed to alarm the authorities, jealous of the legalitarian religion and of the literal truth.

Thus it is not to be wondered at if Ibn 'Arabī had a presentiment that life in Andalusia would soon become impossible for him. There were tragic precedents (Ibn Qasī, Ibn Barrajān). Whoever departed from literalism was suspected of fomenting political disorder. Ibn 'Arabī was not concerned with politics, but once he had started on his path, the alternative was to remain unknown to official circles or to arouse their suspicions. It is no easy matter for a man like Ibn 'Arabī to pass unnoticed. He himself speaks of violent religious discussions between himself and the sultan Ya'qūb al-Manṣūr. His only hope of finding a wider audience, of meeting with greater tolerance, lay in leaving Andalusia, the Maghrib, and the atmosphere created by the Almuhad sultans, for the Eastern Islamic world where indeed so many of his disciples were to thrive down through the centuries.

His decision was taken in consequence of a theophanic vision: He saw God's throne supported by an incalculable number of flashing columns of fire. The concavity of the Throne, which conceals its treasure, the celestial Anthropos, projected a shadow which veiled the light of the Enthroned One, making it endurable and contemplatable; in the softness of this shadow there reigned an ineffable peace. (Thus the vision configures with precision the mystery of divine anthropomorphosis in the celestial world, which is the foundation of the theophanic idea, of the dialectic of love, and also the central secret of Shīʿite imāmology). A bird whose marvelous beauty surpassed the beauty of all other celestial birds was circling round the Throne. It was the bird who communicated to the visionary the order to set out for the Orient: he himself would be his companion and celestial guide. At the same time he disclosed to Ibn ʿArabī the name of an earthly companion who was awaiting him in Fez, a man who had expressed the desire to leave for the Orient but who had received a divine premonition that he should wait for the companion who had been reserved for him. In this bird with his celestial beauty, it is not difficult to recognize a figuration of the Holy Spirit, that is, of the Angel Gabriel, Angel of Knowledge and Revelation, to whom the philosophers "traced back" their active Intelligence. This is an infinitely precious datum, enabling us at this decisive moment to appreciate the form of Ibn ʿArabī's spiritual experience. The visionary image that rose to his consciousness shows us that this was the very Figure whose identity under many variants has been disclosed to us in connection with the Uwaysīs. He is the personal Holy Spirit, in his own words the "companion and celestial guide"; we shall meet with him elsewhere in other forms, notably "around the mystic Kaʿaba." Against this visionary setting Ibn ʿArabī, the pilgrim to the Orient, seems to stand out as a personification of the hero of Suhrawardī's "Recital of Occidental Exile."

With this departure begins the second phase of our *shaikh*'s life of wandering. Between 597/1200 and 620/1223 it would lead him to various regions of the Near East, until at last he settled in Damascus, where he was to pass the last seventeen years of his life in peace and arduous labors. In 598/1201 when he reached Mecca, the first goal of his pilgrimage, Ibn ʿArabī was thirty-six years of age. This first stay in the holy city was to be so profound an experience that it formed the basis of what we shall read later on about the "dialectic of love." He received the hospitality of a noble Iranian family from Ispahān, the head of the house being a *shaikh* occupying a high post in Mecca. This *shaikh* had a daughter who combined extraordinary physical beauty with great spiritual wisdom. She was for Ibn ʿArabī what Beatrice was to be for Dante; she was and remained for him the earthly manifestation, the theophanic figure, of *Sophia aeterna*. It was to her that he owed his initiation into the *Fedeli d'amore*. We shall find ample traces of this incident below (Ch. II). Not to understand, or to affect not to take seriously Ibn ʿArabī's conscious intention, in addressing the young girl Sophia, of expressing a divine love, would be neither more nor less than to close one's eyes to the theophanism on which this book insists because it is the very foundation of our *shaikh*'s doctrine, the key to his feeling for the universe, God and man, and for the relationships between them. If, on the other hand, one has understood, one will perhaps by that same token, glimpse a solution to the conflict between symbolists and philologists in connection with the religion of the *Fedeli d'amore*, Dante's companions. For theophanism there is no dilemma, because it is equally far removed from allegorism and literalism; it presupposes the existence of the concrete person, but invests that person with a function which transfigures him, because he is perceived in the light of another world.

His frequentation of the *shaikh*'s family and of the small élite circle surrounding it, gave Ibn ʿArabī the quiet intimacy, the confident peace of which he seems to have been deprived during his years in the West. His stay in Mecca was the beginning of his extraordinary productivity. His mystic life became more intense; his circumambulations, real or imagined, of the Kaʿaba internalized as a "cosmic center," nourished a speculative effort to which inner visions and theophanic perceptions lent experimental confirmation. Ibn ʿArabī was received into the Ṣūfī brotherhood as he had been years before in Seville. But this, after all, was only an outward sign.

The real and decisive event was similar to that which had been at the source of his departure for the Orient. It could be only provoked by meditation "around the Kaʿaba," because such events occur only "in the center of the world," that is, at the pole of the internal microcosm, and the Kaʿaba is the "center of the world." It was here that the visionary once again met his personal Holy Spirit, who, in communicating to him the order to undertake his pilgrimage, had announced himself as Ibn ʿArabī's companion and celestial guide. Later on we shall examine the form of this encounter, this theophany of the divine Alter Ego which is at the origin of the immense book of the *Futūḥāt,* the book of the divine revelations received in Mecca. These privileged theophanic moments cut across the continuity of profane, quantified and irreversible time, but their *tempus discretum* (the time of angelology) does not enter into that continuity. This must be borne in mind when we attempt to link the theophanies together, that of the young girl Sophia, for instance, with that of the mystic youth in the prologue to the *Futūḥāt.* An encounter with theophanic persons always postulates a return to the "center of the world," because communication with the *ʿālam al-mithāl* is possible only at the "center of the world." Many other statements of our *shaikh* bear witness to this fact.[17] Finally, it is to the order of things implied by theophanies that we must relate the dominant trait of Ibn ʿArabī's character, the trait which made him not only, like most of the Ṣūfīs, a disciple of human masters, but above all and essentially the "disciple of Khiḍr."

The Disciple of Khiḍr

This trait in Ibn ʿArabī has already been seen to be a symbol guiding the curve of his life, and it has given us occasion to

17. For example (Asín, "Ibn Masarra," I, 83): The son of the Caliph Hārūn al-Rashīd, Aḥmad al-Sabati, a great spiritual who died in the second century of the Hegira, appeared to Ibn ʿArabī in corporeal form and spoke to him: "I met him when I was performing the ritual circumambulations of the Kaʿaba, one Friday in the year 599, after public prayer. I questioned him and he replied; but it was his spirit that had taken on sensible form in order to appear to me as I was turning about the temple, just as the Angel Gabriel appeared in the form of a young Arab."

identify him with those Ṣūfīs who are termed Uwaysīs. The spiritual individuality which this qualification presupposes has already enabled us to anticipate the existential choices on which are grounded, most often implicitly, the solutions given to the technical problem of the intellects, to the problem of the relation between the individual soul with the active Intelligence as the Holy Spirit which bestows existence and light. The mere fact that Ṣūfism recognized and approved the situation typical of the Uwaysīs (we have mentioned the cases of Abu'l-Ḥasan Kharraqānī and of Farīduddīn ʿAṭṭār) would suffice to forestall any hasty comparison between Ṣūfism and Christian monachism, for the latter does not seem capable of offering anything comparable.

It has seemed to us that the fact of having Khiḍr for a master invests the disciple, as an individual, with a transcendent, "transhistorical" dimension. This is something more than his incorporation into a brotherhood of Ṣūfis in Seville or Mecca; it is a personal, direct, and immediate bond with the Godhead. What remains to be established is the place of Khiḍr in the order of theophanies: How is he, as an unearthly, spiritual guide, related to the recurrent manifestations of that Figure in which, under various typifications, we can recognize the Holy Spirit, or in other words, what is his relation to the supreme theophany proclaimed in the *ḥadīth* which we shall meditate below: "I contemplated the Lord in the most beautiful of forms" (cf. below, Ch. VI). In seeking an answer to this question we are led to ask whether the disciple's relation to Khiḍr is similar to the relation he would have had with any visible earthly *shaikh*—a relation implying a numerical juxtaposition of persons, with the difference that in the one case one of these persons is perceptible only in the *ʿālam al-mithāl.* In other words, does Khiḍr in this relationship figure as an archetype, according to the definition established by analytical psychology, or as a distinct and enduring personality? But is the dilemma involved in our question not dissipated once we become aware that the answers to two questions—*Who is Khiḍr?* and *What does it mean to be a disciple of Khiḍr?*—illuminate each other existentially.

For a complete answer to the question *Who is Khiḍr?* we should have to compile a very considerable mass of material from very divergent sources: prophetology, folklore, alchemy, etc.; but since we here consider him essentially as the invisible spiritual master, reserved for those who are called to a direct unmediated relationship with the divine world—that is, a bond seeking no historical justification in a historical succession of *shaikhs*—for those who owe their investiture to no authority, we can confine ourselves to certain essential points: his appearance in the Koran, the meaning of his name, his connection with the prophet Elijah,[18] and in turn the connection between Elijah and the Imām of Shīʿism.

In Sūra XVIII (vv. 59–81) Khiḍr figures in a mysterious episode, a thorough study of which would require an exhaustive confrontation with the earliest Koran commentaries. He is represented as Moses' guide, who initiates Moses "into the science of predestination." Thus he reveals himself to be the repository of an inspired divine science, superior to the law (*sharīʿa*); thus Khiḍr is superior to Moses in so far as Moses is a prophet invested with the mission of revealing a *sharīʿa*. He reveals to Moses precisely the secret, mystic truth (*ḥaqīqa*) that transcends the *sharīʿa*, and this explains why the spirituality inaugurated by Khiḍr is free from the servitude of the literal religion. If we consider that Khiḍr's mission is likewise related to the spiritual mission of the Imām through the identification of Khiḍr with Elijah, it becomes evident that we have here one of the scriptural foundations on which the deepest aspiration of Shīʿism is built. And indeed Khiḍr's pre-eminence over Moses ceases to be a paradox only if we consider it in this light; otherwise, Moses remains one of the six pre-eminent prophets

18. On this important point, see Louis Massignon's study "Élie et son rôle transhistorique, *Khadirīya*, en Islam," *Élie le prophète*, II, 269–90.

charged with revealing a *sharīʿa,* while Khiḍr is merely one of the hundred and eighty thousand *nabīs,* mentioned in our traditions.

True, his earthly genealogy raises a problem which defies historical analysis. According to certain traditions, he is a descendent of Noah in the fifth generation.[19] In any case, we are far from the chronological dimension of historical time. Unless we situate these events in the *ʿālam al-mithāl,* we shall never find a rational justification of the Koran episode in which Khiḍr-Elijah meets Moses as if they were contemporaries. The event partakes of a different synchronism, whose peculiar qualitative temporality we have already noted. And moreover, how can "objective" historical methods be applied to the most characteristic episode of Khiḍr's career? He is described as he who has attained the source of life, has drunk of the water of immortality, and consequently knows neither old age nor death. He is the "Eternal Youth." And for this reason no doubt, we should discard the usual vocalizations of his name (Persian *Khezr,* Arabic *Khiḍr*) in favor of *Khāḍir* and follow Louis Massignon in translating it as "the Verdant One." He is indeed associated with every aspect of Nature's greenness. But let us not, for that reason, interpret him as a "vegetation myth," which would be meaningless unless we presupposed the special mode of perception implied by the presence of *Khāḍir.*

Such a mode of perception is indeed involved; it is bound up with the extraordinary pre-eminence, still unexplained it must be admitted, accorded to the color green in Islam. Green is "the spiritual, liturgical color of Islam"; it is the color of the ʿAlids, that is, the Shīʿite color par excellence. The twelfth, "hidden Imām," the "lord of this Time," dwells on the Green Island in the middle of the Sea of Whiteness. The great Iranian Ṣūfī Semnānī (fourteenth century) inaugurated a subtile physiology, whose *centers* are typefied by "the seven prophets of thy being."

19. Cf. ʿAbbās Qummī, *Safīnat Biḥār al-Anwār,* I, 389.

1 *Elijah and Khiḍr at the Fountain of Life*

Persian, School of Herāt, late fifteenth century

Each has its specific color. Whereas the subtile center of the arcanum, the "Jesus of thy being" has luminous black (*aswad nūrānī*, "black light") as its color, the color of the supreme center, the "mystery of mysteries," the "Muḥammad of thy being," is green.[20]

It is impossible within the limits of this introduction to explain why Khiḍr and Elijah are sometimes associated to form a pair and sometimes identified with one another.[21] The Shī'ite traditions, notably certain dialogues with the Fifth Imām, Muḥammad Baqīr, tell us something concerning the persons of Elijah and Elisha.[22] What concerns us here, in connection with the person of Khiḍr-Elijah as initiator of the mystic truth which emancipates one from literal religion, is the bond with the person of the Imām which these traditions establish. One must have read certain of the homilies attributed to the First Imām in order to understand what Shī'ism is: there is incomparable power in its incantation of the prophetic Word, its flashing lyricism. If the "historicity" of these homilies has been doubted, such doubt perhaps is merely the profane aspect of the impression made by a speaker who seemed to be uttering the Word of an eternal Imām rather than that of an empirical and historical person. In any case they exist, and their content is by no means the legitimist political polemic to which certain writers have tried to reduce Shī'ism, forgetting that it is a religious phenomenon, hence a primordial, original datum (like the perception of a color or of a sound) which cannot be "explained" by a causal derivation from something else.

In these homilies Shī'ism shows its power to encompass the secret meaning of all Revelations. In one of them the Imām utters the names under which he has been successively known by all nations, those who have a revealed Book (*ahl al-Kitāb*) and those who have none. Speaking to the Christians, he says: "I

20. See our "L'Intériorisation du sens."
21. Cf. Massignon, "Élie et son rôle transhistorique."
22. Cf. 'Abbās Qummī, *Safīnat*, I, 27–29; II, 733.

am he whose name in the Gospel is Elijah."[23] Here Shīʿism in the person of Imām proclaims itself to be the witness to the Transfiguration, the metamorphosis; Moses' meeting with Elijah-Khiḍr as his initiand in the eighteenth Sūra has as its counterpart the colloquy between Moses and Elijah (that is, the Imām) on Mount Tabor. This typology is extremely eloquent as to the intentions of the Shīʿite mind. It would be a simple matter to compile testimonies showing how Shīʿite thinking, if we hearken to it, upsets our current idea of the relations between Christianity and Islam. Ismailian esoterism has another homily in which the Imām proclaims: "I am the Christ who cures the blind and the lepers [which means the second Christ, we read in a gloss]. I am he and he is I."[24] And if elsewhere the Imām is designated as Melchizedek, we easily discern the connection between this imāmology and the christology of the Melchizedekian Christians who saw in this supernatural person the true "Son of God," the Holy Spirit.

Here we have only thrown out a few indications concerning the person of Khiḍr-Elijah. Set in context, they suffice to give us an idea of the vast sum of human experience concealed behind this theme. But in the presence of such complexity, of a Figure that discloses so many associations and undergoes so many metamorphoses, our only hope of arriving at a significant result lies in the phenomenological method. We must lay bare the implicit intentions of the mystic consciousness, discern what it *shows* itself of itself when it shows itself the figure of Khiḍr-Elijah in all its many aspects and implications. In the present instance, however, our sole purpose in envisaging such a phenomenology is to suggest an answer to the question of *who is* Khiḍr, considered as the invisible spiritual master of a mystic subordinated to the teaching of no earthly master and of no collectivity—precisely what Averroes had admired in the young

23. Ibid., I, 389 and Majlisī, *Biḥār al-Anwār*, IX, 10.
24. Jaʿfar b. Mansūri'l Yaman, *Kitābu'l Kashf*, p. 8.

Ibn ʿArabī. Phenomenologically speaking, the question is equivalent to this other question: What does it mean to *be* the disciple of Khiḍr? To what act of self-awareness does the fact of recognizing oneself to be the disciple of Khiḍr correspond?

We have already intimated that the question thus formulated enables us to dispel in advance the dilemma that might be stated in these terms: are we dealing with an archetype or with a real person? It is not hard to see how great a loss either answer would involve. If, taking the standpoint of analytical psychology, we speak of Khiḍr as an archetype, he will seem to lose his reality and become a figment of the imagination, if not of the intellect. And if we speak of him as a real person, we shall no longer be able to characterize the difference in structure between Khiḍr's relationship with his disciple and the relationship that any other *shaikh* on this earth can have with his. In this case Khiḍr, numerically one, faces a plurality of disciples in a relationship which is hardly compatible with the fervent sentiment of the one consorting with the one. In short, these answers are not adequate to the *phenomenon* of Khiḍr's person.

But perhaps there is another path that will lead us to an understanding of the phenomenon as it occurs among our Ṣūfīs. Suhrawardī seems to open up such a path in an intention that is quite consonant with that of Ibn ʿArabī. In one of the recitals that make up Suhrawardī's spiritual autobiography, that of "The Purple Archangel," the mystic is initiated into the secret which enables him to ascend Mount Qāf, that is, the cosmic mountain, and to attain to the Spring of Life. He is frightened at the thought of the difficulties of the Quest. But the Angel says to him: "Put on the sandals of Khiḍr." And his concluding words: "He who bathes in that spring will be preserved forever from all taint. If someone has discovered the meaning of the mystic Truth, it means that he has attained to the Spring. When he emerges, he has gained the aptitude that makes him resemble that balm, a drop of which distilled in the palm of the hand, if you hold it up to the sun, passes through to the back of the hand. If you *are Khiḍr*, you too can ascend Mount Qāf without difficulty." And the "Recital of Occidental Exile" describes the journey leading to the summit of Mount Qāf, at the foot of the *emerald* rock, the mystic Sinai, where resides the Holy Spirit, the Angel of mankind, whom the philosopher in this same recital identifies as the "Active Intelligence" and situates at the base of the hierarchy of the cherubic Intelligences. The essence of this answer is to be sought in the words: *If you are Khiḍr.* For this *assimilation* fits in with the meaning which, as we shall soon see, Ibn ʿArabī was to attribute to his own investiture with the "mantle" of Khiḍr, a happening which he relates to the general significance of the rite, for its effect indeed is to identify the *spiritual* state of him who receives the investiture with the spiritual state of him who confers it upon him.

This suggests what it means to *be* the disciple of Khiḍr. And this meaning is such that though the person of Khiḍr does not resolve itself into a simple archetypal schema, the presence of his person is experienced in a relationship which transforms it into an archetype; if this relationship is to *show* itself phenomenologically, a situation corresponding to its two fundamental terms is required. Such a relationship implies that Khiḍr be experienced simultaneously as a person and as an archetype, as a person-archetype. Because he is an archetype, the unity and identity of Khiḍr's person is compatible with the plurality of his exemplifications in those who *are* by turn Khiḍr. To have him as a master and initiand is to be obliged to *be* what he himself *is*. Khiḍr is the master of all those who are masterless, because he *shows* all those whose master he is how to *be* what he himself is: he who has attained the Spring of Life, the Eternal Youth, is, as Suhrawardī's recital makes it clear ("If you are Khiḍr . . ."), he who has attained *ḥaqīqa*, the mystic, esoteric truth which dominates the Law, and frees us from the literal religion. Khiḍr is the master of *all* these, because he shows *each one* how to attain the spiritual state which he himself has attained and which he typifies. His relationship with each one is the relationship of the exemplar or the exemplified with him who exemplifies it. This is what enables him to be at once his own person and an archetype, and it is by being one and the other that he is able to be each man's master, because he exemplifies himself as many times as he has disciples, and his role is to reveal each disciple to himself.

Indeed, Khiḍr's "guidance" does not consist in leading all his disciples uniformly to the same goal, to one theophany identical for all, in the manner of a theologian propagating his dogma. He leads each disciple to his own theophany, the theophany of which he personally is the witness, because that theophany corresponds to his "inner heaven," to the form of his own being, to his eternal individuality (*'ayn thābita*), in other words, to what Abū Yazīd Basṭāmī calls the "part allotted" to each of the Spirituals and which, in Ibn 'Arabī's words, is that one of the divine Names which is invested in him, the name by which he knows his God and by which his God knows him; that is the interdependence between *rabb* and *marbub,* between the lord of love and his vassal (see Ch. I). In Semnānī's words, we should say that the Khiḍr's mission consists in enabling you to attain to the "Khiḍr of your being," for it is in this inner depth, in this "prophet of your being," that springs the Water of Life at the foot of the mystic Sinai, pole of the microcosm, center of the world, etc. This is also in keeping with the vision of our Uwaysīs: Guided and initiated by Manṣūr Ḥallāj's being-of-light, his "Angel," 'Aṭṭār attains to the "Manṣūr of his being," becomes Manṣūr in the course of the fifty passionate last pages of his *Haylāj-Nāma*. It also falls in with 'Alī Wafā's (fourteenth century) saying to the effect that in the voice of a Khiḍr every Spiritual hears the inspiration of his own Holy Spirit, just as every prophet perceives the spirit of his own prophecy in the form of an Angel Gabriel. And this merely echoes the words of 'Abd al-Karīm Jīlī (which we shall read below) concerning the Holy Spirit, the divine Face, of every being. To become Khidr is to have attained an aptitude for theophanic vision, for the *visio smaragdina*, for the encounter with the divine Alter Ego, for the ineffable dialogue which the genius of Ibn ʿArabī will nevertheless succeed in recounting.

Once again we are carried back to the Figure whose recurrences we have noted not only in mystic theosophy but also in the philosophers when through the problems of noetics the Active Intelligence makes itself known to them as the intelligence of the Angel of Knowledge and Revelation, that is to say, the Holy Spirit (according to Koranic Revelation itself, which identifies Gabriel, the Angel of the Annunciation, with the Holy Spirit). We have pointed out the existential implications of this problem (in Abu'l-Barakāt, in Avicenna, in Averroes), insofar as each individual's solution of it defines the status of his spirituality. Khiḍr as a personal invisible guide, free, and in turn freeing the man he guides from any legalistic or authoritarian servitude, bears a marked kinship to the "Perfect Nature" of Abu'l-Barakāt and Suhrawardī, while for Avicenna no doubt the "Khiḍr of his being" took the name of Ḥayy ibn Yaqẓān. The panic aroused by Latin Avicennism among the orthodox believers of the West might perhaps be defined as the fear of having to recognize the individual ministry of Khiḍr. It is true that Avicennan noetics and angelology led to an exaltation of the idea of the Angel, which was utterly shocking to orthodox scholasticism; but in reality Avicennism and scholasticism were in every way worlds apart: in their vocabulary, their ideas, and their existential situations. This Angel is not a simple messenger transmitting orders, nor the usual "guardian angel," nor the angel evoked by the Sunnites in their discussions of which is superior, the man or his angel. This angel is bound up with the idea that the Form under which each of the Spirituals knows God is also the form under which God knows him, because it is the form under which God reveals Himself to Himself in that man. For Ibn ʿArabī the Angel represents the essential correlation between the form of a theophany and the form of him to whom it is disclosed. He is the "part allotted" to each Spiritual, his absolute individuality, the divine Name invested in him. He is the essential *theophanism;* every theophany has the form of an angelophany, because it is determined by this correlation; and precisely in this essential determination, without which the divine Being would remain unknown and inaccessible, lies the significance of the *Angel.* Once this has been understood, the way in which Ibn ʿArabī as a disciple of Khiḍr meditates the philoxeny of Abraham (see below, Ch. I, §3), leads to the very heart of his theosophy and mystic experience, to a secret which is also that of the *Cherubinic Wanderer* of Angelus Silesius, which to the mystic means: to feed the Angel from one's own substance.

It remains for us only to single out, in Ibn ʿArabī's life, a few *memorabilia* concerning his encounters with Khiḍr. Two episodes of his youth bear witness to Khiḍr's latent presence in his mind. This presence, manifested by a piety which was so much a part of his life and person that it never wavered, attained its culmination on the day when, in a garden in Mosul, Ibn ʿArabī was invested with the "mantle" (*khirqa*) of Khiḍr at the hands of a friend, who had himself been directly invested with it. The ritual of this investiture is shrouded in mystery.

A first memorable encounter took place in the days of his youth, when he was studying in Seville, but it was not until afterward that the young Ibn ʿArabī knew *whom* he had met. He had just left his master (Abu'l Ḥasan al-Uryānī), with whom he had had a rather violent discussion concerning the identity of the person whom the Prophet had favored with his apparition. The disciple had stood firm and then, somewhat vexed and dissatisfied, taken his leave. At a turn in the street a stranger spoke to him affectionately: "O Muḥammad! Trust your master. It was indeed that person." The young man retraced his steps, meaning to inform his master that he had changed his mind, but on seeing him the *shaikh* stopped him with these words: "Must Khiḍr appear to you before you trust your master's words?" Then Ibn ʿArabī knew whom he had met. Later in Tunis, on a warm night of full moon, Ibn ʿArabī went to rest in the cabin of a boat anchored in the port. A feeling of uneasiness awakened him. He went to the edge of the vessel while the crew was still plunged in sleep. And he saw coming toward him, dry-shod over the waters, someone who approached and talked with him for a moment and then quickly withdrew into a grotto in the mountainside, some miles distant. The next day in Tunis a holy man unknown to him asked him: "Well, what happened last night with Khiḍr?"[25]

And now comes the far more important episode of his mystic investiture, which occurred in the year 601/1204. After a brief stay in Baghdād Ibn ʿArabī had gone to Mosul, whither he had been attracted by the reputation of the Ṣūfī master ʿAlī ibn Jāmiʿ, who had been invested with the *khirqa,* the Ṣūfī mantle by Khiḍr "in person." On the occasion of what theophanic event, with what ceremonial? Ibn ʿArabī does not tell us, but he does say that in investing him with the mystic mantle the *shaikh* had observed the same ceremonial in every detail. Here again it will be best to let Ibn ʿArabī speak for himself.

"This consociation with Khiḍr," he writes,[26] "was experienced by one of our *shaikhs,* the *shaikh* ʿAlī ibn ʿAbdillāh ibn Jāmiʿ, who was one of the disciples of ʿAlī al-Mutawakkil and of Abū Abdillāh Qaḍīb Albān. He lived in a garden he owned in the outskirts of Mosul. There Khiḍr had invested him with the mantle in the presence of Qaḍīb Albān. And it was in that very spot, in the garden where Khiḍr had invested him with it that the *shaikh* invested me with it in turn, observing the same ceremonial as Khiḍr himself had observed in conferring the investiture upon him. I had already received this investiture, but more indirectly, at the hands of my friend Taqiuddīn ibn ʿAbdirraḥman, who himself had received it at the hands of Sadruddīn, *shaikh* of *shaikhs* in Egypt, whose grandfather had received it from Khiḍr. It was then that I began to speak of the investiture with the

25. *Futūḥāt,* I, 186.
26. *Futūḥāt,* I, 187.

mantle and to confer it upon certain persons, because I discovered how much importance Khiḍr attached to this rite. Previously I had not spoken of the mantle which is now so well known. This mantle is for us indeed a symbol of confraternity, a sign that we share in the same spiritual culture, in the practice of the same *ethos*. It has become customary among the masters of mysticism that when they discern some deficiency in one of their disciples, the *shaikh* identifies himself mentally with the state of perfection he wishes to communicate. When he has effected this identification, he takes off the mantle he is wearing at the moment of achieving this spiritual state, and puts it on the disciple whose spiritual state he wishes to make perfect. In this way the *shaikh* communicates to the disciple the spiritual state he has produced in himself, and the same perfection is achieved in the disciple's state. Such is the rite of investiture, well known among us; it was communicated to us by the most experienced among our *shaikhs*."

This commentary shows that the rite of investiture with the mantle, whether at the hands of Khiḍr himself or through an intermediary, effects not only an affiliation, but an actual identification with Khiḍr's spiritual state. From that moment on the initiate fulfils the requisite condition—the condition indicated to Suhrawardī by the Angel—for ascending Mount Qāf and attaining at the Spring of Life: "If you are Khiḍr . . ." Henceforth the mystic is Khiḍr, he has attained the "Khiḍr of his being." Phenomenologically speaking, the real presence of Khiḍr is experienced simultaneously as that of a person and as that of an archetype, in other words as a person-archetype. This is the situation we have analyzed above, showing how it resolves the dilemma presented in terms of formal logic.

Let us carefully note the significance of the circumstances indicated by Ibn ʿArabī: investiture with the mantle can be conferred directly by Khiḍr, by an intermediary who has himself received it directly from Khiḍr, or even by one who has received it from the first intermediary. This does not detract from what we have shown to be the *transhistorical* significance of the rite, but provides, rather, a striking illustration of it. The ceremonial of investiture is always the ceremonial observed by Khiḍr himself; unfortunately Ibn ʿArabī leaves it shrouded in mystery. The rite implies in any case that the desired identification is not with a spiritual state or a state of perfection acquired from any other source by the *shaikh* who transmits the investiture, but only with the state of Khiḍr himself. Whether there are one or several intermediaries or none, the affiliation by identification with Khiḍr's state is accomplished in the longitudinal order connecting the visible with the invisible, an order cutting vertically across the latitudinal order of historical successions, generations, and connections. It is and remains a direct affiliation with the divine world, transcending all social ties and conventions. Accordingly, its significance remains transhistorical (a kind of antidote to the widespread obsession with the "trend of history").

It is also significant that Ibn ʿArabī accepted the investiture more than once. The first time there had been three intermediaries between Khiḍr and himself; now, in the garden in Mosul, there was only one. This implies the possibility of abridging the distance, the possibility of a contraction tending toward perfect synchronism (as in the case of the meeting between Khiḍr-Elijah and Moses in Sūra XVIII or on Mount Tabor). This synchronism results from a quantitative intensification which modifies temporal relations and is conceivable only in purely qualitative psychic time; in quantitative, continuous, and irreversible physical time such a bridging of distances is inconceivable. If, for example, you are chronologically separated from a spiritual master by several centuries, it is not possible for one of your contemporaries to bring you chronologically closer to him, as though he were that master's sole intermediary in time. We cannot do away with the intervals of quantitative time that serve to measure historical events; but the events of the soul are themselves the qualitative measure of their own characteristic time. A synchronism impossible in historical time is possible in the *tempus discretum* of the world of the soul or of the *ʿālam al-mithāl.* And this also explains how it is possible, at a distance of several centuries, to be the direct, synchronous disciple of a master who is only chronologically "in the past."

We have seen what it means "to be the disciple of Khiḍr" (as were all the Uwaysīs), and this is what Ibn ʿArabī meant when he said that he attached the utmost importance to the rite of investiture with the mantle and stated his intention of conferring it in turn on other persons. Through this rite he makes known his intention of guiding each one of his disciples to the "Khiḍr of his being." "If you *are* Khiḍr . . ." you can indeed do what Khiḍr *does*. And this is perhaps the secret reason for which the doctrine of Ibn ʿArabī was so feared by the adepts of the literal religion, of the historical faith hostile to the *ta'wīl,* of the dogma imposed uniformly upon all. He, on the other hand, who is the disciple of Khiḍr possesses sufficient inner strength to seek freely the teaching of all masters. Of this the biography of Ibn ʿArabī, who frequented all the masters of his day and welcomed their teachings, offers living proof.

This biography, whose characteristic measure we have endeavored to grasp in the rhythm of its three symbols, discloses an exemplary coherence. In the witness to Averroes' funeral, becoming the "pilgrim to the Orient" at the call of his "Holy Spirit," we have discerned a living exemplification of Suhrawardī's "Recital of Occidental Exile." The hero of the recital is led to the Spring of Life, to the mystic Sinai, where, having attained to the esoteric Truth, the *ḥaqīqa,* he passes through and beyond the darkness of the Law and of the exoteric religion, just as the drop of balm, in the light of the sun which induces transparence, passes through to the back of the hand. And it was likewise to the Spring of Life that the "pilgrim to the Orient," Ibn ʿArabī the "disciple of Khiḍr," was led when he forsook Andalusia, his earthly homeland.

His Maturity and the Completion of His Work

Ibn ʿArabī had now attained the age of maturity; he was in his fortieth year, which most masters (the "Brothers of Purity," for example, in their "philosophical ritual") regard as the earliest age at which the spiritual state entailing the decisive encounter with the personal "Guide" and all those tendencies involved in "being the disciple of Khiḍr" can come to fruition. Now we are in a position to follow our *shaikh* through the prodigiously full years of his maturity. Two years after the mystical investiture in the garden in Mosul (in 1204), we find him in Cairo in the company of a small group of Ṣūfīs, some of whom were his compatriots. The little community seems to have cultivated an intense mystical life, accepting the phenomena manifested among its members (photism, telepathy, mind reading) with simplicity and enthusiasm. One night Ibn Arabī contemplated a vision which seems to have reproduced certain traits of the vision which figures in the prelude to his great book, the *Futūḥāt* (see below, Ch. VI). A marvelously beautiful being entered the house and announced to him: "I am the messenger whom the Divine Being sends you." What the heavenly messenger revealed to him would be his own doctrine.

But to relate such visions and their teachings in hermetic language is one thing; to indulge in over-transparent allusions that may come to the ears of the redoubtable doctors of the Law, the *fuqahā'* of Cairo, is another. Undoubtedly Ibn ʿArabī held the *fuqahā'* in horror; he made no secret of his disgust at their stupidity, ignorance, and depravity, and such an attitude was not calculated to win their favor. The tension rose, giving rise to denunciations and arrests; our *shaikh* was in mortal peril. At this critical moment the irreducible antagonism between the spiritual Islam of Ṣūfism and legalitarian Islam became patent. Saved by the intervention of a friendly *shaikh*, Ibn ʿArabī had but one concern, to flee far from Cairo and its hateful, bigoted canonists. Where was he to seek refuge? He returned to Mecca

(1207). Six years after his first arrival in that city, he revisited the small élite group that had been his refuge on the first occasion, when he had known peace for the first time in his life and his literary production had soared. Once again he found the figure of pure beauty which for his contemplative imagination had been the theophany of divine Beauty, the figure of *Sophia aeterna*. He resumed his circumambulations of the Ka'aba, the "center of the world."

And yet this was to be merely a stage in his journey. Three years later (1210) he was in the heart of Anatolia, in Qunya, where the Seljuk emperor, Kay Kaus I accorded him a magnificent reception (similar to that which some thirty years before another Seljuk, the amir of Kharput, had given Suhrawardī, the resurrector of the philosophy of ancient Persia). Ibn 'Arabī's stay in Qunya was to assume an extraordinary importance for the destiny and orientation of the spiritual life of Ṣūfism in eastern Islam. Here his principal disciple was the young Ṣadruddīn Qunyawī (who became his son-in-law). It was in the person of Ṣadruddīn that the teachings of Ibn 'Arabī and Oriental Ṣūfism found their meeting place. Ṣadruddīn's work was considerable in itself; like that of many other Orientals, it was waiting for a "pilgrim to the Orient" who would reveal it to the West. He constitutes a nodal point in the spiritual topography outlined in the early pages of this book. The still-unpublished correspondence between him and Naṣīruddīn Ṭūsī, one of the great figures of Iranian Imāmism, treats of high questions of philosophy and mysticism; he was the teacher of Quṭbaddīn Shīrāzī, one of the most famous commentators on Suhrawardī's "philosophy of Light"; he was the friend of Sa'duddīn Hammū'ī, of whom we have spoken above; he was the teacher of one of the greatest Iranian mystic poets and *Fedeli d'amore*, Fakhruddīn 'Irāqī of Hamadān, whose famous theosophical poem in Persian (*Lami'āt*, "Divine Reflections") was directly inspired by the lessons of Ṣadruddīn commenting on one of Ibn 'Arabī's books. This poem, on which numerous commentaries were written, helped to introduce the doctrines of Ibn ʿArabī into Iran and India. Ṣadruddīn, the disciple of Ibn ʿArabī, was the intimate friend of Mawlānā Jalāluddīn Rūmī and died in the same year as he (1273).

This friendship was of the utmost importance, for through it Ṣadruddīn became the connecting link between the Shaikh al-Akbar and the author of the immense mystic *Mathnawī*, which the Iranians call the *Qorān-e fārsī*, the Persian Koran, and cultivate as such. An interval of ten years prevented physical encounter between the two men, who were perhaps the most representative figures of Ṣūfī spirituality. As a child, Mawlānā had fled from the Mongol invaders of Transoxania with his father, the venerable *shaikh* Bahā'uddīn Walad (whose ample collection of mystic sermons, the *Maʿārif*, cannot be disregarded if we wish to understand his son's spiritual doctrine). Their travels had carried them through Iran (where their meeting, in Nishapur, with the great mystic poet Farīduddīn ʿAṭṭār assumes a prophetic character) to Mecca; thence they had made their way slowly, by way of Damascus, to Asia Minor.

At first sight the teachings of Jalāluddīn Rūmī and of Ibn ʿArabī seem to reflect two radically different forms of spirituality. Mawlānā took no interest whatever in philosophers or philosophy; certain of his remarks might even have been compared with Ghazālī's attacks on philosophy in his "Destruction of the Philosophers." From this point of view he contrasts sharply with Suhrawardī, who wished his disciples to combine philosophical education with mystic experience, because both are necessary to the perfect Sage. A similar synthesis is effected in the work of Ibn ʿArabī, where pages of high theosophy alternate with the pages of a *Diarium spirituale*, so that the aim of speculation becomes a metaphysic of ecstasy. Yet it would be quite superficial to dwell on the contrast between the two forms of spirituality cultivated by Mawlānā and Ibn ʿArabī. Both are inspired by the same theophanic sentiment, the same nostalgia for beauty, and the same revelation of love. Both tend toward the same absorption of the visible and invisible, the physical and the spiritual, into an *unio mystica* in which the Beloved becomes a mirror reflecting the secret face of the mystic lover, while the lover, purified of the opacity of his ego, becomes in turn a mirror of the attributes and actions of the Beloved. Of this Ṣadruddīn, as well as Mawlānā's disciples, were well aware. References to the works of Ibn ʿArabī are frequent in the abundant commentaries on the *Mathnawī* produced in India and Iran. Indeed, it is necessary to study these commentaries if we wish to learn what Mawlānā's spirituality meant to his mystic following.

Ibn ʿArabī then continued on toward eastern Anatolia. We find him in Armenia, on the banks of the Euphrates, and subsequently in Diyarbekr. In the course of this journey he almost reached Iran; actually, he was to penetrate Iran in another way, invisibly and all the more durably (just as Suhrawardī, who never saw Iran again but nevertheless caused the ideas he had lived for to flower anew in Iran). In 1211 we find him in Baghdad, where he met the famous *shaikh* Shihābuddīn ʿUmar Suhrawardī (a celebrated Ṣūfī, not to be confused with the famous *shaikh* Shihābuddīn Yaḥyà Suhrawardī, the *shaikh al-Ishrāq*, so often mentioned in these pages). In 1214 he revisited Mecca, where "the interpreter of ardent desires" became his own commentator (see Ch. II), in order to confound his old adversaries the *fuqahā'* and expose the hypocrisy of their censure of the *Dīwān* in which, thirteen years before, he had sung his pure love for the young girl Sophia. Next he went to Aleppo, where he made friends with the amir al-Mālik al-Ẓāhir, one of Saladin's sons, who twenty years before had also been the friend of Suhrawardī, approximately his contemporary, whom he had tried in vain to save from the fanaticism of the *fuqahā'* and of his own father. The young *shaikh al-Ishrāq* must have been evoked more than once in intimate conversations between Ibn ʿArabī and the prince, whose guest and friend he in turn had become.

Numerous princes had tried to attract Ibn ʿArabī, whose reputation had spread throughout the Orient, and showered him with gifts, which, jealously guarding his freedom, he gave away in alms. Finally, Ibn ʿArabī acceeded to the pleas of the sovereign of Damascus; it was there that he settled in 1223 and spent the remaining seventeen years of his life. The prince and his brother who succeeded him (al-Mālik al-Ashraf) became his disciples, attended his lessons and obtained from him a certificate (*ijāza*) permitting them to instruct others in his books. So we learn that at that time Ibn ʿArabī's bibliography (the "list of his writings") comprised more than four hundred titles, though he was far from having completed his work.[27] His labors had been enormous during the whole period of his travels. Yet he surmounted his weariness as well as the illness brought on by his long and arduous journeys, and perhaps also by the physiological repercussions of his frequent mystical experiences. From this time on the *shaikh* lived in material security and peace of mind, surrounded by his family and his numerous disciples. He was able to complete his work, if such a work, whatever limits it may attain, can ever be said to be completed.

Here I shall discuss only two of his principal works, those which will be often cited here and which are at present the best known, no doubt because they are the most representative. The *Fuṣūṣ al-Ḥikam* ("The Gems of the Wisdom of the Prophets") was written in consequence of a vision that came to him in a dream during the year 627/1230. The Prophet had appeared to Ibn ʿArabī, holding a book whose title he pronounced and had bidden him to write down its teachings for the greater good of his disciples. After relating the vision that had inspired his book, the author describes the spirit in which he had set to work: "I am neither a prophet (*nabī*) nor an envoy (*rasūl*); I am simply an heir, someone who plows and sows the field of

27. For further details about the personal bibliography of Ibn ʿArabī (which far exceeds the above-mentioned figure), see ʿOsmān Yaḥià, *L'Histoire et la classification des œuvres d'Ibn ʿArabī.*

his future life." The twenty-seven prophets (from Adam to Muḥammad), to each of whom a chapter is devoted, are not envisaged in their empirical reality as historical persons. They are meditated upon as typefying "wisdoms," to which their names serve as indices and titles, or mark their respective tonality. Thus it is to the metaphysical individuality, the "eternal hexeity," of these prophets that their various wisdoms must be related. This book is no doubt the best compendium of Ibn ʿArabī's esoteric doctrine. Its influence was enormous. It elicited a large number of commentaries in all the languages of Sunnite as well as Shīʿite Islam; a comparative study of these commentaries will provide us with valuable lessons.

It still remained for the *shaikh* to complete his *Futūḥāt*, the book that has been called the "Bible of esoterism in Islam" (very much as the mystic *Mathnawī* of Jalāluddīn Rūmī has been termed the "Persian Koran"). The complete title is: *Kitāb al-Futūḥāt al-Makkīya fī maʿrifat al-asrār al-malikīya wa'l-mulkīya* ("The Book of the Revelations Received in Mecca concerning the Knowledge of the King and the Kingdom"). (We shall here have occasion, following an indication of the great mystic Jāmī, to suggest a variant of this translation, permitting us to dispense with the word "revelations" which already serves as an equivalent for so many terms of the Arabic Ṣūfī vocabulary, whose shadings it is difficult to capture in our languages.) He originally conceived this work during his first stay in Mecca; the idea was related to the inspirations and visions which burgeoned in his soul during his ritual circumambulations of the Kaʿaba, though we do not know whether to think of an internalization of a physically accomplished rite or of its mental repetition. Here we have already noted the relationship between the theophanic moments experienced while circumambulating a mentally transfigured Kaʿaba, imaginatively perceived and actualized as the "center of the world": the apparition of Sophia emerging from the night, the vision of the mystic Youth rising up from the Black Stone, and the vision at the source of the

Futūḥāt, which will be evoked in detail at the end of the present book.

The enormous work was not composed in a continuous flow. The beginning of Volume IV was written in 1230, the end of Volume II in 1236, Volume III in the following year. The work took several years to write, and this is explained not only by its length but also by Ibn ʿArabī's method of composition: "In this work, as in all my works," he writes, "the method followed in the works of others is not observed, nor do we conform to the method ordinarily employed by the authors of other works, regardless of their nature. Indeed, every author writes under the authority of his free will, although it is said that his freedom is subordinated to divine decree, or under the inspiration of the science that is his specialty. . . . But an author who writes under the dictation of divine inspiration often registers things that are without (apparent) relation to the substance of the chapter he is engaged in writing; they will strike the profane reader as incoherent interpolations, although to my mind they pertain to the very soul of the chapter, though perhaps for reasons of which others are unaware."[28] And again: "Know that the composition of the chapters of the *Futūḥāt* was not the outcome of a free choice on my part or of deliberate reflection. Indeed God, through the Angel of Inspiration, dictated everything I have written, and that is why between two developments I sometimes insert another that is connected neither with what precedes nor with what follows."[29]

In short, the process of composition appears to be a hermeneutics of the individual, alert to the secret sympathies between the concrete examples it juxtaposes. The method of thought shows an affinity with Stoic logic; it resists the conceptual dialectic of a development carried on according to the laws of Aristotelian logic. This marks the difference between this book

28. Asín Palacios, "Ibn Masarra," p. 102.

29. al-Shaʿrānī, *Kitāb al-Yawāqīt*, I, 31 (according to chs. 89 and 348 of the *Futūḥāt*).

and the books of the *falāsifa*, of Avicenna, for example. And for this reason it is virtually impossible to sum up or even to outline such a work. It is a *summa* of mystic theosophy, at once theoretical and experimental. It comprises speculative developments often highly abstruse and bearing witness to the author's thorough grounding in philosophy; it also includes all the elements of a *Diarium spirituale;* and finally it contains an abundance of information about Ṣūfism and the spiritual masters known to Ibn ʿArabī.[30] It is a voluminous work; its five hundred and sixty chapters in the Cairo edition (1329/1911) take up some three thousand pages in quarto.[31] And yet Ibn ʿArabī confesses: "Despite the length and scope of this book, despite the large number of sections and chapters, I have not exhausted a single one of the ideas or doctrines put forward concerning the Ṣūfī method. How, *a fortiori*, can I have exhausted the entire subject? I have confined myself to a brief clarification of some small part of the fundamental principles on which the method is based, in an abridged style, holding a middle course between vague allusion and clear, complete exposition."

A fortiori, we may say with Ibn ʿArabī, it is impossible in the present work to exhaust any theme or aspect of Ibn ʿArabī's teachings. We have meditated in his company some of the basic themes of his thinking and of his practical doctrine. Truly to *understand* them, it seems to us, presupposes the will to evaluate them positively. It goes without saying that the form in which each of us receives the master's thought *conforms* to his "inner heaven"; that is the very principle of the theophanism of Ibn ʿArabī, who for that reason can only guide *each* man individually to what he alone is capable of *seeing*, and not bring him to any

30. The six main sections announced at the beginning of the work treat of the following themes: (1) the doctrines (*maʿārif*); (2) the Spiritual practices (*muʿāmalāt*); (3) the Mystic States (*aḥwāl*); (4) the degrees of mystic perfection (*manāzil*); (5) the consociations of the Godhead and the soul (*munāzalāt*); (6) the esoteric abodes (*maqāmāt*).

31. And it is well known that an Arabic text at least doubles in length when translated into a European language.

collective pre-established dogma: *Talem eum vidi qualem capere potui*. The truth of the individual's vision is proportional to his fidelity to himself, his fidelity to the one man who is able to bear witness to his individual vision and do homage to the guide who leads him to it. This is no nominalism or realism, but a decisive contemplation, far anterior to any such philosophical choice, a distant point to which we must also return if we wish to account for the deformations and rejections which the spirituality of Ibn ʿArabī has so often incurred, sometimes for diametrically opposed reasons, but always because men have sidestepped the self-knowledge and self-judgment that this spirituality implies.

Ibn ʿArabī died peacefully in Damascus on the 28th day of Rabiʿ II, A.H. 638 (November 16, A.D. 1240), surrounded by his family, his friends, and his Ṣūfī disciples. He was buried north of Damascus in the suburb of Salihīya, at the root of Mount Qāsiyūn. The curve of his life ended in accordance with its immanent norm, for the place where Ibn ʿArabī was buried, where his remains still repose with those of his two sons, was already a place of pilgrimage, sanctified in Muslim eyes by all the prophets, but especially by Khiḍr. In the sixteenth century Selim II, sultan of Constantinople, built a mausoleum and *madrasa* over Ibn ʿArabī's tomb.

Today pilgrims still flock to the tomb of the "disciple of Khiḍr." One day we were among their number, savoring in secret—but who knows with how many others?—the paradoxical triumph: the honors and popular cult devoted to this man whose disciples traditionally salute him as *Muḥyi'd-Dīn*, "Animator of the Religion," but whom so many doctors of the Law in Islam have attacked, inverting his honorific surname into its antitheses: *Māḥī'd-Dīn*, "he who abolishes the religion," or *Mumītuddīn*, "he who kills the religion." What the paradox of his tomb guarantees is the presence of an undeniable testimony, perpetuating something which, in the very heart of the religion of the letter and the Law, prophetically surmounts and transcends them both. And another paradoxical image comes to the mind of the pensive pilgrim: Swedenborg's tomb in the cathedral of Uppsala—a mental diptych attesting the existence of an *Ecclesia spiritualis* reuniting all its own in the triumphant force of a single paradox.

3. *The Situation of Esoterism*

This title merely states the theme of the inquiry that would normally follow from the preceding pages, which in suggesting it also limit its scope. Our purpose here should be to analyze the situations of esoterism in Islam and in Christianity in order to determine in what degree these situations are comparable. But even in thus restricting our field of inquiry we find that it would require a minimum of preliminary investigation that is still lacking. Moreover, every student is necessarily limited by the range of his own experience and observation. What we shall have to say here can be no more than a sketch.

Insofar as the Ṣūfism of Ibn ʿArabī leads us to raise it, the question becomes essentially an inquiry into the position, the function, and the significance of Ṣūfism as an esoteric interpretation of Islam. To deal with it exhaustively would require a large volume, for which the time is not yet ripe: the writings of Ibn ʿArabī have been insufficiently explored; too many works emanating from his school or preparing the way for it are still in manuscript; too many of the connections and relationships to which we have referred remain to be investigated in detail. But at least it will be worthwhile to specify the meaning of the question, for it involves very different tasks from those undertaken by history and sociology. It concerns the phenomenon of Ṣūfism as such, in its essence. To create a phenomenology of Ṣūfism is not to derive it causally from something else or to reduce it to something else, but to look for what reveals itself to itself in this phenomenon, to distinguish the intentions implicit in the act which causes it to reveal itself. To that end we must consider it as a spiritual perception and by that same token as a phenomenon as basic and irreducible as the perception of a sound or of a color. What is made manifest in this phenomenon is the act of mystic consciousness disclosing to itself the inner, hidden *meaning* of a prophetic revelation, for the characteristic situation of the mystic is a confrontation with a prophetic message and revelation. The situation of Ṣūfism as such is characterized by the interpenetration of mystic religion and prophetic religion. Such a situation is conceivable only in an *Ahl al-Kitāb*, a "people of the book," that is to say, a community whose religion is grounded on a book revealed by a prophet, for the existence of a celestial Book imposes the task of fathoming its *true meaning*. Parallels can no doubt be established between certain aspects of Ṣūfism and, for example, of Buddhism; but such parallels will not be as profound as those that can be drawn with the Spirituals in another community of *Ahl al-Kitāb*.

This is the basis of the fundamental kinship between Shīʿism and Ṣūfism. Some may impute the stress I put upon this tie to the long years I have spent in Iran, to my familiarity with Shīʿite Ṣūfism, to my cherished friendships with Shīʿites. I make no secret of my heartfelt debt to Shīʿism; there are too many things of which I should never have become aware if not for my familiarity with the spiritual world of Iran. And it is precisely this that leads me to insist on a fact which has too seldom been taken into account. The conviction that to everything that is apparent, literal, external, exoteric (*ẓāhir*) there corresponds something hidden, spiritual, internal, esoteric (*bāṭin*) is the scriptural principle which is at the very foundation of Shīʿism as a religious phenomenon. It is the central postulate of esoterism and of esoteric hermeneutics (*taʾwīl*). This is not to doubt that the prophet Muḥammad is the "seal of the prophets and of prophecy"; the cycle of prophetic Revelation is closed, no new *sharīʿa*, or religious Law, is awaited. But the literal and apparent text of this ultimate Revelation offers something which is still a potency. This potency, calls for the action of persons who will transform it into act, and such is the spiritual mission of the Imām and his companions. It is an initiatic mission; its function is to initiate into the *ta'wīl,* and initiation into the *ta'wīl* marks spiritual birth. Thus prophetic Revelation is closed, but precisely because it is closed, it implies the continued openness of prophetic hermeneutics, of the *ta'wīl,* or *intelligentia spiritualis.* Upon the homology between the celestial and terrestrial hierarchies Ismailian Gnosis founded this idea of the Sacred Book whose meaning is potential. It finds the same relationship between the esoteric potential meaning and the Imām as between that one of the angelic intelligences (the third) which is the celestial Anthropos, the Adamic form of the pleroma, and that other Intelligence, emanating directly from the archangel Logos, which transforms it into act. Here we cannot even list all the forms and ramifications of esoterism in Islam. We merely note the impossibility of dissociating them, of studying separately Ismailian Gnosis, the theosophy of Duodeciman Shīʿism (notably Shaikhism), and the Ṣūfism of Suhrawardī, Ibn ʿArabī, or Semnānī.

The *intelligentia spiritualis* brings about the union between prophetic religion and mystic religion (see below, Ch. I). From this complex derives a threefold preoccupation with the *method, organ,* and *source* of this hermeneutics. We have tried to characterize the method above by drawing a careful distinction between symbol and allegory.[32] As for the organ which the spiritual perception of symbols presupposes, it motivates the most characteristic chapters of Shīʿite and of Ṣūfī theosophy, dealing with themes that can be subsumed under the title "prophetic psychology." We have already noted the importance accorded to this organ by the Avicennans in their noetics. Here the con-

32. For further details on the following, see our "L'Intériorisation du sens."

templative intellect in its higher form, designated as holy intellect or holy spirit, is the organ common to the perfect Sage and to the prophet, the vehicle of a perception whose object is no longer the logical concept or universal, but presents itself in the form of a typification. Ḥamīduddīn Kermānī (eleventh century), one of the most profound thinkers of Ismailian Shīʿism, gives an extraordinary explanation of this prophetic psychology and its noetics. He related it to the motion of the eternal emanation in the archangelic pleroma, a movement *ab intra ad extra*, which also characterizes the operations of the Imagination as an active power, independent of the physical organism. Unlike common knowledge, which is effected by a penetration of the sense impressions of the outside world into the interior of the soul, the work of prophetic inspiration is a projection of the inner soul upon the outside world. The active Imagination guides, anticipates, molds sense perception; that is why it transmutes sensory data into symbols. The Burning Bush is only a brushwood fire if it is merely perceived by the sensory organs. In order that Moses may perceive the Burning Bush and hear the Voice calling him "from the right side of the valley"—in short, in order that there may be a theophany—an organ of trans-sensory perception is needed. We shall hear Ibn ʿArabī repeat the same remarks in connection with the apparitions of the Angel Gabriel in the form of Daḥyā Kalbī, the beautiful Arab youth.

This theophanic perception is accomplished in the *ʿālam al-mithāl*, whose organ is the theophanic Imagination. That is why we have alluded here to the consequences to the Western world of the disappearance of the *Animae coelestes* which were still retained in Avicennism. Since the Imagination is the organ of theophanic perception, it is also the organ of prophetic hermeneutics, for it is the imagination which is at all times capable of transmuting sensory data into symbols and external events into symbolic histories. Thus the affirmation of an esoteric meaning presupposes a prophetic hermeneutics; and this hermeneutics postulates an organ capable of perceiving theophanies, of investing visible figures with a "theophanic function." This organ is the active Imagination. And a study of the creative Imagination in Ibn ʿArabī will disclose this same thematic sequence. All this calls for a prophetic philosophy going hand in hand with an esoterism to which the philosophical oppositions by which we tend to "explain" everything (nominalism and realism, for example) may well seem absurd. Such a prophetic philosophy moves in the dimension of a pure theophanic historicity, in the inner time of the soul; external events, cosmologies, the histories of the prophets, are perceived as the history of spiritual man. Thus it obliterates the "historical trend" with which our epoch is obsessed. Prophetic philosophy looks for the meaning of history not in "horizons," that is, not by orienting itself in the latitudinal sense of a linear development, but vertically, by a longitudinal orientation extending from the celestial pole to the Earth, in the transparency of the heights or depths in which the spiritual individuality experiences the reality of its celestial counterpart, its "lordly" dimension, its "second person," its "Thou."

As to the source of this hermeneutics, we must first go back to what has been said above concerning the figure of the Active Intelligence as Holy Spirit, Angel of Knowledge and of Revelation, and then follow the connecting lines leading from Avicennan or Suhrawardian noetics to Shīʿite and Ṣūfī esoterism. Here we can deal with this subject only allusively. In Ismailian Gnosis the Imām is the terrestrial pole of the Tenth Intelligence, corresponding functionally to the Angel Holy-Spirit of the Avicennan or Suhrawardian philosophers. In Duodeciman Shīʿism the "hidden Imām," hidden between Heaven and Earth in the *ʿālam al-mithāl*, assumes a similar function, acting upon what Mullā Ṣadrā calls the treasure of celestial origin, the Imāmate concealed within every human being. Other parallels will present themselves in the course of this book, notably in respect of the Holy Spirit, the divine Face of every being.

Thus recalled in broad outlines, these aspects of esoterism in Islam, seen as an initiation into the meaning hidden beneath the literal appearance of Revelation and shown to postulate a prophetic philosophy, already provide us with a basis of comparison permitting us to raise the question of whether there is in Christianity an analogous situation pointing to a "Christian esoterism." Insofar as this term may strike some readers as odd or even offensive, a question of fact imposes itself. Can we, in a community of *Ahl al-Kitāb* such as Christianity, find a phenomenon comparable to that of esoterism in Islam? In regard to the affirmation of a hidden meaning and the necessity of a prophetic hermeneutics, such as we have just found attested in the esoterism of Islam, a first observation is in order. Christian Gnosis has left us texts embodying the secret teachings which Jesus, in his body of light, dispensed to his disciples after his resurrection. The idea of this gnosis has its parallel in the Shī'ite idea of the esoteric meaning of Koranic revelation, whose initiator is the Imām. But the fact which dominates Christianity and relates to the question here raised is that with the condemnation of the Montanist movement in the second century any possibility of a new prophetic revelation dispensed by the Angels, or of a prophetic hermeneutics, was cut off, at least for and by the Great Church. From that time on the authority of the Great Church substituted itself for individual prophetic inspiration; this authority presupposes and at the same time legitimizes the existence of a dogmatic magistery, and the dogma states everything that can or should be said. There is no room for "the disciples of Khiḍr"; esoterism has lost its concept and justification. Nevertheless it persevered, and from time to time prophetic hermeneutics exploded irrepressibly, but outside the confines of the established orthodoxy. At first sight this suffices to mark a profound difference from Islam, which never knew either a dogmatic magistery or a Council. Not even the Shī'ite Imāmate has the character of a dogmatic pontifical authority; it is the source, not of dogmatic definitions, but of the inspiration of the *ta'wīl*, and it is all the adepts, from degree to degree of the esoteric hierarchy, who form the "Temple of light" of the Imāmate, which from degree to degree repeats the aspect of an initiatic companionship (that of Salmān the Persian with the Prophet).

The contrast is striking. And in view of the phenomenology of this contrast, any speculative dogmatic construction tending to reduce one of these forms to the other can only falsify the phenomenon to the great detriment of what each of the two forms represents and expresses. The theosophy of Ṣūfism invests with the dignity of *nabī* every Spiritual who allies himself with the Active Intelligence because it is the Holy Spirit; a corresponding promotion occurs in certain circles of Christian Spirituals. In both cases analysis discloses the idea of a spiritual state that can be termed contemplative prophetism. Falsification sets in when, by a deliberate confusion, an attempt is made to find it in contexts where it is not present. Some writers then feel obliged to reconstruct it arbitrarily, to show that such a phenomenon can only exist within an ecclesiastic reality, that it must not transgress against the law of the community but must subordinate itself to the dogmatic magistery, which is its repository par excellence. But we have just pointed out why the whole idea of contemplative prophetism presupposes precisely the absence of such a magistery. The calling of a *nabī* is the most personal of callings; it is never a function conferred (and still less exercised) by a collectivity or a magistery. Theophanies reveal no dogmatic proposition, nor is anything in the nature of a "Council of prophets," that would decide on such a proposition by majority vote, even conceivable. The phenomenon of "orthodoxy" presupposes the end of prophecy. The coming of dogma puts an end to prophetism, and at this stage men conceive the idea of a "past," of a latitudinal direction, an "expansion" in history.

The coming of historical consciousness is concomitant with the formation of a dogmatic consciousness. In the official form given to it by the definitions of the Councils, the fundamental dogma of Christianity, that of the Incarnation, is the most characteristic symptom of this, because the Incarnation is a unique and irreversible fact; it takes its place in a series of material facts; God in person was incarnated at a moment in history; this "happened" within the framework of a set chronology. There is no more mystery, consequently esoterism is no longer necessary; and that is why all the resurrected Christ's secret teachings to his disciples have been piously relegated to the *Apocrypha* along with the other Gnostic books; they had no connection with history. Such an Incarnation of "God in person" in empirical history and, consequently, the historical consciousness which goes hand in hand with it, are unknown to the traditional Orient. Some have expressed this by saying that the traditional Orient was fundamentally monophysite, others have used the word "docetic"; both qualifications apply to the same way of looking at the phenomenon.

All esoterism in Islam, in Shīʿism and in Ṣūfism, recognizes a divine anthropomorphosis, a divine Manifestation in human form; this anthropomorphosis is essential to the Godhead, but it takes place "in heaven," on the plane of the angelic universes. The celestial Anthropos is not "incarnated" on earth; he is manifested on earth in theophanic figures which draw his followers, those who recognize him, toward their celestial assumption. All the traits which reveal an affinity between Imāmology and a Christology of the Ebionite or Gnostic type underline its remoteness from every variety of Pauline Christology. The theophanism of Ibn ʿArabī will show us why no history, or philosophy of history, can be made with theophanies. Their time does not coincide with historical time. God has no need of coming down to earth, because He "removes" His people, just as He "removed" Jesus from the hatred of those who had the illusion of putting him to death (Koran IV: 156). Gnostic esoterism in Islam has always known this, and that is why it can never regard the fatidic cry "God is dead!" as anything more than the pretention and delusion of people blind to the profound truth of the "docetism" that is so much ridiculed in our history books.

These are only a few of the differences that must be noted before, replying to the question stated above, we can go on to determine what parallels there may be in the respective situations of esoterism in Islam and in Christianity. By now one thing has become clear: a theoretical reply to the question cannot be adequate; we must start from the view of esoterism taken by the religious mind both in Islam and in Christianity. Phenomenology discerns very different "intentionalities" accordingly as it investigates the phenomenon of esoterism from the standpoint of a radically hostile mind or from that of the adept. To this distinction we must add another, that which manifests itself accordingly as we consider mystic esoterism in relation to a pure prophetic religion, moving in the pure theophanic dimension (the dimension in which Khiḍr-Elijah and Moses are contemporaries), or in relation to a religion of Incarnation involving all the implications of historical consciousness. In the first case the demands of the *ta'wīl* shake the stability of the Law, though preserving the letter as the foundation of its symbols. In the second case, the same demands shake the authority of the magistery in bond with the historicity which it establishes and from which it derives justification. For this reason we can discern in both quarters a common hostility to the very postulate of esoterism, just as in both quarters we find minorities which adhere fervently to this same esoterism. Taking the differences into account, we may then, pursuing our phenomenological approach, try to determine what there may be in common between the implicit intentions expressed in both quarters by these positions. Accordingly, the problem of parallels raised above will lead necessarily to the search for a religious typology which will thematize the data while removing them from the state in which they present themselves to positive history or sociology.

One is struck by the way in which the adversaries of esoterism recognize and agree with one another, as do its adepts. Islam offers us numerous examples of implacable adversaries. Ibn Taymīya made himself famous by his virulent polemic against the *ta'wīl* of the esoterics of all shadings. The theologian Ghazālī is responsible, through his unfounded polemic, for the idea of Ismailian esoterism that long prevailed.[33] As for the attacks and *takfīr* (anathemas) leveled against Ibn 'Arabī and his school, this is not the place to enumerate them. But it is striking to see how these condemnations of esoterism by the Islamic doctors of the Law appeal to the adversaries of esoterism in the Christian camp. They seem to be overjoyed at the good work done by the doctors of the Law, the *fuqahā'*, in disposing of interlocutors whom the Christian doctors would find it embarrassing to meet. And this same embarrassment reveals what there is in common between the disturbers who are thrust aside in both camps, as though they threatened to trouble the program of the dialogue or controversy between Islam and Christianity.

As for this program, it suffices to apply the Ismailian principle of the Scales to gain an idea of its broad outlines. Once such esoterism as that of Ibn 'Arabī, with all it implies in Islam, is put aside, it is thought that the tenets of orthodox Christianity will weigh more heavily in the scales. The Christians will then be in a better position to play the doctors of the Law and the Ṣūfīs against each other. They will support the first when they say that the ultimate revelation is definitive in its literal accept-

33. Indeed, it has remained virtually unknown to this day that as early as the twelfth century a monumental work was written by the fifth Yemenite Dā'ī in response to Ghazālī's polemic. We shall have more to say of this unpublished work of 1400 pages. It will provide us with an occasion to observe the misunderstandings to which we were exposed in regard to Ismailian Gnosis as well as to ancient Gnosticism as long as we were deprived of the original texts and were dependent for our information on polemicists whose ignorance of the substance of Gnosticism was equalled only by the psychological unsoundness of their method.

ance, that the supposition of an esoteric meaning or any effort at internalization aimed at accomplishing this meaning transgresses the *sharīʿa* and falls under a well-deserved *takfīr*. On the other hand, they will recognize the legitimacy of the Ṣūfīs' striving for an inner religion, but only to make them admit that such an inner religion is attainable only by transgressing the law. Then it will be a simple matter to turn against the *fuqahā'* once again, precisely on the basis of what has been conceded: prophetic religion is not self-sufficient, God cannot be encountered through the sole intermediary of a book, even revealed; abstract monotheism and religion of the Book do not provide a sufficient counterweight to the other pan of the scales: the idea of the Incarnation and the phenomenon of the Church.

Even this bare outline may suffice to suggest why the intervention of esoterism threatens to upset the scales, that is, the conditions of dialogue between the doctors of the two faiths, and why the Christian doctors try so hard to discredit it by citing the condemnations of esoterism by the authorities of Islam. Suddenly, indeed, the religious values which the doctors have put in their own pan of the scales are opposed by the counterweight which was lacking in the orthodoxy of the *fuqahā'*. In other words, one of the parties in the dialogue triumphed too easily; in choosing to eliminate esoterism, it deliberately set aside everything in Islam that might have constituted an answer to the questions which the Christians raised with a view to proposing "objective" answers. Abstract monotheism and literalist religion do not suffice to permit an effective divine encounter—but it is precisely this insufficiency that Shīʿism and all related varieties of spirituality set out to remedy. To ignore Shīʿism in its various forms or to put aside the esoterism of an Ibn ʿArabī is to refuse from the outset to consider the replies given in Islam itself to the questions asked of Islam. The hostility of orthodox Islam to these replies originating in esoteric Islam detracts in no way from their importance.

Let us recapitulate a few of these answers: the idea of an eternal Imām (primordial theophany, divine anthropomorphosis "in Heaven," but also designated by many other names), exemplified in earthly persons who are not its incarnations but its theophanic figures; the idea of the "awaited Imām," the Resurrector, explicitly identified with the Paraclete of the Gospel of St. John (xv:26); the idea of the *ta'wīl,* which is not an allegorical exegesis but a transfiguration of the literal texts, referring not to abstract truths, but to Persons; initiation into the *ta'wīl*; initiation into the encounter with Persons, spiritual birth; the transformation of all history of events into a symbolic history of spiritual man, enacted in a temporality in which are accomplished all the synchronisms that are inconceivable in historical time; the pre-eminence of the Active Imagination, that organ of prophetic inspiration which perceives, and at the same time confers existence upon, a reality of its own, whereas for us it secretes only "imaginings"; an organ without which we can apprehend neither the meaning of the extraordinary sermons of the first Imām, nor the *ḥadīth* in which God speaks in the first person through the intermediary of the Angel, nor those in which the holy Imāms, speaking in the plural, bear witness to their theophanic investiture, nor those theophanic visions that exemplify the *ḥadīth* of the vision upon which we shall meditate in the last pages of this book, nor even, finally, the paradoxical phenomenon of Shī'ite religious iconography, which upsets all our notions about the official iconoclasm of Islam (notably the iconography of the "hidden Imām," the Awaited One, represented by the figure of a youth closing the circle of the Twelve). All these are matters that cannot be taught uniformly to all, because each man is the measure of what he can understand and of what, in accordance with the "economy" of esoterism, it is fitting to set before him.

Shī'ite Imāmology is equally far removed from the abstract monotheism of Sunnite Islam and from the Christianity of the historical Incarnation. It bears witness to an originality which should lead us to reopen our history of dogmas, even chapters that are regarded as closed and in which the dogmatists feel fully secure. Accordingly, if we are to compare the situations of esoterism in Islam and in Christianity, we must start by situating what the contestants in both camps rejected as a corruption. The reasons for this rejection, the intentions it implies, show what the adversaries of esoterism in Islam and in Christianity have in common. And consequently the comparative question must, at some point, be formulated in terms of religious *typology*.

Such a typology becomes still more imperative when we turn to the adepts of esoterism in both camps. Still more, because in considering the adversaries we were dealing largely with a community of negative traits; here we have positive affinities. Such studies in comparative esoterism are extremely complex and are thus far in their barest beginnings. They require familiarity with a vast body of literature in several languages. The first point in the program will, in any case, have to be a study in comparative *ta'wīl*. Investigations aimed at a religious typology are obliged to transgress such frontiers as are imposed by the very nature of their subject matter on the historical sciences, because the types which a philosophical anthropology will be looking for are distributed on either side of the historical frontiers. The lines of cleavage corresponding to such a typology do not by any means coincide with historical frontiers; they cut across the formations officially and denominationally defined by history. Here above all we must not be too sanguine in our judgments. Ineluctably every spiritual formation that achieves official status becomes ensnared in orthodoxy and literalism. Even Shīʿism, which in the beginning and for many centuries was the refuge of bold spirits, preserving in Islam the heritage of the older Gnoses, was sorely tried when it became a State religion. Under the Ṣafavids in Iran there developed a Shīʿite neo-orthodoxy, which persecuted the philosophers of the school of Mullā Ṣadrā, the Ṣūfīs and theosophists as well as the *shaikhis*, all more authentically Shī'ite than the *mullās* who harassed them. Once again the invisible frontier separated mind from mind, but the mere fact that we can speak of such a cleavage shows that the prophetic leaven was preserved and continued to act.

While in Christianity the inspiration of new prophetic revelations was definitively closed with the condemnation of the Montanist movement, one thing was never stifled: a prophetic hermeneutics attesting the vitality of the Word in each spiritual individual, a vitality too powerful to be contained within the limits of pre-established dogmatic definitions. We shall speak in the present book of the striking consonance between certain utterances of Ibn 'Arabī and certain distiches of the *Cherubinic Wanderer* of Angelus Silesius. But what we must insist on if we are to assemble the data that will make possible a comparison between the situations of esoterism in Islam and in Christianity is the community of prophetic hermeneutics, the community of the *ta'wīl*.

To understand what such an invisible and always virtual community can mean we must bear in mind the existential implications of the *ta'wīl;* we have recalled some of them above. Just as it is clearly contradictory to invest a dogmatic magistery with a prophetic function, so it is hopeless to attempt to integrate an esoteric tradition with the dogmatic tradition of a magistery, which by its very nature excludes it. Such an esoterism may be tolerated thanks to its caution; it will never be recognized. It will have to attune itself to the "historical trend," to a latitudinal (horizontal) expansion, to that obsession of the historical mind, the notion of a linear and irreversible progression. The "transgressive" vigor of symbolism will inevitably wither away into inoffensive allegory. What we have learned about the "disciples of Khiḍr," the transhistorical meaning of the affiliation which unites them vertically with the invisible celestial assembly, implies the idea of a *tradition* whose line is vertical, longitudinal (from Heaven to Earth), a tradition whose moments are independent of the causality of continuous physical time but relate to what Ibn ʿArabī calls the *tajdīd al-khalq*, the recurrence of the creative act, that is, the Theophany. Iconographically speaking, the contrast between the two concepts of tradition might be likened to the contrast between an image whose elements are disposed according to the laws of classical perspective and an image in which they are superimposed in accordance with a vertical projection, as in Chinese painting or in the image of the Kaʿaba reproduced in the frontispiece of the present book.[34]

34. This image is drawn from a Persian manuscript (Bibliothèque nationale, Paris, supplément persan 1389, fol. 19) of the sixteenth century; the manuscript contains the Persian poem "Futūḥ al-Ḥaramayn" of Muḥyī Lārī (d. 1527) describing the holy places of Medina and Mecca and the practices to be observed in the course of a pilgrimage to them. It is not without reason that the iconographic method here followed has been compared to the Iranian representations of *paradise* (a word which comes to us, through the Greek *paradeisos*, from Persia, where it figures in the *Avesta* in the form of *pairi-daêza*, Persian *ferdaws*); the iconography of this Iranian motif par excellence figures an enclosure planted with trees, *hortus conclusus*, at the center of which ("center of the world") stands a pavilion, which here seems to have its correspondence in the Kaʿaba (cf. L. I. Ringbom, *Graltempel und Paradies*, pp. 54 ff.). The iconographic method embodied in this image calls for the following brief remark, in reference to the contrast of which we here take it as a symbol. There is not, as in classical perspective, a foreground behind which the secondary levels recede in foreshortening (as the past and future in relation to the present, the historic *nunc*, in our linear, evolutionary representation). All the elements are represented in their real dimensions ("in the present"), in each case perpendicularly to the axis of the viewer's vision. The viewer is not meant to immobilize himself at a particular point, enjoying the privilege of "presentness" and to raise his eyes from this fixed point; he must *raise himself* toward each of the elements represented. Contemplation of the image becomes a mental itinerary, an inner accomplishment; the image fulfills the function of a *mandala*. Because each of the elements is presented not *in* its proper dimension but *being* that same dimension, to contemplate them is to enter into a multidimensional world, to effect the passage of the *ta'wīl* through the symbols. And the whole forms a unity of qualitative time, in which past and future are simultaneously in the *present*. This iconography does not correspond to the perspectives of the historical consciousness; it does respond to the "perspective" by which the disciple of Khiḍr orients himself, and which permits him, through the symbolic rite of circumambulation, to attain to the "center of the world." Here, unfortunately, it will not be possible to speak at length of the relationship between *ta'wīl* and the treatises on perspective.

If we wish to inquire where in Christian spirituality the *dimension* of such a tradition can be found, there is no lack of signs by which to recognize the witnesses. We shall accord special mention to the Protestant representatives of mystic theosophy because of the amplitude of their works and because they are very seldom asked the questions we shall put to them here. The idea of assembling this community of the *ta'wīl* in a single study does not so far seem to have figured in the program of the religious sciences; the main reason for this is perhaps the inaccessibility of the sources; it is to be hoped that the little we shall be able to say here will suffice to show how valuable such an inquiry would be.

For the way in which Jacob Boehme, J. G. Gichtel, Valentin Weigel, Swedenborg, and their disciples read and understand the story of Adam in Genesis, for example, or the story of the prophets, as the invisible history of the "celestial" and spiritual man, enacted in a time of its own and always "in the present" —this has something in common with the way in which an Ismailian theosophist, Ibn ʿArabī, Semnānī, or Mullā Ṣadrā, for example, understands this same story as he reads it in the Koran (and in so doing raises the standing of those books which we call apocryphal but certain fragments of which were taken into the text of the Koran). But this must be clearly understood: the inquiry we are undertaking has nothing in common with what is ordinarily disparaged as syncretism or eclecticism. We do not wish to confuse elements that should be kept apart or reduce them to their poorest common denominator; quite the contrary, our purpose is to recognize the most personal originalities, because all notion of divergence or deviation is done away with where it is admitted that individual spontaneities arise freely from a mode of perception common to all of them, from the participation of all in a common prophetic religion. It is this community of perception, this unpremeditated mode of perception which remains to be studied typologically in its variants, because its perspectives develop according to the laws of one and the same vision. There is no syncretism to be constructed, but only isomorphisms to be noted when the axis of symmetry is governed by one and the same *intelligentia spiritualis,* when, unbeknownst to them, a pre-established harmony gathers all these "esoterics" fraternally in the same temple of Light, the same kingdom of spiritual man, which is limited by no other frontiers than those set up against it by In-science, *a-gnosia.* For in Christianity as in Islam, in Islam as in Christianity, there have always been "disciples of Khiḍr."

What they have in common is perhaps the perception of an over-all unity, calling for perspectives, depths, transparencies, appeals, which the "realists" of the letter or of dogma have no need of or reject. And this contrast is far more fundamental than any opposition conditioned by time or climate, for in the eyes of "esoterics" all this "realism" lacks a dimension or rather the many dimensions of the world which are revealed by the *ta'wīl* (the seven levels of esoteric meaning, or, in Semnānī, the "seven prophets of thy being"). There is no need to construct this multidimensional world; we discover it by virtue of a principle of equilibrium and of harmony. Ismailian Gnosis effects this intuitive discovery through the universal science of the Scales, which indicates the invisible that is the necessary counterweight to the visible. The theosophies of Light have merely applied the laws of their own perspective, interpreting esoterically the geometrical laws of optics; the *ta'wīl* is this esoteric science of the Scales and of optics. Here again it would be fitting to illustrate the function of the active Imagination, for this is a science which eludes rational demonstrations and dogmatic theorems alike. Nor should it be condemned as a mere theoretical view. It is not theory; it is an initiation to vision. Is it possible to see without *being* in the place where one sees? Theophanic visions, mental visions, ecstatic visions in a state of dream or of waking are in themselves *penetrations* into the world they *see.* These penetrations into a world of another dimension will be described for us in a fine text of Ibn ʿArabī:

And it is likewise the sense of a twofold dimension of individual being, implying the idea of a celestial counterpart, its being "in the second person," that provides the foundation of the mystical anthropology which has been so much misunderstood, because it has been judged in terms of the common anthropology which places individualities, reduced to the single dimension of their selves, equidistant from a universal God standing in the same relation to all. It is for this reason that the greatest importance should be attached to the pages in which Ibn ʿArabī distinguishes between *Allah* as God in general and *Rabb* as the particular Lord, personalized in an individualized and undivided relation with his vassal of love. This individualized relationship on both sides is the foundation of the mystical and chivalric ethic of the *fedele d'amore* in the service of the personal Lord whose divinity depends on the adoration of his faithful vassal and who, in this interdependence, exchanges the role of lord with him, because he is the First and the Last. It is impossible to see how what we call monism or pantheism in the West could have led to anything comparable to Ibn ʿArabī's method of theophanic prayer, the prayer which draws its inspiration from a God whose secret is sadness, nostalgia, aspiration to know Himself in the beings who manifest his Being. A passionate God, because it is in the *passion* that his *fedele d'amore* feels for him, in the theopathy of his *fedele*, that He is revealed to himself. And this always individually, in an "alone to alone," which is something very different from universal logic or from a collective participation, because only the knowledge which the *fedele* has of his Lord is the knowledge which this personal Lord has of him.

This is the very relationship we outlined above in the idea of the Angel compounded with the idea that every theophany necessarily has the form of an angelophany. This should avoid any misunderstanding when we come to speak of the "Self" and the knowledge of "self." The "Self" is a characteristic term by which a mystic spirituality underlines its dissociation from all the aims and implications of denominational dogmatisms. But it enables these dogmatisms to argue in return that this Self, experienced as the pure act of existing, is only a natural phenomenon and consequently has nothing in common with a supernatural encounter with the revealed God, attainable only within the reality of the Church. The term "Self," as we shall employ it here, implies neither the one nor the other acceptance. It refers neither to the impersonal Self, to the pure act of existing attainable through efforts comparable to the techniques of yoga, nor to the Self of the psychologists. The word will be employed here solely in the sense given it by Ibn ʿArabī and numerous other Ṣūfī theosophists when they repeated the famous sentence: He who knows himself knows *his* Lord. Knowing one's self, to know *one*'s God; knowing one's Lord, to know one's self. This Lord is not the impersonal self, nor is it the God of dogmatic definitions, *self*-subsisting without relation to *me*, without being experienced by *me*. He is the he who knows himself through myself, that is, in the knowledge that I have of him, because it is the knowledge that he has of me; it is alone with him alone, in this syzygic unity, that it is possible to say *thou*. And such is the reciprocity in which flowers the creative Prayer which Ibn ʿArabī teaches us to experience simultaneously as the Prayer of God and the Prayer of man.

Then it will become clear to some of us that the problems which our philosophical systems exhaust themselves trying to deal with have been left far behind. To others the rational foundations of this transcending will seem very fragile. But can it be otherwise? There are so many troubling facts: there is the fact that Imāmology and Koranic Christology are docetic; and we are in the habit of ridiculing the docetism of the Gnostics, which, it seems to us, has reduced the reality of Jesus, the man, to a "phantasm," when in truth this docetism is a strictly theological critique of knowledge, of the law governing the *apparition* of religious phenomena to a religious consciousness and governing the reciprocity of which we have just spoken.

There is the idea of a God whose divine personal reality depends on the service of his *fedele d'amore;* this seems so much in contradiction with the imperial idea of the Pantokrator, that it may well seem absurd to claim not only that such a God is meaningful, but also that it is meaningful to pray to such a God. We learn in the company of Ibn ʿArabī how this rejection can be rejected. There is finally the shattering of all the self-evident truths concerning the historicity of history, of those truths which bear so heavily on our modern minds that failure to attach importance to the historical meaning or to the *historical* reality of a religious phenomenon may seem equivalent to denying it *all* reality. Here we have tried to show that there is another "historicity." But the modern passion for material facts stops at nothing; it has fictions of its own, such as the supposed "eyewitness reports," which would have seemed blasphemous to a pious Gnostic reader of the Acts of St. John, well aware that on the evening of Good Friday the Voice revealed the mystery of the Cross of Light to the disciple who had been drawn into the Grotto. "For the True Cross is not this wooden cross that you will see when you come down here again." And this is a truth which was well known to Ismailian Gnosis.[35]

If the cry "God is dead" has left many on the brink of the abyss, it is because the mystery of the Cross of Light was long ago done away with. Neither pious indignation nor cynical joy can alter the fact. There is only one answer, the words that Sophia, emerging from the night, murmured in the ear of the pensive pilgrim circumambulating the Kaʿaba: "Can it be that you yourself are already dead?" The secret to which Ibn ʿArabī and his companions initiate us impels those whom that cry has shaken to the depths of their being to recognize *what* God has died and *who* are the dead. To recognize this is to understand the secret of the empty tomb. But the Angel must have removed the stone, and we must have the courage to look into the bottom

35. See our article, "L'Ismaélisme et le symbole de la Croix."

of the tomb if we are to know that it is indeed empty and that we must look for Him elsewhere. The greatest misfortune that can befall the shrine is to become the sealed tomb before which men mount guard and do so only because there is a corpse in it. Accordingly, it takes the greatest courage to proclaim that it is empty, the courage of those able to dispense with the evidence of reason and authority because the only secret they possess is the secret of love that has seen.

Our meaning is expressed in the following anecdote which we owe to Semnānī, the great Iranian Ṣūfī: Jesus was sleeping with a brick for pillow. The accursed demon came and stopped at his bedside. When Jesus sensed that the accursed one was there, he woke up and said: Why hast thou come to me, accursed one?—I have come to get my things.—And what things of thine are there here?—This brick that thou restest thine head on.—Then Jesus (*Rūḥ Allāh, Spiritus Dei*) seized the brick and flung it in his face.

The purpose of an introduction as of a prelude is to announce, to give an intimation of, the themes of a work. It is thus to be hoped that certain of our leitmotivs have been set forth with some clarity in the foregoing pages. In concluding our introduction, we shall make no attempt to summarize the book itself, but merely indicate the link between its two parts.[36]

Part One. We start by noting the encounter—characteristic, as we have seen, of Ṣūfism in Islam—between prophetic religion and mystic religion. It is this encounter which gives mystic religion its prophetic resonance (the "seven prophets of thy Being" in Semnānī); and through it, conversely, prophetic religion ceases to be dissociated from mystic experience: the

36. Parts One and Two appeared previously in a somewhat different form in *EJ* XXIV (1955) and XXV (1956), with the titles "Sympathie et théopathie chez les 'Fidèles d'Amour' en Islam" and "Imagination créatrice et prière créatrice dans le soufisme d'Ibn 'Arabī."

celestial assumption of the Prophet (*Mi'rāj*) becomes the prototype of a spiritual experience which the mystic in turn must relive in a mental vision or assumption, which makes of him too a *nabī*. The spirituality thus established develops what we have characterized as theophanism. From this encounter between prophetic religion and mystic religion rises the idea of *unio mystica* as *unio sympathetica;* far from conflicting with such a "sympathetic union," it is the co-passion of the *fedele d'amore* and his God; the *praesentia realis* of his God is in the passion that this *fedele* experiences for Him, his *theopathy*, which puts him into sympathy with the being or beings which have been invested by him and for him with the theophanic function. The prayer of the heliotrope in Proclus is perhaps the most subtle prefiguration and annunciation of this sympathy; it is a prelude to that other Prayer which is simultaneously the Prayer of God and the Prayer of man. As for the theophanic function invested in men, it is the secret of the dialectic of love. In the nature of mystic love this dialectic discovers the encounter (con-spiration) between sensory, physical love and spiritual love. Beauty is the supreme theophany, but it reveals itself as such only to a love which it transfigures. Mystic love is the religion of Beauty, because Beauty is the secret of theophanies and because as such it is the power which transfigures. Mystic love is as far from negative asceticism as it is from the estheticism or libertinism of the possessive instinct. But the organ of theophanic perception, that is, of the perception through which the encounter between Heaven and Earth in the mid-zone, the *'ālam al mithāl* takes place, is the active Imagination. It is the active Imagination which invests the earthly Beloved with his "theophanic function"; it is essentially a theophanic Imagination and, as such, a creative Imagination, because Creation is itself theophany and theophanic Imagination. From this idea of Creation as theophany (the idea of *creatio ex nihilo* being excluded) arises the idea of a sophiology, the figure of *Sophia aeterna* (the Eternal Womanly) as she appears in the theosophy of Ibn 'Arabī.

Part Two. Recapitulation of the basic theme: Imagination and theophany. If Creation is understood as a divine theophanic Imagination, how does the mystic communicate through the organ of the Imagination with the worlds and interworlds? What are the events perceived by the active Imagination? How does it create, that is, manifest, Being? This question introduces the motif of the "subtile physiology," whose center is the heart; the heart is the focus in which creative spiritual energy, that is, theophanic energy, is concentrated, whereas the Imagination is its organ. Our analysis then culminates in the experimental verification of a twofold demonstration: on the one hand, the method of theophanic prayer by which he who prays becomes aware that his prayer is simultaneously Prayer of man and Prayer of God; on the other hand, the theophanic vision which surmounts the void and hiatus, the contradictions which abstract monotheism leaves wide open: on the one hand, the impossibility of vision and the people's rejection of Moses; on the other, the testimony of the Prophet and of all those who ground their spiritual experience in his celestial assumption: "I have seen my Lord in the most beautiful of forms." And the secret of the Imagination which configures the features of this *Forma Dei* must be sought in experimental verification of the maxim commented above: "He who knows himself knows his Lord."

Perhaps a word is in order about the unfamiliar vocabulary employed in this book. We have learned it from our authors themselves. If it seems unusual, it is because, writing in Arabic or Persian, Suhrawardī, Ibn ʿArabī, Semnānī and others say things which our customary philosophical language is not always equipped to express. The most characteristic Arabic or Persian terms have been interpolated in parentheses. In the course of the present introduction the terms "theophany" and "theopathy" have already been employed in contexts that make their meanings clear.

Still, there is one term which perhaps calls for special justification: *Fedeli d'amore.* We have already had occasion to speak of the *Fedeli d'amore,* Dante's companions, and we shall speak of them again, for the *theophanism* of Ibn 'Arabī has a good deal in common with the ideas of the symbolist interpreters of Dante (Luigi Valli), though it is secure against such criticism as that of the literalist philologists, who were alarmed to see the person of Beatrice fade into a pale allegory. We have suggested that both the *Fedeli d'amore* and their critics can be reproached with one-sidedness. In any case, the young girl who was for Ibn 'Arabī in Mecca what Beatrice was for Dante, was a real young girl, though at the same time she was "in person" a theophanic figure, the figure of *Sophia aeterna* (whom certain of Dante's companions invoked as *Madonna Intelligenza*). The problem is similar to that raised by the person of Khiḍr the prophet, both individual person and, by virtue of his investiture with a theophanic function whose organ is the active Imagination, an archetype. If we fail to grasp this twofold dimension simultaneously, we lose the reality both of the person and of the symbol.

It has not been our intention to re-open the great debate, inaugurated by Asín Palacios, concerning the actual historical relations between those to whom we can give the name of *Fedeli d'amore* in the East and West. It has seemed more important to indicate the undeniable typological affinities between them. We shall observe that this term *Fedeli d'amore* (the Arabic or Persian equivalents will be given below) does not apply indiscriminately to the entire community of Ṣūfīs; it does not, for example, apply to the pious ascetics of Mesopotamia, who in the first centuries of Islam took the name of Ṣūfī. In making this distinction we only conform to the indications provided by the great Iranian mystic Rūzbehān Baqlī of Shīrāz (d. 1209) in his beautiful Persian book entitled *The Jasmin of the Fedeli d'amore.* Rūzbehān distinguishes between the pious ascetics, or Ṣūfīs, who never encountered the experience of human love, and the *Fedeli d'amore,* for whom the experience of a cult of love dedicated to a beautiful being is the necessary initiation to divine love, from which it is inseparable. Such an *initiation* does not indeed signify anything in the nature of a monastic conversion to divine love; it is a unique initiation, which transfigures *eros* as such, that is, human love for a human creature. Rūzbehān's doctrine falls in with Ibn ʿArabī's dialectic of love. It creates a kinship between him and Fakhr ʿIrāqī, the Iranian who was Ibn ʿArabī's disciple through the intermediary of Ṣadr Qunyawī, and also makes Rūzbehān the precursor of that other famous man of Shīrāz, the great poet Ḥāfiẓ, whose *Dīwān* is still observed today by the Ṣūfīs of Iran as a Bible of the religion of love, whereas in the West it has been solemnly debated whether or not this *Dīwān* has a mystic meaning. This religion of love was and remained the religion of all the minstrels of Iran and inspired them with the magnificent *ta'wīl* which supplies a link between the spiritual Iran of the Ṣūfīs and Zoroastrian Iran, for according to this *ta'wīl* the Prophet of Islam in person proclaims Zarathustra to be the prophet of the Lord of love; the altar of Fire becomes the symbol of the Living Flame in the temple of the heart.

PART ONE

SYMPATHY AND THEOPATHY

I DIVINE PASSION AND COMPASSION

1. *The Prayer of the Heliotrope*

In a treatise on "the hieratic art of the Greeks," Proclus, that lofty figure of late Neoplatonism whom scholars have so unjustly neglected, writes the following:

> Just as in the dialectic of love we start from sensuous beauties to rise until we encounter the unique principle of all beauty and all ideas, so the adepts of hieratic science take as their starting point the things of appearance and the sympathies they manifest among themselves and with the invisible powers. Observing that all things form a whole, they laid the foundations of hieratic science, wondering at the first realities and admiring in them the latest comers as well as the very first among beings; in heaven, terrestrial things according both to a causal and to a celestial mode and on earth heavenly things in a terrestrial state.

Example: the heliotrope and its *prayer*.

> What other reason can we give for the fact that the heliotrope follows in its movement the movement of the sun and the selenotrope the movement of the moon, forming a procession within the limits of their power, behind the torches of the universe? For, in truth, each thing prays according to the

> rank it occupies in nature, and sings the praise of the leader of the divine series to which it belongs, a spiritual or rational or physical or sensuous praise; for the heliotrope moves to the extent that it is free to move, and in its rotation, if we could hear the sound of the air buffeted by its movement, we should be aware that it is a hymn to its king, such as it is within the power of a plant to sing.[1]

This passage by a philosopher and poet endowed with a hieratic sense of Beauty, strikes us as an exemplary text eminently suited to preface the themes which will here be at the center of our meditation. It establishes a connection between the "dialectic of love" and hieratic art, which are grounded on the same principle: the essential community between visible and invisible beings. "On earth," Proclus goes on to say, "suns and moons can be seen in an earthly state and in the heavens all the plants, stones, animals in a heavenly state, living spiritually."[2] This common essence, which is distributed among several beings, is not perceived through argument proceeding from effect to cause; it is the perception of a *sympathy*, of a reciprocal and simultaneous attraction between the manifest being and his celestial prince, that is, one of those whom Proclus elsewhere designates as creative, generative, and saving angels; grouped into choirs, they escort the Archangel or God who leads them,[3] just as the flowers of earth form a train behind the Angel who is the leader of the "divine series" to which they belong. Here indeed community of essence is perceived in the visible phenomenon of a flower, in the *tropism* that gives it its name: *heliotrope*. But taken as a phenomenon of sympathy, this tropism in the plant is at once *action* and *passion:* its action (that is to say, its *tropos*, its "conversion") is perceived as the action (that is, the attraction) of the Angel or celestial prince whose name for that very reason it bears. Its *heliotropism* (its "conversion" toward its celestial prince) is thus in fact a *heliopathy* (the passion it experiences for him). And this passion, this πάθος, is disclosed in a prayer, which is the *act* of this *passion* through which the invisible angel draws the flower toward him. Accordingly, this prayer is the *pathos* of their *sympatheia* (here we must take the word in its etymological sense, for the word "sympathy" as currently employed has lost much of its force); and in this *sympatheia* is actualized the reciprocal aspiration based on the community of essence.

But since sympathy here is also a condition and mode of perception—for it is safe to say that not everyone perceives this silent prayer offered up by a plant—we must also speak of the poetic or cognitive function of sympathy in a man like Proclus. As such, it opens up a new dimension in beings, the dimension of their invisible selves; perhaps, indeed, it is the only means by which we may know, or gain an intimation of, this invisible self, just as a fragment of an arch arouses a mental image of the missing part of the arch. Thus we may speak of a *pathos* experienced by Proclus in common with the flower, a *pathos* necessary to his perception of the *sympathy* which aroused it and which, when he perceived it, invested the flower with a theophanic function.

This notion of a *tropos* which in the heliotrope *is* a *heliopathy* (in the sense of sympathy with its Angel), and the idea that the perception of this heliopathy presupposes a sympathy directed toward the sympathy of the flower, a sympathy which makes Proclus aware of the *hierophanic dimension* of the flower's sympathy (whereupon he perceives the movement of the flower as a prayer whose impulse culminates in a transcending which it shows him with a gesture that speaks without the help of language), provide us with the essential elements by which to orient our investigation. Our orientation will be all the surer if we start out on our own at the point where other investigations intersect with our own.

The passage from Proclus has led us to associate the terms

tropos and sympathy. These same terms were employed to good advantage in a highly original study undertaken in a different religious context, its purpose being to establish, in new terms, a phenomenology of prophetic religion.[4] This excellent study, which I shall not be able to discuss at length, is distinguished by its application of a phenomenology of sympathy to an analysis of prophetic religion and by the antitheses it works out between the categories of prophetic religion and those of mystical religion. In contrast to the deist God who had paled to an empty concept, or to the ethical God, guardian of the moral law, it sets forth, with penetrating vigor, the notion of a *pathetic God,* that is, a suffering and passionate God, a notion which has at all times been a dreaded stumbling block to the rational theology and philosophy of Christianity, Islam, and Judaism alike. The notion of a God who is affected by human events and feelings and reacts to them in a very personal way, in short, the idea that there is a divine πάθος in every sense of the word (affection, emotion, passion), led the author to regard this *pathos* as a special category.[5] He wished it to be considered, not as an attribute of an independent essence, but as a *transitive passion,* that is, a relationship, the relationship between man and his God in a συμπαθεῖν, a συμπάθησις (*sym-pathesis,* here again we go back to the etymology of the word).

Taken in this sense, the category of *pathos* spontaneously gave rise to the category of the *tropos,* that is to say, the revelation of God to man as the "conversion" of a God turning toward man; a divine initiative, an anthropotropism reserving and sanctioning the divine sovereignty, or theonomy, and contrasting with any idea of a "conversion" of man toward God, that is, a *theotropism* which would be a movement resulting from human initiative.

The contrast thus established was developed in a series of antitheses comprehensible only if we reduce the infinitely diversified concept of mystic religion to a single type, for example, a certain form of Yoga. This highly questionable reduction led to the contention that the prophet essentially experiences a dialogical relationship and situation, and that the prophetic state calls for a theophany which contrasts with mystical ecstasy; mystical religion on the other hand would lead to an ecstasy in which the human personality dissolves into the infinite divine Unity, whereby the entire basis of sympathy would be done away with. In support of this thesis it can be argued that the prophet is blind to the subtleties of negative theology, to its notion of a *superessence,* while the mystic holds to a negative theology which denies all relation between the divine Being and the world. And a contrast is drawn between the basic emotional tonalities of prophetic and mystical religion: in the prophet of Israel, militant support of the divine cause in the world; in the mystic, nostalgia and enthusiasm, aspiration to ecstasy, indifference to earthly affairs, the passion for personal salvation. In short, on the one hand unification of will and feeling; on the other, unification of essence. Finally, it can be argued that the prophet's idea of *unio sympathetica* is the direct opposite of the ecstatic's *unio sympathetica.*[6]

I have dwelled by design on these categories of a religious experience analyzed as a phenomenon of sympathy, that is, as man's response to the demands of a *pathetic* God. For the crux of the question is whether amid the wide diversity of mystical experience there is not some region where mystical religion proves precisely to be a *sympathetic* religion, that is to say, where, far from providing an antithesis to the categories of prophetic religion, it assimilates them and thereby surmounts the opposition we have just seen formulated in connection with an isolated type of mystical experience. Perhaps the flower, whose heliotropism proves to be its "heliopathy," will put us on the path, if we open our ears to an echo of the Koran verse: "Every being has his own appropriate mode of prayer and glorification" (XXIV:41). The question is: Does a mystical theology of *superessence* preclude the experience of a pathetic God; does ecstasy preclude every dialogical situation; can there be a *sym-patheia* without a community of essence; in short, is *unio mystica*, far from being its antithesis, not the privileged mode of *unio sympathetica;* and is not the metaphysic of ecstasy grounded precisely in a theophanism? We shall see that theophanism stands in fundamental opposition to the idea of Incarnation in its current dogmatic form. But the possibility that the two types of experience elsewhere represented as antitheses may on the contrary imply one another and be understood through one another, presupposes a mystical experience developing in a religious environment built on a prophetology, an environment where prophetology itself is conceived as the prototype of a mystical experience.

Islamic Ṣūfism meets this condition. Here we are not speaking of official, orthodox Islam; there is a gulf between the two. And by Ṣūfīs we mean precisely all those whom, for reasons set forth above, we group as *Fedeli d'amore.* This group is dominated by two great figures: Ibn ʿArabī, the incomparable master of mystic theosophy, and Jalāluddīn Rūmī, the Iranian troubadour of that religion of love whose flame feeds on the theophanic feeling for sensuous beauty.[7] *Fedeli d'amore* struck us as the best means of translating into a Western language the names by which our mystics called themselves in Arabic or Persian (*ʿāshiqūn, muḥibbūn, arbāb al-hawà,* etc.). Since it is the name by which Dante and his companions called themselves, it has the power of suggesting the traits which were common to both groups and have been analyzed in memorable works.[8] We can observe how the experience of the Muslim Neoplatonists (the followers of Avicenna and Suhrawardī's *Ishrāqīyūn*) and that of the disciples of Ibn ʿArabī and Jalāluddīn Rūmī converge toward the symbol of an identical archetype. The teaching that is common to all of them suggests the following: if there is any fact in experience which justifies us (if justification is needed) in speaking of a divine *pathos*, of a divine passion for man (a divine "*anthropopathy*") motivating the "conversion" of the divine being toward man (his "anthropotropism"), this fact of experience can only be a corresponding, complementary, and as it were sym-pathetic, state in man, a state in which the divine *pathos* is revealed. In other words, the divine *pathos* is accessible, it has existential reality, only in a state experienced by man as a theopathy and theotropism. Man cannot directly grasp a question asked him from outside (that would be pure speculation); he grasps it through his response, and this response is his being, his very own mode of being, as he wills it and assumes it (just as the tropism of the heliotrope expresses that flower's very own being).

This response depends then on the degree to which man renders himself "capable of God," for it is this capacity which defines and measures sympathy as the necessary medium of all religious experience. Here again the movement of the heliotrope, which in its totality exceeds the visible, can instruct us. We shall need a divination, as in the case of Proclus "listening" to the flower pray, in order to perceive its meaning, and this divination is precisely a presentiment of unfulfilled virtualities. Though we speak with Max Scheler of the cognitive function of sympathy,[9] we actually have in mind a divination that surpasses actual reality, because it is the meaning of virtual existences.[10]

In short, the path we shall now follow passes through these two stages; first, to recognize the presence of the *pathetic* God in a mystical theosophy which maintains the twofold notion of *Theos agnostos* (unknowable God) and of the *Deus revelatus;* second, to understand how, since the mystery of the origin of beings is expressed as a divine com-passion, a *sympathesis*, which frees beings from their nonbeing, there arises from this *sympathesis* a human-divine sympathetism which unites the divine lord and his *fedele d'amore* in their very being; in other words, how, since there is a constant reciprocity between divine anthropopathy and human theopathy, *unio mystica* is not in opposition to, but must be identified with, *unio sympathetica.*

2. *The "Pathetic God"*

The premises of negative theology are far from excluding a dialogical situation; on the contrary, they are essential to the authenticity of such a situation. This is the case of Islamic Gnosis, whose premises have a number of features in common with those of gnosis in general, those precisely which are the most irritating to any dogmatism concerned with rational definitions. The structure is constant: There is "That which originates"; beyond being, "which is," there is the "God who is not" (the οὐκ ὢν θεός of Basilides) that is, the *Theos agnostos*, the unknowable and impredicable God;[11] and there is the revealed God, His Νοῦς who thinks and acts, who maintains the divine attributes and is capable of relation. However, it is not by looking for a compromise favoring one or the other of these notions, but by firmly maintaining the simultaneity of the vision, that we come to speak of a *pathetic God*, not as a theoretical demand in opposition to the positive theologies concerned with the dogma of divine immutability, but as an internal progression by which to effect, in our experience, a passage from the silent emptiness of Above-Being to Figures and statements possessed of a positive foundation.

In this respect Ismailian Gnosis has more than one trait in common with the doctrine of Ibn ʿArabī. The etymology it suggests for the divine name *Al-Lāh* projects a flash of light on the path we are attempting to travel. Despite the reticence of Arabic grammar on this point, it derives the word *ilāh* from the root *wlh* connoting to be sad, to be overwhelmed with sadness, to sigh toward, to flee fearfully toward.[12] And in support of this etymology, which gives the divine name (*ilāh* = *wilāh*) the meaning of "sadness," our Ismailians adduce another etymology, which is still stranger because in it grammar is disregarded, but ceases to seem arbitrary when we consider the imperious preoccupation it reflects. This etymology consists in considering the word *ulhānīya* (formed, like the words *ilāha, ulūha,* and *ulūhīya,* from the root *'lh* and signifying the Godhead) as an *ideogram* which, by introducing a trifling orthographic sign (a *tashdīd,* which doubles the *n*) we can read as *al-hān(n)īya.* We then have an abstract noun denoting state, mode of being, formed from the verbal noun of the root *hnn* (= *ḥnn*) meaning to desire, to sigh, to feel compassion.[13]

Thus the true name of the Divinity, the name which expresses His hidden depths, is not the Infinite and All-Powerful of our rational theodicies. Nothing can better bear witness to the feeling for a "pathetic God," which is no less authentic than that disclosed (as we have seen above) by a phenomenology of prophetic religion. Here we are at the heart of a mystical gnosis, and that is why we have refused to let ourselves be restricted to the above-mentioned opposition. For Ismailian Gnosis, the supreme Godhead cannot be known or even named as "God"; *Al-Lāh* is a name which indeed is given to the created being, the Most-Near and sacrosanct Archangel, the Protokistos or Archangel-Logos.[14] This Name then expresses sadness, nostalgia aspiring eternally to know the Principle which eternally initiates it: the nostalgia of the revealed God (i.e., revealed *for man*) yearning to be once more *beyond* His revealed being. This is an inscrutable intradivine mystery: we can speak of it only allusively. Nevertheless we in our meditation can perceive that (since this revelation itself is only *for* us and *through* us) the aspiration of the Angel, the aspiration of the revealed God yearning to know the God He reveals, is, in the first and highest of creatures, identical with the Sadness of the *Theos agnostos* yearning *to be known* by and in that same creature. The intradivine mystery remains none the less inviolate; we can know only as much of it as it reveals of itself in us. However, through the *action* of an always incomplete knowledge, responding to an always unslaked passion to be known, we grasp an aspect which can also situate for us the starting point of Ibn ʿArabī's personal theosophy.

The dimensions of this study oblige us to treat of this matter with concision at the risk of being obscure and, still worse, incomplete. Nevertheless, let us try.

What is the foundation, what is the meaning of this sadness of a "pathetic God"? How does the mystic come to regard it as determining the sympathy between the invisible and the visible, as the secret of a human-divine *sym-pathetism?*

To begin with, let us recall the *ḥadīth* which all our mystics of Islam untiringly meditate, the *ḥadīth* in which the Godhead reveals the secret of His passion (his *pathos*): "I was a hidden Treasure and I yearned to be known. Then I created creatures in order to be known by them." With still greater fidelity to Ibn ʿArabī's thought, let us translate: "in order to become in them the object of my knowledge." This divine passion, this desire to reveal Himself and to know Himself in beings through being known by them, is the motive underlying an entire divine dramaturgy, an eternal cosmogony. This cosmogony is neither an Emanation in the Neoplatonic sense of the word nor, still less, a *creatio ex nihilo*. It is rather a succession of manifestations of being, brought about by an increasing light, within the originally undifferentiated God; it is a succession of *tajalliyāt*, of theophanies.[15] This is the context of one of the most characteristic themes of Ibn ʿArabī's thinking, the doctrine of *divine Names* (which has sometimes been termed, rather inexactly, his "mythology" of the divine Names).

The Names, which are the divine Essence itself, because, though not identical with the divine Essence as such, the attributes they designate are not different from it, have existed from all eternity: these Names are designated as "Lords" (*Arbāb*), who often have all the appearance of hypostases though they cannot strictly be defined as such.[16] We know them only by our knowledge of ourselves (that is the basic maxim). God describes Himself to us through ourselves. Which means that the divine Names are essentially relative to the beings who name them, since these beings discover and experience them in their own mode of being. Accordingly these Names are also designated as Presences (*Ḥaḍarāt*), that is, as the states in which the Godhead reveals Himself to his faithful in the form of one or another of His infinite Names.[17] Thus the divine Names have meaning and full reality only *through* and *for* beings who are their epiphanic forms (*maẓāhir*), that is to say, the forms in which they are manifested. Likewise from all eternity, these forms, substrate of the divine Names, have existed in the divine Essence (*A 'yan thābita*).[18] And it is these latent individualities who from all eternity have aspired to concrete being *in actu*. Their aspiration is itself nothing other than the nostalgia of the divine Names yearning to be revealed. And this nostalgia of the divine Names is nothing other than the sadness of the unrevealed God, the anguish He experiences in His unknownness and occultation.[19]

And from the inscrutable depths of the Godhead this sadness calls for a "Sigh of Compassion"[20] (*Nafas Raḥmānī*). This *Sigh* marks the release of the divine Sadness *sym-pathizing* with the anguish and sadness of His divine names that have remained unknown, and in this very act of release the Breath exhales, arouses to active being, the multitude of concrete individual existences by which and for which these divine names are at last actively manifested. Thus in its hidden being every existent is a Breath of the existentiating divine Compassion,[21] and the divine Name *Al-Lāh* becomes purely and simply equivalent to *al-Raḥmān*, the Compassionate. Thus mystical gnosis starts from the *Theos agnostos* of negative theology to open up a path to the "pathetic God," and that is what concerns us here. On the one hand, the Sigh of divine Compassion expresses here the divine *pathos*, delivers the divine Names, that is to say, emancipates beings from the virtuality in which, anguished over their latent existentiating energy, they were confined, and they in turn deliver the God whose Names they are from the solitude of His unknownness. There, in pre-eternity, is joined the pact of that *sympathetism* which will forever unite the Godhead and his *fedele*, the Worshiped and the Worshiper, in "compassionate" dialogue.

We are already in a position to note that the idea of divine Sympathy as an emancipator of beings is far removed from the attribute of Compassion known to exoteric theologies as pity or mercy toward servants, as indulgence or forgiveness toward sinners. This is no moral or moralizing conception, but a metaphysical conception, or more precisely, the initial act of a metaphysic of love.[22] Moreover, this Breath of Compassion as a phenomenon of primordial Love is at once an active, creative, and liberating potency and a passive potency, that is to say, it is the very substance, the "immaterial matter" constitutive of all beings from the angelic Spirits to the beings of supra-elementary Nature and those of sublunar Nature.[23] This twofold dimension is encountered at every degree of being, just as the divine Names are at once active, insofar as they determine the attribute which they invest in the concrete form to which they aspire, and passive insofar as they are determined in and by that form which manifests them according to the requirement of its eternal condition.[24] And it is this structure which both posits and fulfils the conditions of an Understanding that is not a theoretical inspection but a *passion* lived and shared with the understood object, a com-passion, a sympathy. For the divine Names are not the attributes conferred by the theoretical intellect upon the divine Essence as such; they are essentially the vestiges of their action in us, of the action by which they fulfil their being through our being, and which in us then assumes the aspect of what, in accordance with the old medieval terminology, may well be called their *significatio passiva*.[25] In other words, we discover them only insofar as they occur and are made within us, according to what they make of us, insofar as they are our *passion*. As we said a little while ago: God describes himself to us through ourselves.

In this essential point Ibn ʿArabī declares concisely: "Those to whom God remains veiled pray the God who in their belief is their Lord to have compassion with them. But the intuitive mystics [*Ahl al-Kashf*] ask that divine Compassion be fulfilled [come into being, exist] through them."[26] In other words, the Gnostic's prayer does not tend to provoke a change in a being outside him who would subsequently take pity on him. No, his prayer tends to actualize this divine Being as He aspires to be *through* and *for* him who is praying and who "in his very prayer" is the organ of His passion. The Gnostic's prayer means: Make of us, let us be, Compassionate ones, that is to say, "become through us what thou hast eternally desired to be." For the mystic has come to know that the very substance of his being is a breath (*spiritus*) of that infinite Compassion; he is himself the epiphanic form of a divine Name. Accordingly his prayer does not consist in a request (the Ṣūfīs have always stood in horror of that kind of prayer)[27] but in his actual mode of being (like the prayer of the heliotrope turning toward its heavenly Lord); it has the value of clarifying the degree of spiritual aptitude he has attained, that is, the measure in which he has become "capable of God." But this measure is itself determined by his own eternal condition, his archetypal individuality. "As thou wert in pre-eternity, that is to say, in thine eternal virtuality, so wert thou manifested in thy present condition. Everything that is present in the manifest being is the form of what he was in his state of eternal virtuality."[28] It would be a mistake to find here the source of a causal determinism of the current variety; more appropriately we might liken this conception to Leibniz' "pre-established harmony."[29]

From it a number of consequences, both far-reaching and magnificent, will follow. With Ibn ʿArabī we have just spoken of the "God created in the faiths,"[30] and the expression recurs more than once in his writings. In one sense (pejorative) it designates the God created by the man who remains veiled to God and to whom in turn God remains veiled, and who with all the more exclusive intransigence sets up the God of his faith as the one and absolute God. And yet we must ask: Is this "God created in the faiths" not a consequence of the eternal virtuality of the being who thus creates Him? Is He not at least the rough sketch of a theophany? And in embracing the infinity of the divine Names does not the divine Compassion also embrace the virtualities of the beings who were given to them as forms of their manifestation? For unquestionably we must follow out the consequences to their end. Ibn ʿArabī says as much: "The divine Compassion also embraces the God created in the faiths."[31]

To become a Compassionate One is to become the likeness of the Compassionate God experiencing infinite sadness over undisclosed virtualities; it is to embrace, in a total religious *sympathy,* the theophanies of these divine Names in all faiths. But this sympathy, precisely, does not signify acceptance of their limits; it signifies rather that in opening ourselves to them we open them to the expansion that the primordial divine *sympathesis* demands of them; that we increase their divine light to the maximum; that we "emancipate" them—as the divine Compassion did in pre-eternity—that is, emancipate them from the virtuality and the ignorance which still confine them in their narrow intransigence. By thus taking them in hand, religious *sympathy* enables them to escape from the impasse, that is, the sin of metaphysical idolatry. For this sympathy alone renders a being accessible to the light of theophanies. Mankind discloses the refusal of the divine Names in many forms, ranging from atheism pure and simple to fanaticism with all its variants. All come from the same ignorance of the infinite divine Sadness, yearning to find a *compassionate*[32] servant for His divine Names. The Gnostic's apprenticeship consists in learning to practice fidelity to his own Lord, that is, to the divine Name with which he, in his essential being, is invested, but at the same time to hear the precept of Ibn ʿArabī: "Let thy soul be as matter for all forms of all beliefs." One who has risen to that capacity is an *ʿārif*, an initiate, "one who through God sees in God with the eye of God."[33] Those who accept and those who decline are subject to the same authority: the God in function of whom you live is He for whom you bear witness, and your testimony is also the judgment you pronounce on yourself.

Let us not be in too much of a hurry to speak of relativism or monism or syncretism for here we are not dealing with a philosophical point of view or with the history of religions. The problem is to determine *who* is the real agent in the religious act and actualization par excellence disclosed by a phenomenology of prayer regulated in accordance with the premises of Ibn ʿArabī's mystical theosophy, though here we shall be able to give only the barest outline of such a phenomenology. The fundamental idea is this: visible, apparent, outward states, in short, phenomena, can never be the causes of other phenomena. The agent is the invisible, the immaterial. Compassion acts and determines, it causes things to be and to become like itself, because it is a spiritual state,[34] and its mode of action has nothing to do with what we call physical causality; rather, as its very name indicates, its mode of action is *sympatheia*. In each particular instance, this *sympatheia* is further specified by the name of the being whose passion (*patheia*) is undergone: for example, heliopathy in the case of the heliotrope praying to its heavenly lord, theopathy pure and simple in the case of the mystic.

This prayer activates a response, an *active passion* in one of the two components of the total being of him who prays, namely in the dimension of his manifest being. The prayer in turn is activated by his invisible (*bāṭin*) being, that is, his transcendent dimension, the celestial counterpart of his being, his eternal individuality, hence in essence the very breath of that divine Compassion which through it has summoned one of the divine Names to active being. Such indeed are the two existences which constitute a being's total existence; Ibn ʿArabī calls them *lāhūt* and *nāsūt*, the divine nature or condition and the human or created condition.[35] This is too readily forgotten by those who speak of existential monism in connection with Ibn ʿArabī, as though *lāhūt* and *nāsūt* were two garments which the mystic selects or alternates at will. To get to the bottom of the matter (and the problem is of the utmost import for our understanding of an entire school of spirituality), we must begin at least to understand that if the experience of the Prophet has been meditated and relived as the prototype of mystical experience, it is because of the exemplary character of the conjunction of *lāhūt* and *nāsūt* in his person. But this conjunction is conceived not as a hypostatic union of two natures (after the manner of the Christology of the Church Councils),[36] but as a theophanic union, that is, as the union of a divine Name and of the sensible form, or appearance, in which this Name *becomes visible*. The two together, not the one without the other or mistaken for the other, compose the totality of a divine Name, the one as this Name's lord (*rabb*), the other as its servant (*ʿabd*); the one is attached to the other by a pact of suzerainty and vassaldom or love service, which makes the two "co-respondents"—and this pact is born with the initial act of divine Love, with the Sigh of Sadness, com-passionate with the nostalgia of the divine Names crying out for the beings who would will them. Then we shall stop thinking in the *incarnationist* terms familiar for many centuries to our theology; then we shall truly envisage the conditions and structures of theophanies; and then *unio mystica* will appear to us as the true realization of an *unio sympathetica*.[37]

3. *Of* Unio Mystica *as* Unio Sympathetica

These two terms were set before us as an antithesis (§1, above). Our investigations seem to have led us to a schema of spiritual experience in which, far from excluding one another, the one is interpreted through the other. Let us recapitulate the stages in this development: each being is an epiphanic form (*maẓhar, majlà*) of the Divine Being, who in it is manifested as invested in one or more of His Names. The universe is the totality of the Names by which He is named when we name Him by His Names. Each divine Name manifested is the lord (*rabb*) of the being who manifests it (that is, who is its *maẓhar*). Each being is the epiphanic form of his own Lord (*al-rabb al-khāṣṣ*), that is, he manifests only that aspect of the divine Essence which in each case is particularized and individualized in that Name. No determinate and individualized being can be the epiphanic form of the Divine in its totality, that is to say, of all the Names or "Lords." "Each being," says Ibn ʿArabī, "has as his God only his particular Lord, he cannot possibly have the Whole."[38]

Here we have a kind of *kathenotheism* verified in the context of a mystic experience; the Divine Being is not fragmented, but wholly present in *each* instance, individualized in *each* theophany of His Names, and it is invested in *each* instance with one of these Names that He appears as Lord. Here we encounter another motif essential to the spirituality of Ibn ʿArabī's school, namely the secrecy which is constitutive of this Lord as Lord, the *sirr al-rubūbīya*. By way of suggesting the chivalric bond between the divine lord and the vassal of his Name and since it is impossible to form an abstract term from the word *seigneur* (lord),[39] we render these words by "the secret of divine suzerainty." What is meant by them? A saying of Sahl Tustarī, quoted by Ibn ʿArabī, reveals their depth: "The divine suzerainty has a secret, and it is *thou*—this *thou* is the being to whom one speaks; if (this thou) should disappear, this suzerainty would also cease to be."[40] And in a similar passage we find an implicit reference to the phenomenon of primordial Love evoked in the *ḥadīth:* "I was a hidden Treasure, I longed to be known" —for His being-known depends on *thee* (which means that when He is known *by thee*, it is because He knows Himself *in thee*)—and here we find an essential dialogical situation which no imputation of monism can impair.

The *sirr al-rubūbīya* initially implies a distinction, which is also current in common exoteric religion, between divinity (*ulūhīya*) as an attribute of the God (*Al-Lāh*) we worship, and "suzerainty" (*rubūbīya*) as attribute of the Lord to whom we appeal for help.[41] But in Ibn 'Arabī's own terminology Al-Lāh is the Name which designates the divine Essence qualified and invested with the sum of His attributes, whereas *al-Rabb,* the Lord, is the personified and particularized Divine in *one* of its attributes (hence the divine Names designated as so many "lords," *arbāb*.[42]

As more detailed analysis[43] shows, there are names of divinity relating to Al-Lāh, and names of suzerainty (*rubūbīya*) relating to the lord (*rabb*); "Lord" is the divine Name considered in respect of the relations between the divine Essence and concrete individual beings both spiritual and corporeal.[44] On the one hand the relations of the divine essence with these individuations in their state of eternal hexeity are the sources of the "Names of divinity" (such as the Mighty, the Willer, etc.), while the relations of these Names with objectified, actualized beings *in concreto* are the source of the "Names of suzerainty" (such as *al-Razzāq,* "the Provider"; *al-Ḥāfiẓ,* "the Preserver"; etc.).[45]

It follows that "lord" is a particular divine Name (*ism khāṣṣ*) postulating the actuality of a being whose Lord He is, in other words, his *fedele* or "vassal" (*'abd,* ὑπήκοος), designated as *marbūb,* a word which is the passive participle, the *nomen patientis,* of the verbal root. Each manifest being is the form (*ṣūrat*) of a "lordly name" (*ism rabbānī*), the name of the particular God who governs him, by whom he acts, to whom he appeals. The *rabb,* or lord, has no essential reality in himself but becomes a reality in relation to a being who is designated in the corresponding passive form, and this is the most eminent example of the phenomenon analyzed above in connection with the *significatio passiva.* The phenomenon is equally evident in the case of the divine Name *Al-Lāh,* for this Name postulates the positive reality, which is at least latent in His Essence, of someone whose God He is. The person through whom he thus *becomes* God is designated in a way that seems rather strange at first, as *ma'lūh,* which term is the passive participle of the primitive verb of the root *'lh.* The term, however, does not, as its grammatical aspect might lead one to suppose, designate the Worshiped One (the *ma'būd*); the divine Name here put "in the passive" designates precisely the being in whom and by whom the positive reality of the godhead is accomplished; the *ma'lūh* is the worshiper, he through whom the Divine Being is constituted as a worshiped one *in actu.*[46] Here language itself reflects the feeling that the divine *pathos,* the passion of the "pathetic God" who "yearned" to be known, presupposes as its correlate a *theopathy* in the human being whose God He *is.* Thus the abstract word *ma'lūhīya,* formed from the passive participle, seems to find a faithful equivalence in the word theopathy; and indeed a commentator on Ibn 'Arabī, struck by the unaccustomed use of the word (when our *shaikh* declares that "it is by our theopathy that we constitute Him as God"), associates it with *shaṭḥ,* that is, considers this statement as an instance of "theopathic parlance."[47]

It is this *sym-pathetism* that is expressed in such a text as the following. "The divinity [*ulūhīya*] seeks [desires, yearns for] a being whose God it is [a *ma'lūh*]; suzerainty [*rubūbīya*] seeks [desires, yearns for) a being whose lord it is [a *marbūb*]; without these both are deprived of actual or even virtual reality."[48] This is an eminently "pathetic" text, which serves to remind us on the one hand of the primordial Sadness of the divine Names anguished in the expectation of beings who "will name" them, that is, whose being will manifest them *in concreto* —and on the other hand of the Compassion of the Divine Being, "sympathizing" with the Sadness of the Names which name His essence, but which no being yet names, and triumphing over His solitude in this Sigh (*nafas*) that actualizes the reality of the "thou" which is henceforth the secret of His divine Suzerainty;

consequently it is to "thee" that the divinity of thy lord is entrusted, and it is up to thee to "make thyself capable of thy God" by answering *for* Him. And it seems to us that for this correspondence between the divine lord and his *fedele*, this *passion* of the one for the other, each actualizing through the other the *significatio passiva* of his Name, there can be no better term than *unio sympathetica*.

Here undoubtedly we are touching upon the secret of a spirituality whose paradoxical expressions formulate for us the dialogical relations which are its experience and at the same time invite us to meditate and to reproduce the example of certain prefigurations, or archetypal Figures, of the divine service in which the *fedele d'amore* "gives being" to his divine lord.

Among many other such expressions there is, for example, this line in one of Ibn ʿArabī's poems: "By knowing Him, I give Him being."[49] This does not mean that man existentiates the divine Essence, which transcends all naming and all knowledge; it refers to the "God created in the faiths" (*al-Ilāh al makhlūq fī'l-mu ʿtaqadāt*), that is to say, the God who in every soul takes a form determined by that soul's belief, knowledge, and aptitude, becoming a symbol that reflects the very law of that soul's being. The line means roughly this: I know God in proportion to the Names and attributes which are epiphanized in me and through me in the forms of beings, for God epiphanizes Himself to each of us in the form of what we love; the form of your love is the form of the faith you profess.[50] Out of all this I "create" the God in whom I believe and whom I worship. Ibn ʿArabī said: "To one who understands the allusion, God is a meaningful designation."[51]

This, however, is only one aspect of *unio sympathetica*, precisely that aspect which, considered in itself, can be a source of malicious glee to the rationalist critic and a stumbling block to the orthodox theologian, but in any case does not wholly express the mystical experience involved. For when there is mention of the "created God," we must ask: *who* in reality is the active subject who creates? It is true, of course, that without the divine (*ḥaqq*) which is the cause of our being, and without us who are the cause of its manifestation, the order of things would not be what it is and God would be neither God nor Lord. But on the other hand, though it is *you*, the vassal of this Lord, who hold the "secret of his suzerainty" because it is realized through you, nevertheless, because your *action* in positing Him is His *passion* in you, your passion for Him, the active subject is in reality not you, your autonomy is a fiction. In reality you are the subject of a verb in the passive (you are the *ego* of a *cogitor*). And that is what our mystics mean when they declare that this "secret of the divine suzerainty" has itself in turn a secret (*sirr sirr al-rubūbīya,* the secret of the secret of suzerainty).[52]

By making this clear they forestall the consequence that might be drawn by a critic under the influence of psychologism or sociologism: the Godhead as a projection of consciousness. The "secret of the secret" corresponds here to our contention that, contrary to these deductive explanations, we are dealing here not with an *a posteriori* fabrication but with an *a priori* fact of experience, posited along with the very fact of our being. The *totality* of a divine Name is this Name as lord *along with* the Name's vassal or servant (whose very name expresses the service of devotion with which he is invested: ʿAbd al-Raḥmān, ʿAbd al-Karīm, etc.; strictly speaking, only the supreme Spirit or Archangel, *ʿAql awwal,* of whom the prophet is the theopathy, *maẓhar,* is entitled to the name ʿAbd Allāh, because he totalizes all the Names).[53]

There are two aspects to the "secret of the secret"; the first is that if the servant of the Name is the man who manifests it and through whom the name subsists in the visible universe, it is because that man is the Name's action, the executant of its intention and will.[54] In us this action fulfils its *significatio passiva:* it is the *marbūbīya* of the Name's servant, its *maʾlūhīya,* its theopathy; man discovers that his own being is the accomplishment of this *pathos;* in it he discovers the trace of his own lord, and it is this knowledge by "sympathetism" that is also its supreme guarantee. This is what we mean when we say that *rabb* and *marbūb* confirm one another.[55]

The second aspect is that this correlation between the divine lord and his *fedele* did not originate in time. If the *fedele*'s *ma'lūhīya*, or theopathy, posits the existence of the God he worships,[56] it is because the Worshiped makes himself into the Worshiper, and this act did not begin with the existence of the *fedele* in time; it was accomplished in preeternity in the virtual essences of these two beings. The question which the Divine Being addressed to the primordial mass of these archetypal existences—"Am I not your Lord?" (*a-lastu bi-rabbikum?*)—is in this sense a dialogue of the Divine Being with His "self," a question which He asked of Himself in them and answered through them.[57] A pre-eternal pact of *sym-pathesis*. That is why it is impossible that the Divine Being should detach himself (and absurd that we should detach Him) from the forms of the universe,[58] that is, from the beings who in worshiping Him make him into God, because their adoration, that is, their theopathy, is the form of the divine Compassion (*sym-pathesis*) sympathizing with them: He praises Himself in all *His* beings who are His theophanies, though all do not apprehend them as such, for many beings do not apprehend the prayer of the Silent One (*al-Sāmit*), the prayer of the heliotrope, for example, of which Proclus was so well aware.[59]

And this theopathy lent its form to the divine service through which the *Fedeli d'amore* gave being to the "pathetic God" whose passion they were—by feeding this passion with their entire being. The life of the mystic striving to realize this *unio sympathetica* then became what, by way of fixating and safeguarding its content, we shall have to designate, by another Latin term, as a *devotio sympathetica*. Later on we shall see what its primordial image, its archetypal Figure, is. But even now Ibn 'Arabī invites us to meditate its prefiguration par excellence in the person of an ideal Abraham who, it must be admitted, bears only the most remote relationship to the historical Abraham. It is the designation of Abraham as *Khalīl Allāh*—the intimate friend, the beloved, of God—which leads our *shaikh* to take him as the type of a wisdom that is "ecstasy of love" (*ḥikmat muhayyamīya*);[60] and it is a similar typification that motivates the presence of an equally ideal Abraham in the books of *futuwwat*, the manuals of "spiritual chivalry" in use among the Ṣūfīs.[61]

We know of philosophers in the West whose lofty feeling for philosophy led them to say that philosophy too was a divine service. Ibn 'Arabī and his group would have agreed on condition that "philosophy" were interpreted very differently from what philosophers in the restricted sense tend to mean by the word, and it is this condition which permits Ibn 'Arabī to dismiss both the philosopher Avicenna (at least the exoteric philosopher, not the Avicenna of the "Visionary Recitals" or of "Oriental Wisdom") and the theologian Ghazālī, because both thought it possible for the pure intellect to demonstrate the existence of a Necessary Being outside of time, space, and form, in short, to prove the existence of a God who has not, or not yet, any relation with the man whose God He is (the *ma'lūh*).[62] But this cannot satisfy our mystical theosophists (*al-ilāhīyūn*), who find their God not by constructing proofs of His abstract existence, but in what they experience or undergo (or "suffer") of Him, that is to say, in their theopathy (*ma'lūhīya*). To know God and His attributes is to define this theopathy, to verify experimentally the maxim "He who knows himself knows his Lord," for in this theopathy the divine Lord is *to* himself and *by* himself His own proof *for* his *fedele*.

A definition of this state is suggested by the etymology of Abraham's surname (*Khalīl Allāh*), at least as analyzed in Ibn 'Arabī's personal philology, which is consciously indifferent to the contingencies of grammar. Our *shaikh* relates the word *Khalīl* to the fifth form of the verbal root (*takhallala*), connoting to mix, to mingle. What mixes with a thing is veiled by the thing that incurs the mixture; this thing, which is in a passive situation, corresponds to the Apparent (*ẓāhir*), while the agent, the active subject (that which mixes) corresponds to the Hidden (*bāṭin*), which is likened to the food that feeds the former, just as water that is mixed with wool takes possession of it and permeates it. This is pure symbolism, but it imperatively raises the questions: Shall we say that God is the Apparent? In that case it is the creature who is veiled in Him. Or shall we say that the creature is the Apparent? Then it is God who is veiled and hidden in him.[63] This gives rise to a meditation which, instead of arguing rationally from effect to cause, apprehends the Giver in the given, that is to say, apprehends the subject who is *active* in his own *theopathy*.

This meditation passes through three phases:[64] to experience and mediate this theopathy (our *ma'lūhīya*) in order to discover how, through the mediation of our worship, which expresses the form of our being since its pre-eternal virtuality, it is God who makes Himself into God and precisely into the God of this worship which posits Him as Worshiped; to discover that in this worship He himself, as the *a priori* fact of my being, is His own proof, because if there is a God, it is because there is a God for us; and finally, to discover that the knowledge of ourselves by ourselves as the "place" of this theopathy is accomplished *in Him;* in this place He is Presence of Himself to Himself, since the being who knows is the very same being in whom He knows Himself. That is why the theopathic maxim of the disciples of Ibn ʿArabī was not *Anā'l Ḥaqq* "I am God" (*Ḥallāj*), but *Anā sirr al-Ḥaqq*, "I am the secret of God,"[65] that is to say, the secret of love that makes His divinity dependent on me, because the hidden Treasure "yearned to be known" and it was necessary that beings exist in order that He might be known and know Himself. Thus this secret is nothing other than the Sigh which appeases His Sadness by giving existence to beings and which, by investing the primordial Image, the Name that each of them bears as his secret nostalgia, with their image, leaves to each one the task of recognizing Him in that Image, and of making Him recognize Himself in it. This is not the movement of a dialectical pendulum, oscillating between two terms. It is rather a movement describing the area of His Compassion in an ellipse, one focus of which is the being of God for and through me, while the other is my being for and through Him, in other words, the area enclosing the two of us, the area in which He is for me in proportion to my capacity for Him and in which *my* knowledge of *Him* is *His* knowledge of *me.*

In the mystic area delimited by the *unio sympathetica* of this *unus ambo* is accomplished the divine service typified by Abraham's name and hospitality. For it is to the Perfect Man whom Abraham prefigures that these verses address their imperative: "Feed then God's Creation on Him, For thy being is a breeze that rises, a perfume which He exhales; We have given Him the power to manifest himself through us, Whereas He gave us (the power to exist through Him). Thus the role is shared between Him and us."[66] This perfume He exhales is the Breath of His Compassion which emancipates beings enclosed in their unburgeoned virtuality; it is this perfume that all breathe and that is the nourishment of their being. But because in their secret being they *are* this Compassion itself, the Compassion does not move only in the direction from the Creator to the creature whom He feeds with his existentiating Breath; it also moves from the creature toward the Creator (from the *ma'lūh* toward *Al-Lāh,* from the Worshiper to the Worshiped, the Lover to the Beloved), so that the created universe is the theophany of His Names and attributes, which would not exist if the creature did not exist.[67] The same idea is formulated in different ways: "If He has given us life and existence by His being, I also give Him life by knowing Him in my heart,"[68] which means: "To give life to God in one's heart is to cause a form among the forms of belief to exist in my heart."[69] And these formulas are in harmony with the most striking paradoxes of Angelus Silesius: "I know that without me, the life of God were lost; / Were I destroyed, he must perforce give up the ghost."[70]

But once we grasp the interdependence, the *unio sympathetica* between the "pathetic God" and the *fedele* who feeds Him with his own theopathy, does it not cease to be a paradox? For to nourish all creatures with Divine Being is at the same time to nourish this God through and with all the determinations of being, through and with His own theophanies.[71] This mystic task can be fulfilled only by the sympathy of a "com-passionate" love, the love connoted by Abraham's surname of "God's intimate," which Ibn ʿArabī relates etymologically to the radical connoting the idea of interpenetration.[72] Creator and creatures (*ḥaqq* and *khalq*), divine Names and theophanic forms of beings, appearances and apparitions, intermingle and nourish one another without any need for an Incarnation (*ḥulūl*), since "sympathetic union" differs essentially from "hypostatic union"; we must at all times remain on the plane of theophanic vision,[73] for which Junayd, Jāmī, and many others favored and often invoked the following symbol: it is like the color of water, which takes the coloration of the vessel that holds it.

It is incumbent on the Spiritual to preside over this mystic Supper at which all beings feed on the pre-eternal sympathy of their being. And it is there that the act of Abraham, whose surname of "God's intimate" marks and predestines him for this mystic role, takes on its exemplary significance. I am referring to the repast which he hospitably offers the mysterious strangers, the episode which our sacred history calls the *philoxeny* of Abraham; the Koran (xi:72) also mentions it in terms whose appropriate docetism fittingly preserves its theophanic character.[74] The episode is especially favored in the iconographic art of Oriental Christianity; among the numerous images in which it figures, Andrei Rublev's (fifteenth century) masterpiece occupies a place of honor. And now, unexpectedly, the symbolic Imagination of Ibn ʿArabī invites us to meditate and perceive it in an entirely new way. His mental iconography represents the service incumbent on the *fedele d'amore* in the person of Abraham ministering to the three Angels[75] seated at the mystic banquet to feed God or His Angel on His creatures, and that service is at the same time to feed the creatures on God.

For to feed on our being is to feed on *His* being, with which precisely He has invested us. It is to "substantiate" with our own passion the passion of the "pathetic God." It is for His *fedele* "to make himself capable of God," who though Beloved is nevertheless the first Lover, who though adored has summoned Himself to adoration in the adoration of His creatures and in them has brought to flowering the Image of primordial beauty which in them is the secret of suzerainty of love and at the same time the pledge of this secret. But to feed God's creatures on Him is to reinvest them with God, is therefore to make their theophanic radiance flower within them; it is, one might say, to make oneself capable of apprehending the "angelic function" of beings, to invest them with, and perhaps awaken them to, the angelic dimension of their being. And this is itself an angelic service, as is suggested by the consociation of Abraham with the Archangel Michael, that one of the four Archangels, pillars of the cosmic Throne, who concerns himself with the substantiation of the universe of being.[76] Abraham's philoxeny, the mystic repast presented to the Angels, becomes here the most perfect image of *devotio sympathetica*.

As such, it is for the mystic a plastic symbol signifying the degree of spiritual realization that he must attain in order to become a *Khalīl*, his God's intimate. Here then, in conclusion, it will be incumbent on us to define the complex but characteristic notion of the Perfect Man, *Anthropos teleios, Insān-i-kāmil*.[77] First of all, we must be on our guard against the illusory pretentions arising from a conception of the universal which may satisfy the intellect but which, measured by the limits of our human modality, strikes us as an overweening and absurd spiritual pride.[78] The first question is this: Should it be supposed that the mystic realizes the type of the Perfect Man *ontologically*, in his very being, that is, can he in person become the perfect theophany of all the divine Names and attributes? Or should it be supposed that he realizes it *noetically* by having realized the meaning of the Names in his mystic consciousness, that is, by having mystically experienced the meaning of his essential unity with the Divine Being?[79] If in experience the truth of the first concept is conditioned by the second, experience must also show us the way to a solution of the apparent contradiction between the two terms, neither of which can or should be done away with. They represent on the one hand the totality that the Perfect Man typifies mystically and on the other hand the singularity which attaches each particular divine Name to the *fedele* who is invested with it and whose Lord it is.

Far from being dispensable, the singularity of this tie is so precious that the Koran verse which is the expression par excellence of individual eschatology refers to it: "O serene soul! Return to your Lord, joyful and pleasing in His sight" (LXXXIX: 27). We have already explored the significance of this mutual pleasure: the Lord to which the soul is enjoined to return is *its* Lord, the Lord whose Name it bears and whom it has invoked,[80] having distinguished Him among all others, because it recognized itself in the image it bore of Him, while He recognized Himself in it. As our texts observe, the soul is not enjoined to return to God in general, to *Al-Lāh*, who is the All, but to its own Lord, manifested in it, the Lord to whom it replied: *Labbayka*, Here I am![81] "Enter my Paradise" (LXXXIX:29), that Paradise which is none other than yourself, that is to say, the divine form hidden in your being, the secret primordial Image in which He knows himself in you and by you, the image you must contemplate in order to become aware that "he who knows himself knows his Lord." And to the Gnostic who in this "himself" attains the coalescence of the Creator and the creature, this is the supreme joy, unknown not so much to the believer pure and simple as to the theologian and philosopher.[82] For they posit a contingent creature, whom they oppose to the Necessary Being, thereby disclosing an inferior knowledge of God (for in it the soul knows itself only as a *mere creature*), a purely negative knowledge which cannot comfort the heart. The authentic mystic wisdom (*maʿrifa*) is that of the soul which knows *itself* as a theophany, an individual form in which are epiphanized the divine Attributes which it would be unable to know if it did not discover and apprehend them in itself.[83] "When you have entered into my Paradise, you have entered into yourself (into your "soul," *nafs*), and you know yourself with another knowledge, different from that which you had when you knew *your* Lord by the knowledge you had of yourself," for now you know Him, and it is through Him that you know yourself.[84]

Thus there can be no contradiction between your fidelity to your own Lord and the mystic vocation which is to tend toward the archetype of the Perfect Man, or rather, the contradiction was apparent only on the plane of rational evidences and contradictions. The divine commandment is to "return to *your* Lord" (not to *Al-Lāh* in general); it is through and in *your* Lord that you can attain to the Lord of Lords who manifests Himself in each Lord, that is to say, it is by your fidelity to this Lord who is absolutely your own, it is in His divine Name which you serve, that the totality of the Names becomes present to you, for spiritual experience does not achieve this totality as one gathers the pieces of a collection or the concepts of a philosophical system. The mystic's fidelity to *his own* Lord frees him from the dilemma of monism or pluralism. Thus the divine Name to which and for which he responds, performs the "function of the Angel," to which we alluded above (see n. 10), as a safeguard against the sin of metaphysical idolatry.

Indeed, because the mystic can attain the Lord of Lords *through* and *in* his Lord, this "kathenotheism" is his safeguard against all metaphysical idolatry, that two-faced spiritual infirmity which consists in either loving an object without transcendence, or in misunderstanding that transcendence by separating it from the loved object, through which alone it is manifested. These two aspects spring from the same cause: in both cases a man becomes incapable of the sympathy which gives beings and forms their transcendent dimension. The cause may be a will to power, dogmatic or otherwise, which wishes to immobilize beings and forms at the point where the man has immobilized himself—perhaps out of secret fear of the infinite successions of perpetual transcendences which we must accept if we profess that the revealed Lord can never be anything other than the Angel of the *Theos agnostos*, and that to be faithful to the Angel is precisely to let ourselves be guided by him toward the transcendences he announces. Or the cause may be an asceticism or puritanism which, isolating the sensible or imaginable from the spiritual, divests beings of their *aura*. And it is precisely by investing the beloved being with this *aura*, this dimension of transcendence, that the dialectic of love of Ibn ʿArabī, Rūzbehān, or Jalāluddīn Rūmī preserves itself from the idolatry which its ascetic critics, precisely because they were blind to this transcendent dimension, were so ready to find in it. And this no doubt is the most fecund paradox of the religion of the *Fedeli d'amore*, which in every Beloved recognizes the one Beloved and in every divine Name the totality of Names, because between the divine Names there is an *unio sympathetica*.

A life in *sympathy* with beings, capable of giving a transcendent dimension to their being, to their beauty, to the forms of their faith, goes hand in hand with that theopathy which makes the spiritual a being of Compassion (a *Raḥmān*), and which through him realizes the divine *Sym-pathy* (*Nafas Raḥmānī*), which is the compassion of creative love, because it is at once passion and action. In what Image can we contemplate at once the type and the object of this *devotio sympathetica?* To what mode of being does this contemplation summon us? That will be the theme of the second part of our inquiry. But we are now in a position to introduce it. In Ibn ʿArabī's great *sophianic* poem, the *Dīwān*, the whole of which is secretly dominated by the Figure which during his memorable stay in Mecca appeared to him as the Figure of Wisdom or of divine Sophia —in this *Dīwān* there bursts forth the following profession of faith of a *fedele d'amore*, capable of taking upon himself all the transcendences that open beyond each form, because his love transmutes them into the brilliance of a "Fire which neither consumes itself nor consumes him, for its flame feeds on his nostalgia and his quest, which can no more be destroyed by fire than can the salamander":

O marvel! a garden among the flames . . .
My heart has become capable of all forms.
It is a meadow for gazelles and a monastery for Christian monks,
A temple for idols and the pilgrim's Kaʿaba,
The Tables of the Law and the book of the Koran.
I profess the religion of Love, and whatever direction
Its steed may take, Love is my religion and my faith.[85]

II SOPHIOLOGY AND *DEVOTIO SYMPATHETICA*

1. *The Sophianic Poem of a* Fedele d'amore

In the prologue to the *Dīwān*, which he entitled "The Interpreter of Ardent Desires,"[1] Ibn ʿArabī relates the circumstances of its composition as follows: "While sojourning in Mecca in the course of the year A.H. 598 [A.D. 1201], I frequented a group of outstanding men and women, an élite of culture and virtue. Although they were all persons of distinction, I found none among them to equal the wise doctor and master Zāhir ibn Rustam, a native of Ispahān who had taken up residence in Mecca, and his sister, the venerable ancient, the learned woman of Hijāz, whose name was Fakhr al-Nisā' [Glory of Women] Bint Rustam." Here Ibn ʿArabī expatiates on pleasant memories, mentioning among other things the books he studied under the *shaikh*'s guidance and in the company of his sister. With all this he is merely leading up to the motive underlying the poems that make up the *Dīwān*.

Among all the delightful persons who frequented the home of this noble Iranian family established in Mecca, there was one who stood out: a figure of pure light. The passage is one of those that cannot be summarized.

> Now this *shaikh* had a daughter, a lissome young girl who captivated the gaze of all those who saw her, whose mere

3 *The Philoxeny of Abraham* *Detail from a mosaic, Cathedral of St. Mark, Venice, thirteenth century*

presence was the ornament of our gatherings and startled all those who contemplated it to the point of stupefaction. Her name was Niẓām [Harmonia] and her surname "Eye of the Sun and of Beauty" [*'ayn al-Shams wa'l-Bahā'*]. Learned and pious, with an experience of spiritual and mystic life, she personified the venerable antiquity of the entire Holy Land and the candid youth of the great city faithful to the Prophet.[2] The magic of her glance, the grace of her conversation were such an enchantment that when, on occasion, she was prolix, her words flowed from the source; when she spoke concisely, she was a marvel of eloquence; when she expounded an argument, she was clear and transparent. . . . If not for the paltry souls who are ever ready for scandal and predisposed to malice, I should comment here on the beauties of her body as well as her soul, which was a garden of generosity. . . .

At the time when I frequented her, I observed with care the noble endowments that graced her person and those additional charms conferred by the society of her aunt and father. And I took her as model for the inspiration of the poems contained in the present book, which are love poems, composed in suave, elegant phrases, although I was unable to express so much as a part of the emotion which my soul experienced and which the company of this young girl awakened in my heart, or of the generous love I felt, or of the memory which her unwavering friendship left in my memory, or of the grace of her mind or the modesty of her bearing, since she is the object of my Quest and my hope, the Virgin Most Pure [*al-Adhrā' al-batūl*]. Nevertheless, I succeeded in putting into verse some of the thoughts connected with my yearning, as precious gifts and objects which I here offer.[3] I let my enamored soul speak clearly, I tried to express the profound attachment I felt, the profound concern that tormented me in those days now past, the regret that still moves me at the memory of that noble society and that young girl.

II. *Sophiology and* Devotio Sympathetica

But now come the decisive remarks revealing the content of the poem, the intentions which the reader is asked to bear in mind:

> Whatever name I may mention in this work,[4] it is to her that I am alluding. Whatever the house whose elegy I sing, it is of her house that I am thinking. But that is not all. In the verses I have composed for the present book, I never cease to allude to the divine inspirations [*wāridāt ilāhīya*], the spiritual visitations [*tanazzulāt rūḥānīya*], the correspondences [of our world] with the world of the angelic Intelligences; in this I conformed to my usual manner of thinking in symbols; this because the things of the invisible world attract me more than those of actual life, and because this young girl knew perfectly what I was alluding to [that is, the esoteric sense of my verses].

Hence this solemn warning: "May God preserve the reader of this *Dīwān* from any temptation to suppose things unworthy of souls who despise such vileness, unworthy of their lofty designs concerned solely with things celestial. Amen—by the power of Him who is the one Lord."

No doubt he was too optimistic, for malicious words, especially those of a certain learned moralist of Aleppo, were carried back to the author by two of his closest disciples. He was baldly accused of dissimulating a sensual love in order to preserve his reputation for austerity and piety. This is what led Ibn ʿArabī to write a long commentary on his *Dīwān* in which he tried to show that the amatory imagery of his poems as well as the central and dominant feminine figure are nothing more nor less than allusions, as he says, "to the spiritual mysteries, to the divine illuminations, to the transcendant intuitions of mystic theosophy, to the awakenings provoked in the hearts of men by religious admonitions."[5]

In order to understand him and to avoid any hypercritical questioning of his good faith, we must bear in mind what may be termed the theophanic mode of apperception, which is so characteristic of the *Fedeli d'amore* that without this key one cannot hope to penetrate the secret of their vision. We can only go astray if we ask, as many have done in connection with the figure of Beatrice in Dante: is she a concrete, real figure or is she an allegory? For just as a divine Name can be known only in the concrete form of which it is the theophany, so a divine archetypal Figure can be contemplated only in a concrete Figure —sensible or imagined—which renders it outwardly or mentally visible. When Ibn ʿArabī explains an allusion to the young girl Niẓām as, in his own words, an allusion to "a sublime and divine, essential and sacrosanct *Wisdom* [Sophia], which manifested itself *visibly* to the author of these poems with such sweetness as to provoke in him joy and happiness, emotion and delight,"[6] we perceive how a being apprehended directly by the Imagination is transfigured into a symbol thanks to a theophanic light, that is, a light which reveals its dimension of transcendence. From the very first the figure of the young girl was apprehended by the Imagination on a visionary plane, in which it was manifested as an "apparitional Figure" (*ṣūrat mithālīya*) of *Sophia aeterna*. And indeed it is as such that she appears from the prologue on.[7]

Meditating the central event of this prologue, we are struck first of all by the "composition of the scene": it is night, the author is performing his ritual circumambulations of the Kaʿaba. He himself will later remark on the importance of this sign: its situation in a memorable Night discloses the visionary nature of the event.[8] To the rhythm of his stride the poet is inspired with a few verses. Suddenly a Presence hitherto invisible is revealed, and in that Presence the narrative enables us to discern a real woman transfigured by a celestial aura; speaking with the stern authority of a divine initiatrix, she divulges the entire secret of the sophianic religion of love. But the verses which provoke her lesson are so enigmatic that in order to understand it we shall have perhaps to learn from the poet himself the secret of a language which closely resembles the *langage clus* (or arcane language) of our troubadours. In so doing, moreover, we shall gain the means of deciphering the entire poem, which may be regarded as a celebration of his meeting with the mystic Sophia or as an inner autobiography moving to the rhythm of his joys and fears.

> One night [the poet relates,] I was performing the ritual circumambulations of the Ka'aba. My spirit savored a profound peace; a gentle emotion of which I was perfectly aware had taken hold of me. I left the paved surface because of the pressing crowd and continued to circulate on the sand. Suddenly a few lines came to my mind; I recited them loudly enough to be heard not only by myself but by someone following me if there had been anyone following me.
>
> Ah! to know if *they* know what heart *they* have possessed!
> How my heart would like to know what mountain paths *they* have taken!
> Ought you to suppose them safe and sound, or to suppose that *they* have perished?
> The *fedeli d'amore* remain perplexed in love, exposed to every peril.
>
> No sooner had I recited these verses than I felt on my shoulder the touch of a hand softer than silk. I turned around and found myself in the presence of a young girl, a princess from among the daughters of the Greeks.[9] Never had I seen a woman more beautiful of face, softer of speech, more tender of heart, more spiritual in her ideas, more subtle in her symbolic allusions. . . . She surpassed all the people of her time in refinement of mind and cultivation, in beauty and in knowledge.

Of course we recognize the silhouette in the half-darkness, but in the beloved Presence suddenly disclosed to his vision on that memorable Night the mystic poet also discerned a transcendent Figure, visible to him alone, a Figure of which sensuous beauty was only the forerunner. To intimate this the poet requires only one delicate touch: the young *Iranian* girl is saluted as a *Greek* princess. Now the sophiology of the poems and their commentaries presents this remarkable feature: the woman whom the poem invests with an angelic function because she is for him the visible manifestation of *Sophia aeterna* is as such a theophany. As a theophany she is assimilated to the example of Christ as understood by Ibn ʿArabī and all the Spirituals of Islam, namely, in accordance with a docetic Christology, or more precisely, an "angel Christology" such as that held by certain very early Christians. The young girl in turn is the typification (*tamthīl*) of an Angel in human form and this is sufficient reason for Ibn ʿArabī to identify her with the "race of Christ," to qualify her as "Christic Wisdom" (*ḥikmat ʿisawīya*) and to conclude that she belongs to the world of Rūm, that is, to the world of the Greek Christians of Byzantium. These mental associations were to have far-reaching consequences for our author's sophiology. But the point that concerns us for the present is that the Figure which has appeared to Ibn ʿArabī is identified as Wisdom or divine Sophia; and it is with the authority of the divine Sophia that she will instruct her *fedele*.

To appreciate her teaching it will be necessary for us to decipher to some extent, with the help of the poet himself, the four lines with which he was inspired to the rhythm of his nocturnal perigrination and which are written, like all the poems of "the interpreter of ardent desires," in his own special arcane language. To whom does the feminine plural pronoun "they" refer? We learn from Ibn ʿArabī's own commentary that he is alluding to the "supreme Contemplated Ones" (*al-manāẓir al-ʿulà*). Were we to translate simply by "divine ideas," we should run the risk of immobilizing ourselves in the area of conceptual philosophy. The contexts in which they occur suggest those Figures designated as Wisdoms (*ḥikam*),[10] individuations of eternal Wisdom (*Ḥikmat*), each one imparted to one of the twenty-seven prophets typified in the book of the *Fuṣūṣ*—Wisdoms for which in pre-eternity the cherubinic Spirits were taken with ecstatic love,[11] just as the hearts of the mystics are taken with love for them in time.

The meaning of the poet's questions becomes clear if we recall what we have learned about the "secret of divine suzerainty" (*sirr al-rubūbīya*), that secret which is *thou*, that is, which is the theopathy of its *fedele* or "vassal," because this theopathy establishes the God of his faith, the God whom he nourishes with the substance of his being, following the example of Abraham offering his hospitality to the mysterious strangers[12]—and because in and by his being he gives substance to the divine Name with which he has been invested since pre-eternity and which is his own Lord. In the privileged hours of his spiritual life, the mystic knows and feels this without need of any other pledge than the *sympathetic passion* which gives him, or rather which *is*, this Presence, for love asks no questions. But then come the hours of weariness or lukewarmness in which the reasoning intellect, through the distinctions it introduces, through the proofs it demands, insinuates between the Lord of love and his *fedele* a doubt that seems to shatter their tie. The *fedele* no longer has the strength to feed his Lord on his Substance; he loses his awareness of their secret, which is their *unio sympathetica*. Then, like critical reason informing itself of its object, he asks whether the "supreme Contemplated Ones" are of his own essence, whether they can know what heart they have invested? In other words: Has the divine Lord whom I nourish with my being any knowledge of me? Might the bond between them not be comparable to those mystic stations (*Maqāmāt*) which exist only through him who stops (*muqīm*) in them? And since the spiritual visitations have ceased, *at best* perhaps they have taken some mountain path leading them to the inner heart of other mystics; or *at worst* might they not have perished, returned forever to nonbeing?

§ 1. *The Sophianic Poem*

Suddenly Ibn ʿArabī's gentle melancholy is interrupted by the reprimand of the mystic Sophia, whose apparition emerges from the very Night which had inspired his reverie without issue: "How, O my Lord [*sayyidī*]," [13] the young girl asks, "can you say: 'O, to know if they know what heart they have possessed?'—You, the great mystic of your time, I am amazed that you can say such a thing. . . . Is not every object of which one is the master [*mamlūk*] by that very fact an object that one knows [*maʿrūf*]? [14] Can one speak of being master [*mulk*] unless there has been Knowledge [*maʿrifa*]? . . . Then you said: 'How my heart would like to know what mountain paths they have taken!'—O my Lord, the paths that are hidden between the heart and the subtile membrane that envelops the heart, those are things that the heart is forbidden to know. How then can one such as you desire what he cannot attain? . . . How can he say such a thing? And what did you ask after that: Ought you to suppose them safe and sound, or to suppose that they have perished?—As for them, they are safe and sound. But one cannot help wondering about you: Are you safe and sound, or have you perished, O my Lord?"

And unsparingly reversing the question, Sophia recalls her *fedele* to the truth of his mystic state. He has given in for a moment to the philosopher's doubt; he has asked questions that can only be answered by rational proofs similar to those applying to external objects. He has forgotten for a moment that for a mystic the reality of theophanies, the existential status of the "supreme Contemplated Ones," depends not on fidelity to the laws of Logic, but on fidelity to the service of love. Do not ask *them* whether they have perished; the question is whether you have perished or whether you are still alive, whether you can still "answer for" them, still permit them to invest your being. And that is the crux of the matter: what to a philosopher is doubt, the impossibility of proof, is to the *fedele d'amore* absence and trial. For on occasion the mystic Beloved may prefer absence and separation while his *fedele* desires union; yet must the *fedele* not love what the Beloved loves? Accordingly, he falls a prey to perplexity, caught between two contradictories.

This is the decisive point on which Sophia continues to initiate her *fedele* with lofty and at the same time passionate rigor. " 'And what was the last thing you said? The *fedeli d'amore* remain perplexed in love, exposed to every peril?' Then she cried out and said: 'How can a *fedele d'amore* retain a residue of perplexity and hesitation when the very condition of adoration is that it fill the soul entirely? It puts the senses to sleep, ravishes the intelligences, does away with thoughts, and carries away its *fedele* in the stream of those who vanish. Where then is there room for perplexity? . . . It is unworthy of you to say such things.' "[15]

This reprimand, concluding with words of stern reproach, states the essential concerning the religion of the *Fedeli d'amore.* And what is no less essential is that, by virtue of the function with which she who states its exigencies in that Night of the Spirit, in the shadow of the Temple of the Kaʿaba, is invested, the religion of mystic love is brought into relation with a sophiology, that is to say, with the sophianic idea.

In the dramatic prologue with which the "interpreter of ardent desires" heads his *Dīwān*, we note two indications which will guide us in our present inquiry.

First of all, we note the visionary aptitude of a *fedele d'amore* such as Ibn ʿArabī, who invests the concrete form of the beloved being with an "angelic function" and, in the midst of his meditations, discerns this form on the plane of theophanic vision. How is such a perception, of whose unity and immediacy we shall have more to say in a moment, possible? To answer this question we must follow the progress of the dialectic of love set forth by Ibn ʿArabī in an entire chapter of his great work (the *Futūḥāt*); it tends essentially to secure and test the sympathy between the invisible and the visible, the spiritual and the sensible, that sympathy which Jalāluddīn Rūmī was to designate by the Persian term *ham-damī* (litt. σύμπνοια, *conflatio*, blowing-together), for only this "con-spiration" makes possible the spiritual vision of the sensible or sensible vision of the spiritual, a vision of the invisible in a concrete form apprehended not by one of the sensory faculties, but by the Active Imagination, which is the organ of theophanic vision.

And secondly we note that this prologue reveals a psycho-spiritual experience that is fundamental to the inner life of our *shaikh*. This encounter with the mystic Sophia prefigures the goal to which the dialectic of love will lead us: the idea of the feminine being (of which Sophia is the archetype) as the theophany par excellence, which, however, is perceptible only through the sympathy between the celestial and the terrestrial (that sympathy which the heliotrope's prayer had already announced to Proclus). This conjunction between Beauty and Compassion is the secret of the Creation—for if divine "sympathy" is creative, it is because the Divine Being wishes to reveal His Beauty, and if Beauty is redeeming, it is because it manifests this creative Compassion. Thus the being invested by nature with this theophanic function of Beauty will present the most perfect Image of Divinity. From this intuition will follow the idea of the *Creative Feminine*, not only as an object, but also as an exemplary Image of the *devotio sympathetica* of the *fedele d'amore*. The conjunction between the spiritual and the sensible realized in this Image will lead to admirable paradoxes, whence will emerge the figure of Maryam as the prototype of the mystic, fixating the features of the "Christic Sophia" (which for the present are still concealed beneath the symbols of the "interpreter of ardent desires") because it is she who holds the *sirr al-rubūbīya*, the secret of the Godhead that we analyzed above.[16]

2. *The Dialectic of Love*

Of all the masters of Ṣūfism it is Ibn ʿArabī (except perhaps for Rūzbehān of Shīrāz) who carried furthest the analysis of the phenomena of love; in so doing he employed a very personal dialectic, eminently suited to revealing the source of the total devotion professed by the *Fedeli d'amore*. From the context thus far outlined the question rises: What does it mean to love God? And how is it possible to love God? Ordinarily the religious language employs such formulas as though they were self-explanatory. But the matter is not so simple. Ibn ʿArabī carries us forward by means of two observations: "I call God to witness that if we confined ourselves to the rational arguments of philosophy, which, though they enable us to know the divine Essence, do so in a negative way, no creature would ever have experienced the love of God. . . . Positive religion teaches us that He is this and that; the exoteric appearances of these attributes are absurd to philosophical reason, and yet it is because of those positive attributes that we love Him." But then it becomes incumbent upon religion to say that nothing resembles Him.[17] On the other hand God can be known to us only in what we experience of Him, so that "We can typify Him and take Him as an object of our contemplation, not only in our innermost hearts but also before our eyes and in our imagination, as though we saw Him, or better still, *so that* we really see Him. . . . It is He who in every beloved being is manifested to the gaze of each lover . . . and none other than He is adored, for it is impossible to adore a being without conceiving the Godhead in that being. . . . So it is with love: a being does not truly love anyone other than his Creator."[18] Ibn ʿArabī's whole life provides a pledge of personal experience on all these points.[19]

But if the one Beloved is never visible except in a Form which is His epiphany (*maẓhar*), if He is indeed unique in *each* instance for each unique individual, it is because this Form, though revealing Him, also conceals Him, because He always transcends it. How then can He show Himself in that Form if it is true that the Form hides Him and yet that without that Form he would be unable to disclose Himself? What relation is there between the real Beloved and the concrete form that makes Him visible?

Between the two there must necessarily be a *con-spiration* (Persian *ham-damī*) a sym-pathy. And further, what sort of love is really addressed to this form that manifests Him? When is it true love, and when does it err by becoming engrossed in the Form? And finally, *who* is the real Beloved, but also *who* in reality is the Lover?

The entire work of Ibn ʿArabī is an experiential answer to these questions. In specifying their content, we may be guided by what we have meditated upon thus far, which may be summed up as follows. What we call "divine love" (*ḥibb ilāhī*) has two aspects: in one aspect it is the Desire (*shawq*) of God for the creature, the passionate Sigh (*ḥanīn*) of God in His essence (the "hidden Treasure"), yearning to manifest Himself in beings, in order to be revealed for them and by them; in its other aspect, divine love is the Desire of the creature for God, or in actual fact the Sigh of God Himself epiphanized in beings and yearning to return to himself. In reality the being who sighs with nostalgia (*al-mushtāq*) is *at the same time the being toward whom His nostaglia sighs* (*al-mushtāq ilayhi*), although in his concrete determination (*ta ʿayyun*) he differs from Him. They are not two heterogeneous beings, but one being encountering himself (at once *one* and *two*, a bi-unity, something that people tend to forget). One and the same ardent Desire is the cause of the Manifestation (*ẓuhūr*) and the cause of the Return (*ʿawda*). If God's Desire is more intense, it is because God experiences this desire in its two aspects, whereas to be a creature is to experience it only in its second aspect. For it is God who, determined in the form of the *fedele*, sighs toward Himself, since He is the Source and Origin which yearned precisely for this determinate Form, for His own anthropomorphosis. Thus love exists eternally as an exchange, a permutation between God and creature: ardent Desire, *compassionate* nostalgia, and encounter exist eternally, and delimit the area of being. Each of us understands this according to his own degree of being and his spiritual aptitude. A few men, such as Ibn ʿArabī, have experienced this encounter visually for prolonged periods of time. For all those who have experienced it and understood it, it is a yearning for the vision of divine Beauty which appears at every moment in a new form (the "divine days" of which the "interpreter of ardent desires" speaks), and it is the infinite desire to which Abū Yazīd Basṭāmī alludes: "I have drunk the potion of love, goblet after goblet. It is not exhausted and my thirst has not been slaked."[20]

This relationship inherent in divine love is exemplified by the relationship, analyzed above, of every human being with *his* own Lord. With this as our starting point we shall be able, by following Ibn ʿArabī's own developments and the questions he puts to himself to advance our design, which is to show how, since *unio mystica* is in itself *unio sympathetica* (that is to say, a sharing in that com-passion which joins the being of the lord and the being of his vassal of love into a unity which an essential *passion* splits into two terms, each yearning for the other, the Creator and the creature in their bipolarity) the fidelity in love which nourishes and guarantees this "suzerainty" by attaching the two terms that are essential to it, assumes for us the aspect of the *devotio sympathetica*. What do we learn from the dialectic of love underlying the situation we have outlined? And what mode of being fulfils and exemplifies this "devotion"?

Since in both its aspects, whether consciously or not, the love whose mover is Beauty has God alone as its object—since "God is a beautiful Being who loves beauty"[21] and who in revealing Himself to Himself has produced the world as a mirror in which to contemplate His own Image, His own beauty—and since if it is written that "God will love you" (Koran III:29), it is because He loves Himself in you[22]—all love would seem *eo ipso* to warrant the epithet "divine." Virtually, no doubt; but to suppose this to be the actual reality would be to suppose the existence of an ideal humanity, made up entirely of *Fedeli d'amore*, that is, of Ṣūfīs.

Thus it is fitting to distinguish with Ibn ʿArabī three kinds of love which are three modes of being: (a) a divine love (*ḥibb ilāhī*), which is on the one hand the love of the Creator for the creature in which He creates Himself, that is, which arouses the form in which He reveals Himself, and on the other hand the love of that creature for his Creator, which is nothing other than the desire of the revealed God within the creature, yearning to return to Himself, after having yearned, as the hidden God, to be known in the creature; this is the eternal dialogue of the divine-human *syzygia;* (b) a *spiritual love* (*ḥibb rūḥānī*), situated in the creature who is always in quest of the being whose Image he discovers in himself, or of which he discovers that he himself is the Image; it is, in the creature, a love which has no other concern, aim, or will than to be adequate to the Beloved, to comply with what He wishes to do *with* and *by* His *fedele;* (c) the natural love (*ḥibb ṭabīʿī*) which desires to possess and seeks the satisfaction of its own desires without concern for the satisfaction of the Beloved. "And that, alas," says Ibn ʿArabī "is how most people understand love today."[23]

This classification contains its own motivation. Love considered in relation to the creature differs from love considered in relation to God, to the Being who is at once subject and object, Lover and Beloved. Considered in relation to us, according to the demands of our essence, which is at once spiritual and corporeal, love is twofold: spiritual and natural or physical, which are so different as to pursue opposing ends. The first problem is to find a way to reconcile spiritual love with physical love; only when the two aspects of creatural love have been reconciled can we ask whether a conjunction is possible between it and the divine love which is love in its true essence; only then can we ask whether it is possible for us to love God with this twofold, spiritual and physical love, since God Himself is never visible except in a concrete form (imagined or sensible) that epiphanizes Him. A *sympathy* must be restored between the spiritual and the physical if love is to flower in the creature as a *theopathy* corresponding to the divine yearning to be known, in other words, if the bi-unity, the *unio sympathetica*, of the lord of love (*rabb*) and of his vassal of love (*marbūb*) is to be realized.[24]

The first step will have been taken when we are able to answer the question: Must we suppose that we love Him for Himself or for ourselves? or for Him and ourselves at once, or neither for Him nor for ourselves? For this question will prove to be appropriate and answerable only on condition that we ask this second question: *through whom* do we love Him? In other words, *who* is the real subject of Love? But this second question is tantamount to inquiring into the origin and end of love, a question which, says Ibn ʿArabī, was never asked him except by a woman of subtle mind, who was a great mystic, but whose name he passes over in silence.[25]

The answer to the first question will automatically postulate a reconciliation of the two, spiritual and natural, aspects of love. Ibn ʿArabī observes that the most perfect of mystic lovers are those who love God simultaneously *for* himself and *for* themselves, because this capacity reveals in them the unification of their twofold nature (a resolution of the torn "conscience malheureuse").[26] He who has made himself capable of such love is able to do so because he combines mystic knowledge (*ma ʿrifa*) with vision (*shuhūd*). But in mystic experience all vision is a mode of knowledge presupposing a Form of the object experienced; this Form, which is itself "composite," corresponds to the lover's being. For since the soul is dual in structure, its love for God or for any other being proceeds from its physical nature in so far as it is inspired by the hope of finding itself (or by the fear of losing itself); a love whose only aim is to satisfy the Beloved, proceeds from the spiritual nature of the soul.

In order to "synchronize" this dual nature by joining the two forms of love springing from the two facets of the soul, the divine Beloved, who defines Himself as admitting of no division, as desiring that the soul should love no one but Him and should love Him for Himself, manifests Himself to the soul, that is, produces Himself for the soul in the *physical form* of a *theophany*.[27] And He grants him a *sign* (*'alāma*), which makes it so plain that it is He who is manifesting Himself to the soul in this Form, that the soul cannot possibly deny it. Of course it is the kind of sign that is identified not by the senses but by another organ; it is an immediate, *a priori* evidence (*'ilm ḍarūrī*). The soul apprehends the theophany; it recognizes that the Beloved *is* this physical Form (sensible or mental, identified by the Active Imagination); at once in its spiritual and its physical nature, it is drawn toward that Form.[28] It "sees" its Lord; it is aware of seeing Him in this ecstatic vision that has been bestowed upon its inner faculties, and it can only love Him for Himself: this love is "physical" since it apprehends and contemplates a concrete Image, and at the same time a spiritual love, for it is not concerned with taking possession of the Image, but is itself wholly invested with that Image. This conjunction of spiritual love and the natural love it transmutes, is the very definition of mystic love.

Nevertheless this magnificent impulse might prove to exceed the mystic's capacity and therefore come to nothing if the mystic did not at the same time know *who* the real Subject is that moves this love within him, that is, who the *real lover* is, a knowledge which anticipates and resolves the question: who is the real Beloved? The answer is quite precise: the soul gains awareness that it "sees" God not *through* itself, but *through* Him; it loves only *through* Him, not *by* itself; it contemplates God in all other beings not *through* its own gaze, but because it *is* the same gaze by which God sees them; the soul's "Lord of love" is the image acting within it, the organ of *its* perception, whereas the soul itself is *His* organ of perception. The soul's vision of its divine Lord *is* the vision which He has of the soul. *Its sympathy with* being *is* the theopathy it experiences in itself, the *passion* which this Presence arouses in the soul and which to the soul is its own proof. Accordingly it is not by itself or even in conjunction with Him that the soul contemplates and loves, but through Him alone. Thus since the soul is His organ, the organ of *Him* who demands a total devotion in *sym-pathy* with Him, how could the soul love anyone but Him? It is He who seeks and is sought for, He is the Lover and He is the Beloved.[29]

To state this identity is simply to recall the nostalgia of the "Hidden Treasure" yearning to be known, the nostalgia which is the secret of the Creation.[30] It is with Himself that the Divine Being sympathized in sympathizing with the sadness of His Names, with the sadness of our own latent existences yearning to manifest those Names, and that is the first source of His love for us who are "His own beings." Conversely, the love that these beings experience for Him without even knowing it, is nothing other than a vibration of His being in their being, set in motion by His love when he freed them from their expectancy by putting their being into the imperative (*KuN*, *Esto!*). It is precisely therein that Ibn ʿArabī discerns the cause of the emotion we experience when we listen to music, for there is *sympathy* between on the one hand the response of our eternal virtuality to the Imperative that has awakened it to being and on the other hand our presentiment of the virtualities which the musical incantation seems to evoke and release.[31] Still, we must never forget that if He is the Lover and the Beloved, it is because it is in His essence to be *both* one and the other, just as He is the Worshiped, the Worshiper, and the eternal dialogue between the *two*. But, as we have already pointed out, we should lose sight of this essential bi-unity by reducing the doctrine of Ibn ʿArabī purely and simply to what is known to us elsewhere as philosophical monism, or by confusing it with an existential monism of mystic experience.[32]

Indeed, our usual philosophical categories as well as our official theological categories fail us in the presence of a theosophy such as that of Ibn ʿArabī and his disciples. It is no more possible to perceive the specific dialogue that this theosophy establishes if we persist in reducing it to what is commonly called "monism" in the West, than to understand the *consocia-*

tion of the physical and the spiritual on the theophanic plane or, *a fortiori*, to understand how Maryam can be a substitute for the mystic, if we think in terms of Incarnation (in the sense which official Christian dogma has given to this word). There is an essential structural connection between the theological docetism of Islamic esoterism (in its Christology transposed into prophetology and Imāmology) and the theophanic idea professed by our mystics. The *subjectum Incarnationis*, if it is necessary to speak of it, will never be found on the plane of materially realized existences, of events accomplished and known once and for all, but always in the transcendent dimension announced by theophanies—because "true reality" is the internal event produced in each soul by the Apparition that impresses it. In this domain we require a faculty of perception and mediation very different from the demonstrative or historical reasoning which judges the sensible and finite data relating to rationally defined dogmas or to the irreversible events of material history. It is not in the realm of an already given and fixated reality that this mediating faculty brings about the theophanic union of the divine and the human and the reconciliation between the spiritual and the physical which, as we have seen, is the condition of perfect, that is to say, mystic love. This mediating faculty is the active or creative Imagination which Ibn ʿArabī designates as "Presence" or "imaginative Dignity" (*Ḥaḍrat khayālīya*). Perhaps we are in need of a neologism to safeguard the meaning of this "Dignity" and to avoid confusion with the current acceptance of the word "imaginative." We might speak of an *Imaginatrix*.[33]

It is through this Imaginatrix that the dialectic of love attains its culminating phase when, after finding out who the real Lover is, it opens the way to the transcendent dimension in order to discover *who* the *real Beloved* is.

Here the spiritual aspect, the Spirit, must manifest itself in a physical form; this Form may be a sensible figure which the Imagination transmutes into a theophanic figure, or else it may be an "apparitional figure" perceptible to the unaided imagination without the mediation of a sensible form in the instant of contemplation. In this theophanic figure it is the real Beloved who *manifests Himself;* He can do so only in the figure which at once reveals Him and veils Him, but without which He would be deprived of all concrete existence, of all relatedness. Thus the *real* and invisible *Beloved* has to be *typified* (*mumaththal*) in a concrete figure by the Active Imagination; through it He attains a mode of existence perceptible to the vision of that privileged faculty.[34] It is in this sense that the *concrete* figure toward which the volitional act of love is directed is called the Beloved; but it is also called the Beloved in the sense that what is really loved in the figure is something which it discloses as being the Image of the Beloved, but which is not a datum existing *in actu*, despite the illusion to the contrary held by simple natural love which, since it is interested only in itself, strives only for the possession of what it looks upon a given object.

But of course this nonexistent (*maʿdūm*) is not a mere nothing; it is hardly conceivable that a nothing should exert an influence and certainly not that it should be invested with a theophanic function. It is *something not yet existent* in the concrete form of the Beloved, something which has not yet happened, but which the lover desires with all his strength to make exist or cause to happen. It is here precisely that originates the highest function of human love, that function which brings about the coalescence of the two forms of love that have been designated historically as chivalric love and mystic love. For love tends to transfigure the beloved earthly figure by setting it against a light which brings out all its superhuman virtualities, to the point of investing it with the theophanic function of the Angel (so it was with the feminine Figures celebrated by Dante's companions, the *Fedeli d'amore;* and so it was with her who appeared to Ibn ʿArabī in Mecca as the figure of the divine Sophia). Ibn ʿArabī's analysis goes ever deeper: whether the Lover tends to contemplate the beloved being, to unite with that being, or to perpetuate its presence, his love strives always to bring into existence something which does not yet exist in the Beloved.[35] The real object is not what he has obtained, but duration, persistence or perpetuation (*dawām wa'stimrār*); duration, persistence, perpetuation, however, are something nonexistent, they are a *not yet;* they have not yet entered into being, into the category of the real. The object of loving adhesion in the moment when the lover has achieved union (*ḥāl al-waṣla*) is again something nonexistent, namely, the continuation and perpetuation of that union. As the Koran verse— "He will love them and they will love him" (v:59)—suggests to our *shaikh,* the word love never ceases to anticipate something that is still absent, something deprived of being.[36] Just as we speak of a *Futurum resurrectionis,* we must speak of a *Futurum amoris.*

Thus the experience of mystic love, which is a conjunction (σύμπνοια, "conspiration") of the spiritual and the physical, implies that imaginative Energy, or creative Imagination, the theory of which plays so large a part in the visionary experience of Ibn 'Arabī. As organ of the transmutation of the sensible, it has the power to manifest the "angelic function of beings." In so doing, it effects a *twofold* movement; *on the one hand* it causes invisible spiritual realities to descend to the reality of the Image (but no further, for to our authors the *Imaginalia* are the maximum of "material" condensation compatible with spiritual realities); and it also effects the only possible form of assimilation (*tashbīh*) between Creator and creature, so resolving the questions we asked at the outset: What does it mean to love God? How can one love a God one does not see? For it is this Image that enables the mystic to comply with the Prophet's precept: "Love God as if you saw Him." And on the other hand the image itself, though distinct from the sensible world, is not alien to it, for the Imagination transmutes the sensible world by raising it up to its own subtile and incorruptible modality. This *twofold* movement, which is at the same time a descent of the divine and an assumption of the sensible, corresponds to what Ibn ʿArabī elsewhere designates etymologically as a "condescendence" (*munāzala*). The Imagination is the scene of the encounter whereby the supersensory-divine and the sensible "descend" at one and the same "abode."[37]

Thus it is the Active Imagination which places the invisible and the visible, the spiritual and the physical in sym-pathy. It is the Active Imagination that makes it possible, as our *shaikh* declares, "to love a being of the sensible world, in whom we love the manifestation of the divine Beloved; for we spiritualize this being by raising him (from sensible form) to incorruptible Image (that is, to the rank of a theophanic Image), by investing him with a beauty higher than that which was his, and clothing him in a presence such that he can neither lose it nor cast it off, so that the mystic never ceases to be united with the Beloved."[38] For this reason the degree of spiritual experience depends on the degree of reality invested in the Image, and conversely. It is in this Image that the mystic contemplates *in actu* the full perfection of the Beloved and that he experiences His presence within himself. Without this "imaginative union" (*ittisāl fī'l-khayāl*), without the "transfiguration" it brings about, physical union is a mere delusion, a cause or symptom of mental derangement.[39] Pure "imaginative contemplation" (*mushāhadat khayālīya*), on the other hand, can attain such intensity that any material and sensible presence would only draw it down. Such was the famous case of Majnun, and this, says Ibn ʿArabī, is the most subtile phenomenon of love.[40]

Indeed this phenomenon presupposes that the *fedele d'amore* has understood that the Image is not outside him, but within his being; better still, it *is* his very being, the form of the divine Name which he himself brought with him in coming into being. And the circle of the dialectic of love closes on this fundamental experience: "Love is closer to the lover than is his jugular vein."[41] So excessive is this nearness that it acts at first as a veil. That is why the inexperienced novice, though dominated by the

Image which invests his whole inner being, goes looking for it outside of himself, in a desperate search from form to form of the sensible world, until he returns to the sanctuary of his soul and perceives that the real Beloved is deep within his own being; and, from that moment on, he seeks the Beloved only through the Beloved. In this *Quest* as in this ***Return***, the active subject within him remains the inner image of unreal Beauty, a vestige of the transcendent or celestial counterpart of his being: it is that image which causes him to recognize every concrete figure that resembles it, because even before he is aware of it, the Image has invested him with its theophanic function. That is why, as Ibn ʿArabī puts it, it is equally true to say that the Beloved is in him and not in him; that his heart is in the beloved being or that the beloved being is in his heart.[42] This reversibility merely expresses the experience of the "secret of divine suzerainty" (*sirr al-rubūbīya*), that secret which is "thou,"[43] so that the divine service of the *fedele d'amore* consists in his *devotio sympathetica*, which is to say, the "substantiation" by his whole being of the theophanic investiture which he confers upon a visible form. That is why the quality and the fidelity of the mystic lover are contingent on his "imaginative power," for as Ibn ʿArabī says: "The divine Lover is spirit without body; the purely physical lover is body without spirit; the spiritual lover (that is, the mystic lover) possesses spirit and body."[44]

3. *The Creative Feminine*

Now perhaps we are in a position to follow the second indication we discerned above in the sophianic experience of the "interpreter of ardent desires." By setting in motion the active, creative Imagination, the dialectic of love has, in the world of the creative Imagination, that is, on the theophanic plane, brought about a reconciliation of the spiritual and the physical, a unification of spiritual love and physical love in the one experience of mystic love. On this reconciliation depends the possibility of "seeing God" (for we have been expressly reminded that one can neither worship nor love a God whom "one does not see"),[45] not, to be sure, with the vision that is meant when it is said that man cannot see God without dying, but with the vision without which man cannot live. This vision is life and not death, because it is not the impossible vision of the divine Essence in its nakedness, but a vision of the Lord appertaining to each mystic soul, who bears the Name corresponding to the particular virtuality of the soul which is its concrete epiphany. This vision presupposes and actualizes the eternal co-dependence (*taʿalluq*) of this Lord (*rabb*) with the being who is also *His* being, for whom and by whom He is the Lord (his *marbūb*), since the totality of a divine Name comprises the Name and the Namer, the one supplying being, the other revealing it, those two who put each other mutually "in the passive," each being the action of the other, and that action is compassion, *sympathesis*. It is this interdependence, this unity of their bi-unity, of the dialogue in which each obtains his role from the other, that we have designated as an *unio sympathetica*, which is in the fullest sense an *unio sympathetica*. This union holds the "secret of the divinity" of the Lord who is your God (*sirr al-rubūbīya*), this secret which is "thou" (Sahl Tustarī), and which it is incumbent on you to sustain and to nourish with your own being; union in this *sympathesis*, in this passion common to the Lord and to him who makes him (and in whom He makes Himself) *his* Lord—this union depends on the devotion of your love, of your *devotio sympathetica*, which was prefigured by Abraham's hospitality to the Angels.[46]

Prefiguration—or perhaps better still an exemplary Image, concerning which it has not yet been explained how the mystic can reproduce it, exemplifying it in his own being. Initiation into this mode of being must be sought in the sophiology which first appears in the prologue of the *Dīwān* orchestrated by the "interpreter of ardent desires" and is consolidated in the final chapter of the *Fuṣūṣ*. The itinerary from one to the other is represented by the dialectic of love whose principal stages we have just traversed. If the Godhead must be contemplated in a concrete form of mental vision, this form must present the very Image of His being. And the contemplation must be effective, that is, its effect must be to make the contemplator's being conform to this same Image of the Divine Being. For it is only after his being has been molded to this Image, only after he has undergone a second birth, that the mystic can be faithfully and effectively invested with the secret on which rests the divinity of his Lord.

But, as we recall, the Breath of the Divine Compassion (*Nafas Raḥmānī*), which liberates the divine Names still confined in the occultation of their latent existence, this Compassion which makes itself into the substance of the forms whose being it puts into the imperative—the forms which the divine Names invest and which manifest the Names—suggests a twofold, active and passive dimension in the being of the Godhead who reveals himself. Necessarily then, the being who will be and reveal His perfect image will have to present this same structure: He will have to be at once *passion* and *action*, that is, according to the Greek etymology of these words, *pathetic* and *poïetic* (*munfaʿil-fāʿil*), receptive and creative. That is the intuition which dominates the final chapter of the *Fuṣūṣ*, from which it follows that a mystic obtains the highest theophanic vision in contemplating the Image of feminine being, because it is in the Image of the Creative Feminine that contemplation can apprehend the highest manifestation of God, namely, creative divinity.[47]

Thus where affirmation of the dual, active-passive structure would have led us to expect some recurrence of the myth of the androgyne, the spirituality of our Islamic mystics is led esoterically to the apparition of the Eternal Womanly as an Image of the Godhead, because in her it contemplates the secret of the compassionate God, whose creative act is a liberation of beings. The *anamnesis*, or recollection, of *Sophia aeterna*, will start from an intuition set forth with the utmost clarity in our authors, namely, that the Feminine is not opposed to the Masculine as the *patiens* to the *agens*, but encompasses and combines the two aspects, receptive and active, whereas the Masculine possesses only one of the two. This intuition is clearly expressed in a distich of Jalāluddīn Rūmī:

Woman is a beam of the divine Light.
She is not the being whom sensual desire takes as its object.
She is Creator, it should be said.
She is not a Creature.[48]

And this sophianic intuition is perfectly in keeping with that of the extreme Shī'ites, the Ismailians and Nuṣayrīs, who in the person of Fāṭima, considered as "Virgin-Mother" giving birth to the line of the Holy Imāms, perceive a theophany of *Sophia aeterna*, the mediatrix of Creation celebrated in the books of wisdom, and attach to her name the demiurgic qualification in the masculine (*Fāṭima fāṭir*): Fāṭima-Creator.[49]

This intuition of the Feminine Creator and hence of feminine being as Image of creative divinity is by no means a pure speculative construction; it has an "experiential" origin which can be discovered by meditating the words so famous in Ṣūfism: "He who knows himself knows his Lord." This Lord of his own to whom the *fedele* attains by self-knowledge (knowledge of his own *nafs*, which means at once *self* and *soul*), this Lord, we repeat once again, is obviously not the Godhead in His essence, still less in His quintessence, but the God manifested in the *fedele*'s "soul" (or self), since each concrete being has his origin in the particular divine Name which leaves its trace in him and is his particular Lord. It is this origin and this Lord which he attains and knows through self-knowledge—or which through ignorance or lack of self-knowledge he fails to attain.[50] When in pre-eternity the Divine Being yearned to be revealed and known, He yearned for the revelation of His Names still enclosed in nonknowledge. Similarly, when the *fedele* attains self-knowledge, it means that he has attained knowledge of the divine Name which is his particular Lord—so that the world of the divine Names represents, in both quarters, the world of the Self to which aspires the nostalgia of the divine Being desiring to be known, and for which he himself still yearns and will yearn forever, with the nostalgia, akin to God's desire to return to Himself, of the creature searching for the divine Name he reveals.

It is at this point that we discover with our *shaikh* why, insofar as this self-knowledge is for the *fedele* an experiential knowledge of his Lord, it reveals to him the truth of the Creative Feminine. Indeed, if the mystic apprehends the Sigh of Divine Compassion, which was at once the creator, the liberator and the substance of beings, it is because he himself, yearning to return to his Lord, that is, to have the revelation of himself, meditates on himself in the person of Adam. The nostalgia and sadness of Adam were also appeased by the projection of his own Image which, separating from him, becoming independent of him like the mirror in which the Image appears, finally revealed him to himself. That, our *shaikh* holds, is why we can say that God loved Adam as Adam loved Eve: with the same love; in loving Eve, Adam imitated the divine model; Adam is a divine exemplification (*takhalluq ilāhī*); that is also why in his spiritual love for woman (we have examined the nature of "spiritual love" above) man in reality loves his Lord.[51] Just as Adam is the mirror in which God contemplates His own Image, the Form capable of revealing all His Names, the Names of the "treasure hidden" in the divine unrevealed Self (*dhāt al-Ḥaqq*), so Woman is the mirror, the *maẓhar*, in which man contemplates his own Image, the Image that was his hidden being, the Self which he had to gain knowledge of in order to know his own Lord.

Thus there is a perfect homology between the appeasement of divine sadness represented by the existentiating and liberating Compassion in beings, and Eve as Adam's nostalgia, leading him back to himself, to his Lord whom she reveals. They are similar mediums in which phenomenology discovers one and the same intention. When the Divine Being achieves the perfect revelation and contemplation of Himself, he achieves them by demiurgic Energy, by his own creative divinity (*al-ḥaqq al-makhlūq bihi*), which is at the same time the substance and spiritual matter of beings and consequently reveals Him as invested with a twofold, active and passive *potentia*, a twofold poïetic and pathetic dimension. Or, to cite another parallel: though there is a threefold contemplation by which man, Adam, can seek to know himself and thereby know his Lord, there is only one which can offer him the perfect Image. That is what Ibn ʿArabī states in the page of the *Fuṣūṣ* to which we have already alluded and which especially captured the attention of the commentators of the *Mathnawī* of Jalāluddīn Rūmī.[52]

Man, "Adam," can contemplate his Lord in himself, considering himself as he by whom Eve was created; then he apprehends Him and apprehends himself in his essentially *active* aspect. He can also meditate on himself without recourse to the thought that Eve was created by him; then he apprehends himself in his purely creatural aspect, as purely *passive*. In each case he obtains only a one-sided knowledge of himself and of his Lord: In order to attain to the contemplation of his totality, which is *action* and *passion*, he must contemplate it in a being whose very actuality, in positing that being as *created*, also posits that being as creator. Such is Eve, the feminine being who, in the image of the divine Compassion, is creatrix of the being by whom she herself was created—and that is why woman is the being par excellence in whom mystic love (combining the spiritual and the sensible by reciprocal transmutation) attaches to a theophanic Image (*tajallī*) par excellence.

This deduction of the Creative Feminine—in which we can discern the "experiential" foundation of all sophiology—and from which it follows that feminine being is the theophany par excellence, could not, it goes without saying, be reconciled with the traditional exegesis of the mytho-history of Adam. And indeed our mystics were led to express the event which they experienced in themselves by grouping the symbolic figures in a new way, and it is a matter of great significance to religious psychology, it seems to me, that they should have arrived at the configuration of a *quaternity*. To the couple Adam-Eve they opposed as a necessary complement the couple Maryam-Jesus (allowing for differences, we should say "Sophia-Christos" in Christian Gnosis). Just as a Feminine had been existentiated by a Masculine without the mediation of a mother, namely, Eve created by Adam and standing in a passive relation to Adam, so it was necessary that a Masculine should be borne by a Feminine without the mediation of a father; and so Jesus was borne by Maryam. In the person of Maryam the Feminine is invested with the active creative function in the image of the divine Sophia. Thus the relation of Maryam to Jesus is the antitype to the relation of Eve to Adam. Thus, says Ibn ʿArabī, Jesus and Eve are "brother and sister," while Maryam and Adam are the two parents. Maryam accedes to the rank of Adam, Jesus to that of Eve (it is superfluous to note how far removed this typology is from that current in Christian exegesis). What this *quaternity* expresses (with the exchange of the qualifications of masculine and feminine) is the symbol and "cipher" of the sophiology which we shall here analyze.[53]

The emergence of this quaternity which marks the "cipher" of sophiology also announces the ultimate fruition of the dialectic of love; indeed, the substitution of the figure of Maryam for Eve is ordained by the intuition of the Creative Feminine—and this intuition marks the moment in which the motif of Beauty as theophany par excellence develops into an exaltation of the form of being which is invested with Beauty, because that form of being is the image of the divine Compassion, creator of the being by which it was itself created.

The tradition provides frequent reminders that Beauty is the theophany par excellence: God is a beautiful being who loves beauty. This, of course, can be verified only on the basis of the mystic love defined and experienced by our Spirituals, for whom the sympathy they discerned between the invisible and the sensible meant that the one "symbolized with" the other. This fact more than any other, it seems to me, invalidates the argument raised against the love mystics by an asceticism utterly closed to this sympathy and this symbolism, which could think of nothing better than to accuse them of *aestheticism*. The pious outrages which hostility or cowardice hurled at our fragile theophanies prove only one thing: how far removed the critics were from the sacral feeling for sensible Beauty professed by all the Ṣūfīs of the school of Ibn ʿArabī or Jalāluddīn Rūmī—a feeling which also prevented them from conceiving such an episode as the fall of Sophia in the form given it by other gnostic systems.

A veritable *spiritual potency* invests the human Image whose beauty manifests in sensible form the Beauty that is the divine attribute par excellence, and because its power is a spiritual power, this potency is *creative*. This is the potency which creates love in man, which arouses the nostalgia that carries him beyond his own sensible appearance, and it is this potency which, by provoking his Active Imagination to produce for it what our troubadours called "celestial love" (Ibn ʿArabī's spiritual love), leads him to self-knowledge, that is, to the knowledge of his divine Lord. That is why feminine being is the Creator of the most perfect thing that can be, for through it is completed the design of Creation, namely, to invest the respondent, the *fedele d'amore*, with a divine Name in a human being who becomes its vehicle.[54] That is why the relation of Eve to Adam as represented in exoteric exegeses could not satisfy the theophanic function of feminine being: it was necessary that feminine being should accede to the rank assigned it by the *quaternity*, in which Maryam takes the rank of creative Sophia. Here of course we see the sophiology of a Christianity very different from the official Christianity presented by history; yet, it was this *other* Christianity which the mystical gnosis of Islam understood and assimilated, a fact confirmed by Ibn 'Arabī's designation of Sophia as the "Christic Sophia" (*ḥikmat 'īsawīya*).[55]

Thus it is important to note the profound particularity of the sophiology here presented. Because Beauty is perceived as the theophany par excellence—because feminine being is contemplated as the Image of Wisdom or Creative Sophia—we must, as we remarked a moment ago, not expect to find here a motif such as that of the fall of Sophia in the form it took in other gnostic systems. For, fundamentally, the conjunction of *lāhūt* and *nāsūt*, of the divine and the human, or more exactly the epiphany of *lāhūt* and *nāsūt*, is not brought about by the idea of a fall, but corresponds to a necessity immanent in the Divine Compassion aspiring to reveal its being. It is not within the power of man to "explain" the tragedy of the human adventure, to explain the vicissitudes and obstacles encountered by the theophanic will, to explain, in other words, why men in the mass prefer the anonymity of their nonbeing, why they reject the Name which aspired to find in them a vessel, a compassionate organ.

In any case it is not by an incarnation on the sensible plane of material history and its chronological events, but by an assumption of the sensible to the plane of theophanies and events of the soul that the Manifestation of *lāhūt* in the attributes of *nāsūt* is accomplished; and to this fundamental intuition we must return over and over again, whether we call it "docetic" or not. The coming of the Prophet had as its aim to realize this conjunction which we have found intimated in mystic love as a conjunction (by transmutation) of physical love and spiritual love. This event is always accomplished on the plane of reality established by the active Imagination. This coming of the Prophet, whose personal experience was the prototype of mystic experience, must then mark the coming of this pure love, that is, inaugurate what Jalāluddīn Rūmī, in a particularly memorable text, designates by the Persian term already cited: *ham-damī*, sympathy (σύμπνοια, *conflatio*), a "conspiration" of the spiritual and the sensible. In a mysterious appeal addressed in pre-eternity by the Prophet to the Eternal Feminine (Holy Spirit or Mother of the Faithful, according to the commentator), we hear these words: "May I be enchanted by your beauty and drawn to you, in order that the incandescence of pure love, penetrating the mountain (of my being), transform it into pure ruby." Thus Beauty, in this context, is by no means an instrument of "temptation"; it is the manifestation of the Creative Feminine, which is not a fallen Sophia. The appeal addressed to her is rather an appeal to the transfiguration of all things, for Beauty is the redeemer. Fascinated by Beauty, the Prophet, in his pre-eternal existence, aspired to issue forth from the invisible world "in order to manifest in sensible colors and forms the rubies of gnosis and the mysteries of True Reality." And that is how the Ṣūfīs understood *their* Islam, as a harmony, a sympathy (*ham-damī*) between the spiritual elements and the sensible elements in man, a harmony achieved by mystic love as *devotio sympathetica.*[56]

This pre-eminence of the Creative Feminine as epiphany of divine Beauty was expressed in admirable paradoxes: she was apprehended on the metaphysical plane of eternal birth and on the plane of second birth, the birth which by modeling the mystic's being on this preeminent Image, causes the supreme secret of spiritual life to flower within him. Sometimes Ibn ʿArabī seizes upon simple lexicographical or grammatical facts, which for him are not inoffensive matters of language but disclose a higher metaphysical reality, and treats them with the methods of a highly personal philology, which may well baffle a philologist but are eminently suited to the detection of symbols. In a *ḥadīth* of the Prophet, he notes a grave breach of grammatical convention: in disregard of a fundamental rule of agreement the feminine outweighs the masculine in the sentence.[57] This is the point of departure for remarks which were to be amplified by the commentators. Ibn ʿArabī points out that in Arabic all terms indicating origin and cause are feminine. Thus we may assume that if the sentence attributed to the

Prophet is grammatically incorrect, it is because the Prophet wished to suggest that the Feminine is the origin of all things.[58] And indeed the origin or source of anything is designated in Arabic by the word *umm*, "mother." This is the most striking case in which a lexicographical fact discloses a higher metaphysical reality.

It is indeed a feeling that cannot be gainsaid if we stop to meditate on the feminine term *ḥaqīqa*, which designates the reality that is true, the truth that is real, essential Reality, in short the essence of being, the origin of origins, that beyond which nothing is thinkable. ʿAbd al-Razzāq Kāshānī, one of the great figures of the school of Ibn ʿArabī, devotes a page of dense reflections to the connotation of this term. We may say that as "absolute agent" (*fāʿil muṭlaq*) this *ḥaqīqa* is the "father of all things" (*ab al-kull*); but it is no less fitting, indeed it is still more fitting, to say that it is their Mother, because in accordance with the connotation of its name which is feminine, it combines action and passion (*jāmiʿa bayna'l-fiʿl wa'l-infiʿāl*), which also signifies that it implies balance and harmony between Manifestation and Occultation. Insofar as it is the Hidden (*bāṭin*) in every form and is the *determinant* which determines itself in every determinate thing of which it is the origin, it is *agens;* insofar as it is the Manifested and Apparent (*ẓāhir*) and consequently the *determined* in this epiphanic form (*maẓhar*) which at once manifests it and veils it, it is *patiens;* and every epiphanic form presents the same structure in the eyes of him who knows.[59] The intent of these speculative considerations is condensed by Ibn ʿArabī as follows: "Whatever may be the philosophical doctrine to which we adhere, we observe, as soon as we speculate on the origin and the cause, the anteriority and the presence of the Feminine. The Masculine is placed between two Feminines: Adam is placed between the Divine Essence (*dhāt al-Ḥaqq*) from which he issues and Eve, who issues from him."[60]

These last words express the entire structure and order of

being, beginning with the heights of the celestial pleroma; in terms of spiritual experience, they were translated into paradoxes, and these paradoxes merely stated a situation which reverses the mytho-history of Adam and by reversing it completes it. But the Adam to whom we have just alluded is first of all the spiritual Adam, the *Anthropos* in the true sense (*Adam al-ḥaqīqī*),[61] the first degree of determinate being, the *Nous*, the First Intelligence. The second degree is the universal Soul (*Nafs kullīya*), which is the celestial Eve. Thus the original masculine *Nous* is placed between two feminines: the Divine Essence (*dhāt al-Ḥaqq*) and the universal Soul. But on the other hand this first Intelligence is also called the Muḥammadic Spirit (*Rūh Muḥammadī*, pure Muḥammadic Essence, or Holy Spirit, Archangel Gabriel). As First-Created (Protokistos), this Spirit was created in a state of pure passivity (*infiʿāl maḥd*), then was invested with demiurgic *activity* (*fāʿilīya*). That is the significance of its enthronement and its investiture with the divine Name par excellence, *al Raḥmān*, the Compassionate[62] (which also developed the name with the angelic suffix *Raḥmānial*). In these characteristic traits of the supreme figure of the pleroma, of the figure whose Name encompasses the entire secret of divine Compassion, we can thus discern the features of the Creative Sophia. And indeed another famous master of Ṣūfism, ʿAbd al-Karīm Jīlī, records an ecstatic colloquy in the course of which the "Pure Muḥammadic Essence" or the "Angel called Spirit" evoked the words in which the Divine Being had informed *her* that *she* was the reality symbolized by the feminine figures in Arabic chivalric poetry, those figures who also lent their name to the Sophia celebrated by the "interpreter of ardent desires."[63] We recognize her again in a *ḥadīth qudsī* attributed to the Imām Jaʿfar al-Ṣādiq, as her to whom the divine imperative was addressed in the feminine (first divine, emanation, perfect Hūrī): "Be (*kūnī*) Muḥammad —and *she* became (Muḥammad)."[64] Here we have a few indications of the way in which the Prophet's experience was meditated in its "sophianic" aspect as the prototype of mystic experience.

And such again is the fundamental intuition that is expressed in a famous line attributed to Ḥallāj: "My mother gave birth to her father; that is a marvel indeed." Among the commentators on this verse—which states the secret of the origin of beings in the form of a paradox because it cannot be stated otherwise—were two celebrated Iranian Ṣūfīs, two great names of the mystic religion of love: Fakhruddīn ʿIrāqī in the thirteenth century, and Jāmī in the fifteenth. On the plane of eternal birth, they hold, "my mother" designates my eternal existence latent in the Divine Being, what in the vocabulary of ancient Zoroastrian Iran we should call my *Fravashi,* my archetype and individual angel. This individuation of my eternal individuality is produced by an epiphany (*tajallī*) of the Divine Being within his secret self and witnessed by Him alone. In this aspect, He is its "father" (*wālid*). But if we consider Him as He was when this epiphany produced this individuation of mine in His being, that is, when His being incurred and received its determinations and was "colored" by them, in this aspect He is the *child* (*walad*) of my eternal individuality, that is, the child of "*my* mother," who seen in this aspect is "*his* mother." What this paradox aims to suggest is that the essence of the Feminine is to be the creatrix of the being by whom she herself is created, just as she is created only by the being whose creatrix she herself is. If we recall here the initial act of the cosmogony, we shall understand that the paradox expresses the mystery of intra-divine life as well as the mystery of the Eternally Feminine.[65]

Accordingly it is not only on the plane of his eternal individuality that this secret presents itself to the mystic, but also as a mode of being which he must inwardly exemplify in order to exist in the divine manner, in order to make his concrete existence into the path of his Return to his origin. Seen in this aspect, the line attributed to Ḥallāj refers to the second birth—the birth alluded to in a line of the Gospel of St. John (III:3), which all the Spirituals of Islam knew and meditated upon: "Except a man be born again, he cannot see the kingdom of God."[66] But in our context this new birth will signify that the mystic soul in turn "creates" its Creator, or in other words: that the mystic's exemplification of the Creative Feminine, his "sophianity," determines the degree in which he is fit to assume the secret of his Lord's divinity (the secret which is "thou"), that is to say, in which his *theopathy* posits ("gives birth to") the God whose passion it is to be known by the mystic. The fruition of the paradox perceived on the metaphysical plane in Ḥallāj's verse is shown us in the invocation addressed by Suhrawardī to his "Perfect Nature" (*al-ṭibāʿ al-tāmm*, the spiritual entity which in Hermetism is known as the philosopher's personal Angel): "You are my spiritual father (*ab rūḥānī*) and you are my mental child (*walad maʿnawī*),"[67] that is to say, you engendered me as spirit, and I engendered you by my thought, my meditation. This is the very situation which Ḥallāj's paradox related to the origin ("my mother engendered my father"), but transposed from the pre-eternal plane to the actual plane of the mystic's concrete existence. If the mystic thus came to exemplify the Image of the Creative Feminine, we understand how Maryam could become its prototype and how, in one of the finest pages of his *Mathnawī*, Jalāluddīn Rūmī could substitute her for the mystic.[68] The episode of the Annunciation now becomes one of the symbols verifying the maxim that he who knows himself knows his Lord: Essentially it is the "sophianity" of the mystic's being (typified by Maryam) which conditions his vision of the Angel, that is, which defines his capacity for theophanic vision, his capacity for the vision of a form in which the invisible and the sensible are conjoined, or symbolize one another.

Let us now attempt to discern the sonorities set in vibration in the lines in which Jalāluddīn Rūmī, with all the resources of Persian lyricism, describes the apparition of the Archangel.

> Before the apparition of a superhuman beauty,
> Before this Form which flowers from the ground like a rose before her,
> Like an Image raising its head from the secrecy of the heart,

Maryam, beside herself with fear, seeks refuge in divine protection. But the Angel says to her:

> "Before my visible Form you flee into the invisible . . .
> But truly my hearth and swelling are in the Invisible . . .
> O Maryam! Look well, for I am a Form difficult to discern.
>
> I am new moon, and I am Image in the heart.
> When an Image enters your heart and establishes itself,
> You flee in vain, the Image will remain within you,
> Unless it is a vain Image without substance,
> Sinking and vanishing like a false dawn.
> But I am like the true dawn, I am the light of your Lord,
>
> For no night skulks around my day . . .
> You take refuge from me in God,
> I am for all eternity the Image of the sole Refuge,
> I am the Refuge that was often your deliverance,
> You take refuge from me, and I am the Refuge."[69]

"I am the light of your Lord"—is there any better way of saying *what* the Angel is than in these words in which the Angel, himself revealing *who* he is, at the same time announces that he who knows himself knows his Lord? For is there any better way of saying what the Angel says through the Imagination of Jalāluddīn Rūmī, namely, that to seek refuge from His Apparition would have been for Maryam and would be for the mystic to retreat from oneself, to take refuge from oneself? To seek refuge is perhaps the first movement of the novice Spiritual, just as he tends to look outside of himself for the Image which, as he still fails to realize, is the very form of his inner being. But to persevere in this evasion, in this flight, is to consent to subterfuges, to call for proofs, at the end of which no imperious presence will come to save you from doubt and anguish, for to the question asked of the "interpreter of ardent desires" by the nocturnal Apparition of Sophia in the shadow of the Temple there is only one reply, the reply which the *Mathnawī* typifies in the person of Maryam. Because it is impossible to prove God, there is no other answer than to "make oneself capable of God." Indeed, as Jalāluddīn Rūmī also says, each of our eternal individualities is a word, a divine Word, emitted by the Breath of Divine Compassion. When this Word penetrates the mystic's heart (as it penetrates Maryam through the Angel's Breath), that is, when the "secret of his Lord" unfolds to his consciousness, when divine inspiration invests his heart and soul, "his nature is such that there is born within him a spiritual Child (*walad maʿnawī*) having the breath of Christ which resuscitates the dead."[70]

What Jalāluddīn Rūmī taught is almost word for word what Meister Eckhart was to teach in the West little more than a century later.[71] And this motif of the Spiritual Child, of the mystic soul giving birth to itself, or in the words of Jalāluddīn Rūmī meditating the sublime symbol, "engendering himself to his Angel"—this motif is so much a spiritual dominant that we also find it in the mystic theologians and philosophers of the Avicennan or Suhrawardian tradition of Iran, as we learn from the testimony of Mīr Dāmād, master of theology in Ispahān in the seventeenth century. This motif also defines without ambiguity the meaning and intention of the sophiology that we have here attempted to disclose and shows us how very much it differs from the theosophies which in recent times have contributed to the emergence in the West of a sophiological thought such as that of Vladimir Soloviev, whose intention amounts in the end to what he himself called a "social Incarnation." This,

I am fully convinced, is a formula that would have been unintelligible to a disciple of Ibn ʿArabī or Jalāluddīn Rūmī—whereas for us, alas, it is infinitely difficult to establish our thought on the theophanic plane—no doubt because we must first overcome a habit of thought engrained by centuries of rationalistic philosophy and theology, and discover that the totality of our being is not only the part which we at present call our person, for this totality also includes another person, a transcendent counterpart which remains invisible to us, what Ibn ʿArabī designates as our "eternal individuality"—our divine Name—what in ancient Iran was termed *Fravashi.* There is no other means of experiencing its presence than to undergo its attraction in a *sympatheia* which the heliotrope's prayer expresses so perfectly in its way. Let us not wait until this invisible presence is proved objectively to us before entering into dialogue with it. Our dialogue is its own proof, for it is the *a priori* of our being. This is the lesson which, considering this dialogue as *unio sympathetica,* we have here sought to distil from the "secret of divinity," the secret that is *thou.*

For the apparent monism of Ibn ʿArabī gives rise to a dialogue, to a dialogical situation. To convince ourselves of this, let us listen to the final canto of the *Book of Theophanies.* Certain Jewish mystics interpreted the Song of Songs as a passionate dialogue between the human soul and the active angelic Intelligence (who is also called Holy Spirit, Angel Gabriel, or Madonna Intelligenza). And in this poem we hear the adjuration of a passion no less intense. In it we discern the voice of Divine Sophia, of the Angel, the Fravashi, or more directly, the voice of the "apparitional figure" invested by the mystic with its "angelic function," for in the threefold *why* of a sorrowful interrogation we hear a kind of echo of the question asked of the "interpreter of ardent desires" in the shadow of the Kaʿaba: Have you yourself perished that you can ask whether the invisible Beloved has gone away, or whether he whose Name, whose secret you alone know, ever was?

II. *Sophiology and* Devotio Sympathetica

Listen, O dearly beloved!
I am the reality of the world, the center of the circumference,
I am the parts and the whole.
I am the will established between Heaven and Earth,
I have created perception in you only in order to be the
object of my perception.

If then you perceive me, you perceive yourself.
But you cannot perceive me through yourself.
It it through my eyes that you see me and see yourself,
Through your eyes you cannot see me.

Dearly beloved!
I have called you so often and you have not heard me:
I have shown myself to you so often and you have not seen me.
I have made myself fragrance so often, and you have not
smelled me,
Savorous food, and you have not tasted me.
Why can you not reach me through the object you touch
Or breathe me through sweet perfumes?
Why do you not see me? Why do you not hear me?
Why? Why? Why?

For you my delights surpass all other delights,
And the pleasure I procure you surpasses all other
pleasures.
For you I am preferable to all other good things,
I am Beauty, I am Grace.

Love me, love me alone.
Love yourself in me, in me alone.
Attach yourself to me,
No one is more inward than I.
Others love you for their own sakes,
I love you for yourself.
And you, you flee from me.

§ 3. *The Creative Feminine*

Dearly beloved!
You cannot treat me fairly,
For if you approach me,
It is because I have approached you.

I am nearer to you than yourself,
Than your soul, than your breath.
Who among creatures
Would treat you as I do?
I am jealous of you over you,
I want you to belong to no other,
Not even to yourself.
Be mine, be for me as you are in me,
Though you are not even aware of it.

Dearly beloved!
Let us go toward Union.
And if we find the road
That leads to separation,
We will destroy separation.
Let us go hand in hand.
Let us enter the presence of Truth.
Let it be our judge
And imprint its seal upon our union
For ever.[72]

PART TWO

CREATIVE IMAGINATION AND CREATIVE PRAYER

Prologue

"The notion of the imagination, magical intermediary between thought and being, incarnation of thought in image and presence of the image in being, is a conception of the utmost importance, which plays a leading role in the philosophy of the Renaissance and which we meet with again in the philosophy of Romanticism."[1] This observation, taken from one of our foremost interpreters of the doctrines of Boehme and Paracelsus, provides the best possible introduction to the second part of the present book. We wish to stress on the one hand the notion of the *Imagination* as the *magical* production of an *image*, the very type and model of magical action, or of all action as such, but especially of creative action; and, on the other hand, the notion of the image as a body (a *magical* body, a *mental* body), in which are incarnated the thought and will of the soul.[2] The Imagination as a creative magical potency which, giving birth to the sensible world, produces the Spirit in forms and colors; the world as *Magia divina* "imagined" by the Godhead, that is the ancient doctrine, typified in the juxtaposition of the words *Imago* and *Magia*, which Novalis rediscovered through Fichte.[3] But a warning is necessary at the very outset: this *Imaginatio* must not be confused with *fantasy*. As Paracelsus already observed, fantasy, unlike Imagination, is an exercise of thought without foundation in nature, it is the "madman's cornerstone."[4]

This warning is essential. It is needed to combat the current confusion resulting from conceptions of the world which have brought us to such a pass that the "creative" function of the Imagination "is seldom spoken of and then most often metaphorically." Such vast efforts have been expended on theories of knowledge, so many "explanations" (partaking of one form or another of psychologism, historicism, or sociologism) have had the cumulative effect of annulling the objective significance of the *object,* that our thinking, measured against the *gnostic* conception of an Imagination which posits real being, has come to be an *agnosticism* pure and simple. On this level all terminological rigor is dropped and Imagination is confounded with fantasy. The notion that the Imagination has a noetic value, that it is an organ of knowledge because it "creates" being, is not readily compatible with our habits.

No doubt a preliminary question is in order: What, essentially, is the creativity we attribute to man? But is an answer possible unless we presuppose the meaning and validity of his creations? How can we accept and begin to elucidate the idea that man feels a need not only to surpass given reality but also to surmount the solitude of the self left to its own resources in this imposed world (to surmount his only-I-ness, his *Nur-Ich-Sein,* which can become an obsession bordering on madness), unless we have first, deep within ourselves, experienced this need to go beyond, and arrived at a decision in that direction? True, the terms "creative" and "creative activity" are part of our everyday language. But regardless of whether the purpose of this activity is a work of art or an institution, such objects, which are merely its expressions and symptoms, do not supply an answer to the question: What is the *meaning* of man's creative need? These objects themselves have their places in the outside world, but their genesis and meaning flow primarily from the inner world where they were conceived; it is this *world* alone, or rather the creation of this inner world, that can share in the dimension of man's creative activity and thus throw some light on the meaning of his creativity and on the creative organ that is the Imagination.

Accordingly, everything will depend on the degree of reality that we impute to this imagined universe and by that same token on the real power we impute to the Imagination that imagines it; but both questions depend in turn on the idea that we form of *creation* and the creative act.

As to the imagined universe, the reply will perhaps take the form of a wish or challenge, because there has ceased to be a schema of reality admitting of an intermediate universe between, on the one hand, the universe of sensory data and the concepts that express their empirically verifiable laws, and, on the other hand, a spiritual universe, a kingdom of Spirits, to which only faith still has access. The degradation of the Imagination into fantasy is complete. An opposition is seen between the fragility and gratuitousness of artistic creations and the solidity of "social" achievements, which are viewed as the justification and explanation of developments in the artistic world. In short, there has ceased to be an intermediate level between empirically verifiable reality and unreality pure and simple. All indemonstrable, invisible, inaudible things are classified as creations of the Imagination, that is, of the faculty whose function it is to secrete the *imaginary*, the unreal. In this context of agnosticism the Godhead and all forms of divinity are said to be creations of the imagination, hence unreal. What can prayer to such a Godhead be but a despairing delusion? I believe that we can measure at a glance the enormity of the gulf between this purely negative notion of the Imagination and the notion of which we shall be speaking if, anticipating our analyses of the ensuing texts, we answer as though taking up the challenge: well, precisely because this Godhead is a Godhead, it is real and exists, and that is why the Prayer addressed to it has meaning.

A thorough understanding of the notion of Imagination to which we have been introduced by a brief allusion to our theosophists of the Renaissance would call for a vast study of their works. It would be necesary to read or reread, with this intention in mind, all the testimonies to visionary mystic experience. We are obliged by the design of the present book to confine our inquiry to a circumscribed zone: that of Ṣūfism and esoterism in Islam, and in particular to the school of Ibn ʿArabī. But between the theosophy of Ibn ʿArabī and that of a theosophist of the Renaissance or of Jacob Boehme's school, there are correspondences sufficiently striking to motivate the comparative studies suggested in our introduction, outlining the respective situation of esoterism in Islam and in Christianity. On both sides we encounter the idea that the Godhead possesses the power of Imagination, and that by imagining the universe God created it; that He drew this universe from within Himself, from the eternal virtualities and potencies of His own being; that there exists between the universe of pure spirit and the sensible world an intermediate world which is the idea of "Idea Images" as the Ṣūfīs put it, the world of "supersensory sensibility," of the subtile magical body, "the world in which spirits are materialized and bodies spiritualized"; that this is the world over which the Imagination holds sway; that in it the Imagination produces effects so real that they can "mold" the imagining subject, and that the Imagination "casts" man in the form (the mental body) that he has imagined. In general we note that the degree of reality thus imputed to the *Image* and the creativity imputed to the Imagination correspond to a notion of *creation* unrelated to the official theological doctrine, the doctrine of the *creatio ex nihilo*, which has become so much a part of our habits that we tend to regard it as the only authentic idea of creation. We might even go so far as to ask whether there is not a necessary correlation between this idea of a *creatio ex nihilo* and the degradation of the ontologically creative Imagination and whether, in consequence, the degeneration of the Imagination into a fantasy productive only of the imaginary and the unreal is not the hallmark of our laicized world for which the foundations were laid by the preceding religious world, which precisely was dominated by this characteristic idea of the Creation.

Be that as it may, the initial idea of Ibn ʿArabī's mystic theosophy and of all related theosophies is that the Creation is essentially a *theophany* (*tajallī*). As such, creation is an act of the divine imaginative power: this divine creative imagination is essentially a theophanic Imagination. The Active Imagination in the gnostic is likewise a theophanic Imagination; the beings it "creates" subsist with an independent existence *sui generis* in the intermediate world which pertains to this mode of existence. The God whom it "creates," far from being an unreal product of our fantasy, is also a theophany, for man's Active Imagination is merely the organ of the absolute theophanic Imagination (*takhayyul muṭlaq*). Prayer is a theophany par excellence; as such, it is "creative"; but the God to whom it is addressed because it "creates" Him is precisely the God who reveals Himself to Prayer in this Creation, and this Creation, at this moment, is one among the theophanies whose real Subject is the Godhead revealing Himself to Himself.

A number of notions and paradoxes follow in strict sequence. We must recall some of the essential ones before considering the organ of this theophanic Imagination in man, which is the heart and the creativity of the heart.

III THE CREATION AS THEOPHANY

1. *The Creative Imagination as Theophany or the "God from Whom All Being Is Created"*

It will first be necessary to recall the acts of the eternal cosmogony as conceived by the genius of Ibn ʿArabī.[1] To begin with: a Divine Being alone in His unconditioned essence, of which we know only one thing: precisely the sadness of the primordial solitude that makes Him yearn to be revealed in beings who manifest Him to Himself insofar as He manifests Himself to them. That is the Revelation we apprehend. We must meditate upon it in order to know *who* we are. The *leitmotiv* is not the bursting into being of an autarchic Omnipotence, but a fundamental sadness: "I was a hidden Treasure, I yearned to be known. That is why I produced creatures, in order to be known in them." This phase is represented as the sadness of the divine Names suffering anguish in nonknowledge because no one names them, and it is this sadness that descended in the divine Breath (*tanaffus*) which is Compassion (*Raḥma*) and existentiation (*ījād*), and which in the world of the Mystery is the Compassion of the Divine Being with and for Himself, that is, for His own Names. Or, in other terms, the origin, the beginning is determined by love, which implies a movement of ardent desire (*ḥarakat shawqīya*) on the part of him who is in love. This ardent desire is appeased by the divine Sigh.[2]

By an analysis in which he discovers the mystery of being in the experience of his own being, the theosophist avoids from the outset the theological opposition between *Ens increatum* and an *ens creatum* drawn from nothingness, an opposition which makes it doubtful whether the relationship between the *Summum Ens* and the *nothingness* from which He causes creatures to arise has ever been truly defined. Sadness is not the "privilege" of the creature; it is in the Creator Himself, it is indeed the motif which, anticipating all our deductions, makes the primordial Being a creative Being; it is the secret of His creativity. And His creation springs, not from nothingness, from something other than Himself, from a not-Him, but from His fundamental being, from the potencies and virtualities latent in His own unrevealed being. Accordingly, the word *tanaffus* also connotes "to shine," "to appear" after the manner of the dawn. The Creation is essentially the revelation of the Divine Being, first to himself, a luminescence occurring within Him; it is a theophany (*tajallī ilāhī*). Here there is no notion of a *creatio ex nihilo* opening up a gulf which no rational thought will ever be able to bridge because it is this profoundly divisive idea itself which creates opposition and distance; here there is not so much as a fissure capable of growing into an area of uncertainty that no arguments or proofs can ever traverse. The Divine *Breathing* exhales what our *shaikh* designates as *Nafas al-Raḥmān* or *Nafas Raḥmānī*, the Sigh of existentiating Compassion; this Sigh gives rise to the entire "subtile" mass of a primordial existentiation termed Cloud (*ʿamā*). Which explains the following *ḥadīth:* "Someone asked the Prophet: Where was your Lord before creating His (visible) Creation?—He was in a Cloud; there was no space either above or below."[3]

This Cloud, which the Divine Being exhaled and in which He originally was, *receives* all forms and at the same time *gives* beings their forms; it is active and passive, receptive and existentiating (*muḥaqqiq*); through it is effected the differentiation within the primordial reality of the being (*ḥaqīqat al-wujūd*) that is the Divine Being as such (*Ḥaqq fī dhātihi*). As such, it is the absolute unconditioned Imagination (*khayāl muṭlaq*). The initial theophanic operation by which the Divine Being reveals Himself, "shows Himself" to Himself, by differentiating Himself in his hidden being, that is, by manifesting to Himself the virtualities of His Names with their correlata, the eternal *hexeities* of beings, their prototypes latent in His essence (*a 'yān thābita*)[4]—this operation is conceived as being the creative Active Imagination, the theophanic Imagination. Primordial Cloud, absolute or theophanic Imagination, existentiating Compassion are equivalent notions, expressing the same original reality: the Divine Being from whom all things are created (*al-Ḥaqq al-makhlūq bihi kull shay'*)—which amounts to saying the "Creator-Creature." For the Cloud is *the Creator*, since it is the Sigh He exhales and since it is *hidden* in Him; as such the Cloud is the invisible, the "esoteric" (*bāṭin*). And it is the manifested creature (*ẓāhir*). Creator-Creature (*khāliq-makhlūq*): this means that the Divine Being is the Hidden and the Revealed, or also that He is the First (*al-Awwal*) and the Last (*al-Akhir*).[5]

Thus in this Cloud are manifested all the forms of being from the highest Archangels, the "Spirits ecstatic with love" (*al-muhayyamūn*), to the minerals of inorganic nature; everything that is differentiated from the pure essence of the Divine Being as such (*dhāt al-Ḥaqq*), genera, species and individuals, all this is created in the Cloud. "Created," but not produced *ex nihilo*, since the only conceivable nonbeing is the latent state of beings, and since even in their state of pure potentiality, hidden within the unrevealed essence, beings have had a positive status (*thubūt*) from pre-eternity. And indeed, "creation" has a negative aspect, since it puts an end to the privation of being which holds things in their occultation; this double negativity, the nonbeing of a nonbeing, constitutes the positive act. In this sense it is permissible to say that the universe originates at once in being and in nonbeing.[6]

Thus Creation is Epiphany (*tajallī*), that is, a passage from the state of occultation or potency to the luminous, manifest, revealed state; as such, it is an act of the divine, primordial Imagination. Correlatively, if there were not within us that same power of Imagination, which is not imagination in the profane sense of "fantasy," but the Active Imagination (*quwwat al-khayāl*) or *Imaginatrix*, none of what we show ourselves would be manifest. Here we encounter the link between a recurrent creation, renewed from instant to instant, and an unceasing theophanic Imagination, in other words, the idea of a succession of theophanies (*tajalliyāt*) which brings about the continuous succession of beings. This Imagination is subject to two possibilities, since it can reveal the Hidden only by continuing to veil it. It is a veil; this veil can become so opaque as to imprison us and catch us in the trap of idolatry. But it can also become increasingly transparent, for its sole purpose is to enable the mystic to gain knowledge of being as it is, that is to say, the knowledge that delivers, because it is the gnosis of salvation. This occurs when the gnostic understands that the plemulti successive forms, their movements and their actions, appear to be separate from the One only when they are veiled by a veil without transparency. Once transparency is achieved, he knows what they are and why they are; why there is union and discrimination between the Hidden and the Manifest; why there is the Lord *and* his vassal, the Worshiper *and* the Worshiped, the Beloved *and* the Lover; why any unilateral affirmation of a unity that confounds them, or of a discrimination that opposes their two existences as though they were not of the same essence, is a betrayal of the divine intention and hence of the Sadness which in each being yearns for appeasement in the manifestation of His secret.

The Creature-Creator, the Creator who does not produce His creation outside Him, but in a manner of speaking clothes Himself in it as the Appearance (and transparency) beneath which He manifests and reveals Himself first of all to Himself, is referred to by several other names, such as the "imagined

God," that is, the God "manifested" by the theophanic Imagination (*al-Ḥaqq al-mutakhayyal*), the "God created in the faiths" (*al-Ḥaqq al-makhlūq fi'l-iʿtiqādāt*). To the initial act of the Creator imagining the world corresponds the creature imagining his world, imagining the worlds, his God, his symbols. Or rather, these are the phases, the recurrences of one and the same eternal process: Imagination effected in an Imagination (*takhayyul fī takhayyul*), an Imagination which is recurrent just as—and because—the Creation itself is recurrent. The same theophanic Imagination of the Creator who has revealed the worlds, renews the Creation from moment to moment in the human being whom He has revealed as His perfect image and who, in the mirror that this Image is, shows himself Him whose image he is. That is why man's Active Imagination cannot be a vain fiction, since it is this same theophanic Imagination which, in and by the human being, continues to reveal what it showed itself by first imagining it.

This imagination can be termed "illusory" only when it becomes opaque and loses its transparency. But when it is *true* to the divine reality it reveals, it liberates, provided that we recognize the function with which Ibn ʿArabī endowed it and which it alone can perform; namely, the function of effecting a *coincidentia oppositorum* (*jamʿ bayna'l-naqīḍayn*). This term is an allusion to the words of Abū Saʿīd al-Kharrāz, a celebrated Ṣūfī master. "Whereby do you know God?" he was asked. And he replied: "By the fact that He is the *coincidentia oppositorum*."[7] For the entire universe of worlds is at once He and not-He (*huwa lā huwa*). The God manifested in forms is at once Himself and other than Himself, for since He is manifested, He is the limited which has no limit, the visible which cannot be seen. This manifestation is neither perceptible nor verifiable by the sensory faculties; discursive reason rejects it. It is perceptible only by the Active Imagination (*Ḥaḍrat al-Khayāl*, the imaginative "Presence" or "Dignity," the *Imaginatrix*) at times when it dominates man's sense perceptions, in dreams or better still in the waking state (in the state characteristic of the gnostic when he departs from the consciousness of sensuous things). In short, a mystic perception (*dhawq*) is required. To perceive all *forms* as epiphanic forms (*maẓāhir*), that is, to perceive through the figures which they manifest and which are the eternal hexeities, that they are other than the Creator and nevertheless that they are He, is precisely to effect the encounter, the coincidence, between God's descent toward the creature and the creature's ascent toward the Creator. The "place" of this encounter is not outside the Creator-Creature totality, but is the area within it which corresponds specifically to the Active Imagination, in the manner of a bridge joining the two banks of a river.[8] The crossing itself is essentially a hermeneutics of symbols (*ta'wīl, ta'bīr*), a method of understanding which transmutes sensory data and rational concepts into symbols (*maẓāhir*) by making them effect this crossing.

An intermediary, a mediatrix: such is the essential function of the Active Imagination. We shall have more to say of it further on. The intellect (*'aql*) cannot replace it. The First Intelligence (*'Aql awwal*) is the first determination (*ta'ayyun awwal*) that opens within the Cloud, which is itself the absolute theophanic Imagination. The intermediary between the world of Mystery (*'ālam al-ghayb*) and the world of visibility (*'ālam al-shahādat*) can only be the Imagination, since the plane of being and the plane of consciousness which it designates is that in which the Incorporeal Beings of the world of Mystery "take body" (which does not yet signify a material, physical body),[9] and in which, reciprocally, natural, sensuous things are spiritualized or "immaterialized." We shall cite examples to illustrate this doctrine. The Imagination is the "place of apparition" of spiritual beings, Angels and Spirits, who in it assume the figures and forms of their "apparitional forms"; and because in it the pure concepts (*ma'ānī*) and sensory data (*maḥsūsāt*) meet and flower into personal figures prepared for the events of spiritual dramas, it is also the place where all "divine history" is accomplished, the stories of the prophets, for example, which have meaning because they are theophanies; whereas on the plane of sensory evidence on which is enacted what we call *History*, the meaning, that is, the true nature of those stories, which are essentially "symbolic stories," cannot be apprehended.

2. *The God Manifested by the Theophanic Imagination*

Mystic "cosmography" designates the intermediate world or plane of being specifically corresponding to the mediating function of the Imagination, as the luminous world of Idea-Images, of apparitional figures (*ʿālam mithālī nūrānī*). Ibn ʿArabī's first preoccupation is with the connections between visions and on the one hand the imaginative faculty and on the other hand divine inspiration. For indeed, the entire metaphysical concept of the Imagination is bound up with the intermediate world. Here all the essential realities of being (*ḥaqā'iq al-wujūd*) are manifested in real Images; when a thing manifested to the senses or the intellect calls for a hermeneutics (*ta'wīl*) because it carries a meaning which transcends the simple datum and makes that thing a symbol, this symbolic truth implies a perception on the plane of the active Imagination. The wisdom which is concerned with such meanings, which makes things over as symbols and has as its field the intermediate world of subsisting Images, is a wisdom of light (*ḥikmat nūrīya*), typified in the person of Joseph, the exemplary interpreter of visions. Ibn ʿArabī's metaphysics of the Imagination borrows a good many features of Suhrawardī's "Oriental theosophy."[10] The Active Imagination is essentially the organ of theophanies, because it is the organ of Creation and because Creation is essentially theophany. The Divine Being is a Creator because He wished to know Himself in beings who know Him; thus the Imagination cannot be characterized as "illusory," because it is the organ and substance of this auto-revelation. Our manifest being *is* the divine Imagination; our own Imagination *is* Imagination in His Imagination.

The theosophy of Light suggests the metaphor of the mirror and the shadow. But "shadow" must not be taken to imply a dimension of Satanic darkness, an Ahrimanian antagonist; this shadow is essentially a reflection, the projection of a silhouette or face in a mirror. Our authors even speak of a "luminous shadow" (in the sense that color is shadow in the context of absolute Light: *Ẓill al-nūr* as opposed to *Ẓill al-ẓulma*, dark shadow). And that is how we must take the following statement: "Everything we call other than God, everything we call the universe, is related to the Divine Being as the shadow (or his reflection in the mirror) to the person. The world is God's shadow."[11]

The function of Light as a cosmogonic agent begins in the world of Mystery. It is Light which reveals to the Divine Being the latent determinations and individuations contained in His essence, that is to say, the eternal hexeities which are the contents of the Divine Names. What these archetypes of virtual Creation receive is the shadow, the reflection, of the Divine Essence (*dhāt ilāhīya*), projected upon them by the light of the Names. This is the first mirror in which the Divine Being contemplates Himself; He reveals Himself to Himself in the virtualities of His many Names. But the Names aspire to be fully revealed: this epiphany is the function of the Divine Name "Light" (*Nūr*), whose epiphanic form (*maẓhar*), to wit, sensuous light, the Sun, opens up the forms that correspond to these Names in the world of visibility (*shahāda*). Light is the agent of the cosmogony, because it is the agent of Revelation, that is to say, of knowledge. Hence "we know the world only as we know shadows (or reflections); and we are ignorant of the Divine Being insofar as we are ignorant of the person who projects this shadow. The shadow is at once God and something other than God. Everything we perceive is the Divine Being in the eternal hexeities of the possibles." And Ibn ʿArabī concludes: "Thus the world is pure representation (*mutawahham*), there is no substantial existence; that is the meaning of the Imagination. . . . Understand then who you are, understand what your selfhood is, what your relation is with the Divine Being; understand whereby you are He and whereby you are other than He, that is, the world, or whatever you may choose to call it. For it is in proportion to this knowledge that the degrees of preeminence among Sages are determined."[12]

This suggests a reciprocal relationship: the relation of the shadow with the Divine Being is the Divine Being inaugurating the manifestation of the world of Mystery as absolute theophanic Imagination (*khayāl muṭlaq*); the relation of the Divine Being to the shadow constitutes the individuations and personalizations of the Divine Being as God, who discloses Himself to and by the theophanic Imagination in the unlimited number of His Names. This process has been compared to the coloration of glass receiving light: the light is impregnated with a shadow which is the glass itself. And the twofold implication of the divine Names must also be taken into account. All these Names refer to one and the same Named One. But each one of them refers to an essential determination, different from all the rest; it is by this individualization that each Name refers to the God who reveals himself *to* and *by* the theophanic Imagination.[13] To confine oneself to the plurality of the Names is to be with the divine Names and with the Names of the world. To confine oneself to the unity of the Named One is to be with the Divine Being in the aspect of His Self (*dhāt*), independent of the world and of the relationships between His Names and the Names of the world. But the two stations are equally necessary; one conditions the other. To reject the first is to forget that the Divine Being reveals Himself to us only in the configurations of the theophanic Imagination, which gives an effective reality to those divine Names whose sadness yearned for concrete beings in whom to invest their activity, whom they have made what they are, beings thanks to whom and for whom these Names have become hypostases, "Lords." But to miss the second of the two stations is to fail to perceive the unity in plurality. To occupy both simultaneously is to be equidistant from polytheism and from monolithic, abstract and unilateral monotheism. To recognize the plurality that attaches to the Imagination is neither to devaluate it nor to negate it, but on the contrary to establish it. Similarly, he who is the servant of a divine Name is the *shadow* of that Name, his *soul* is its epiphanic form (*maẓhar*). But in recognizing that this is so the servant does not negate his own existence. There is indeed a *ḥadīth* concerning the servant who never ceases to move closer to his Lord; his Lord says of him: "I am *his* hearing by which he hears, *his* eyesight by which he sees. . . ." This servant does not become what he was not; what happens is that the "luminous shadow" becomes increasingly transparent. Moreover, the possessive adjective "his" refers explicitly to the reality of the servant or rather presupposes it.[14]

These brief indications as to the twofold function of the theophanic Imagination as creative Imagination imagining the Creation and as creatural Imagination imagining the Creator, enable us to formulate a few thoughts that will serve as guides for the analyses that follow.

(a) It is thanks to the Active Imagination that the multiple and the other exist, in short, that theophanies occur, so that the Active Imagination carries out the divine intention, the intention of the "Hidden Treasure" yearning to be known, to appease the distress of His Names. Any purely negative critique of the Imagination would be untenable, for it would tend to negate this revelation of God to Himself and to drive Him back into the solitude of nonknowledge, to refuse His Names the assistance they have expected of us since pre-eternity. And that is beyond the power of man. The most that man can do is to reject this revelation, that is, make himself incapable or unworthy of it.

(b) Still, because what is Other than the Divine Being is

not absolutely other (a *no* without a *yes*), but is the very form of the theophany (*maẓhar*), the reflection or shadow of the being who is revealed in it, and because this form is Imagination, it announces something other, which is more than itself; it is more than appearance, it is apparition. And that is why a *ta'wīl* is possible, because there is symbol and transparency. This form itself presupposes an exegesis which carries it back to its source, or rather which apprehends simultaneously the many planes on which it is manifested. Without the Active Imagination the infinite exaltations provoked in a being by the succession of theophanies which that being bestows on himself would be impossible.

(c) There is no ground for setting down the Active Imagination as illusion. The error consists in not seeing what it is, in supposing that the being it manifests is something added, something that subsists in itself outside the Divine Being. But it is through the Active Imagination that the manifested being becomes transparent. On the other hand, if the sensory data or the concepts of the intellect are taken at their face value and nothing more, as perfect expressions of what they have to "say," and no more, if they are stripped of their symbolic function and therefore thought to have no need of a *ta'wīl,* in that case the world is raised to an autonomous status that does away with its theophanic transparency.

(d) And such precisely is the God formulated by the intellect of the dogmatic theologians. Invested with the Names and Attributes held to be most worthy of Him, He is the *Summum Ens*, beyond which nothing more can be imagined. Divested of its transcendent function, the Active Imagination then seems to produce only the unreal, the "imaginary," for it is isolated, just as a creature created *ex nihilo* is isolated from his Creator. In order to know in his heart that the Creator Himself has become creature because His Creation is the absolute Imagination, man must experience the human Imagination as an energy responding to the same creative need, the same creativity. Thus in order to understand what the God manifested by the theophanic Imagination is, man must understand himself. To dogmatic rationalism this God may seem "imaginary"; and yet the God professed in this dogmatic faith is Himself raised to His truth only by the theophanic Imagination, which, because it sees Him in transparency, transmutes doctrine into symbol (*maẓhar*). On this condition, the "God created in the faiths" can become a theophany for the heart.

3. *The "God Created in the Faiths"*

The initial Epiphany (*tajallī*) that appeases the sadness of the Divine Being, the "Hidden Treasure" yearning to go forth from his solitude of nonknowledge, is twofold: one epiphany takes place in the world of Mystery (*ʿālam al-ghayb*), the other in the phenomenal world (*ʿālam al-shahādat*). The first is the Epiphany of the Divine Being to Himself and for Himself in the archetypal essences, the eternal hexeities of His Names which aspire toward their concrete Manifestation. This is the sacrosanct Effusion (*fayḍ aqdas*) in the "Presence of the Names" (*Ḥaḍrat al-Asmā'*). The second is the Epiphany in the manifest world, that is, in the beings who are the epiphanic (*maẓhar*) forms or receptacles of the divine Names. This is the holy, "hieratic" and "hierophanic" Effusion (*fayḍ muqaddas*) which brings to Light those forms which, like mirrors, receive the reflection of the pure divine Essence in proportion to their respective capacities. This twofold Epiphany is typified in the divine Names "the Hidden and the Revealed, the First and the Last," of which Ibn ʿArabī offers experiential verification in his theosophical practice of Prayer.[15]

But to speak of an Epiphany of the divine Names proportional to the capacity of the forms which receive them and reflect them in the manner of a mirror, implies beings to which these forms disclose themselves as such (that is, beings who know themselves), and whose capacity for vision will in turn condition the proportion of epiphany invested in the world in them and by them. Here then we encounter the notion of the *heart,* whose importance as the "subtile organ" of theophanic visions will become apparent to us in a little while. The gnostic's *heart* is said to be encompassed by Divine Compassion; in other words, it is said to be one of the things to which the Divine Compassion lends existence, because Divine Compassion (*Raḥma*) is the equivalent of existentiation (*ījād*).[16] And yet, vast as is this Compassion which embraces all things, the gnostic's heart is still greater, since it is said: "Neither my Heaven nor my Earth contains me, but the heart of my faithful believer contains me,"[17] this because the heart is a mirror in which the manifested "Form of God" is at each moment reflected on the scale of the microcosm.

Here we encounter two inverse and complementary explanations. Many Ṣūfīs maintain that the Divine Being is epiphanized in the heart of every faithful believer in accordance with the aptitude of his heart,[18] or in other words, that it always takes a Form corresponding to the exigence and receptivity constituting this aptitude. In speaking of the gnostic (*ʿārif*), Ibn ʿArabī seems to prefer an inverse explanation of this "mystic kathenotheism." It is not the heart that gives its "color" to the Form it receives, but on the contrary, the gnostic's heart "is colored" in every instant by the color, that is, the modality of the Form in which the Divine Being is epiphanized to him. He then resembles a pure "spiritual matter" informed by the faiths, or a mirror receiving the forms and colors reflected in it, but expanding and contracting to their measure. And he reveals his heart to the Divine Being in the same form which the Divine Being has chosen to disclose Himself to him. No doubt because the revelation or knowledge he has of God is the same as that which God has of him and because the gnostic's heart is predisposed to the reception of all forms of theophany, whereas the non-gnostic is predisposed to the reception of only a single one, it is true to speak of an aptitude or capacity (*istiʿdād*) of the gnostic's heart, for it is in this heart and there alone that the "God created in the faiths" shows His truth.

For indeed neither the heart nor the eyes of the believer ever see anything other than the Form of the faith he professes in respect of the Divine Being. This vision is the degree of theophany that is given to him personally, in proportion to his capacity. As such, it is part of the Creation which is itself theophany, that is, the theophanic Imagination of the Creator, imagining to himself the world and the forms that reveal Him to Himself. The form here assumed by the Creator-Creature, the "God of whom all things are created"—that is the "God created in the faiths." The God who discloses Himself to Himself in His ipseity, in His own knowledge of His Names and of His Attributes (that is, in the "first Epiphany"), still isolated from any relation with their manifested existence—this God is visible to no one; here Ibn ʿArabī disavows those of the Ṣūfīs who claim to *see* such a God in their state of ecstasy and of *fanā'*.[19] This God becomes visible only in the forms of His epiphanies (*maẓāhir, majallī*), which compose what we call the universe.

"The God who is in a faith," says Ibn ʿArabī, "is the God whose form the heart contains, who discloses Himself to the heart in such a way that the heart recognizes Him. Thus the eye sees only the God of the faith."[20] Since the form in which He discloses Himself in a faith is the form of that faith, the theophany (*ẓuhūr, tajallī*) takes the dimension of the receptacle that receives it (*maẓhar*), the receptacle in which He discloses Himself. The faith reveals the measure of the heart's capacity. That is why there are many different faiths. To each believer, the Divine Being is He who is disclosed to him in the form of his faith. If God manifests Himself in a different form, the believer rejects Him, and that is why the dogmatic faiths combat one another. "But when you meditate upon His words (alluding to His *fedele*): I am His foot on which he walks, his hand with which he feels, his tongue with which he speaks . . . then you will say: the reality is the Creature-Creator (*Ḥaqq-Khalq*), Creator in one dimension, creature in another, but the concrete totality is one. The form that discloses itself is the form of the receptacle. It is both that which discloses itself (*mutajallī*) and that to which it is disclosed (*mutajallà lahu*)."[21]

But of this dogmatic believers are unaware. They are unaware of the metamorphoses (*taḥawwul*) of theophanies.[22] They believe the form of their vision to be the only true form, for they are unaware that it is one and the same divine creative Imagination that shows itself this "God created in the faiths," who in every instance is a theophany configured by it. Knowledge of this requires *himma*, creativity of the heart, and this *himma* is itself the Creator's theophanic Imagination at work in the heart of the gnostic. To the gnostic all faiths are theophanic visions in which he contemplates the Divine Being; according to Ibn ʿArabī, a gnostic possesses a true sense of the "science of religions." Are we to infer that such an "ecumenism" does away with the personal tie between the *fedele* and his own Lord (*Rabb*)? To this question there can be no satisfactory theoretical answer; it calls for an answer in experience, and such an answer is obtainable through a Prayer which is itself a theophany (cf. below, Ch. V). It is characteristic of Ibn ʿArabī's theosophy that it gives rise to corresponding paradoxes; the solutions too are analogous. His Divine Being transcends all representation and all qualification, and yet he speaks of the "Form of God" (*ṣurat al-Ḥaqq*). The gnostic unravels the knots of all the particular faiths, and yet he too has a theophanic vision of his Lord. For this vision is no longer given him in the form of this or that faith prescribed and imposed by a religious or social collectivity. What is disclosed to the gnostic is the form in which he himself is known to Him who evoked his being, that is, his eternal *hexeity*, whose knowledge of him has the same form as his knowledge of it. This is attested by

Ibn ʿArabī's visionary experience, and he calls upon his disciples to share in this experience.

An often cited *ḥadīth* typifies the situation. On the day of the Resurrection (*Qiyāma*), God will show Himself to His servants in a form they have not known.[23] It will not be the form of the God of their faiths, but some form from among the divine determinations in which other believers have known their God. The servants deny and reject Him; they take refuge in God against this "false" God, until at last God discloses Himself to them in the form of their own faith. Then they recognize Him. What, indeed, would a Muʿtazilite theologian think if on the day of Resurrection he perceived that even a rebel who had died unconverted is received by the Divine Compassion? How could he recognize the God of his faith in so shocking a form?

The mystic interpretation of this *ḥadīth* finds another profound meaning, far removed from the letter of Islamic dogma. Unquestionably the "day of Resurrection"[24] refers to the end of time, but it also has an initiatic meaning: it is the moment when the individual soul comes to understand his unity of essence (which does not mean his existential unity) with the divine totality, the day on which the forms of the particular faiths cease to be veils and limitations and become manifestations (*maẓāhir*) in which God is contemplated because they express the capacities of men's hearts. It is the day on which is confirmed the paradoxical depth of the bond between the Lord and His *fedele* (*Rabb* and *marbūb*), a bond so strong that neither can exist without the other,[25] a notion which inevitably strikes dogmatic religion as scandalous. The day on which what Schelling was to call "unilateral monotheism" is surmounted is the day on which Ibn ʿArabī's gnostic becomes aware that the "God created in the faiths" is also, in every instance, encompassed in the divine existentiating Compassion, that He is one of the forms of the Divine Imagination revealing Himself to Himself and giving His Names the Manifestation to which they aspire. To understand dogma as a *maẓhar*, a symbol, is to "unravel" its dogmatism,[26] and that is the meaning of Resurrection, of the other world, or rather, this understanding is already Resurrection. And that is why Ibn ʿArabī declares: "The knowledge of God has no limit at which the gnostic may stop. How can it have a limit, since it feeds on the theophanic forms of being, which are in perpetual metamorphosis, and since the recurrence of Creation, which signifies these metamorphoses of theophanies (*taḥawwul al-Ḥaqq fi'l-ṣuwar*) is the very rule of being (*qānūn al-wujūd*)?

4. *The Recurrence of Creation*

This is one of the key terms in the theosophical system of Ibn ʿArabī; the idea of recurrent creation, new creation (*khalq jadīd*) calls the very nature of creation into question.[27] We have already seen that there is no place in Ibn ʿArabī's thinking for a *creatio ex nihilo*, an absolute beginning preceded by *nothing*. The existentiation of a thing which had no existence before, a creative operation which took place once and for all and is now complete is for him a theoretical and practical absurdity. *Creation* as the "rule of being" is the pre-eternal and continuous movement by which being is manifested at *every instant* in a new cloak. The *Creative Being* is the pre-eternal and post-eternal essence or substance which is manifested at every instant in the innumerable forms of beings; when He hides in one, He manifests Himself in another. *Created Being* is the *manifested*, diversified, successive, and evanescent forms, which have their substance not in their fictitious autonomy but in the Being that is manifested in them and by them. Thus creation signifies nothing less than the Manifestation (*ẓuhūr*) of the hidden (*bāṭin*) Divine Being in the forms of beings: first in their eternal *hexeity*, then—by virtue of a renewal, a recurrence that has been going on from moment to moment since pre-eternity—in their sensuous forms.[28] This is the "new creation" to which, according to the theosophist, the following Koran verse alludes: "Were we wearied by the first creation? Yet they are uncertain about a new creation" (L:14).[29]

Nevertheless, we never cease to see what we are seeing;[30] we do not notice that there is existentiation and passing away at every moment, because when something passes away, something like it is existentiated at the same moment. We look upon existence, our own for example, as continuous, past-present-future, and yet at every moment the world puts on a "new creation," which veils our consciousness because we do not perceive the incessant renewal. At every *breath* of the "Sigh of Divine Compassion" (*Nafas al-Raḥmān*) being ceases and then is; we cease to be, then come into being. In reality there is no "then," for there is no interval. The moment of passing away is the moment in which the like is existentiated (of this we shall encounter an example later on, in the episode of the throne of the Queen of Saba). For the "Effusion of being" that is the "Sigh of Compassion" flows through the things of the world like the waters of a river and is unceasingly renewed.[31] An eternal hexeity takes on one existential determination after another, or changes place, yet remains what it is in the world of Mystery. And all this happens in the instant (*al-ān*), a unit of time that is indivisible *in concreto* (though divisible in thought), the atom of temporality which we designate as the "present" (*zamān ḥāḍir*, not as the *nunc*, the ideal limit between the past and future, which is pure negativity), though the senses perceive no interval.

The positive foundation of these metamorphoses is the perpetual activation of the divine Names calling for the concrete existentiation of the hexeities which, though they manifest what the Names are, are in themselves pure possibles, which in themselves do not demand concrete existence.[32] Here, unquestionably, we have a primordial Image which interprets the nature of being in advance of all empirical sense perception, for succession in the instant provides the senses with no perceptible anteriority or posteriority; this is pure, intelligible, ideal "succession"—on the one hand, a perpetual negativity, since the possible postulates no necessity of being; on the other hand, perpetual existentiation by virtue of Divine Epiphany. Consequently the possibles are an area of pure discontinuity; here there is recurrence not of the same, but of the like. Continuity is limited to the realm of the divine Names and the eternal hexeities (*a'yān thābita*). In the realm of phenomena (*maẓāhir*) there are only *connections without cause*; no phenomenon is the cause of another. All causality is in the divine Names, in the incessant renewal of their epiphanies from instant to instant. The recurrence of Creation consists in this recurrence of epiphanies. Thus the identity of a being does not stem from any empirical continuity of his person; it is wholly rooted in the epiphanic activity of his eternal hexeity. In the realm of the manifest, there is only a succession of likes from instant to instant.[33]

We are now in a position to foresee the technical meaning that the word *fanā'* (annihilation), so frequently employed in Ṣūfism, will assume in the theosophy of Ibn 'Arabī.[34] It will not designate the destruction of the attributes that qualify the Ṣūfī's person, nor his passage into a mystic state that annuls his individuality, merging it with the so-called "universal" or the pure inaccessible Essence. The word *fanā'* will be the "cipher" (*ramz*), symbolizing this passing away of the forms that appear from instant to instant and their perpetuation (*baqā'*) in the one substance that is pluralized in its epiphanies. In this sense *fanā'* is not incompatible with an activity on the part of the creature, or more precisely, it is one aspect of this activity, the other being its perpetuation (*baqā'*) in the Divine Being. Since Creation is a concatenation of theophanies (*tajalliyāt*), in which there is no causal nexus between one form and another, each creation is the beginning of the manifestation of one form and the occultation of another. This occultation (*ikhtifā'*) is the *fanā'* of the forms of beings in the One Divine Being; and at the same instant their *baqā'*, their perpetuation, is their manifestation in other theophanic forms, or in nonterrestrial worlds and planes of existence. Here again we may say: this is the other world, or rather, this already is the other world. Clearly this is a far cry from the dogmatic religious definition of the "other world," for this world has no beginning or end; the other world is perpetually engendered in this world and from this world.

Far removed as we are from the meaning which these words assume in the usual religious language, we cannot close our eyes to the parallels suggested by this doctrine of a recurrence of creation from instant to instant. The Ashʿarites, a representative school of Islamic orthodoxy, taught a similar cosmology; but it soon becomes evident that among the Ṣūfīs the Ashʿarite concepts are employed in a very different edifice.

The Ashʿarites profess that the cosmos is composed of substances and accidents; the accidents are engaged in a process of change and renewal, so that none of them endures for two successive moments. It would not be inaccurate to say[35] that despite a fundamental difference between the two modes of thought the atomist theory of the Ashʿarites, because it necessitates the assumption of an unceasingly renewed creative action, implied the theory of the transcendental unity of being (*waḥdat al-wujūd*). Or perhaps we should speak of a fatal tendency in monotheism—a secularization of concepts suffices—to degenerate into monism. Ibn ʿArabī's thinking falls into neither of these categories. He professed neither the abstract monotheism of the orthodox Islamic theologians nor what in the Western history of philosophy is commonly termed monism. Abstract monotheism and monism, which is its secularization as social philosophy, reveal a common totalitarian trend; the theosophy of Ibn ʿArabī, on the other hand, proceeds from a theophanic sense of the universe of being, which leaves no room for such possibilities. For though the coherence of theophanies postulates an essential unity of being, one cannot negate the diversity and plurality of theophanies without denying the manifestation of this One Being to Himself and in His creatures. And who has the power to negate this twofold manifestation which is the "appeasement of His sadness"? As we have seen, to understand this necessary diversity, plurality, and differentiation, is to escape the "unilateral monotheism" which adulterates the truth of the "God created in the faiths," destroys the transparency of symbols, and succumbs to the very idolatry it denounces.

It will be remembered[36] that the Ashʿarites carry the existential multiplicity of the world back to a single substance composed of atoms infinite in number, which are known to us only by the accidents they acquire through their momentary association with this or that form. These accidents have neither duration nor continuity; they change in every instant. For the Ashʿarites this incessant change is decisive proof that the world is renewed (*muḥdath*) and contingent, that it needs a Creator, and such indeed is the idea of Creation embodied in the common acceptance of the word. For Ibn ʿArabī this perpetual coming into being and renewal take place in the particular forms; they do not postulate the notion of a Creator of substance in general. The Ashʿarites fail to see the true reality of the world: a body of accidents, of "apparitions," which are "essentified" by a single essence, the Divine Essence, which is alone self-subsisting. They presuppose still another substance, if not several substances, side by side with this Essence (*dhāt*), failing to recognize that these supposed substances must inevitably be devoid of all substantiality. The "Divine Face" (*wajh al-Ḥaqq*), in which the *multitude* of forms, "apparitions," determinations are existentialized, remains veiled to them. They are unaware that the phenomenon of the world is this aggregate of "apparitions" and forms. They are unaware of the unity of the One God *and* of His necessary pluralization in His manifestations. The idea of a one created substance professed by these orthodox believers cannot account for, or perhaps even tolerate, plurality. The theosophist's theophanic idea postulates and grounds this plurality.

The Ashʿarite position is an impasse, witness the contradictions in which they become involved as soon as they begin to define things. They define them by their accidents. But these accidents (spatiality, receptivity, etc.) are the very reality of things as they are; accidents are not something that is added to a thing, but simple relationships established by thought (cf. the "incorporeals" of the Stoics). But in that case the thing itself becomes pure accident and therefore cannot subsist for two successive instants. How then can they speak of substances, that is, substances other than the Divine Being?[37] Every "substance" other than He is a mere aggregate of accidents without other stability or duration than the "recurrence of His Creation." But, it may be argued, the very idea of the Creator, as understood by the Ashʿarites, disappears as soon as the Divine Being is substituted for their idea of "substance." Ibn ʿArabī's answer is that such an objection can be raised only by people, orthodox or not, who are unable to take cognizance of unceasingly recurrent Creation, of the multitude of theophanies—wherein they differ from the intuitive mystics (*ahl al-kashf*), who "see" God epiphanized in each soul by the renewal of His theophanies. And precisely that is what we mean by recurrent Creation or the recurrence of Creation. Of course such vision is not sensory experience, but it is far more: for he who has understood the reality of this recurrence of Creation has also understood the secret of Resurrection (*sirr al-baʿth wa'l-ḥashr*).

This conception is the key to an entire system of thought; it opens the highest perspective of that system, namely, the idea of a *continuous ascension* of beings, beginning with the untying of the knot (*ʿaqd*) of the dogmatic faiths (*iʿtiqād*), when dogmatic science (*ʿilm al-iʿtiqād*) gives way to the science of vision (*ʿilm shuhūdi*): "When the Divine Being is epiphanized to the believer in the form of his faith, this faith is true. He professes this faith in this world. But when the veil is lifted in the other world, the knot (*ʿaqd*), that is to say, the dogma (*ʿaqīda*) which binds him to his particular faith, is untied; dogma gives way to knowledge by direct vision (*mushāhada*). For the man of authentic faith, capable of spiritual vision, this is the beginning of an ascending movement after death."[38] This is unquestionably an eschatological statement; but we have seen above that in Ibn ʿArabī Resurrection (*Qiyāma*) must also be taken in the initiatic sense of a new spiritual birth in *this* world. These "resurrected ones" obtain from God something which previously, before the lifting of the veil of ignorance, they had not seen in the Divine Ipseity, namely, an increasing capacity for acceptance of forms forever new. And Ibn ʿArabī also speaks of a mysterious kind of spiritual mutual aid between the living and the dead, that is to say, between the living of this world and the living of the other worlds. Indeed, even in this world, thanks to mystic encounters in the intermediate world (*barzakh*), there are spirituals who are able to come to the help of certain of their brothers in gnosis by unbinding ties that have remained secret; and by instructing them in matters that had remained hidden to them, they help them to rise from degree to degree. To this Ibn ʿArabī bore personal witness in one of his books.[39]

This ascending movement involves not only man;[40] every being is in a state of perpetual ascension, since its creation is in a state of perpetual recurrence from instant to instant. This renewed, recurrent creation is in every case a Manifestation (*izhār*) of the Divine Being manifesting *ad infinitum* the possible hexeities in which He essentializes His being. If we consider the creature in relation to the Creator, we shall say that the Divine Being *descends* toward concrete individualizations and is epiphanized in them; inversely, if we consider these individualizations in their epiphanic function, we shall say that they *rise*, that they ascend toward Him. And their ascending movement never ceases because the divine descent into the various forms never ceases. The ascent is then the Divine Epiphany in these forms, a perpetually recurrent Effusion, a twofold intradivine movement. That is why ***the other world already exists in this world;*** it exists in every moment, in relation to every being.[41]

Every being ascends with the "instant," provided that he receives theophanies, and each theophany increases his capacity, his aptitude, for receiving a new one. This is no repetition of the identical but a recurrence of likes: like is not identical. To "see" this is to see the multiple subsisting in the one; just as the divine Names and their essences are multiple whereas the Essence they modalize is one, and just as matter receives all forms. And so the man who knows himself with this knowledge, that is, who knows that his "soul" (*nafs*), is the reality of the Real Being, manifesting Himself in this form—such a man knows his Lord. For according to this form of his, that is, according to his epiphanic function, his creator *is* His own creature, since He is manifested according to the exigency of that creature's eternal hexeity, and yet without his Creator-Creature, this creature would be nothing. "And that is why none of the scholars, none of the rational theoreticians and thinkers, none of the ancient philosophers or scholastics of Islam (*Mutakallimūn*) suspected the true knowledge or true reality of the soul; only the theosophists (*Ilāhīyūn*) among the Prophets and the masters among the Ṣūfīs have known it."[42]

5. *The Twofold Dimension of Beings*

"If you say that a certain form is God, you are homologating that form, because it is one among the forms in which He manifests Himself (*maẓhar*); but if you say that it is something else, something other than God, you are interpreting it, just as you are obliged to interpret forms seen in a dream."[43] But homologation and interpretation are valid only when taken together, for then to say that the theophanic form is other than God is not to deprecate it as "illusory," but on the contrary to prize it and establish it as a symbol relating to something symbolized (*marmūz ilayhi*), which is the Divine Being. Indeed, revealed being (*ẓāhir*) is theophanic Imagination, and its true hidden (*bāṭin*) reality is the Divine Being. It is because revealed being is Imagination that we require a hermeneutics of the forms manifested in it, that is to say, a *ta'wīl* which carries them back (as the etymology of the word *ta'wīl* indicates) to their true reality. The world of dreams and what we commonly call the waking world are equally in need of hermeneutics. Nevertheless it should be borne in mind that if the world is recurrent creation (*khalq jadīd*) and recurrent epiphany, if as such it is theophanic Imagination and therefore requires a hermeneutics, or *ta'wīl*, we must conclude that the ultimate reason why the world is Imagination and like dreams demands a hermeneutics, is to be sought in the recurrent creation, imperceptible to the senses. The saying attributed to the Prophet: "Men are asleep, they awaken at their death,"[44] implies that everything human beings see in their earthly lives is of the same order as visions contemplated in dream. The advantage of dreams over the positive data of waking life is that they permit, or rather require, an interpretation that transcends all data, for data signify something other than what is *disclosed*. They *manifest* (and herein lies the entire significance of the theophanic functions). We do not interpret something that has nothing to teach us and signifies no more than what it is. Because the world is theophanic Imagination, it consists of "apparitions" which demand to be interpreted and transcended. And for that very reason it is only through the Active Imagination that consciousness, awakened to the true nature of the world as "apparition," can transcend its data and thereby render itself capable of new theophanies, that is, of a continuous ascent. The initial imaginative operation is to typify (*tamthīl*) the immaterial and spiritual realities in external or sensuous forms, which then become "ciphers" for what they manifest. After that the Imagination remains the motive force of the *ta'wīl* which is *the continuous ascent of the soul.*

In short, because there is Imagination, there is *ta'wīl;* because there is *ta'wīl,* there is symbolism; and because there is symbolism, beings have two dimensions. This apperception reappears in all the pairs of terms that characterize the theosophy of Ibn 'Arabī: Creator and Creature (*Ḥaqq* and *Khalq*), divinity and humanity (*lāhūt* and *nāsūt*), Lord and vassal (*Rabb* and *'Abd*). Each pair of terms typifies a union for which we have suggested the term *unio sympathetica.*[45] The union of the two terms of each pair constitutes a *coincidentia oppositorum,* a simultaneity not of contradictories but of complementary opposites, and we have seen above that it is the specific function of the Active Imagination to effect this union which, according to the great Ṣūfī Abū Sa'īd al-Kharrāz, defines our knowledge of the Godhead. But the essential here is that the *mysterium coniunctionis* which unites the two terms is a theophanic union (seen from the standpoint of the Creator) or a theopathic union (seen from the standpoint of the creature); in no event is it a "hypostatic union." It is perhaps because our age-old Christological habits prevent us from conceiving a union other than hypostatic that so many Western writers have characterized Ibn 'Arabī as a "monist." They overlook the fact that such fundamentally docetic thinking is hardly compatible with what Western philosophy has defined as "monism." As "Lord," a divine Name invests the hexeity (its *'abd*) which manifests it, and in that hexeity achieves its *significatio passiva;*[46] the total being is the union of this Lord and of His vassal. Thus each being, as a totality, has two dimensions. It is not possible to say *Ḥaqq-Khalq* or *lāhūt-nāsūt* with the implication that the two dimensions are equivalent. The two dimensions refer indeed to the same being, but to the totality of that being; one is added to (or multiplied by) the other, they cannot negate one another, one cannot be confounded with, or substituted for the other.

This two-dimensional structure of a being seems to depend on the notion of an eternal hexeity (*ʿayn thābita*) which is the archetype of each individual being in the sensible world, his latent individuation in the world of Mystery, which Ibn ʿArabī also termed the Spirit, that is, the "Angel," of that being. Thus the individuations "essentified" by the Divine Essence revealing itself to itself, burgeon eternally, beginning in the world of Mystery. To know one's eternal hexeity, one's own archetypal essence, is to know one's "Angel," that is to say, one's eternal individuality as it results from the revelation of the Divine Being revealing Himself to Himself. In "returning to *his* Lord" a man constitutes the eternal pair of the servant and his *Lord*, who is the Divine Essence not in its generality but individualized in one or another of His Names.[47] Consequently to deny this individuation that takes place in the world of Mystery is to deny the archetypal or theophanic dimension specific to each earthly being, to deny one's "Angel." No longer able to appeal to *his* Lord, each man is at the mercy of a single undifferentiated Omnipotence, from which all men are equidistant, lost in the religious or social collectivity. When this happens, each man tends to confound *his* Lord, whom he does not know as He is, with the Divine Being as such, and to wish to impose Him upon all. As we have seen, this is what happens in the "unilateral monotheism" characteristic of the "God created in the faiths." Having lost his bond with his specific Lord-archetype (that is, having lost his knowledge of himself), each ego is exposed to a hypertrophy that can easily degenerate into a spiritual imperialism; this kind of religion no longer aims to unite each man with his own Lord, but solely to impose the "same Lord" upon all. Such "imperialism" is forestalled by the *coincidentia oppositorum* expressed by Ibn ʿArabī in innumerable forms, all of which concur in preserving simultaneously the unity and plurality without which the twofold dimension of each being, that is to say, his theophanic function, is inconceivable. When we consider each of these expressions carefully, we find that

Ibn ʿArabī does not speak entirely like the monotheist he is supposed to be or like the pantheist he is so often accused of being.

"This Presence (*ḥaḍra*) which remains for you in the present (*ḥuḍūr*) at the same time as the Form [the apparent form corresponding to it] can be likened to the Book, the Koran, of which God has said: *We have neglected nothing in the Book,* for it synthetizes at once that which has happened and that which has not happened. But no one will understand what we have just said except for him who is himself, in his person (*fī nafsihi*), a 'Koran,' for *to him who takes God as his protector discernment* (*furqān*) *will be given* (VIII:29)."[48]

"Koran" is here taken by homonymy in the sense of conjunction, simultaneity, *coincidentia;* and *furqān* in the sense of discrimination, disjunction. This brings us back to our dominant theme. To be a "Koran" is to have achieved the state of the Perfect Man, to whom the totality of the divine Names and Attributes are epiphanized and who is conscious of the essential unity of divinity-humanity or Creator-creature. But at the same time the Perfect Man discriminates between the two modes of existentiation encompassed in the essential unity; by virtue of which he is the vassal without whom his Lord would not be, but also by virtue of which he himself would be nothing without his Lord. Hence the very personal exegesis which Ibn ʿArabī puts on the Koran verse; he does not take the word *mutaqqī* in its usual sense ("He who fears God") but derives it from *wiqāya,* safeguard, preservation. The Divine Lord and His vassal are each the safeguard and guarantor of the other.[49] The state of being "Koran" corresponds to the state of *fanā'*, which has a number of meanings in Ibn ʿArabī, one of which we have discussed above (§ 4 of this chapter). In the present context, it takes on a new meaning. Here, taken as the state in which all distinctions are annulled, *fanā'* is the initial test, because authentic *discrimination* can set in only after a long period of spiritual training. Indeed, when (as in all the dogmatic faiths which postulate the Godhead as an object because they are unable to conceive of it in any other way) the vassal discriminates between divinity and humanity without having experienced this *fanā'*, it is through ignorance of his essential unity with the Divine Being, that is, of the perfect conjunction between *lāhūt* and *nāsūt*. But when he discriminates after his experience of the *fanā'*, it is in true awareness of what *Ḥaqq* and *Khalq*, the Lord and His vassal, *lāhūt* and *nāsūt* are: although there is an essential unity between the two, the creature is distinguished from the Creator as the form is distinguished from the substance of which it is the form. If "to be a 'Koran' " corresponds to the state of *fanā'*, *furqān* corresponds to the state of *baqā'* (perpetuation); here we have discrimination after unification. This is perhaps the most characteristic sense in which Ibn ʿArabī employs the terms *fanā'* and *baqā'*: to return to oneself after dying away, to endure after annulment.[50]

The organ which establishes and perceives this *coincidentia oppositorum*, this simultaneity of complementaries determining the twofold dimension of beings, is man's Active Imagination, which we may term creative insofar as it is, like Creation itself, theophanic. And if, because it is such, its creations are neither fictions nor "fantasies," it is because the Imagination itself, in every instance, is a recurrence of the creation whose nature it bears within itself and expresses. And this conjunction between Imagination and Creation can be verified with the help of still another theme meditated upon by Ibn ʿArabī. This is the theme of the twofold Divine *Raḥma*, the twofold meaning of the existentiating Compassion which gives to the divine Names the concrete manifestations to which they aspire.

There is an unconditioned[51] Compassion, identical with the gift of existence (*ījād*). Independent of any work previously produced by man, it is identified with the Divine Being aspiring to reveal Himself to Himself. It is in this sense that the Divine Compassion contains and embraces all things. And there is also a *conditional* Compassion, the Compassion which the Divine

Being has "imposed" upon Himself, made necessary to Himself (*Raḥmat al-wujūb*), and which invests the vassal's being by virtue of his divine service; through it he acquires a *claim upon* God, resulting from the obligation which God has imposed on Himself. But let us not be misled by the juridical aspect of this definition. Viewed theosophically, it is an aspect of the mutual guarantee (*wiqāya*), analyzed above, between the Lord and His vassal. The conditional Compassion relates here to the guarantee of the Lord who answers *for* His vassal. But if the vassal is a disciple who has properly understood Ibn ʿArabī, he knows that his Lord is the true agent of his own works.[52] We have already read the *ḥadīth:* "I am his hearing, his eyesight, his tongue. . . ." This means that the visible form belongs to the vassal, whereas the Divine Ipseity is as it were "interpolated" (*mundarija*) into the vassal, or more precisely into the Name which the vassal "bears." So that ultimately the conditional Compassion returns to the absolute Compassion, which is the Compassion of the Divine Being with and for Himself.

But in speaking of an "interpolation" into the Name that the vassal "bears" in his soul, we must understand it in the same sense as if we were to say that our own person is "interpolated" into the form of it manifested in a "mirror,"[53] that is to say, that we must always think in terms of theophany and not of Incarnation or ἐνοίκησις (*ḥulūl*). Since this interpolation is a manifestation, an "apparition," the creature is what is manifested of the Divine Being. Thus, for example, divine Names such as the Apparent, the Manifested (*al-Ẓāhir*), the Last (*al-Akhir*) are given to the vassal because his being and the production of his action are grounded in the Creator. But reciprocally, the manifestation of the Creator and the production of His action are grounded in the creature, and in this sense the divine Names such as the Hidden (*al-Bāṭin*), the First (*al-Awwal*), belong to the vassal. Thus he too is the First and the Last, the Apparent and the Hidden; the divine Names are shared by the Lord and His vassal.[54] The Lord is the secret of the vassal's ipseity, his *self;* it is the Lord who acts in him and through him: "When you see the creature, you see the First and the Last, the Manifested and the Hidden."

This sharing, this "communication of Names," results from the twofold Divine Compassion, from what was presented to us above as a twofold movement of descent and ascent: *descent,* which is Epiphany, the primordial existentiating Imagination; *ascent* or return, which is the vision dispensed proportionally to the capacity of the receptacle created at the time of the "descent." And it is this sharing, this mutual guarantee, which is the work of theophanic prayer, itself "creative" in the same way as the theophanic Imagination because in every instance it brings about a recurrence of Creation. For one and the same agent underlies the secret of Prayer and the secret of the Imagination, although outwardly both spring from the vassal; and that is why they are not vain. This is expressed in a Koran verse: "It is not you who cast the dart when you cast it, but Allah who casts it" (VIII:17). And yet, yes, it is you who cast it; and yet, no, it is not you who cast it.

Mystically meditated, this verse is a condensation of what we have been trying to say about the *coincidentia oppositorum.* It is our Active Imagination (and, it goes without saying, not the "fantasy") that does this imagining, and then again it is not; our Active Imagination is a moment, an instant, of the Divine Imagination that is the universe, which is itself total theophany. Each of our imaginations is an instant among theophanic instants, and it is in this sense that we call it "creative." ʿAbd al-Karīm Jīlī (Persian: Gīlānī), one of Ibn ʿArabī's most illustrious disciples, formulated the context in a statement remarkable for its density: "Know that when the Active Imagination configures a form in thought, this configuration and this imagination are created. But the Creator exists in every creation. This imagination and this figure exist in you, and you are the creator (*al-Ḥaqq*) in respect of their existence in you. Thus the imaginative operation concerning God must be yours, but simultaneously God exists in it. On this point I awaken you to a sublime secret, from which a number of divine secrets are to be learned, for example, the secret of destiny and the secret of divine knowledge, and the fact that these are one and the same science by which the Creator and the Creature are known."[55]

These ideas are strictly related: When you create, it is not you who create, and that is why your creation is true. It is true because each creature has a twofold dimension: the Creator-creature typifies the *coincidentia oppositorum*. From the first this *coincidentia* is present to Creation, because Creation is not *ex nihilo* but a theophany. As such, it is Imagination. The Creative Imagination is theophanic Imagination, and the Creator is one with the imagining Creature because each Creative Imagination is a theophany, a recurrence of the Creation. Psychology is indistinguishable from cosmology; the theophanic Imagination joins them into a psycho-cosmology. Bearing this in mind, we can now investigate the human organ of visions, of transferences, and of the transmutation of all things into symbols.

IV THEOPHANIC IMAGINATION AND CREATIVITY OF THE HEART

1. *The Field of the Imagination*

The doctrine of the imagination in its psycho-cosmic function has two aspects: the one is cosmogonic or theogonic, (the "theogony" of the divine Names). In connection with this aspect we must bear in mind that the idea of "genesis" here expressed has nothing to do with a *creatio ex nihilo* and is equally far removed from the Neoplatonic idea of emanation; we must think rather of a process of increasing illumination, gradually raising the possibilities eternally latent in the original Divine Being to a state of luminescence. The second aspect or function is specifically psychological. It should be remembered, however, that the two aspects are inseparable, complementary, and subject to homologation. A complete analysis would have to embrace the entire opus of Ibn ʿArabī and would require a work of imposing dimensions. But in a chapter of his great book, the "Spiritual Conquests (or Revelations) of Mecca,"[1] Ibn ʿArabī outlines a "science of the Imagination" (*ʿilm al-khayāl*) and provides a schema of the themes involved in such a science. This chapter also shows how difficult it is to articulate clearly the two aspects distinguished above. But regardless of the aspect, degree, or phase in which we consider the Imagination, whether we consider it in its cosmic function, according to its degree of "Presence" or of "Imaginative Dignity" (*Ḥaḍrat khayālīya*), or consider it as an imaginative potency in man, one characteristic remains constant. We have already spoken of it: I have in mind its function as an intermediary, a mediatrix.

As we have seen, the Primordial Cloud, the divine, existentiating Sigh of Compassion, is the intermediary between the Divine *Essentia abscondita* and the manifest world of multiple forms; similarly the world of Idea-Images, the world of apparitional forms and of bodies in the subtile state (*ʿālam al-mithāl*) to which our imaginative faculty specifically relates, is the intermediary between the world of pure spiritual realities, the world of Mystery, and the visible, sensible world. Dream is intermediary between the real (in the mystic sense, that is) "waking" state, and the waking consciousness in the common, profane sense of the world. The Prophet's vision of the Angel Gabriel in the form of Daḥyā al-Kalbī, an Arab youth known for his beauty, the images seen in mirrors, which were neither objects nor abstract ideas—these are intermediary realities. And because they are intermediary, they culminate in the notion of the symbol, for the intermediary "symbolizes with" the worlds it mediates. There is no incoherence, as has been claimed, in Ibn ʿArabī's doctrine of the Imagination; but there is an extreme complexity to reckon with. The "field" encompassed in the "science of the Imagination" is so vast that it is difficult to enumerate all its sectors.[2]

The science of the Imagination is theogony when it meditates on the Primordial *Cloud,* the theophanies of the "God from whom all being is created"; it is again theogony when it meditates on the theophanies of the "God created in the faiths," since these are still manifestations and occultations of the divine Names. But here it is also cosmology, since it is knowledge of being and of the universe as theophany. It is again cosmology when it thematizes the intermediary world perceived by our imaginative faculty, the world in which occur visions, apparitions, and in general all the symbolic histories which reveal only their material aspect to perception or sensory representation.

It is the science of the theophanies that are dispensed specifically to mystics, and of all the related thaumaturgies; it gives existence to the Improbable, to what reason rejects, and above all to the fact that the Necessary Being, whose pure Essence is incompatible with all form, is nevertheless manifested in a form belonging to the "Imaginative Presence." It has the specific power to cause the impossible to exist, and this power is put into effect by Prayer.[3]

The science of the Imagination is also the science of mirrors, of all mirroring "surfaces" and of the forms that appear in them. As the science of the *speculum*, it takes its place in *speculative* theosophy, in a theory of the vision and manifestations of the spiritual, and draws the ultimate consequences from the fact that though forms *appear* in mirrors, they *are* not in the mirrors. To it belongs also mystic geography, the knowledge of this Earth that was created from Adam's surplus clay and on which all the things seen in this world exist in the subtile state of an "immaterial matter," with their figures, their contours and their colors.[4] Hence it is the science of paradisiacal contemplations; it explains how the inhabitants of "Paradise" enter into every beautiful form that they conceive and desire, how it becomes their garment, the form in which they appear to themselves and to others.[5]

All this is confirmed both by the fervor of believers and by the experience of the mystics; but the rational theoreticians (*aṣḥāb al-naẓar*) accept it only reluctantly, as an "allegory," or out of deference for the Divine Book in which the Prophet states it. But if by chance such a testimony comes from you, they reject it and impute it to the disorder of your imagination (*fasād al-khayāl*). Very well, but the disorder of the Imagination presupposes at least its existence, and what these men of theoretical knowledge are unaware of is the intermediary character of the Imagination, which places it at once in the sensible and the intelligible, in the senses and in the intellect, in the possible, the necessary and the impossible, so that it is a "pillar" (*rukn*) of true knowledge, the knowledge that is gnosis (*maʿrifa*), without which there would be only a knowledge without consistency.[6] For it is the Imagination that enables us to understand the meaning of death, in the esoteric as well as the physical sense: an awakening, before which you are like someone who merely dreams that he wakes up.[7] It would be difficult to situate the science of the Imagination any higher.

We now turn to the specifically psychological aspect of the Imagination. Here, it goes without saying, we must reject anything suggesting what is today termed psychologism, and in particular the tendency to consider "imaginations" as products without intrinsic "reality." And indeed our schematization of the imaginative faculty results exclusively from the metaphysical status of the Imagination. Ibn ʿArabī distinguishes an imagination *conjoined* to the imagining subject and inseparable from him (*khayāl muttaṣil*) and a self-subsisting imagination *dissociable* from the subject (*khayāl munfaṣil*). In the first case we must distinguish between the imaginations that are premeditated or provoked by a conscious process of the mind, and those which present themselves to the mind spontaneously like dreams (or daydreams). The specific character of this conjoined Imagination is its inseparability from the imagining subject, with whom it lives and dies. The Imagination separable from the subject, on the other hand, has an autonomous and subsisting reality *sui generis* on the plane of the intermediary world, the world of Idea-Images. "Exterior" to the imagining subject, it can be seen by others in the outside world, but in practice these others must be mystics (for on occasion the Prophet saw the Angel Gabriel when his Companions were present, while they saw only the handsome Arab youth).[8]

The fact that these "separable" Images subsist in a world specific to them, so that the Imagination in which they occur is a "Presence" having the status of an "essence" (*ḥaḍrat dhātīya*) perpetually capable of receiving ideas (*maʿānī*) and Spirits (*arwāḥ*) and of giving them the "apparitional body" that makes possible their epiphany—all this makes it clear that we are far removed from all "psychologism." Even the Imagination *conjoined* to, and inseparable from, the subject is in no sense a faculty functioning arbitrarily in the void, secreting "fantasies." When the form of the Angel, for example, "projects itself" into a human form (in the same sense, as we have seen, as a form "projects" itself upon a mirror), this act takes place on the plane of the autonomous Imagination (*munfaṣil*), which then raises the Image to the plane of the conjoint Imagination. Thus there is only one autonomous Imagination, because it is absolute Imagination (*Khayāl muṭlaq*), that is to say, *absolved* of any condition that would subordinate its subsistence, and it is the Primordial Cloud which constitutes the universe as theophany. It is this same Primordial Cloud which originally inaugurates, maintains and governs the Imagination *conjoined* to the subject. Then come the revealed divine Laws which determine and fixate the modalization of the Divine Being in the *qibla* ("orientation"), in the "face to face" of the believer at prayer. This means moreover that the "God created in the faiths" partakes of this Imagination conjoined to the subject; but because Compassion, that is, the Divine Existentiation, also embraces the "God created in the faiths," the conjoined Imagination, though inseparable from the subject, is also included in the modes of the absolute Imagination, which is the absolutely encompassing Presence (*al-Ḥaḍrat al-jāmiʿa, al-martabat al-shāmila*).[9]

It is the notion of the separable, autonomous Imagination that most directly relates to our theme, namely, the function of the "creative" Imagination in mystic experience. In considering it we must concern ourselves with two technical terms: one is the "heart," the other is *himma*, an extremely complicated notion which cannot perhaps be translated by any one word. Many equivalents have been suggested: mediation,[10] project, intention, desire, force of will; here we shall concentrate on the aspect that encompasses all the others, the "creative power of the heart."

2. *The Heart as a Subtile Organ*

In Ibn ʿArabī as in Ṣūfism in general, the heart (*qalb*), is the organ which produces true knowledge, comprehensive intuition, the gnosis (*maʿrifa*) of God and the divine mysteries, in short, the organ of everything connoted by the term "esoteric science" (*ʿilm al-Bāṭin*). It is the organ of a perception which is both experience and intimate taste (*dhawq*), and although love is also related to the heart, the specific center of love is in Ṣūfism generally held to be the *rūḥ, pneuma,* spirit.[11] Of course, and of this we are reminded at every turn, this "heart" is not the conical organ of flesh, situated on the left side of the chest, although there is a certain connection, the modality of which, however, is essentially unknown. It is a notion to which the utmost importance has been attached by the mystics of all times and countries, of Oriental Christianity (the Prayer of the Heart, the charisma of cardiognosis) as well as India.[12] Here we have to do with a "subtile physiology" elaborated "on the basis of ascetic, ecstatic, and contemplative experience" and expressing itself in symbolic language. This, as Mircea Eliade has pertinently remarked, does not mean "that such experiences were not *real*; they were perfectly real, but not in the sense in which a physical phenomenon is real."[13]

In short, this "mystic physiology" operates with a "subtile body" composed of psycho-spiritual organs (the centers, or Chakras, "lotus blossoms") which must be distinguished from the bodily organs. For Ṣūfism the *heart* is one of the centers of mystic physiology. Here we might also speak of its "theandric" function, since its supreme vision is of the Form of God (*ṣurat al-Ḥaqq*)—this because the gnostic's heart is the "eye," the organ by which God knows Himself, reveals Himself to Himself in the forms of His epiphanies (not as He inwardly knows Himself, for in its quest of the Divine Essence even the highest science can go no further than the *Nafas al-Raḥmān*). It is also true to say that the gnostic, as Perfect Man, is the *seat* of God's divine consciousness and that God is the seat and essence of the gnostic's consciousness[14] (if it were necessary to draw a diagram, the situation would be far better represented by the two focuses of an ellipse than by the center of a circle). To sum up, the power of the heart is a secret force or energy (*quwwat khafīya*), which perceives divine realities by a pure hierophanic knowledge (*idrāk wāḍiḥ jalī*) without mixture of any kind, because the heart contains even the Divine *Raḥma*. In its unveiled state, the heart of the gnostic is like a mirror in which the microcosmic form of the Divine Being is reflected.

This power of the heart is what is specifically designated by the word *himma*, a word whose content is perhaps best suggested by the Greek word *enthymesis*, which signifies the act of meditating, conceiving, imagining, projecting, ardently desiring —in other words, of having (something) present in the θύμος, which is vital force, soul, heart, intention, thought, desire. We recall that in Valentinian gnosis 'ενθύμησις is the *intention* conceived by the thirtieth Eon, Sophia, in its aspiration to understand the greatness of Unengendered Being. This intention detaches itself from Sophia, takes on a separate existence; it is the Sophia external to the pleroma, but of pneumatic substance. The force of an *intention* so powerful as to project and realize ("essentiate") a being external to the being who conceives the intention, corresponds perfectly to the character of the mysterious power that Ibn ʿArabī designates as *himma*.[15]

Accordingly, *himma* is creative, but in the specifically "epiphanic" sense attaching to every idea of creation in the theosophy of Ibn ʿArabī. In practice its function presents two aspects. The first governs a large group of phenomena, many of which are today the concern of parapsychology. The second applies to the mystic perception known as "intimate taste" (*dhawq*), or touch. But since this too is an unveiling, an epiphany, of the heart, it is also an aspect of the gnostic's creativity.

§ 2. *The Heart as a Subtile Organ*

Thus there is no incoherence in Ibn ʿArabī's explanations of *himma,* if only we recall that the human Imagination is enveloped in the unconditioned Imagination, which is the universe as Divine Epiphany, for this envelopment is our guarantee that the intentions arising from the creative power of the heart as an independent being *sui generis,* are not vain fictions.

"Thanks to his representational faculty (*wahm*)," our *shaikh* declares, "every man creates in his Active Imagination things having existence only in this faculty. This is the general rule. But by his *himma* the gnostic *creates* something which exists outside the seat of this faculty."[16] In both cases the imaginative faculty is exercised, though with entirely different results, and in both cases the *shaikh* employs the word "create." We know that the creative operation necessarily implies the manifestation of an outward existence that is conferred upon something which already possessed a latent existence in the world of Mystery. In the two cases, however, the organ of creativity, the Active Imagination, performs very different operations. In the first case, as it is exercised by most men, its function is representational;[17] it produces images which are merely part of the conjoined Imagination (*muttaṣil*), inseparable from the subject. But even here, pure representation does not, *eo ipso,* mean "illusion"; these images really "exist"; illusion occurs when we misunderstand their mode of being. In the case of the gnostic (*ʿārif*), the Active Imagination serves the *himma* which, by its concentration, is capable of *creating* objects, of producing changes in the outside world. In other words: thanks to the Active Imagination, the gnostic's heart projects what is reflected in it (that which it mirrors); and the object on which he thus concentrates his creative power, his imaginative meditation, becomes the *apparition* of an outward, extra-psychic reality. This is precisely what Ibn ʿArabī, as we have seen, designates as the detached Imagination, separable (*munfaṣil*) from the imagining subject, but as we have also seen, only other mystics are able to perceive it. (When the Angel Gabriel took the form of Daḥyā, an Arab youth known for his extraordinary beauty, the Prophet's companions saw only the youth; they did not *see* the Angel).

All this is of the utmost importance for the experience gained in Prayer, namely, the paradoxical vision of the "Form of God." If the heart is the mirror in which the Divine Being manifests His form according to the capacity of this heart, the Image which the heart projects is in turn the outward form, the "objectivization" of this Image. Here indeed, we find confirmation of the idea that the gnostic's *heart* is the "eye" by which God reveals Himself to Himself. We can easily conceive of an application of this idea to material iconography, to the images created by art. When in contemplating an image, an icon, others recognize and perceive as a divine image the vision beheld by the artist who created the image, it is because of the spiritual creativity, the *himma,* which the artist put into his work. Here we have a compelling term of comparison, by which to measure the decadence of our dreams and of our arts.

By giving objective body to *intentions* of the heart (*himma,* ἐνθύμησις), this creativity fulfils the first aspect of its function. This aspect comprises a large number of phenomena designated today as extrasensory perception, telepathy, visions of synchronicity, etc. Here Ibn ʿArabī contributes his personal testimony. In his autobiography (*Risālat al-Quds*), he tells how he was able to evoke the *spirit* of his *shaikh,* Yūsuf al-Kūmī, whenever he needed his help, and how Yūsuf regularly appeared to him, to help him and answer his questions. Ṣadruddīn Qunyawī, the disciple whom Ibn ʿArabī instructed in Qunya, also speaks of his gift: "Our *shaikh* Ibn ʿArabī had the power to meet the spirit of any Prophet or Saint departed from this world, either by making him descend to the level of this world and contemplating him in an apparitional body (*ṣūrat mithālīya*) similar to the sensible form of his person, or by making him appear in his dreams, or by unbinding himself from his material body to rise to meet the spirit."[18]

§ 2. *The Heart as a Subtile Organ*

What explanation does Ibn 'Arabī give for these phenomena? A first explanation invokes the hierarchical *planes* of being, the *Ḥaḍarāt*, or "Presences." There are five of these Presences, namely, the five Descents (*tanazzulāt*); these are determinations or conditions of the divine Ipseity in the forms of His Names; they act on the receptacles which undergo their influx and manifest them. The first *Ḥaḍra* is the theophany (*tajallī*) of the Essence (*dhāt*) in the eternal latent hexeities which are objects, the *correlata* of the Divine Names. This is the world of Absolute Mystery (*'ālam al-ghayb al-muṭlaq, Ḥaḍrat al-Dhāt*). The second and the third *Ḥaḍarāt* are respectively the angelic world of determinations or individuations constituting the Spirits (*ta'ayyunāt rūḥīya*) and the world of individuations constituting the Souls (*ta'ayyunāt nafsīya*). The fourth *Ḥaḍra* is the world of Idea-Images (*'ālam al-mithāl*), typical Forms, individuations having figure and body, but in the immaterial state of "subtile matter." The fifth *Ḥaḍra* is the sensible and visible world (*'ālam al-shahāda*), of dense material bodies. By and large, with minor variations, this schema is constant in our authors.[19]

The relations between these *Ḥaḍarāt*, these Presences or planes of being, are determined by their structure. On each plane the same Creator-Creature (*Ḥaqq* and *Khalq*) relation is repeated, dualizing and polarizing a unitotality, a bi-unity whose two terms stand to one another in a relation of action and passion (*fi'l-infi'āl*, corresponding to *bāṭin-ẓāhir*, hidden and manifest, esoteric and exoteric). Consequently each of these *Ḥaḍarāt* or Descents is also designated as a "marriage" (*nikāḥ*), whose fruit is the Presence or *Ḥaḍra* which follows it in the descending hierarchy.[20] For this reason each lower Presence is the image and correspondence (*mithāl*), the reflection and mirror of the next higher. Thus everything that exists in the sensible world is a reflection, a typification (*mithāl*), of what exists in the world of Spirits, and so on, up to the things which are the first reflections of the Divine Essence itself.[21] Everything that is manifested to the senses is therefore the form of an ideal reality of the world of Mystery (*ma'nā ghaybī*), a face (*wajh*) among the faces of God, that is to say, of the divine Names. To know this is to have the intuitive vision of mystic meanings (*kashf ma'nawī*); he to whom this knowledge is given has received an infinite grace, says 'Abd al-Razzāq Kāshānī, the commentator of the *Fuṣūṣ*. Consequently, all the sciences of Nature are based on the meaning of the typifications of the world of Mystery. And this is one of the interpretations given to the Prophetic maxim: "Men are asleep; at their death they awaken."

Because of their correspondences, these rising or descending planes of being are not isolated or fundamentally different from one another. To say that one and the same human being may be manifested in a sensible form in this world, and in a spiritual form in the world of Spirits, does not imply a radical difference between the physical form and the spiritual form. One and the same being can exist simultaneously on entirely different planes, in forms which are in correspondence by virtue of the homology between the world of Spirits and the sensible world. A thing may exist in the higher *Ḥaḍarāt* but not in the lower, and then again it may exist in all the *Ḥaḍarāt*. When Ibn 'Arabī says that a gnostic *creates* something through his *himma*, through the creativity of his *heart*, he means (since, strictly speaking, neither God nor man "creates" if by creation we mean a *creatio ex nihilo*) that the gnostic causes to appear, in the *Ḥaḍra* of the sensible world, for example, something which already exists *in actu* in a higher *Ḥaḍra*. In other words, the heart creates by "causing to appear," by "preserving" something which already exists in one of the *Ḥaḍarāt*. By concentrating the spiritual energy of *himma* on the form of a thing existing in one or more of the "Presences" or *Ḥaḍarāt*, the mystic obtains perfect control over that thing, and this control preserves the thing in one or another of the "Presences" as long as the concentration of *himma* lasts.[22]

§ 2. *The Heart as a Subtile Organ*

Here we have a first explanation of the projection effected by the mystic's heart with the help of his Active Imagination, which is theophanic Imagination. The object on which it is concentrated *appears* as endowed with an outward reality, even if it is visible only to other mystics. If Ibn 'Arabī compares this *Ḥaḍra*, which becomes present to the gnostic, to the Koran, it is both because its presence (*ḥuḍūr*) presupposes the concentration of all spiritual energies on a form belonging to this *Ḥaḍra*, and because this *Ḥaḍra* then shows him in the manner of a mirror everything that exists in the other *Ḥaḍarāt*, or "Presences." "But," Ibn 'Arabī adds, "what we are saying will be understood only by one who is himself, in his person, a 'Koran.' "[23] A few pages back, we characterized the spiritual state—the state of the Perfect Man—to which in Ibn 'Arabī's vocabulary this expression, "to be as a 'Koran' in one's own person," relates. By an ambivalence of its radicals, the term designates a state of concentration which suspends discrimination between the attributes of the Creator and the attributes of the Creature; in this sense, "to be a 'Koran' " is to be in the state of *fanā'*. This does not signify the annulment or destruction of the Ṣūfī's person but an initial test which is intended to preserve him ever after from false discriminations (e.g., to preserve him from dogmatic embodiments of the "God created in the faiths"). This experience is prerequisite to the authentic *discrimination* which the mystic will subsequently reintroduce between Creator and Creature (corresponding to the state of *baqā'*, persistence).[24] We are now prepared to examine the second function of *himma* as the mystic creativity of the heart, and Ibn 'Arabī's second explanation of it.

This second explanation of the creativity (*quwwat al-khalq*) attributed to the heart of the Ṣūfī, is mentioned by our *shaikh* in one of his first treatises; here *himma* is defined as the "cause" which leads God to create certain things, though *himma* itself, strictly speaking, creates nothing. This interpretation of *himma* enables him to generalize its function and to regard it "as a hidden potency which is the cause of all movement and all change in the world."[25] A simple juxtaposition with the expression "to be a 'Koran' " enables us to understand that here again *himma* corresponds to the state of *fanā'*. But again we must be careful to bear in mind that for Ibn ʿArabī *fanā'* is never absolute annihilation (the failure to do so has been a source of countless misunderstandings in regard both to Ṣūfism and to Buddhism). *Fanā'* and *baqā'* are always relative terms. According to Ibn ʿArabī, one must always state *toward what* there is annihilation, and wherein there is survival, persistence.[26] In the state of *fanā'*, of concentration, of "Koran," in which the essential unity of Creator and Creature is experienced, the Divine Attributes become predicables of the mystic (discrimination is suspended). Then we may say not only that the mystic "creates" in the same sense as God Himself creates (that is to say, causes something which already existed in the world of Mystery to be manifested in the sensible world), but in addition that God creates this effect *through* him. It is one and the same divine operation, but through the intermediary of the gnostic, when he is "withdrawn" (*fanā'*) from his human attributes and when he persists, survives (*baqā'*) in his divine attributes. The mystic is then the medium, the intermediary, through whom the divine creative power is expressed and manifested.[27]

Here we are again reminded of the Ashʿarites, who sought to determine whether man's acts are *created* by man or whether God is the sole agent. A comparison has also been drawn with what, in modern philosophy, has been termed *occasionalism*.[28] There is, indeed, only one Creation, but it *recurs* perpetually, from instant to instant. And since Creation means essentially *theophany*, the relation between the creativity of the heart and perpetually recurrent Creation can again be defined by the idea that the gnostic's heart is the "eye" by which the Divine Being sees Himself, that is, reveals Himself to Himself. Here the question of outer and inner world does not arise, as it would in any other system not based on the idea of epiphany and on the docetic critique of knowledge it implies. Accordingly, when Ibn ʿArabī explains the phenomena of the creativity of the heart by the *Ḥaḍarāt*, there is no ground for accusing him of confusion between the subjective and the objective. Every one of the gnostic's "creative Imaginations," whether produced by him directly on the basis of a *Ḥaḍra* higher than the plane of being on which the Imagination occurs, or whether it is brought about by his *himma*, is a new, recurrent Creation (*khalq jadīd*), that is to say, a new theophany, whose organ is his heart as mirror of the Divine Being.[29]

And this is the crux of the question. The control (*taṣarruf*) of things, the power to work miracles, is a secondary aspect; the greatest mystics refrained from exerting this power, often with contempt,[30] partly because they knew that in this world the servant cannot become the Lord, and that the subject who dominates a thing (*mutaṣarrif*) and the thing he dominates (*mutaṣarraf fīhi*) are essentially one being, but also because they recognized that the form of what is epiphanized (*mutajallī*) is also the form of what the epiphany is revealed (*mutajallà-lahu*). And no one, says our *shaikh*, except for the possessor of *himma* is capable of recognizing the fundamental reality of being (*ḥaqīqat al-wujūd*) as a unity polarized between Creator and Creature, whose interdependence and unity are repeated in the multitude of theophanies which are all recurrences of Creation.[31] Here we are not concerned with the control of magic domination (*taskhīr*) that a mystic can exert over things, but solely with the function of *himma*, the concentration of the heart as the organ which makes it possible to achieve the true knowledge of things, a knowledge inaccessible to the intellect. In this aspect, *himma* designates the perception by the heart which the Ṣūfīs term "inner taste" (*dhawq*). Hence the solemn warning which our *shaikh* finds in a Koran verse, because his personal *ta'wīl* leads him to an esoteric sense which he apprehends thanks to his own *himma:* "Surely in this there is a lesson for him who has a heart and who gives ear and is an eye-witness (*shāhid*)" (L:36).

On the basis of this verse Ibn ʿArabī divides men into three classes: (a) the disciples of the *science of the heart,* those who possess the psycho-spiritual organ which mystic physiology designates as the "heart" (*aṣḥāb al-Qulūb*); these are the mystics, and more particularly the perfect among the Ṣūfīs; (b) the disciples of the rational intellect (*aṣḥāb al-ʿUqūl*); these are the *Mutakallimūn,* the scholastic theologians; (c) simple believers (*mu'minūn*). Under normal circumstances a simple believer can develop into a mystic through spiritual training; but between mystics and rational theologians there is an unbridgeable gulf.

To possess the science of the heart is to perceive the divine metamorphoses, that is to say, the multiplicity and the transformation of the forms in which the Divine Ipseity is epiphanized, whether in a figure of the outward world or in a religious faith. Thus it is to know the Divine Being through intuitive vision (*shuhūd*), to perceive Him in the form in which each of his epiphanies (*tajallī*) shows itself (*maẓhar*)—this thanks to the state of concentration in which the mystic has become as a "Koran," that is, thanks to his *himma,* a Perfect Man as microcosm of God.[32] By contrast, the scholastic theologian formulates a dogma; he proves, he refutes, but he is not an eye-witness (*shāhid*); argumentation and dialectic have no need of vision and consequently cannot lead to it, especially as discussion is hopeless in advance. The God of whom those who are not eye-witnesses speak is an "absent"; they have not seen each other. And for this reason no dogmatist's God can help him against someone else's God; the antagonists can neither defeat nor convince each other, they can only separate, each highly dissatisfied with his adversary.[33] For each particular dogma is no better or worse than any other concept elaborated by the rational intellect; essentially limitation (*taqyīd*), it looks upon every other, equally limited dogma as a contradiction; reduced to analyzing, to decomposing (*taḥlīl*) the whole into its parts, the dogmatic intellect can apprehend *rubūbīya* (the divine lordly condition) and *'ubudīya* (the human condition of vassaldom) only as two contrary and heterogeneous quantities, not as the two poles and complementaries of one and the same *ḥaqīqa*.[34] In short, the science of the heart (*qalb*, as science of the *taqlīb*) transmutes dogma by disclosing its limit; the authoritative statement which closed off the horizon because it said everything it had to say and nothing more, is transmuted into a symbol which shows (*maẓhar*) something else by summoning up other *tajallī*, other visions which make the "God created in the faiths" true, because such visions are never a definition, but only a "cipher" of Him.[35]

Here again we perceive the affinity between simple believers and great mystics. As we have seen, a simple believer can become a mystic. Both simple believers and mystics are people "who lend ear and are eye-witnesses," that is, who have direct vision of what they speak of. True, the simple believers conform (*taqlīd*) to their Prophets, they have set beliefs; in a certain sense, however, they contemplate their God directly in their Prayers and invocations; in typifying (*tamthīl*) Him, they conform to the order of their Prophets. But there are several degrees in the Presence of the heart (*ḥudūr bi'l-qalb*), from the faith of simple believers to imaginative Presence (*ḥaḍrat khayālīya*), to the Prophet's vision of the Angel Gabriel or Maryam's vision at the time of the Annunciation,[36] and still higher to the theophany related in an extraordinary *ḥadīth*, in which the Prophet tells how in ecstasy or in a waking dream he saw his God and describes the form He assumed (*ḥadīth al-rū'ya*, cf. below, Ch. VI). "To lend ear" typifies the function of the imaginative faculty on the plane of being, the *Ḥaḍra*, specific to it. "To be an eye-witness" (*shāhid*) designates the imaginative vision that fulfils the prophetic precept: "Worship God as if you saw Him." The mode of presence conferred by the imaginative power (*ḥudūr khayālī*) is by no means an inferior mode or an illusion; it signifies to see directly what cannot be seen by the senses, to be a truthful witness. The spiritual progression from the state of simple believer to the mystic state is accomplished through an increasing capacity for making oneself present to the vision by the Imagination (*istiḥḍār khayālī*): progressing from mental vision by typification (*tamthīl*) by way of dream vision (*rū'yā*) to verification in the station of *walāya*, imaginative witnessing vision (*shuhūd khayālī*) becomes vision of the heart (*shuhūd bi'l-qalb*), that is to say, vision through the inner eye (*baṣīra*), which is the vision of God by Himself, the heart being the organ, the "eye," by which God sees Himself: the contemplant is the contemplated (my vision of Him is His vision of me).[37]

Consequently, whereas the orthodox dogmatists merely set up limits and merely call upon their followers to attain their own limits, the mystics, as disciples of the science of the heart, follow the Prophets' summons to vision.[38] They carry to increasing perfection the response of the simple believers, which was only a rough beginning. The vision of which the simple believer is capable still corresponds to the "Form of God" which he sees along with those of the same religion and faith: a "God created in the faiths" according to the norms of a collective bond. The mystic's visionary capacity, however, frees him from these norms: to recognize God in each form revealing Him (*maẓhar*), to invest each being, each faith, with a theophanic function—that is an essentially personal experience, which cannot be regulated by the norms common to the collectivity. Indeed, this capacity to encounter Him in every *maẓhar* is regulated by the form of the mystic's own consciousness, for the form of every theophany is correlative to the form of the consciousness to which it discloses itself. It is by grasping this interdependence (*ta'alluq*) in each instance that the mystic fulfils the prophetic precept: "Worship God as if you saw Him." The vision of the "Form of God," as configured for and by the mystic's "Creative Imagination," can no longer be imposed by a collective faith, for it is the vision that corresponds to his

2 *Joseph and His Brothers in Egypt*

Persian miniature from Farīduddīn ʿAṭṭār, Manṭiq al-Ṭayr, *Staatsbibliothek, Marburg, MS or. oct. 268, fifteenth century*

fundamental and innermost being. This is the whole secret of the "theophanic Prayer" practiced by Ibn ʿArabī.

All this demonstrates the extraordinary role of the Image in the spirituality of Ibn ʿArabī. No less extraordinary is the fact that this spirituality is most often ignored or passed over in silence by the phenomenology of mysticism, which seems to reduce the types of mystic experience either to the classical forms of pantheism, or to an encounter with a supreme God who has already been dogmatically defined as a spiritual person who is one and infinite.[39] Indeed, a paradox must be surmounted before the full value of the Image can be recognized. To say that the Image is mere "appearance" seems to conform to realistic common sense, for which it is "nothing other" than the unreal, the fantastic. But this "nothing other" is precisely an avowal of "realistic" impotence, compared with the exigency of "theophanism" (the term which seems best to characterize the type of thought with which we are here concerned). To say that "reality" is itself a "theophanic apparition," whose form (*maẓhar*) reflects the form of him to whom it appears and who is its seat, its *medium*, is to revalorize it to such a degree that it becomes the basic element of self-knowledge. This is what historical realism disregards in its critique of docetism, which it accuses of reducing "facts" to appearances, without so much as suspecting that "appearance" is here raised to the level of "apparition" or upon what stage *spiritual facts* are in *reality* enacted. By their meaning and function, theophanies determine both the relation of the vassal to his personal Lord and the mystic's capacity, expanded to the measure of the Perfect Man. It follows that what is so often classified as "pantheistic monism" is inseparable from a vision of the "Form of God" in a personal form and figure. Perhaps this will provide ground for reflection and encourage the search for a specific category. We have proposed above the term "mystic kathenotheism."[40]

What we wish to signify thereby is precisely this valorization of the Image as the form and condition of theophanies. In its ultimate degree, the Image will be a vision of the "Form of God" corresponding to the innermost being of the mystic, who experiences himself as the microcosm of the Divine Being; a limited Form, like every form (without this limitation there would be no theophany), but a Form which as such, unlike the forms limited by the collective consensus from which they result, emanates an *aura*, a "field" which is always open to "recurrent creations" (cf. below, Ch. VI). This presupposes, of course, a basic visionary Imagination, a "presence of the heart" in the intermediate world where immaterial beings take on their "apparitional bodies" and where material things are dematerialized to become "subtile bodies," an intermediate world which is the encounter (the "conspiration," σύμπνοια) of the spiritual and the physical and which consequently dominates the outward world of "real" objects fixated in their material status.

This visionary capacity which is reflected in a conscious valorization of the Image as such, is discernible throughout Ibn 'Arabī's work. It embraces, for example, his ability to "visualize" certain letters of the Arabic alphabet, comparable to the visualization in Tantrism of the letters of the Sanskrit alphabet as inscribed in the "lotus figures" that represent the *chakras*, the centers of the subtile body.[41] Thus he visualizes the Divine Ipseity, the *huwīya*, in the form of the Arabic letter *ha*, resplendent with light and placed on a red carpet; between the two branches of the *ha* gleam the two letters *hw* (*huwa*, He), while the *ha* projects its rays upon four spheres.[42]

Far more significant is another visualization, because it is situated at the very spiritual degree (*manzila*) where mystic meditation tends toward the absolute divine Unity (*aḥadīya*), which demands the negation, the rejection (*tanzīh*) of all attributes and all relation. In this degree (and it would be impossible to carry the spiritual function of the Image any higher), something endowed with a form and a figure is manifested in the act of illumination of the mystic's soul. It may, for example, be a temple (*bayt*)[43] resting on five columns; the columns are surmounted by a roof which covers the walls of the temple; there is no opening in the walls, it is impossible for anyone to penetrate the temple. Outside the temple, however, there is a column which protrudes from the edifice but adheres to the outer wall. The intuitive mystics (*ahl al-kashf*) touch this column just as they kiss and touch the Black Stone which God placed inside the temple of the Kaʿaba.[44] At this point Ibn ʿArabī's allusions take on greater density. Just as God set up this Stone on the right and attached it to Himself and not to the Temple, so the column is not attached to this mystic degree though it is part of it; it is not an exclusive characteristic of this degree, but exists at *every* spiritual degree. It is in a sense the interpreter (the ἑρμενεύς, the *tarjumān*) between ourselves and the lofty insights which the mystic stages infuse in us.[45] There are indeed certain degrees which we penetrate totally and others to which we do not have access, such as the stage of absolutely negative transcendence (*tanzīh*). This column then instructs us by the infallible discourse it addresses to us in the world of the intuitive imagination (*ʿālam al-kashf*), as does the Prophet in the sensible world. It is the language of the Divine Being (*lisān al-Ḥaqq*). Here the allusion is elucidated: this column is part of the wall which encloses the temple; we perceive only one aspect of it, all the rest is hidden behind the wall. Only the "column" that projects on our side can "translate" the Invisible to us.

We shall see at the end of this essay that the mysterious episode in the course of which Ibn ʿArabī had perhaps his most personal vision of the Forma Dei (*ṣūrat al-Ḥaqq*), his own theophany, attaches to the Black Stone, which has its homologue in the mystic Temple of the Imagination. Then perhaps we shall understand who this so eloquent column, this interpreter of the world of mystery, is. But even now we are in a position to appreciate the noetic validity of the visions of the Active Imagination and its indispensable function, since it is absent from no mystic station. If in the hierarchy of the *Ḥaḍarāt*, the Presences or planes of being, there is, as we have seen, a correspondence between planes, so that each lower plane reproduces, or imitates in the manner of a mirror and in accordance with its own specific structure, what there is on the next higher plane, it is because in the succession of Descents (*tanazzulāt*), all the beings and contents of the higher worlds are concretized in theophanies, that is, in new and recurrent creations. The same is true in the ascending direction. To say that one of our thoughts, sentiments, or desires is concretized in a form specific to the intermediate plane of Idea-Images of subtile matter (*ʿālam al-mithāl*), is the same as to meditate before a flower, a mountain or a constellation in order to discover not what obscure and unconscious force they manifest, but what divine thought, flowering in the world of Spirits, is epiphanized, is "at work" in them. Shall we then, succumbing to the doubt which the "imaginary" arouses in us, ask, for all our wonder at the beauty of these forms in which the best of ourselves is epiphanized "Do they exist?" If, giving in to our habits, we demand a guarantee, a rational proof that these forms existed before us and will continue to exist without us, this will amount to closing our eyes to the epiphanic function of our very own being, to the very thing that constitutes the validity of our Creative Imagination. Of course these forms pre-exist, since nothing begins to be that was not before. But it is no less true that these forms were not *created*, in the sense of the word employed by Ibn ʿArabī, since they did not appear. And this precisely is the function of our *himma*, of our creativity, to make them appear, that is, to give them being. Here our creativity merges with the very core, the *heart*, of our being; what we cause to appear, what we project before us and beyond us—and also what judges us—is our *himma*, our *enthymesis*. And all this subsists with as much reality as any other apparition in any of the universes, because it is new creation, recurrent (*khalq jadīd*) from instant to instant, and because in the last analysis, "it is not you who throw the dart when you throw it" (Koran VIII:17).

3. *The Science of the Heart*

Finally, we must go back to this notion of *recurrent creation* in order to understand Ibn ʿArabī's way of considering and explaining a few examples of Creative Imagination. We shall choose a few relating to *himma*, first in the function that enables it to produce something which breaks away from it (*khayāl munfaṣil*) and subsists in one or several of the *Ḥaḍarāt* as long as the *himma* maintains it there; secondly, in its function as the organ by which we perceive the intermediate world of Idea-Images and apparitional Forms; and finally in the function which assimilates it to *dhawq*, or mystic perception, possessing the capacity to transmute all the objections of our sensory perceptions.

In regard to the first aspect, we shall consider Ibn ʿArabī's way of meditating the episode, narrated in the Koran, in which the throne of Bilqīs, queen of Saba, appeared to Solomon. Solomon asks his companions if one of them can bring him the queen's throne before she herself arrives with her train (Koran xxvii:38 ff.). One of Solomon's companions, "he who was deeply versed in Scriptures,"[46] that is, Asaf ibn Bakhīya, says he will bring it in a twinkling ("even before your glance comes back to you!"). And *instantly*, Solomon sees the throne before him.

Of course there was no actual locomotion. Neither Asaf nor the throne moved from one place to another on the earth; nor can we even speak of an involution of space. What took place was a disappearance, an abolition of the *phenomenon* of the throne in Saba, and its existentiation, that is, manifestation, before Solomon, and the instant in which it ceased to be manifested in Saba was the instant in which it appeared to the eyes of Solomon and his court. There was not even a succession. There was simply a *new creation*, a recurrence or renewal of Creation, a notion concomitant, as we have seen, with the idea of the metamorphosis of theophanies. One and the same essence of the world of Mystery can be manifested in a certain place, then hidden in that place and manifested in another; the identity consists in the hexeity of the essence, not in its recurrent manifestations. Similarly causality comes from the divine Name invested in this hexeity, whereas between phenomena as we have seen, there are only *connections without cause,* since, having neither duration nor continuity, they cannot be the causes of each other. What Solomon and his companions saw was, then, a new creation of the throne, for its disappearance (in Saba) and its apparition (before Solomon) had occurred in an indivisible instant, an atom of time.[47]

As we have also seen, this idea of the recurrence or renewal of Creation implies not a repetition of the identical (identity is in the invisible that is made manifest, not in the manifestation). Between manifestations there is only *resemblance,* and that is the meaning of the queen's exclamation when, in view of the great distance, she recognizes the impossibility of a material transfer: "It is as though it were" (*Ka'annahu huwa,* XXVII:42). And what she says is true: it is the throne in respect of its hexeity, its individuation determined in divine knowledge, but not in respect of its existence as concretized before Solomon. Thus Bilqīs' exclamation formulates a synthesis of plurality and unity.[48] Ibn ʿArabī recognizes that this problem of the throne is one of the most difficult of problems, insoluble without the idea of a recurrent Creation at each "breath" of the Sigh of existentiating Compassion (*Nafas al-Raḥmān*). Concurrently, the incident bears witness to the magical power of Solomon, which his companion "versed in Scriptures" merely exercised at Solomon's order. The operation, no doubt, has all the characteristics of an operation produced by *himma.* And yet Solomon is a unique exception. Invested with a power that belonged to him alone, he was able to provoke the same effects without the mental concentration presupposed by *himma;* he merely had to state an order; but if this power was given to him, it was because he had asked for it by order of his divine lord. We shall find that every effect of "Creative Prayer" is subject to this condition.[49]

As to the nature of this particular effect, namely, that the "transfer" of the throne took place on the plane of Imaginative Presence, it is made clear a moment later when Solomon invites the queen to enter the palace floored with crystal (XXVII:44). Taking the glass floor for a pool of water, the queen picked up her robe for fear of getting it wet. Solomon thereby wished to make it clear to her that her own throne, which she had just recognized, was of the same nature, in other words, to give her to understand that every object, perceived at every instant, is a "new creation" and that the apparent continuity consists in a manifestation of likes and resemblances (*iẓhār al-muthul*). The crystal floor is imagined as water; a form resembling the throne is imagined as being the same throne as in Saba. But precisely because it is "imagined," the Image, once recognized as such, betokens something that is not illusory but real and meaningful: for indeed, to recognize it for what it is is "to wake up," and to invest it with one's marvelous power; because it is not self-subsistent or limited to itself in the manner of the data which the unawakened consciousness looks upon as such, only the diaphanous Image makes possible the *ta'wīl*, that is, enables us to pass from the world of the senses to the higher *Ḥaḍarāt*.

Thus it is the function of ***himma***, utilizing the imaginative faculty, to perceive the intermediate world, and, by there raising sensory data to a higher level, to transmute the outward envelope into its truth, so permitting things and beings to fulfil their theophanic function. And that is the only thing that counts. This lesson is brought home to us strikingly in connection with Joseph's dream. One day the child Joseph said to his father: "I dreamt that eleven stars and the sun and the moon were prostrating themselves before me" (Koran XII:4).[50] Much later, at the end of the story, when Joseph welcomed his brothers in Egypt, he declared: "This is the interpretation (*ta'wīl*) of my old vision. The Lord has fulfilled it" (XII:101). Now what troubles Ibn 'Arabī about this *ta'wīl* is that it is not a *ta'wīl* at all. For Joseph thought he had found the *ta'wīl*—the hidden meaning of dreams which had occurred in the realm of imaginative visions—in the order of sensible things and events. But *ta'wīl* does not consist in bringing down to a lower level; it consists in restoring or raising to a higher plane. In *ta'wīl* one must carry sensible forms back to imaginative forms and then rise to still higher meanings; to proceed in the opposite direction (to carry imaginative forms back to the sensible forms in which they originate) is to destroy the virtualities of the imagination (as one would do, for example, by identifying the Mystic Temple, only one column of which is visible, with some particular material temple, whereas the homologation of a visible temple with the Mystic Temple would be a transcending, a "dematerialization"). Accordingly, the *ta'wīl* that Joseph thought he had discovered was the work of a man who was still asleep, who dreamed that he had awakened from a dream and began to interpret it, though actually he was still dreaming. With this error on the part of Joseph, Ibn 'Arabī contrasted the words of a "Muḥammadan Joseph," that is, a Joseph to whom Ibn 'Arabī himself had taught the science of the heart, the mystic sense of the Prophet's saying: "Humans are asleep; at their death they awaken." We have seen this Muḥammadan Joseph building an entire phenomenology of Light and shade. And it is he who, in the person of the Prophet Muḥammad, will show us a *ta'wīl* of the Imagination carried back and carrying itself back to its underlying truth.

Indeed, the Prophet's words make it clear to us that his young wife 'Ā'isha's misapprehension concerning his revelations had the same origin as Joseph's error in supposing that he had found the *ta'wīl* of his dreams in a "real" event ("real" in the sense in which we call a physical event "real"). 'Ā'isha

4 *Three Angels Offering Three Cups to the Prophet*

Bibliothèque nationale, Paris, MS supplément turc 190

related: "The first sign of inspiration (*waḥy*) that showed itself in the Prophet was his true dreams (*rū'yā*), for he had in dream no vision that did not have for him the clarity of the rising dawn, along with which no darkness endures. So it was with him for six months. Then came the Angel." But in all sincerity 'Ā'isha could speak of these things only within the limits of her knowledge, and like Joseph she was unaware of the Prophet's words about the dream state in which human beings live. She spoke only of six months; for her, the apparition of the Angel was a happening in the world of the senses, putting an end to the series of dreams. She was unaware that in reality the Prophet's whole life had passed in the manner of those six months. For in reality everything which emerges from the world of Mystery to take on a visible form, whether in a sensible object, in an imagination, or in an "apparitional body," is divine inspiration, divine notification and warning.[51]

Everything received by men in this manner is of the same nature as what the Prophet saw during the six months of his true dreams; it was through the Imaginative Presence (*Ḥaḍrat al-Khayāl*) that he not only beheld these visions but also that he saw the Angel. Everything he received in the state that everyday consciousness terms the waking state was also received in a state of dream, which does not mean "sleep" in the sense employed by physiology in agreement with the everyday consciousness—it was dream vision within dream vision, that is to say, Imaginative Presence within the imaginative faculty. And indeed, when the Prophet received the divine inspiration, he was ravished away from sensible things; he was covered by a veil; he left the world of everyday consciousness (of evidences considered as pertaining to the "waking" state), and yet he was not "asleep" (in the profane sense of the word). Everything he apprehended was apprehended in the Imaginative Presence, and that precisely is why it all called for an interpretation (*ta'bīr, ta'wīl*). If it had not been a dream in the true sense, there would have been nothing to interpret, that is, to see beyond it, for this "beyond" is precisely the privilege of the Imaginative Presence as *coincidentia oppositorum*. Similarly, when the Angel took human form before him, the Prophet, thanks to his visionary consciousness, was able both to speak of him to his companions as of a human being, and at the same time to say: it is the Angel Gabriel. And in both cases he was telling the truth.

Moreover, once it is recognized that everything man sees during his earthly life is of the same order (*manzila*) as visions in a dream, then *all* things seen in this world, so elevated to the rank of Active Imaginations, call for a hermeneutics, a *ta'bīr;* invested with their theophanic function, they demand to be carried back from their apparent form (*ẓāhir*) to their real and hidden form (*bāṭin*), in order that the appearance of this Hidden form may manifest it *in truth*. That is *ta'wīl* its application by the Active Imagination is unlimited. So it was that the Prophet applied the divine precept: "Say: Lord, increase my knowledge" (Koran xx:113),[52] and submitted everything that came his way to *ta'wīl*, or symbolic, mystic exegesis. Just as he had done in a dream on the occasion of his assumption to heaven (the night of the *Mi'rāj*) when an Angel had brought him a vessel with milk in it,[53] so every time milk was brought him, he "interpreted" (*yata'awwaluhu*) it as he had done in his dream, for all sensible things become subject to interpretation once they take on the value and meaning of dream visions. His companions asked him: "How do you *interpret* it? (that is, to what idea do you carry it back? What is your *ta'wīl* of it? With what does it symbolize for you?)" He replied: "It is knowledge (*'ilm*)."[54] Such an example shows the universal and liberating function of the active imagination: to typify, to transmute everything into an Image-symbol (*mithāl*) by perceiving the correspondence between the hidden and the visible. And this typification (*tamthīl*) of immaterial realities in the visible realities that manifest them, accomplished by *ta'wīl* as the function par excellence of the Active Imagination, constitutes the renewal, the typological recurrence of similitudes (*tajdīd al-muthul*), and that precisely is creation renewed and recurrent from instant to instant (*tajdīd al-khalq*). The function of the Imagination in this universal process, and with it the twofold dimension of psychocosmology, is thus disclosed in all clarity.

The symbolic exegesis that establishes typifications is thus creative in the sense that it transmutes things into symbols, into typical Images, and causes them to exist on another plane of being. To ignore this typology is to destroy the meaning of vision as such and purely and simply to accept data as they present themselves in the raw.[55] And this is what was done by a certain Taqī ibn Mukhallad, whose attitude contrasts all the more sharply with that of the Prophet in that the concrete happening was identical. In a dream Taqī saw the Prophet, who gave him a cup of milk, but instead of interpreting the *hidden* meaning of the dream, he wanted material verification. He therefore forced himself to vomit and so obtained the proof he desired, for he vomited up a whole cup of milk. He obtained the certainty he wished, the certainty coveted by all those for whom there is no other "reality" than in the physical sense, whereas for the Prophet accomplishing the *ta'wīl*, the earthly substance became spiritual fare. Thus what the Prophet's *ta'wīl*, that is, his Creative Imagination, accomplished was a kind of *transubstantiation*, but this transubstantiation was accomplished in the world of Imaginative Presence, not of material, sensible data. Materially, it was indeed milk, just as Gabriel's form was that of a youth, just as it is you who throw the dart. But one does not look for the Angel on the plane of material evidence; transubstantiation is not a phenomenon of material laboratory chemistry. And for that reason Taqī ibn Mukhallad deprived himself utterly of spiritual fare by demanding material verification, by forcing himself to vomit up what he had absorbed in his dream to prove that it was *materially* true. This manner of thinking, be it said in passing, has its bearing on our manner of envisaging both the meaning and the reality of alchemy and also helps us to appreciate the profound truth of Jacob Boehme's angelology, which leads him to speak of the food of the Angels as true, but immaterial food.[56] But all this, it may once again be argued, is "docetism." Yes. But as we have already stressed, it is a docetism that is far from degrading "reality" by making it an "appearance"; on the contrary, by transforming it into appearance it makes this "reality" transparent to the transcendent meaning manifested in it. This docetism attaches no value to a material fact unless it is appearance, that is, apparition. It is in this sense that the Imagination accomplishes at every instant a "new creation" and that the Image is the recurrence of Creation.

And so the circle of our quest closes. Without Imaginative Presence or "Dignity" there would be no manifest existence, that is, no theophany, or in other words, no Creation. But when the Divine Being manifests Himself in this existence whose being is theophanic Imagination, He is manifested not as He would be in Himself, in His Ipseity, but in a manner conforming with the theophanic Imagination. Hence the verse which states the great principle of theophanic metamorphoses:[57] "Everything shall perish except *His face*" (XXVIII:88). These words, if fully understood, sum up the entire theophanic idea. The orthodox literalists, it goes without saying, take them to refer to the Divine Face. Our theosophists understand: "Every thing . . . except the Face *of that thing*."[58] A striking contrast, to be sure. But what is no less striking is the power characteristic of the theophanic mode of thought, for to our mystical theosophists there is no contradiction whatever between the two meanings, since the Divine Face and the unchanging Face of a being refer to one and the same Face (*wajh*). The Face of a being is his eternal hexeity, his Holy Spirit (*Rūḥ al-Quds*). Between the Divine Face and the Face of this being there is the same relationship as between the increate Holy Spirit and the Angel called Spirit (*Rūḥ*).[59] Here again let us call upon ʿAbd al-Karīm Jīlī to formulate the situation with his usual density of thought: "Each sensible thing has a created Spirit by which its Form is constituted. As Spirit of that form, it is related to the form as a meaning is related to a word. This created Spirit (*Rūḥ makhlūq*) has a divine Spirit (*Rūḥ ilāhī*) by which it is constituted, and this divine Spirit is the Holy Spirit." Or in other terms: it is the Holy Spirit, whose perfection is individualized in each object of the senses or of the intellect; this Holy Spirit designates the divine Face by which the Face of each creature is constituted. But this divine Face in each thing is essential to the being of the divine Lord; the "Form of God" belongs to God as a reality constitutive of Himself. It is to this that allude the two *ḥadīth:* "Adam was created after the form (*ʿalà ṣūrat*) of the Compassionate One," and "God created Adam according to His own Form."[60]

This concludes our study of the theophanic Imagination and of the sense in which it must be termed "creative" in man, the being who is its scene and organ. We are now adequately prepared for a brief inquiry concerning the most perfect example of the "science of the heart," namely Prayer as theophanic, that is, creative, Prayer. It alone surmounts in actual practice the paradox of a theosophy which, though thoroughly imbued with the sentiment that God is hidden, that it is impossible to know or to circumscribe the ineffable Essence, nevertheless summons us to a concrete vision of "the Form of God." What we have just learned, namely, that for every created Spirit there is a Holy Spirit, a divine Spirit by which it is constituted, is perhaps the best key to an appropriate interpretation of Ibn ʿArabī's vision of the mystic Temple. For it was from this temple that, in a vision which for us remains shrouded in mystery, he saw arising the youthful figure who initiated him into everything that the Divine Spirit can teach to *its* created Spirit.

V MAN'S PRAYER AND GOD'S PRAYER

1. *The Method of Theophanic Prayer*

Some have thought it paradoxical that prayer should perform a function in a doctrine such as that of Ibn ʿArab , and what is more, an essential function, while others have denied that this was so. For those who hastened to classify his doctrine of the "transcendental unity of being" as "monism" or "pantheism" in the senses these words have assumed in *our* history of modern philosophy, have made it difficult to understand what function could still be performed by prayer. This is what we shall try to show by speaking of "Creative Prayer" in the light of what has just been disclosed to us, namely, that Creation equals theophany, that is, theophanic Imagination. (Perhaps the foregoing analyses will at least have had the advantage of suggesting certain reservations toward overhasty judgments; but this wish should not be taken to suggest any desire on our part to integrate Ibn ʿArabī's theosophy forcibly with the orthodoxy of exoteric Islam!) True, the theophanic structure of being, the relationship which it determines between Creator and creature, imply the unity of their being (because it is impossible to conceive of any being extrinsic to absolute being). But this being, which is one in *essence*, is "personalized" in two modes of *existence*, corresponding to its hidden being and to its revealed being. True, the revealed being (*ẓāhir*) is the manifestation (*ẓuhūr*) of the hidden (*bāṭin*); the two form an indissoluble unity; but this does not mean that they are existentially identical. For, *existentially*, the manifest is not the hidden, the exoteric is not the esoteric, the vassal is not the lord, the human condition (*nāsūt*) is not the divine condition (*lāhūt*), although the same underlying reality conditions their diversification as well as their mutual correspondence, their bi-unity.

And this is the situation expressed by certain of Ibn ʿArabī's maxims, which are paradoxical only in appearance. "We have given Him to manifest Himself through us, whereas He has given us (to exist through Him). Thus the role is shared between Him and us." And again: "If He has given us life and existence by His being, I also give Him life by knowing Him in my heart." We have already pointed out the consonance of such words with those of Angelus Silesius: "I know that without me, the life of God were lost."[1] Precisely this is the foundation of the idea which imposes upon the mystic (the *fedele d'amore*) a divine service which consists in feeding his lord of love on his own being and on all creation, and it is in this sense that Ibn ʿArabī saw the very prototype of this divine service in the hospitality of Abraham offering the mystic repast to the Angels under the oak of Mamre.[2]

This idea of a *sharing* of roles in the manifestation of being, in the eternal theophany, is fundamental to Ibn ʿArabī's notion of prayer; it inspires what we have termed his method of prayer and makes it a "method of theophanic prayer." The notion of sharing presupposes a dialogue between two beings, and this living experience of a *dialogical situation* confutes any theoretical attempt to reduce the unity of dialogue to an existential monism; the truth is, rather, that the unity of being conditions the dialogical situation. We have seen that the Divine Being's Compassion, the source of a creation that is His theophany, does not move only in the direction from Creator to creature, from Worshiped to worshiper, but at the same time in the opposite direction from worshiper to Worshiped, from lover to Beloved, since, although theophanies respond to the

Desire, the nostalgia of the Godhead to be known, the accomplishment of this Desire depends on the forms (*maẓāhir*) which His light invests in the theophanic function.

True, this reciprocity becomes incomprehensible if we isolate the *ens creatum* outside the *Ens increatum*. And then too Prayer takes on a meaning which would have been profoundly repugnant not only to Ibn ʿArabī but to Ṣūfism in general. For prayer is not a request for something: it is the expression of a mode of being, a means of existing and of *causing to exist*, that is, a means of causing the God who reveals Himself to appear, of "seeing" Him, not to be sure in His essence, but in the *form* which precisely He reveals by revealing Himself by and to that form. This view of Prayer takes the ground from under the feet of those who, utterly ignorant of the nature of the theophanic Imagination as Creation, argue that a God who is the "creation" of our Imagination can only be "unreal" and that there can be no purpose in praying to such a God. For it is precisely because He *is* a creation of the imagination that we pray to him, and that He exists. Prayer is the highest form, the supreme act of the Creative Imagination. By virtue of the *sharing* of roles, the divine Compassion, as theophany and existentiation of the universe of beings, is the *Prayer of God* aspiring to issue forth from His unknownness and to be known, whereas the *Prayer of man* accomplishes this theophany because in it and through it the "Form of God" (*ṣūrat al-Ḥaqq*) becomes visible to the heart, to the Active Imagination which projects before it, in its *Qibla*, the image, whose receptacle, (epiphanic form, *maẓhar*) is the worshiper's being in the measure of its capacity. God prays for us (*yuṣallī ʿalaynā*), which means that He epiphanizes Himself insofar as He is the God *whom* and *for whom* we pray (that is, the God who epiphanizes Himself for us and by us). We do not pray to the Divine Essence in its hiddenness; each faithful (*ʿabd*) prays to *his* Lord (*Rabb*), the Lord who is in the form of his faith.

§ 1. *The Method of Theophanic Prayer*

As we know, this encounter, this *coincidentia oppositorum*, is effected on the intermediate plane of "Imaginative Presence" (*Ḥaḍrat al-Khayāl*). The organ of Prayer is the heart, the psychospiritual organ, with its concentration of energy, its *himma*. The role of prayer is shared between God and man, because Creation like theophany is shared between Him who shows Himself (*mutajallī*) and him to whom it is shown (*mutajallà lahu*); prayer itself is a moment in, a recurrence par excellence of, Creation (*tajdīd al-khalq*). Once this is understood, we gain an insight into the secret of that inner liturgical action which Ibn ʿArabī develops, taking as his text the first sūra of the Koran (the *Fātiḥa*). We witness and participate in an entire ceremonial of meditation, a psalmody in two alternating voices, one human the other divine; and this psalmody perpetually reconstitutes, recreates (*khalq jadīd!*) the solidarity and interdependence of the Creator and His creature; in each instant the act of primordial theophany is renewed in this psalmody of the Creator and the creature. This will enable us to understand the homologations that the ritual gestures of Prayer can obtain, to understand that Prayer is a "creator" of vision, and to understand how, because it is a creator of vision, it is simultaneously Prayer of God and Prayer of man. Then we shall gain an intimation of *who* and *of what nature* is the "Form of God," when it shows itself to the mystic celebrating this inward liturgy.

The *Fātiḥa*, the sūra "which opens" the sacred Book, is, as we know, of fundamental importance in Islamic religion. Here we need envisage it only in the meaning given it by Ibn ʿArabī when he uses it as a personal ritual for the private use of the mystic, as a *munājāt*, that is to say, a colloquy, an "intimate dialogue," a "confidential psalm." This sūra he tells us, "constitutes a divine service (*ʿibāda*), shared half and half by God and His faithful: the one share is God's, the other the worshiper's, as related by this pious record (*khabar*) from an authentic source: I have divided Prayer between Myself and my faithful into two halves; the one is my part, the other is his; to my faithful belongs what he asks."

A "shared divine service": it is first of all this sharing which makes Prayer, Orison (*Ṣalāt*), as understood here, an "intimate dialogue" between the Lord and His personal *fedele;* a second reason is that the most important element in this "intimate dialogue" is *dhikr,* a term which is elsewhere employed in different meanings but must here be taken strictly in its literal sense of *rememoration;* the word means to make remain in the heart, to have in mind, to *meditate.* Thus we have to do neither with "litanies," the mere endless repetition of a certain divine Name (a practice occurring elsewhere in Ṣūfism), still less with collective sessions of *dhikr,* involving certain practices suggesting the technique of Yoga.[3] Nor are we speaking of public Prayer in the mosque. The internalization and individualization of liturgy go hand in hand. Though it is not irrelevant here to evoke what is known technically as "*dhikr* of the heart" and "inner *dhikr,*" we must not lose sight of the fact that this would not suffice to constitute the "divine service" which Ibn ʿArabī designates as "intimate dialogue."

Indeed, to constitute such a dialogue, since by definition it implies two mystic "officiants," the *dhikr,* as rememoration "situated in the present," must not be a *unilateral* and exclusive act on the part of the mystic making himself present to his Lord. The reality of the dialogue, of the *munājāt,* implies that there is also a rememoration, a *dhikr,* on the part of the Divine Lord, having his *fedele* present to Himself in the secret which he communicates to him in response. That is the meaning which Ibn ʿArabī gives to the Koran verse: "Have me present to your heart. I shall have you present to myself" (II:147). Understood and experienced in this way, Prayer, because it is a *munājāt,* an intimate dialogue, implies at its apogee a mental theophany, capable of different degrees; but if it is not unsuccessful, it must open out into contemplative vision.[4]

§ 1. *The Method of Theophanic Prayer*

Here then is the manner in which Ibn ʿArabī comments on the phases of a divine service that is a dialogue, an intimate dialogue which takes as its "psalm" and foundation the recitation of the *Fātiḥa*. He distinguishes three successive moments which correspond to the phases of what we may call his "method of prayer" and provide us with a good indication of how he put his spirituality into practice. First, the faithful must place himself in the company of his God and "converse" with Him. In an intermediate moment the orant, the faithful in prayer, must imagine (*takhayyul*) his God as present in his *Qibla*, that is, facing him. Finally, in a third moment, the faithful must attain to intuitive vision (*shuhūd*) or visualization (*rū'yā*), contemplating his God in the subtile center which is the *heart*, and simultaneously hear the divine voice vibrating in all manifest things, so much so that he hears nothing else. This is illustrated by the following distich of a Ṣūfī: "When He shows Himself to me, my whole being is vision: when he speaks to me in secret, my whole being is hearing."[5] Here we encounter the practical meaning of the tradition which declares: "The entire Koran is a symbolic, allusive (*ramz*) story, between the Lover and the Beloved, and no one except the two of them understands the truth or reality of its intention."[6] Clearly, the entire "science of the heart" and all the creativity of the heart are needed to set in motion the *ta'wīl*, the mystic interpretation which makes it possible to read and to practice the Koran as though it were a variant of the Song of Songs.

The sūra "which opens" the Koran is composed of seven verses. As meditated by our *shaikh*, its liturgical action breaks down into three phases; the first (that is, the first three verses) is the action of the faithful *toward* or *upon* his Lord; the second (the fourth verse) is a reciprocal action between the Lord and his faithful; the third (the three last verses) is an action of the Lord *toward* and *upon* his faithful. In each of these verses, the Divine Presence, to which the faithful makes himself present, and which he makes present to himself, is attested by a divine *response*, vibrating as though in an undertone. This *response* is not a poetic or rhetorical fiction, in which the Godhead is arbitrarily "made to speak." The divine response merely records the event of Prayer from the viewpoint of the being to whom it is addressed; it expresses the *intention* as it attains its object, and does so by virtue of the simple fact that this intention is formulated and assumed. Thus from the standpoint of phenomenology, this divine response is rigorously accurate.[7]

The first three verses state the action of the faithful *toward* and *upon* the personal Lord he worships. Preceded by the ritual invocation: "In the name of Allah, the Compassionate, the Merciful," they are: (1) "Praise be to Allah, Lord of the Creation, (2) The Compassionate, the Merciful, (3) King on the day of Judgment." The divine response to the first verse, preceded by the invocation, sets forth the event, the intention which attains its object: "Now my faithful makes me present to himself. Now my faithful makes of me the Glorified One." The divine response to the second and third verses runs: "Now my faithful sings my praise. Now he exalts my glory and puts his trust in me." (4) "Thee alone we worship, and from thee alone do we await help." Here the divine response says: "Now there is a sharing in common between myself and my faithful; to my faithful belongs what he asks." As meditated by Ibn ʿArabī, this moment of the prayer produces a community (*ishtirāk*), a reciprocal action. To understand what this means, it suffices to recall the principles of our *shaikh*'s theosophy, which here find their application: the personal Lord and his faithful *answering* one for the other, because each is responsible for the other. The three last verses constitute the last phase: (5) "Guide us in the straight path"; (6) "The path of those to whom You have given grace"; (7) "Not of those who have incurred your wrath, or of those who have gone astray." And the divine response: "All that belongs to my faithful, for to my faithful belongs what he asks." Here, in the third phase: the action is from the Lord *toward* and *upon* his faithful.[8] The faithful has and possesses what he asks—this, as we shall see, is the profound meaning of "creative," that is, theophanic, imaginative, or mental Prayer.

To understand the full bearing of the inner liturgical action accomplished by our *shaikh*'s meditation, we must place ourselves at the *center*, at the moment of common, reciprocal action between the Lord and His faithful; the first moment prepares the way for it, the third results from it. The second moment is indeed so much the center that its intention is the *keystone* of Ibn ʿArabī's entire theosophy. We must never forget that this Prayer is addressed not to the Godhead as it is in itself, in its pure, absolute essence, in the virtual, unrevealed totality of its names, but to the Lord manifested under one or another of His names, one or another of His theophanic forms (*maẓāhir*), and for this reason standing in every instance in a unique, undivided, personal relation with the faithful in whose soul this Name is invested, the soul which bears in itself the concrete manifestation of that Name. We have already seen that what establishes His existence as a Lord is our "theopathy" (*ma'lūhiya*), that is, what we experience and suffer *of* Him and *by* Him. And indeed the Koran says: "O pacified soul, return to your Lord, well-pleased and well-pleasing." To your Lord, Ibn ʿArabī observes, not to *Al-Lāh* in general; this means the Lord who called you at the very beginning and whom you recognized from among the totality of the divine Names or Lords (*arbāb*). We have to do then with the manifest God, who can manifest Himself only in a direct and individualized relationship with the being to whom He is manifested, in a form which corresponds to that being's capacity. It is in this sense that the Lord and His faithful acknowledge one another, are one another's pledge and shield (the vassal is the *sirr al-rubūbīya*, the secret of his Lord's suzerainty). And the *shaikh* points out: to return to His Lord is for the faithful "to return to his Paradise," that is, to return to his self, to the divine Name, to *yourself* as you are known by your Lord.[9] Or yet again: "I am known only by you, just as you exist only by me. Who knows you knows me, although no one knows me, so that you too are known by no one."[10] Divine solitude and human solitude: each delivers the other by joining itself to the other.

Thus the beginning of the faithful's liturgical action merely effects a "return," the faithful making himself present to his Lord by making himself present to himself. This prelude establishes their community in the divine Names it utters, since the totality of a divine Name is constituted by this Name itself, or by a divine Lord belonging to the world of Mystery, and by the faithful whose soul is its receptacle, the form by which and to which it is epiphanized, the two standing to one another in a reciprocal relationship of action and passion.[11] It is the community thus resulting from the totality of their two aspects, it is this "theopathic union" between divine Compassion and human passion, that is expressed in the central verse: "Thee alone we worship (that is, thee whom our passion of thee, our theopathy establishes as the compassionate Lord, thee of whom our passion *makes* this Lord), from thee alone we await help (that is to say, from thee who answer for us because we answer for thee). Here no doubt we are far from the ideas of Islamic orthodoxy, but in this conception lies the whole theosophy of Ibn ʿArabī with all its greatness.

The best commentary that can be offered on the divine service celebrated as an "intimate dialogue" by the psalmody of the *Fātiḥa* is a short poem which Ibn ʿArabī inserted in another work.[12]

It is He who glorifies me at the moment when I glorify Him.
It is He who worships me at the moment when I worship Him.

> (Which means that the Prayer of man *is* the Prayer of God, that Prayer of God which is the divine epiphany manifesting the forms in which His Names are invested; in it He manifests Himself and reveals Himself to Himself, calling Himself to the worship of Himself, and is therefore

in reality the active subject of all the actions following from these forms.)

There is a mode of being in which it is I who recognize Him,

(That is, in which He manifests Himself, individualized in the form of the Lord who is my personal Lord.)

Whereas in the eternal hexeities I deny Him.

(Since in the realm of pure essence containing the unrevealed hexeities of His Names, that is, our latent eternal individuations, He is unknowable, He does not exist for us.)

But where I deny Him, it is He who knows me.

(That is, in the world of Mystery, where I am known to Him but He is not known to me, since He is not revealed.)

When it is I who know Him, it is then that I contemplate Him.

(That is, as manifest, *ẓāhir,* visible in the theophany that is accorded me in the measure of my aptitude, which itself is predisposed by my eternal hexeity.)

How can He be He who is sufficient unto Himself (*al-ghānī*),
since I assist Him and come to His help?

(The question does not apply to the divine Essence as such, which is impredicable, but to His revealed Being, which is in every instance determined in the form of a personal Lord, a suzerainty, *rubūbīya,* whose secret is the faithful, since without him the Lord's suzerainty would vanish.)[13]

Then it is God who causes me to exist.

(By manifesting my being, carrying it from my hexeity latent in Him to its visible form.)

But by knowing Him, I in turn cause Him to exist.

(That is, I am he for whom and in whom He exists as revealed God, personal Lord, since the unknown God, the "Hidden Treasure," exists for no one, is pure non-being.)

Of this the report has come down to us.
And in me the word of it is fulfilled.[14]

V. *Man's Prayer and God's Prayer*

This short poem, as we have said, is the best commentary on "divine service" (*ʿibāda*) as meditated by Ibn ʿArabī. With great mastery it states what has always been the torment of mystics and often defied their means of expression. In so doing, it defines the sense in which Prayer, because it is not an act produced unilaterally by the faithful, must be looked upon as *creative;* it is the conjunction of the Worshiper and the Worshiped, of the Lover and the Beloved, a conjunction which is an exchange of divine Names (*communicatio Nominum*) between the faithful and his Lord, and that precisely is the act of Creation. The secret psalmody of the *Fātiḥa* accomplishes the essential unity between the man who prays and the Lord who is "personalized" for him, so that the faithful becomes the necessary complement to his Lord. In this exchange, the Worshiper is the Worshiped; the Lover is the Beloved. Here no doubt we are far from the letter of the Koran as interpreted in the official cult, but we see how its spirit is understood when, in the private ritual of the Ṣūfī, the Koran is experienced as a version of the Song of Songs.

The exchange of Names implies, in particular, an exchange of the Names "the First" and "the Last," shared simultaneously by the faithful and his Lord, because the Prayer of the faithful is at the same time the Prayer of *his* Lord, a Prayer of the Creator-Creature. And we shall soon see that this precisely is the secret of the divine responses and the reason why the God "created" by Prayer is neither an illusion nor a fiction, since He is created *by Himself;* and it is also the reason why the imaginative vision or visualization of the Form of God obtained in Prayer and attested by the visionary experience of Ibn ʿArabī is not vain. Indeed, it reveals to him his own form, the form of his fundamental being, the form secretly and eternally known by his Lord, who knows Himself in it beyond all time, even before the Creation which is the primordial theophanic Imagination, and of which each vision or visualization is only a renewal, a recurrence.

§ 1. *The Method of Theophanic Prayer*

"Guide us in the *straight path* (*ṣirāṭ mustaqīm*)" is the prayer uttered in the third moment of the confidential dialogue. Here the words have no moralistic sense;[15] they designate the *path* by which every being fulfils his aptitude to perform the theophanic function in which he is invested by his own personal Lord; this function consists in the fact that the Lord manifests Himself in him, to him and by him, and that he himself thereby realizes his eternal hexeity, what he should *be*. That is the path his existence follows. And so it is for all beings, for all creatures, insofar as their being is a capacity for being (*imkān*) and as such precisely a divine possibility, a possibility of epiphany. The Divine Being needs His faithful in order to manifest Himself; reciprocally, the faithful needs the Divine Being in order to be invested with existence. In this sense, his Prayer (*duʿā bi'l-istiʿdād*) is his very *being*, his very capacity for being; it is the being of his hexeity demanding full realization; and this prayer implies its fulfilment since it is nothing other than the desire expressed by the Godhead still hidden in the solitude of His unknownness: "I was a Hidden Treasure, I yearned to be known."

2. *Homologations*

Looking more deeply into this *creative* meaning of Prayer, we see how in every instance it accomplishes its share of the Divine Being's desire, of His aspiration to create the universe of beings, to reveal Himself in them in order to be known to Himself—in short, the desire of the *Deus absconditus* or *Theos agnostos*, aspiring to Theophany. Each prayer, each instant in each prayer, then becomes a recurrence of Creation (*tajdīd al-khalq*), a new Creation (*khalq jadīd*) in the sense noted above. The creativity of Prayer is connected with the cosmic meaning of Prayer so clearly perceived by Proclus in the prayer of the heliotrope. This cosmic meaning is apparent in two kinds of homologation suggested by Ibn ʿArabī and his commentators, which possess the extreme interest of showing us how in Islam Ṣūfism reproduced the operations and configurations of mystic consciousness known to us elsewhere, especially in India. In one of these homologations, the man in prayer represents himself as the Imām of his own microcosm. In another the ritual gestures of Prayer (accomplished in *private*) are likened to the acts of the Creation of the universe or macrocosm. These homologations presuppose the meaning of Prayer as creative; they prepare, ground, and justify its visionary dénouement, since precisely as new creation it signifies new epiphany (*tajallī*). Thus we move toward our conclusion: Creative Imagination in the service of Creative Prayer, through *himma,* the concentration of all the powers of the heart.

The first of these homologations introduces the idea of the *Imām*, "he who guides"; in current usage, he "who stands before" the faithful, and after whom they regulate their movements for the celebration of Prayer. In Sunnism, he is simply the officiant in a mosque, a function quite unrelated to the individual's moral and spiritual qualities. In Shīʿism, he is something very different. The word *Imām* designates those persons who in their earthly appearance and apparition were epiphanies of the Godhead,[16] spiritual guides of mankind toward the esoteric and saving meaning of Revelations, while in their transcendent existence they assume the role of cosmogonic entities. So all-important are the ideology and devotion concentrated in the persons of the Holy Imāms that *Shīʿism* is properly designated as *Imāmism* (*Imāmīya*). For the Duodeciman Shīʿites, the Imām of our period, the *twelfth Imām* is in occultation (*ghayba*), having been ravished from this world as Enoch and Elijah were ravished. He alone would have the right to guide Prayer. In his absence, no simple officiants assume this role, but persons who have been put to the test and are known for their high spiritual quality; they are not appointed like functionaries, but are gradually recognized and promoted by the community. But, since such qualified persons are extremely rare, and since after all they are only substitutes for the hidden real Imām, a pious Shī'ite likes just as well to practice his cult in private. Hence the extraordinary development, in Imāmism, of the literature of the *Ad'īya*, or private liturgies.[17]

This form of devotion is certainly, and for profound reasons, in sympathy with the private ritual we have just heard Ibn 'Arabī describe as a *Munājāt*, an intimate dialogue. In it, the mystic himself is invested in the dignity of the Imām in relation to his own universe, his microcosm. He is the Imām for "the angels who pray behind him," in ranks like the faithful in a mosque, but invisible. But the condition of this personal divine service is precisely solitude. "Every orant (*muṣallī*) is an Imām, for the Angels pray behind the worshiper *when he prays alone.* Then his person is elevated during Prayer to the rank of the Divine Envoys, that is, to the rank (of the Imāmate) which is divine vicarate (*niyābat 'an Al-Lāh*)."[18] As Imām of his microcosm, the orant is thus the Creator's vicar. This homologation helps us to understand the meaning of creative Prayer.

What are the "Angels of the microcosm"? Here again we find an intimation of a "subtile physiology" resulting from psychocosmology and cosmophysiology, which transform the human body into a microcosm. As we know, since each part of the cosmology has its homologue in man, the whole universe is in him. And just as the Angels of the macrocosm sprang from the faculties of the Primordial Man, from the Angel called Spirit (*Rūḥ*), so the Angels of the microcosm are the physical, psychic, and spiritual faculties of the individual man.[19] Represented as Angels, these faculties are transformed into subtile centers and organs; the construction of the body envisaged in subtile physiology takes on the aspect of a minor, microcosmic angelology; allusions to it are frequent in all our authors.[20] It is in relation to this microcosm transformed into a "court of Angels" that the mystic performs the function of Imām. His situation is quite similar to that of the *mystes* in the Hymn of

Hermes (*Corpus hermeticum XIII*) in which the elect, regenerated as son of God because the divine Powers reside in him, calls on these same powers to pray with him: "Powers who are in me, sing the hymn . . . sing in unison with my will." And because God, the *Noūs*, has become the spiritual eye of man, we may say that when the regenerated man praises God, it is God who praises Himself.[21] We read exactly the same thing in Ibn ʿArabī. When in the final doxology the Imām pronounces these words: "God hears him who glorifies Him," and those present, that is, the Angels of the microcosm, respond: "Our Lord, glory be to Thee," Ibn ʿArabī declares: "It is God himself who through the tongue of His faithful utters the words: God hears him who glorifies Him."[22]

The second homologation of Prayer with cosmology and the initial cosmogonic act renewed from instant to instant, merely corroborates the first. It is based on the attitudes of the body prescribed in the course of ritual Prayer: erect stance (*qiyām*), profound inclination (*rukūʿ*), prosternation (*sujūd*). On this occasion, we shall learn with all desirable clarity what the *Prayer of man* and the *Prayer of God* are; we shall discover their *synergy*, their complicity, their *co-presence*, the one to the other and by the other. A movement of pure thought (*ḥarakat maʿqūla*) transfers the universe of beings from its state of occultation or potentiality to the manifest state of concrete existence which constitutes theophany in the visible world (*ʿālam al-shahāda*). In this visible and sensible world, the movements of natural beings can be reduced to three categories (that is, three dimensions). And the ritual of Prayer embraces all these movements: (a) There is the *ascending*, vertical movement which corresponds to the faithful's erect stance. This is the movement of the growth of man, whose head rises toward the heavens. (b) There is the *horizontal* movement, which corresponds to the orant's state at the moment of the profound inclination. This is the direction in which animals grow. (c) There is the inverse, *descending* movement, corresponding to the prosternation. This is the movement of the plant, sinking its roots in depth. Thus Prayer reproduces the movements of the creatural universe; it is itself recurrence of Creation and new Creation.

As for the movement of pure thought which is the aspiration of the *Deus absconditus* to theophany, giving rise to the genesis of the cosmos, the same homologations are revealed: (a) There is the *intentional* movement (*ḥarakat irādīya*) of the Divine Being, His "conversion" (*tawajjuh*, ἐπιστροφή) toward the lower world in order to existentiate it, that is, manifest it, bring it to light; this is a movement *descending* in depth (corresponding to prosternation, to the movement of the roots of plants). (b) There is the divine "conversion" toward the higher world, that of the divine Names, the eternal hexeities, and the relations between them. This is pleromatic creation (*ibdāʿ*) by an *ascending* movement epiphanizing the Spirits and Souls (corresponding to the erect stance, the movement of man's growth). (c) There is finally divine conversion toward the celestial bodies intermediate between the two worlds, from one *horizon* to the other (corresponding to the profound inclination, the horizontal movement of animal growth). And all this constitutes the Prayer of God (*Ṣalāt al-Ḥaqq*) as His existentiating theophany (*tajallī ījādī*).

To this whole development, beginning with the *Ibdāʿ* which is the original gift, the creation of the pleroma, the primordial theophany, corresponds, phase for phase, the divine service (*ʿibāda*) of the faithful, by virtue of the three movements it imposes on his body, which reproduce the movements of Creation. The gestures and attitudes of the body in Prayer reproduce exactly the "gestures" of God creating the world, that is to say, manifesting the world and manifesting Himself in it. Thus Prayer is a recurrence of creative Creation. *Ibdāʿ* and *ʿibāda* are homologous; both proceed from the same theophanic aspiration and intention. The *Prayer of God* is His aspiration to manifest Himself, to see Himself in a mirror, but in a mirror which itself sees Him (namely, the faithful whose Lord He is, whom He invests in one or another of His Names). The *Prayer of man* fulfils this aspiration; by becoming the mirror of this Form, the orant sees this "Form of God" in the most secret sanctuary of himself. But never would he see the Form of God (*ṣūrat al-Ḥaqq*) if his vision were not itself the Prayer of God (*Ṣalāt al-Ḥaqq*) which is the theophanic aspiration of the *Deus absconditus*.[23]

We are now very close to the dénouement that will crown the *munājāt*, "confidential psalm," rememoration, meditation, recurrent presence, ἐνθύμησις. One who meditates on his God" in the present" maintains Himself in His company. And a tradition (*khabar ilāhī*) from a reliable source tells us: "I myself keep company with him who meditates on me (maintains me present in himself)." But if the faithful's divine Lord keeps him company when the faithful rememorates Him inwardly, he must, if he is endowed with inner vision, *see* Him who is thus present. This is called contemplation (*mushāhada*) and visualization (*rū'yā*). Of course, one who is without this sense of vision does not see Him. But this, says Ibn ʿArabī with gravity, is the criterion by which each orant (*muṣallī*) can recognize his degree of spiritual progress. Either he sees his Lord who shows Himself to him (*tajallī*) in the subtile organ that is his heart or else he does not yet see Him in this way; then let him worship Him through faith *as though he saw Him*. This injunction which carries a profound savor of Shīʿite Imāmology (the Imām being the theophanic form par excellence),[24] is nothing other than a summons to set the power of the Active Imagination to work. "Let the faithful represent Him by his Active Imagination, face to face in his *Qibla*, in the course of his intimate dialogue."[25] Let him be someone who "lends ear" to the divine responses; in short, let him put the method of theophanic prayer into practice.

3. *The Secret of the Divine Responses*

Thus for a disciple of Ibn ʿArabī a great deal is at stake. Let every man test himself and discern his spiritual state, for a

Koranic verse declares: "Man is a witness who testifies against himself, whatever excuse he may offer" (LXXV:14–15)."[26] If he does not apprehend the divine "responses" in the course of prayer, it means that he is not really *present* with his Lord;[27] incapable of hearing and seeing, he is not really a *muṣallī*, an orant, nor one "who has a heart, who lends ear and is an eye witness' (XL:36). What we have called Ibn ʿArabī's "method of prayer" thus embraces three degrees: presence, audition, vision. Whoever misses one of the three degrees remains outside of Prayer and its effects,[28] which are bound up with the state of *fanāʾ*. As we have seen, this word does not, in Ibn ʿArabī's terminology, signify the "annihilation" of the individual, but his occultation to himself, and such is the condition necessary to the apprehending of the *dhikr*, the divine *response* which is here the action of the Lord putting his Faithful in the presence of His own Presence.

We distinguish one basic motif. The idea that there is a divine *response* without which Prayer would not be an intimate dialogue, and it raises the question of who takes the initiative in the dialogue and in what sense one may speak of an initiative. In other words, who has the first role and who the second? We shall see Ibn ʿArabī at pains to analyze this structure which is implied by the most profound and original intuition of his theosophy.

In the first place, this structure rises from the functioning of the Active Imagination as we have been able to observe it up to this point. The theophany given to the heart of the man who prays originates with the Divine Being, not with the *muṣallī*, because it is itself "Prayer of God." Accordingly, the Prophet spoke in the passive when he said: "My consolation (literally, the freshness of my eyes, *qurrat al-ʿayn*) has been placed for me in prayer," or else, if with Ibn ʿArabī we use the same verbal root in a different meaning: "In Prayer my eyes have been set in place,"[29] for Prayer is the *munājāt*, the secret psalm of the Lover and the Beloved. This also is the meaning of the sacralization of the time of Prayer, the injunction not to interrupt it or pay attention to anything else ("Satan's theft preventing the faithful from contemplating his Beloved").[30] In expressing himself in the passive, the Prophet wished to signify that if a mental theophany is attached to the practice of Prayer, it is because Prayer is first of all "Prayer of God" (it is God who prays and shows himself to Himself).[31] It is impossible to contemplate the Divine Being in His essence; the orant requires a support and an individuation, and that is precisely what the idea of *tajallī*, theophany, implies. The spiritual energy concentrated in the heart, the *himma*, projects the image which is this support.[32] But exactly as this image is the *consequence* of the mystic's being, that is, follows and expresses his capacity, it is no less true that this Image precedes the mystic's being, that is, is predetermined and grounded in the structure of his eternal hexeity. It is indeed this "structural law" which, forbidding us to confuse the theophanic Imagination with what is commonly called "imagination" and disparaged as "fancy," permits us to take up the challenge which in fact applied only to an "imaginary" God. But in order to conceive of the "imaginary" as "unreal," we must begin by cutting off the imagination from its structural law. For this law demands that every image bear witness for or against the man who imagines it; the image is far from being a harmless pastime. And, as we shall see, there is a *ḥadīth* which outlines a kind of canon of the mental iconography implied by the method of theophanic prayer.

Secondly, we can now say that the functioning of the Active Imagination and the structure of theophanies imply the idea that in Prayer there is between God and His faithful not so much a sharing of roles as a situation in which each by turns takes the role of the other. We have just seen that there are Prayer of God *and* Prayer of man. Ibn ʿArabī also finds this attested in the Koranic verse: "There is He who prays for thee and also His Angels, to bring thee out of Darkness to Light" (xxxiii:42). Prayer of God and Prayer of the Angels come then to signify the guiding of man to the light, that is to say, the theophanic process. This illumines in depth the structure of the dialogue and answers the question of *who* is the first and *who* the second or last. Finally, the secret of the divine responses, and with it the guarantee of their truth will be revealed in this structure of Prayer, which gives to each, turn by turn, to the faithful and to his Lord, the role of *First* and the role of *Last.*

Under the inspiration of his personal philology, Ibn ʿArabī stresses a homonymy which, far from being a mere play on words, is one of those profoundly significant homonymies due to the polyvalence of certain Arabic roots; the analogies to which they call attention make possible transitions which rational dialectics by itself would never have been able to discover. Thus the word *muṣallī* comes to signify no longer "he who prays" but "he who comes after," who "is later than" (the word is employed for the horse which in a race comes in second, "behind" the first). This homonymy throws a sudden new light on the relationship between *Prayer of God* and *Prayer of man*, serving to determine in what sense God and His faithful are by turns *muṣallī*, that is to say, receive by turns the divine Names "the First" (*al-Awwal*) and "the Last" (*al-Akhir*), corresponding respectively to the "Hidden" (*Bāṭin*) and the "Revealed" (*Ẓāhir*).

Thus when God is the *muṣallī*, "He who prays" and who "comes last,"[33] He manifests Himself to us under His Name of "the Last" (*Al-Akhir*), that is to say, the Revealed (*al-Ẓāhir*), since His manifestation depends on the existence of the faithful to whom and for whom He is manifested. The "God who prays toward us" is precisely the manifested God (whose manifestation fulfils the aspiration of the "Hidden Treasure" to be known), He is the God whom the faithful *creates* in his *heart*, either by his meditations and reflections or by the particular faith to which he adheres and conforms. To this aspect therefore belongs the God who is designated technically as the "God created in the faiths," that is, the God who determines and individualizes Himself according to the capacity of the receptacle which receives Him, and whose soul is the *maẓhar,* the epiphany, of one or another of His Names. This is the case envisaged by the words of Junayd, the great mystic (relating to gnosis and the gnostic): "The color of the water is that of the vessel which contains it." In this sense, the "God who prays toward us" "is later than" our being; He is posterior to it, dependent on it; He is the God whom our *theopathy* (*ma'lūhīya*) establishes as *theos,* because the Worshiped presupposes the existence of the worshiper to whom He shows Himself ("by knowing Him, I give Him being"). In this sense He is therefore the "Last," the "Manifested." Here the divine Names "the First" and "the Hidden" are appropriate to the faithful.

But when we are the *muṣallī,* "we who pray," the Name "the Last" befits us; it is we who are *posterior* to Him, we who are *later* than He. In this case, we are for Him those whom He manifests (because the "Hidden Treasure" has wished to be known, to know himself in beings). Then it is He who precedes us, who is the First. But the admirable part of all this is that it is precisely the beings whom the "Hidden Treasure" manifests to concrete being from the world of Mystery who manifest Him in the multiple forms of belief, in the infinite multiplicity of His divine Names. It is the Hidden who *is* the Manifested, the First who *is* Last. And that is why our Creative Imagination does not create a "fictitious God." The image of the God whom the faithful *creates* is the Image of the God whom his own being reveals, his own being revealed by the "Hidden Treasure." Thus it is the Image of him who first imagined His being (created it, that is, revealed it to being) as his own form or Image, or more exactly his mirror image. It is this anticipatory, primordial, pre-existential image which the *muṣallī* projects in turn (in his beliefs, in his mental visualizations during Prayer). Thus it is *psychologically* true to say that "the God created in the faiths" is the symbol of the Self.[34] The God to whom we pray can be only the God who reveals Himself to us, by us, and for us, but it is in praying to Him that we cause the "God created in the faiths" to be himself enveloped in the Divine Compassion, that is, existentiated, manifested by it. The theophanies of the "Gods" manifested to the heart or to the faiths are all theophanies of the real One God (*Ḥaqq Ḥaqīqī*). When we are the *muṣallī*, this must be borne in mind; he who knows this is the gnostic who has untied the knot of closed, limited dogmas, because for him they have become theophanic symbols.

And this again is to understand with Ibn ʿArabī the meaning of these Koranic verses: "Each being knows *his* Prayer and his form of glorification" (XXIV:41); "there is no being who does not glorify his glory" (XVII:46), for, our *shaikh* remarks, in a certain sense the adjective "his" refers to this being; the verse then relates to the praise which each being renders unto *himself*.[35] Here, seemingly anticipating the view of those psychologists who regard the "God created in the faiths" as a symbol of the Self, Ibn ʿArabī places us at the crossing of the ways. Taking one path, we find the *self* mistaken for the empiric individual who is unaware of having another dimension, a "celestial pole," whose being is spread flat on the surface of the sensible world or of rational evidences. In this case self-praise will be denounced as the worst of idolatries by collective conformism, which is equally guilty of the same idolatry, for it does not suffice to eliminate the individual to attain to the divine. Taking the other path, we rise in equal measure above the empirical self and above collective beliefs to recognize the Self, or rather, experientially, the Figure who represents it in mental vision, as the *paredros* of the gnostic, his "companion-archetype," that is to say, his eternal hexeity invested with a divine Name in the world of Mystery. For one who takes this path there is a profound significance in the fact that the Prayer recommended by Ibn ʿArabī, while utilizing the ritual of official Prayer, is not a public, collective Prayer, but a "divine service" practiced in private, a *munājāt*, an intimate dialogue. This indeed points up the profound difference between the Imagination of the "God created in the faiths" and the "theophanic vision" dispensed to the heart in the course of the "confidential psalm" between Lover and Beloved.

Thus the "life of prayer" practiced in the spirit and according to the indications of Ibn ʿArabī represents the authentic form of a "process of individuation" releasing the spiritual person from collective norms and ready-made evidences and enabling him to live as a unique individual for and with his Unique God. It signifies the effective realization of the "science of the heart," that is to say, in the last analysis, of Ibn ʿArabī's theosophy. From it we can then distill something in the nature of a "phenomenology of the heart," that is, we can observe how in attaining to the awareness that the "God created in the faiths" is a new creation, "a recurrence of creation," Ibn ʿArabī's gnostic, far from reducing Him to a fiction, illumines the believer with his divine truth by freeing him from his limitations, because he now understands them.

The non-gnostic, the dogmatic believer does not know, and can only be scandalized if it is suggested to him, that the praise he offers to Him in Whom he believes is a praise addressed to himself. This precisely because, not being a gnostic, he is unaware of the process and the meaning of this "creation" which is at work in his faith, and is therefore without knowledge of what constitutes its truth. Moreover he sets up his faith as an absolute dogma, though it is necessarily limited and conditioned. Hence the merciless conflicts between faiths which vie with one another, reject and refute one another. Fundamentally, Ibn ʿArabī holds, the belief of such believers is merely an opinion, and they are without knowledge of what is implied by the divine words "I conform to the opinion that my faithful has of Me."[36]

Nor should we cede to the pious illusion of negative theology which removes (*tanzīh*) from God every attribute judged unworthy of Him or even every attribute as such, for the God who is the object of such a *remotio* or *tanzīh* nevertheless remains the

God created in faith; the operation of *tanzīh* itself depends on opinion, and any "purification" attempted by the rational intellect of the theologians serves only to *mix* divinity with the categories of reason. Indeed anyone who applies himself to *tanzīh* and rejects *tashbīh* (symbolism) is merely succumbing to one of the temptations of "unilateral monotheism"; and here there is a profound agreement between Ibn ʿArabī and the premises of Ismailian theosophy.[37] For neither *tanzīh* (negative theology) nor *tashbīh* (symbolic theology) can attain to God as such, but only to an essence (*ḥaqīqa*) which is "essentiated" in each of our souls, proportionally to the capacity and to the intellectual and spiritual development of that soul. The paradoxical situation that results from the theosophy both of Ibn ʿArabī and of the Ismailians is that when the theosophist speaks of the "God created in the faiths," the dogmatic theologian can only be scandalized, but that the more scandalized he is, the more he betrays himself in the theosophist's eyes as one who has fallen into metaphysical idolatry through the purification (*tanzīh*) of his monotheism (*tawḥīd*).

From an exoteric point of view, it may seem that the conversion, the change of meaning which the theosophy of Ibn ʿArabī brings to dogma or confessional faith degrades them into fictions, since it makes their God a creation of the faith in question. But from the esoteric point of view, if we attentively recapitulate all the phases of his system of thought, we cannot fail to see that in transmuting what was dogma into symbol (*maẓhar*) Ibn ʿArabī establishes the *divine truth* of this *human creation*, and this because he grounds its *human truth* on a *divine creation*. One does not refute symbols; one *deciphers* them. This reciprocal authentification will be the fruit of the experience gained in Prayer, practiced by Ibn ʿArabī as a dialogue in which the two parties continually exchange roles. The truth of the divine responses merely expresses this idea of the reciprocal safeguarding of the Lord and His faithful, which we have pointed out above.[38] That in glorifying his Lord the faithful glorifies himself will then no longer seem a monstrous blasphemy or a case of desperate skepticism, but will be recognized as the mystic secret of the "confidential psalm" in which Worshiper and Worshiped are each in turn the "First" and the "Last," the Glorified-Glorifier.[39] It is here that the faithful gains awareness of the theophanic function of his being. The "God created in the faith" manifests Himself no longer in order to impose Himself on the faithful, but in order to express His limits, for these limits are the condition which makes possible *one* among the many divine epiphanies. The gnostic does not receive a ready-made Image of his Lord, but understands Him in the light of the Image which in the course of his *munājāt,* his intimate dialogue, appears in the mirror of his heart as subtile organ.

Here, in a certain measure, we have indicated the meaning of "Creative Prayer" practiced as a personal "divine service." If it is a "plea," it is such as an aspiration to a "new creation," for such a plea is the spiritual state of the orant who formulates it, and this state is conditioned by his eternal hexeity, his essence-archetype (*'ayn thābita*). What incites him to glorify God is precisely his spiritual state, in other words, that within him which determines this God in one or another form, under one or another divine Name. Thus God gives him, and can give him, only what his hexeity implies. Hence the supreme mystic gift will be to receive an intuitive vision of this hexeity, for such a vision enables the mystic to know his aptitude, his own eternal predisposition defining the curve of a succession of states *ad infinitum*. No theophany (*tajallī*) is possible except in the form corresponding to the predisposition of the subject to which it discloses itself (*mutajallà lahu*). The subject who receives the theophany sees only his own form, yet he knows that it is only in this form as in a divine mirror that he can see the Form of the theophany, and in this theophany recognize his own form. He *does not see* God in His essence; the response given to Moses is still valid: "*Lan tarānī,* thou shalt not see me." It is the same with a material mirror: when you contemplate a form in it, you do not see the mirror, though you know perfectly well that you see forms and your own form only *in* this mirror; you cannot at the same time look at the image which appears in the mirror and at the body of the mirror itself. Ibn ʿArabī regards this comparison as adequate: God (*al-Ḥaqq*) is *your* mirror, that is, the mirror *in* which you contemplate your self (*nafs, anima*), and you, you are *His* mirror, that is, the mirror in which He contemplates His divine Names.[40] Thus it is not possible that the unconditioned God should epiphanize Himself as unconditioned, since such a *tajallī* would dissolve the being to which He showed Himself (*mutajallà lahu*), for then neither determinate existence nor aptitude nor predisposition conditioned by a determinate hexeity could endure for that being. These two terms are incompatible and contradictory.

Thus the individual *hexeity*, as raised to its proper rank in the knowledge which God gains of Himself by revealing to Himself the virtualities of His being, and the Divine Form, the vision of which is conditioned by this hexeity, are the two focuses of the ellipse; they are the two elements termed Prayer of man and Prayer of God. Each in turn is determining and determined. Prayer of God determined by the form of man, Prayer of man determined by the Form of God, are strophe and antistrophe of one and the same "confidential psalm." And this is the situation by virtue of which the mystic's soul is termed "his father's mother" as well as the situation described in Suhrawardī's Hymn to his Perfect Nature: "You are the Spirit which engendered me (my father in respect of the spirit that you formed), *and* you are the child of my thought (he who is engendered, who is created by my thought of you)."[41]

Here we have a reciprocal relationship as between two mirrors facing one another and reflecting the same image back and forth. It is this relationship which governs the mental iconography of theophanies. Of this we shall find two illustrations: in a *ḥadīth* meditated at length by many Ṣūfīs and in Ibn ʿArabī's own visionary experience.

VI THE "FORM OF GOD"

1. *The Ḥadīth of the Vision*

Let us now bear firmly in mind these two leitmotives: God's reply to Moses as recorded in the Koran: "Thou shalt not see me"—and the famous "*ḥadīth* of the vision" (*al-rū'yā*), dream vision or ecstatic vision, in which the Prophet bears witness: "I have seen my Lord in a form of the greatest beauty, as a youth with abundant hair, seated on the Throne of grace; he was clad in a garment of gold [or a green robe, according to a variant]; on his hair a golden mitre; on his feet golden sandals."[1] Refusal of vision and attestation of vision: the two motifs together form a *coincidentia oppositorum*. Further, the Image recurring both in the *ḥadīth* of prophetic vision and in the personal experience of Ibn 'Arabī is an Image of the *puer aeternus*, well known to psychologists as a symbol of the same *coincidentia oppositorum*.[2] And now a threefold question arises: *Who* is this Image? *Where* does it come from and what is its context? *What* degree of spiritual experience does its apparition announce, that is to say, what realization of being is effected in and by this Image?

A theologian such as al-Ghazālī is disarmed, perplexed, by such an Image, and *a fortiori* by a visionary experience of the Image, because with his "nominalist," agnostic conception of the image, he has no other recourse than to misinterpret it as a more or less inoffensive allegory,[3] and this precisely because he has no idea of the theophanism professed by Ibn 'Arabī. On the other hand, a disciple of Ibn ʿArabī, such as ʿAbd al-Karīm Jīlī, is all the more at his ease in commenting on it. He insists on the two fold dimension of the event: the full reality of the determinate Form and *hidden content* which can be embodied only in that form. He analyzes it as a *coincidentia oppositorum* which imposes upon us a homologation of the infinite in finite form, because such is the very law of being.[4] And the "Divine Face," the "Form of God" that is thus manifested—as we have seen above—is also the "imperishable Face" of the being to whom it is manifested, his Holy Spirit. Indeed, we must return at every step to this truth: What a man attains at the summit of his mystic experience is not, and cannot be, the Divine Essence in its undifferentiated unity. And that is why Ibn ʿArabī rejected the pretention of certain mystics who claimed "to become one with God."

What a human being attains in mystic experience is the "celestial pole" of his being, that is, his person as the person in whom and by whom the Divine Being manifested Himself to Himself in the origin of origins, in the World of Mystery, and through whom He made Himself known in the Form which is also the Form in which He knew Himself in that person. What he attains is the Idea or rather the "Angel" of his person, of which his present self is only the terrestrial pole; not, of course, the "guardian Angel" of orthodox theology, but an idea very close to the *Daēnā-fravashi* of Mazdaism, whose recurrence under other names in our mystics (the Angel Azrael, for example, of Jīlī, is most striking). A self-determination of the Divine Being was then the theophany constitutive of this human being's eternal individuality; in this theophany the Divine Being is totally *God,* but God as He is in and for this microcosm, *singulatim.* And if we designate this determination which occurred in the World of Mystery as the "Angel," then the vision of the Self, of the divine Alter Ego as theophanic vision, becomes, precisely, an angelophany. In the course of a secret dialogue, Ibn ʿArabī also heard the words: "Thou shalt not see me"[5] and yet he too came to see Him and recognize Him in the shadow of the mystic Temple. To dismiss the pretention of a mystic who defines the rank of the Perfect Man, the microcosmic realization of the Divine Being as an identification with the Divine Essence, is in no sense an indication of rationalism or "intellectualism"; such an attitude is by no means a negation of mystic experience, but merely an implicit rejection of a schema of mysticism which exoteric monotheism can accept. But does not the schema of unilateral monotheism undergo a decisive change as soon as mystic experience, experienced on each occasion as intimate dialogue between the Lover and the Beloved, postulates *on each occasion* an individuation intrinsic to the Divine Essence and homologous to its totality? In the last analysis the Prophet's vision and that of Ibn ʿArabī are the fulfilment of the desire which Suhrawardī formulated as a prayer addressed to his Perfect Nature (which engendered him and which he at the same time engendered, in their full reciprocal individuation): "May You show yourself to me in the most beautiful (or highest) of theophanies."

And now, in order to provide an iconographic context for the Image visualized both by the Prophet and by Ibn ʿArabī, it will be helpful to group several observations.

The splendor of the vision, the insistence on plastic beauty refer us to the feeling, prevalent throughout a vast area of Ṣūfism, that *Beauty* is the theophany par excellence. Here, it should be noted, we are dealing not with a purely aesthetic pleasure accompanied by a joyful tonality[6] but with the contemplation of human beauty as a *numinous*, sacral phenomenon which inspires fear and anguish by arousing a movement toward something which at once precedes and transcends the object in which it is manifested, something of which the mystic gains awareness only if he achieves the conjunction, the conspiration (σύμπνοια) of the spiritual and the sensory, constitutive of mystic love.[7] That is why the "*ḥadīth* of the vision" has been on the lips of so many Ṣūfīs down through the centuries, to the horror of Muʿtazilite and other theologians. And yet we find one of these theologians, the celebrated Jāḥiẓ (d. 250/864) admiring and explaining the fervor of the Christians by the fact that in the image of Christ they were able to worship their God in a human form similar to their own.[8]

This reflection of Jāḥiẓ opens up a vast perspective on iconography. There is indeed a remarkable comformity between the Image in the "*ḥadīth* of the vision" and the Image of the youthful Christ, *Christus iuvenis,* in which the Christianity of the first centuries represented Christ.[9] It is quite possible that the spiritual circles in which the *ḥadīth* made its appearance knew of this Christian iconography which, precisely, illustrates a theophanic conception according perfectly with that of our Spirituals, but like theirs entirely different from the official dogma of the Incarnation, which was to triumph. Of this "Form of God" as *Christus iuvenis* there are still many exquisite illustrations, notably the mosaics of Ravenna, which, it will be recalled, present a complex problem because they represent iconographically the transition from a theophanic to an incarnationist Christology.[10]

Very briefly we may say this: The theophanic conception (by no means limited to a few speculative scholars, but shared by all the circles in which the Apocrypha made their appearance) is that of an Apparition which is a shining of the Godhead through the mirror of humanity, after the manner of the light which becomes visible only as it takes form and shines through the figure of a stained-glass window. This union is perceived not on the plane of sensory data, but on the plane of the Light which transfigures them, that is to say, in "Imaginative Presence." The Godhead is in mankind as an Image is in a mirror. The *place* of this Presence is the consciousness of the individual believer, or more exactly, the theophanic Imagination invested in him. His *time* is *lived psychic* time. The Incarnation, on the other hand, is a hypostatic union. It occurs "in the flesh," and to mark this reality of the flesh, iconography abandoned the type of the *puer aeternus* (the young Orphic shepherd, the young Roman patrician) in favor of the mature man with the signs of differentiated virility. The Incarnation is a fact of history, which can be situated by historical co-ordinates; it is the meaning of history, of which it is itself the center. Its time is continuous *abstract psychic time,* the time by which calendars are reckoned. But there would be neither meaning nor truth in attempting to compute the date of an "event" such as the utterance to Enoch of the words: "Thou art the Son of Man."

Each theophany is a *new creation;* theophanies are discontinuous; their history is that of psychological individuality and has nothing to do with the sequence or causality of outward facts, which are without reality in themselves, that is, when abstracted from the subjects who experience them. The appreciation of theophanies presupposes a form of thought related to Stoic thought, which looks upon facts and events as mere attributes of the subject. What exists is the subject, whereas the "facts," apart from the subject, are "unreal." But for us who are caught in the trap of dialectics and historical causality, the facts are "objective reality." And the consciousness for which the historical fact of the Incarnation replaces the inner evidences of theophanies ought (unless it has given up trying, once and for all) to have solved the problem of the synchronism between subjective *qualificative* time and *quantitative* time of "objective" factual history.[11] When the concept of Incarnation was so laicized as to make way for a "social Incarnation," what remained was philosophies of history and the obsession with the "trend of history" which overwhelms us today with its mythology. It is not possible to make a philosophy of history, or even history, with theophanies or with the theophanic Imagination. The *Christos* of the theophanies knows no ἐνσάρκωσις nor Passion; he does not become a Pantokrator; he remains the *puer aeternus,* the *Christos Angelos,* the youth of the visions of the Prophet and of Ibn ʿArabī.

§ 1. *The* Ḥadīth *of the Vision*

All these distinctions are of capital importance. In any attempt to compare a non-Christian spirituality with Christianity, the first point to make clear is *what* Christianity is being spoken of. And all the more so as this iconography of Ṣūfism has its roots in the mental iconography of Shīʿism, in which the epiphany of the "Form of God" responds to the very concept of the Imām. And the whole secret of Shīʿism, its *raison d'être*—and by this I mean infinitely more than the "historical reasons" evoked in attempts to provide causal deductions or explanations of Shīʿism—this secret is first and foremost that there were minds that postulated the form of theophany constitutive of Imāmology,[12] just as there were minds that postulated a Christology which rejected the official Christology, and more than one feature of which is reproduced in Imāmology.

2. *Around the Mystic Kaʿaba*

In view of these premises and these contexts, what degree and what form of religious experience are announced by the apparition and visualization of an Image such as that of our *ḥadīth?*[13] Here let us once again recall the vision of the Temple in the realm of "Imaginative Presence" (above, p. 235), its significance, its function, and its persistence at all spiritual degrees: The Temple is entirely closed; only a column emerges from the wall, and this column is the interpreter, the hermeneut between the impenetrable and the mystic visionaries. It is homologated to the Black Stone encased in the material Temple of the Kaʿaba. But the Black Stone is a name for the "mystic Pole" and for all its manifestations. The interpreter of the impenetrable, the hermeneut of the Temple, is therefore the Pole (*Quṭb*), that is, the Holy Spirit (*Rūḥ al-Quds*), the Muḥammadic Spirit (*Rūḥ muḥammadī*) also sometimes identified with the Angel Gabriel, a fact which discloses the secret of prophetic Revelations since, as Ibn ʿArabī tells us, when the mystic visualizes a person who projects upon him the high knowledge he had been unable to attain, such a vision is in reality a vision of his own eternal hexeity, his celestial Pole, his "Angel."[14]

We now find Ibn ʿArabī in the shadow of the Temple of the Kaʿaba, the sensuous typification of the Temple contemplated in the Imagination. It is here that the prayer addressed by Suhrawardī to his Perfect Nature will be answered for Ibn ʿArabī. Our *shaikh* has already experienced a memorable encounter (upon which we have meditated in the first part of this book, Ch. II) in the shadow of the Kaʿaba, on a Night of the Spirit. While circumambulating the Temple he improvised aloud certain verses resonant with the melancholy of his doubts. Suddenly there emerged from the shadows the feminine Figure who was to be for him the earthly manifestation of *Sophia aeterna* (here there can be no question of establishing the chronology of these visions, but psychological analysis might well disclose a superposition of apparitional traits and figures).[15] The visionary event that I should like to evoke in conclusion of the present volume forms both the prelude and the mystic source of Ibn ʿArabī's great book *Spiritual Conquests of Mecca.* Our brief reference to it here will concern the identity of the Apparition as a visualization of the Image in which, because this "Form of God" is his origin and end, his eternal companion, Ibn ʿArabī's whole personal being is fulfilled. Here the situation and experience characterized by the recurrence of the Image of the Temple finds its *dénouement.* Becoming alive and transparent, the Temple reveals the secret it concealed, the "Form of God" which is the Self (or rather the Figure which eminently personifies it) and makes it known as the Mystic's divine *Alter Ego.* And the *dénouement* is this: the period of circumambulation around the Temple comes to an end, and together the two "companions" enter the Temple. (In connection with the following, the reader is referred to the texts translated or summarized in our Notes; they are of inestimable beauty and importance.)

This prelude—which is a prelude only because it is the culmination of an entire spiritual experience—takes the form of an extraordinarily lucid dialogue on the frontier of consciousness and transconsciousness between the human self and his Divine *Alter Ego*. Ibn 'Arabī is engaged in circumambulating the Ka'aba. Before the Black Stone he encounters the mysterious being whom he recognizes and designates as "the Evanescent Youth, the Silent Speaker, him who is neither living nor dead, the composite-simple, the enveloped-enveloping," all terms (with alchemical reminiscences) signifying the *coincidentia oppositorum*. At this moment the visionary is assailed by a doubt: "Might this processional be nothing other than the ritual Prayer of a living man around a corpse (the Ka'aba)?" The mystic youth replies: "Behold the secret of the Temple before it escapes."[16] And the visionary suddenly sees the stone Temple turn into a living being. He becomes aware of his companion's spiritual rank; he lowers his right hand; he wishes to become his disciple, to learn all his secrets; he will teach nothing else. But the Companion speaks only in symbols; his eloquence is all in enigmas. And at a mysterious sign of recognition the visionary is overwhelmed by such a power of love that he loses consciousness. When he comes to himself, his Companion reveals to him: "I am knowledge, I am he who knows and I am what is known."[17]

Thus the being who is the mystic's transcendent self, his divine *Alter Ego*, reveals himself, and the mystic does not hesitate to recognize him, for in the course of his quest, when confronting the mystery of the Divine Being, he has heard the command: "Look toward the Angel who is with you and who accomplishes the circumambulations beside you." He has learned that the mystic Ka'aba is the heart of being. It has been said to him: "The Temple which contains Me is your heart." The mystery of the Divine Essence is no other than the Temple of the heart, and it is around the heart that the spiritual pilgrim circumambulates.[18]

"Accomplish the circumambulations and follow my footsteps," the Youth now commands him. Then we hear an amazing dialogue, the meaning of which seems at first to defy all human expression. For how indeed is it possible to translate what two beings who *are each other* can say to each other: the "Angel" who is the divine *self*, and his other *self*, the "missionary" on earth, when they meet in the world of "Imaginative Presence"? The story which the visionary tells his confidant at his bidding is the story of his Quest, that is to say, a brief account of the inner experience from which grew the fundamental intuition of Ibn ʿArabī's theosophy.[19] It is this Quest that is represented by the circumambulations around the Temple of the "heart," that is, around the mystery of the Divine Essence. But the visionary is no longer the solitary self, reduced to his mere earthly dimension in the face of the inaccessible Godhead, for in encountering the being in whom the Godhead *is* his companion he knows that he himself is the secret of the Godhead (*sirr al-rubūbīya*), and it is their "syzygia," their twoness which accomplishes the circular processional: *seven* times, the *seven* divine Attributes of perfection in which the mystic is successively invested.[20]

The ritual then becomes as it were the paroxysm of that "Prayer of God" which is theophany itself, that is, revelation of the Divine Being to a man in the Form in which He reveals Himself to Himself in that man, and *eo ipso* in which He reveals that man to himself. And then comes the *dénouement:* "Enter into the Temple with me," the Mystic Youth commands. The hermeneut of the Mystery no longer contents himself with *translating* the Mystery, the impenetrable Temple. Once it is recognized *who* he is, he shows the way into the Temple. "I entered at once in his company, and suddenly he laid his hand on my chest and said to me: I am of the seventh degree in my capacity to embrace the mysteries of becoming, of the individual hexeity, and of the *where;* the Divine Being existentiated me as a fragment of the Light of Eve in the pure state."[21] In turn, the divine *Alter Ego,* the "Angel," reveals to his earthly self the mystery of his pre-eternal enthronement. In the Temple which encompasses them *both* is revealed the secret of the Adamic theophany which structures the Creator-Creature as a bi-unity: I am the Knower and the Known, the form *which shows* itself and the form *to which* it is shown—the revelation of the Divine Being to Himself, as determined in you and by you by your eternal hexeity, that is, as He knows Himself in you and through you in the form of the "Angel" who is the Idea, the personal theophany of your person, his eternal Companion.

It is this revelation that is meant when it is said that every theophany is as such an "angelophany."[22] One does not encounter, one does not see the Divine Essence; for it is itself the Temple, the Mystery of the heart; into which the mystic penetrates when, having achieved the microcosmic plenitude of the Perfect Man, he *encounters* the "Form of God" which is that of "His Angels," that is to say, the theophany constitutive of his being. We do not see the Light; it is what makes us see and what makes itself seen in the Form through which it shines. The "Temple" is the scene of theophany, the heart where the dialogue between Lover and Beloved is enacted, and that is why this dialogue is the Prayer of God. The theophany in the heart of the Temple is the answer to the Prayer addressed by Suhrawardī to his "Perfect Nature." It is the outcome of what, by way of contrasting it with the traditional idea of the "combat with the Angel," I have characterized in certain earlier studies as a "combat *for* the Angel": a homologation of the infinite in the finite, of the divine totality in the microcosm of the Perfect Man, and these two simultaneous but paradoxical truths—the divine refusal: "Thou shalt not see me" and the prophetic attestation: "I have contemplated my God in the most beautiful of forms."

EPILOGUE

Here perhaps we have gone as far as it is possible at this time to carry this study of the theophanic Imagination. What we have just analyzed offers us an exemplary and maximal instance of the virtue of that Creative Imagination which, in the Prologue to the second part of this book, we carefully distinguished from fantasy, describing it as the fulfillment of being in an Image and a transposition of the Image into being. It may be that in pursuing this meditation we have confidently allowed ourselves for a moment to be carried away by the flight of our mystic visionaries, only to fall back captive into the world that is imposed upon us. But if we even have energy enough to *create* our world, perhaps our creation will be, if not a desperate challenge, at least an anticipated consentment to the only greatness that our consciousness of a devastated spiritual universe still allows us. One of our contemporary philosophers characterizes the greatness I have in mind in the concluding lines of one of his finest books: "A soul has not the power to make itself immortal, but only to make itself worthy of immortality. . . . To have a soul is to live so that if it must perish its last cry . . . may justly be Desdemona's sigh from beyond the grave: O falsely, falsely murder'd!"[1]

Here we can see how imaginatively and spiritually disarmed we are in comparison with those Spirituals whose certainties we have evoked in the course of these pages. What we experience as an obsession with nothingness or as acquiescence in a nonbeing over which we have no power, was to them a manifestation of divine anger, the anger of the mystic Beloved. But even that was a real Presence, the presence of that Image which never forsook our Ṣūfīs. Saʿdī, one of the greatest poets of Persia, who was also a great mystic though not among the greatest, expressed this best in a few poignant verses:

Epilogue

If the sword of your anger puts me to death,
My soul will find comfort in it.
If you impose the cup of poison upon me,
My spirit will drink the cup.
When on the day of Resurrection
I rise from the dust of my tomb,
The perfume of your love
Will still impregnate the garment of my soul.
For even though you refused me your love,
You have given me a *vision of You*
Which has been the confidant of my hidden secrets.

NOTES AND APPENDICES

Author's Note: The notes are numerous and often have the character of appendices. They have not been enlarged out of a sense of vain erudition. They include observations and citations that could not be included in the text without distorting the architecture of the book. Many of these texts are translated for the first time here; they form the basis of the exposition. The reader should not neglect to read them.

PART ONE

SYMPATHY AND THEOPATHY

CHAPTER I
DIVINE PASSION AND COMPASSION

1. ὃν δύναται φυτὸν ὑμνεῖν. See *Catalogue des manuscrits alchimiques grecs*, VI, 148; Πρόκλου περὶ τῆς καθ' Ἕλληνας ἱερατικῆς τέχνης (the translation cited here is taken from *Recherches de science religieuse*, 1933, pp. 102–06). The original Greek of this text of Proclus was discovered by J. Bidez and published in the *Catalogue;* it was translated into Latin in the Renaissance by Marsilio Ficino (II, 868 ff. of the Paris edn., 1641). "Nowhere else does the last of the ancient Platonists speak of a return of the soul to God, of mystic chains and of theurgy, citing so many examples borrowed, as we see, from the lives of animals, plants, and minerals" (*Catalogue*, VI, 142). The *hieratic science*, placed under the twofold patronage of Plato and of the *Oracula Chaldaica*, originates in the "hieratic" or "angelic" souls, the divine messengers (ἄγγελοι) sent to earth to give us an idea of the supernatural spectacles they have beheld in their pre-existence (cf. the idea of the angelic essence of the Imām in Shīʿite Gnosis). As for the method and principle of this science, which are similar to those of the dialectic of love, they follow from the knowledge that "sympathy attracts just as like acts on like . . . similitude creates a bond capable of attaching beings to one another. . . . The hieratic art makes use of the filiation which attaches beings here below to those on high, so bringing it about that the gods come down toward us and illumine us, or rather that we approach them, discovering them in theopties and theophanies capable of uniting our thought to theirs in the silent hymns of meditation."
2. Ibid., VI, 148. Proclus mentions still other cases. Thus, for example "the *lotus* manifests its affinity and sympathy with the

sun. Before the appearance of the sun's rays, its blossom is closed; it opens slowly at sunrise, unfolds as the sun rises to the zenith, and folds again and closes as the sun descends. What difference is there between the human manner of praising the sun by moving the mouth and lips, and that of the lotus which unfolds its petals? They are its lips and this is its natural hymn" (ibid., VI, 149).

3. Here we must think of the mystic chains or series which explain and justify the prescriptions of the hieratic and theurgic art. Each of these series "is recognizable by resemblances, affinities, and special sympathies, which give rise to kinds of prayer, true prayer being an approach and an assimilation of the lower being toward the god who is the director and patron of his series, and thus we see parallel hierarchies of angels, demons, men, animals, plants, and minerals vying with one another in their religious ascents" (ibid., VI, 144). In this short treatise, Proclus borrows most of his examples from the "heliacal chain"; cf. our book, *Terre céleste et Corps de résurrection: de l'Iran mazdéen à l'Iran Shīʿite*, p. 81, n. 15.
4. We have in mind Abraham Heschel's *Die Prophetie*, an excellent and original phenomenological study, a part of which we ourselves translated in *Hermès*, 3e série, No. 3, pp. 78–110. What is said of it here should not be taken as criticism; the author was not concerned with a parallel phenomenology of mystical religion and consequently dealt only with one aspect of mysticism, the aspect providing the antithesis required by his analysis of the prophetic consciousness in Israel. But if, as we do here, one deals with other regions of mysticism as experienced precisely in a religion the principle of which involves a prophetology, the relations between prophetology and mysticism are radically modified. The antithesis is no longer valid, the same categories become common to both (e.g., in particular, the *Miʿrāj*, the celestial assumption of the Prophet mentioned in Koranic revelation and subsequently meditated upon and experienced by Ṣūfism over a period of many centuries as the prototype of mystic experience).
5. Cf. Heschel, p. 142.

6. Ibid., especially pp. 27–36, 113–19, 130 ff., 139, 142, 144–47, 161, 168–76. Heschel rightly observes (p. 141) that, inversely to the *dialogical* prophetic situation, the relation between Allah and man takes on, in the theology of orthodox Islam, the form of a monologue on the part of God, a unilateral power so incomparable that the Muʿtazilites reject all the attributes as anthropomorphisms. It is superfluous to state that the mystic theosophy we shall be speaking of here is far removed from Islamic orthodoxy, in which the theory of Names and Attributes professed by an Ibn ʿArabī can only inspire the keenest alarm. Furthermore, it would be irrelevant to maintain that Allah is too exalted ever to become the "father of mankind"; for that is a "paternalistic" notion alien to all *nuptial mysticism;* the divine image which here invests consciousness and "transcends transcendence" is not that of the Father, but that of the *Beloved* (as in the Song of Songs).
7. The two modes of teaching, that of Ibn ʿArabī and that of Jalāluddīn Rūmī, correspond to two psychologically different types, but, as we have pointed out, it would be a mistake to contrast them in regard to content or inner experience. And indeed the greatest commentators on the *Mathnawī* (notably Walī Muḥammad Akbarābādi and Bahr al-ʿUlūm in eighteenth-century India and Mullā Hādī Subzavārī in nineteenth-century Iran, all authors of voluminous commentaries in Persian) refer frequently to the work of Ibn ʿArabī, who plays an at least equal role in their spiritual life. As to the precise meaning in which the term *Fedeli d'amore* should be taken in connection with Ṣūfism, see the indications given in the introduction to the present book. We owe to Hellmut Ritter a first survey of the successive representations of this love-mysticism in Islam (cf. "Philologika VII," pp. 84–89); to exploit the identified sources a large book would be needed and large amounts of unpublished material would have to be worked over. The principal names to be remembered are: Suhrawardī (d. 587/1191), Rūzbehān Baqlī of Shīrāz (d. 606/1209, cf. the edition of his Persian works cited above in n. 7 of the Introduction), Aḥmad Ghazālī, Fakhruddīn ʿIrāqī, Sadruddīn Qunyawī, Jāmī, etc. We have seen that Ibn ʿArabī is not only

al-Shaikh al-Akbar (Doctor Maximus); he also bears the title of honor Ibn Iflātūn, "son of Plato," or the Platonist.

8. See primarily Asín Palacios, *La Escatología musulmana en la Divina Comedia* (1919), a work which in its day aroused a furore among Romance scholars; see the appendix to the second edition, "Historia y crítica de una polémica." Thirty years later Enrico Cerulli's great work *Il "Libro della Scala" e la questione delle fonti arabo-spagnole della Divina Commedia* provided decisive confirmation of Asín's theses and intimations. See also Luigi Valli, *Il Linguaggio segreto di Dante e dei "Fedeli d'amore,"* in which the symbolist thesis confronts the traditional conceptions of positive philology; we shall have occasion here to cite Valli's arguments, though without allowing ourselves to be imprisoned in the dilemma that may result from them.
9. Cf. Max Scheler, *The Nature of Sympathy*, tr. Heath.
10. We must also stress the great importance in this connection of the work of Étienne Souriau, an eminent contemporary philosopher. As an indication of the "sympathy" between our present investigations and his work and in token of our indebtedness to Souriau, I shall refer, in particular, to three of his books: *Les différents modes d'existence; Avoir une âme, essai sur les existences virtuelles; L'Ombre de Dieu.* I shall briefly indicate a series of motifs, each of which tends to confirm my own thesis. As a prelude let us take the reminder that though it is not in man's power to prove the existence of God, he is at least able to "make himself capable of God" (cf. *Ombre*, pp. 119–25). The only *proof* accessible to man is then to accomplish His presence. This does not mean to make himself receptive to a God such as that professed by dogmatic theologies, to begin by postulating His existence and go on to prove it rationally by endowing Him with attributes. The only divine reality to be postulated is that which leaves man the responsibility of making it actual or non-actual by his own mode of being. We shall see that the "secret of divine suzerainty" (*sirr al-rubūbīya*) analyzed below, the secret which is your *self* (Sahl Tustarī), confronts the *Fedele d'amore* with precisely this responsibility, of which Ibn ʿArabī is reminded on a Night of the Spirit in Mecca (Ch. II, §1, below),

postulates "the directed oblative attitude" (*Ombre*, p. 125) which is a safeguard at once against the narcissistic attitude and against "the panic dissolution of the person in an impersonal totality." As for the transition from the notion of *virtual existence* (*Modes*, pp. 83 ff.) to that of *supraexistence* as an *act* (as the "fact of transcendence" which alone invests with real existence the problematic transcendent being to whom it bears witness and for whom it answers), I believe that there is in the mental operation of *ta'wīl* (etymologically, the exegesis which *carries back* and sublimates an image, concept, person, or event to its original secret, *bāṭin*, significance) something which corresponds to this act (hence the parallel course of the *ta'wīl* and of the *anaphora* which M. Souriau describes, endowing that old liturgical term with an entirely new meaning). Very striking too is the equally new meaning he gives to angelology (*Ombre*, pp. 133–44, 152, 153, 260, 280–82, 318), which confirms us in intimations that came to us in the course of earlier angelological investigations. First of all, we find a refutation of the view that modern philosophy began with the disappearance of the Angel from philosophy (we should then have to exclude Leibniz, Christian Wolf, and Fechner from modern philosophy). Then we encounter the observation that the *modern* idea of the Angel is embodied in statements such as those alluding to the "Angel of a work," that is to say, its "spiritual form," its "transcendent content," its "transnatural" substance, which, though it cannot be found in the sensuous elements of the work, provides an intimation of the virtualities which transcend them. To these virtualities we are in every instance called upon to respond, that is, either to assume them or to reject them, in short, all the "spiritual powers" of that work ("the invisible aspect of a painting, the inaudible aspect of a symphony"), which are not simply the artist's message but which have been transferred by him to this work and which he himself received from "the Angel." To respond to "the *Angel of a work*" is to "render oneself capable of the entire content of its *aura* of love" (*Ombre*, p. 167). Ibn 'Arabī's dialectic of love (analyzed below, Ch. II, § 2) carries us to this same vision of the invisible Beloved (still virtual) in the visible Beloved who alone can manifest Him, an invisible whose actuality depends on an Active Imagination which makes physical love and spiritual love "conspire" in a single mystic love. It is the "angelic function of a being" (*Ombre*, pp. 161, 171) which predetermines the notion of theophanic figure or form (*mazhar*) in the entire school of Ibn ʿArabī as in the speculative Imāmology of Ismailism. The mediation of the Angel tends to preserve us from a twofold idolatry, which forever threatens us (whereas inversely the monotheistic dogmatists would tend to find this same danger in the mediation of the Angel), and this is the foremost reason why the idea of the Angel is so imperiously necessary (*Ombre*, pp. 170–72). The twofold peril: either the impasse, the failure, which immobilizes us in an object without transcendence (it may be a God, a dogma), or else a misunderstanding of this transcendence which creates a gulf between it and the object of love and condemns us to asceticism with all its furies and rejections. The idea of the *Fravashi-Daēnā* in Zoroastrianism, the dialectic of love in Ibn ʿArabī, the sophiology of the creative Feminine and the birth of the spiritual Child, the simultaneity of the *Theos agnostos* (unknowable God) and of the determinate proper Name which is as it were His Angel—all these are homologous expressions tending not to annul, but to compensate for this infinitely nostalgic gulf; their experiential content accords with what Souriau has analyzed with so much penetration, distinguishing *unconditional investiture* (the trap of all metaphysical idolatries) and *functional investiture* (*Ombre*, 170–72): The angelic function, the Angel's mediation, which precisely liberates us for undiscovered, unforeseeable, unsuspected transcendences and prevents us from becoming immobilized in definite, definitive happening; it is the same contrast as between the idea of Incarnation (a unique event, situated in history) and the idea of theophanies (forever inexhaustible events of the soul). Finally, when M. Souriau expresses his belief that the only idea of Creation which cuts across all the philosophical aporias is the idea of the creative act as a "universal emancipation of being, an acquiescence in each being's exercise of his right to existence in the measure of his capacity" (*Ombre*, p. 284), how can one fail to see a consonance with the idea of the Divine Nostalgia, the Sigh of Compassion (*Nafas Raḥmānī*), which frees from their sadness the divine Names yearning in their pure virtuality for the concrete being that will manifest them (§ 2, below)? And when we look for the existential foundation of this experience of the Divine as an unknown God yearning to become known to Himself in and through the creatures which know him, do we not find it typified in the wish (whether cry or sigh) of a character in Gabriel Marcel: "Oh, to be known as one is!" (*Modes*, p. 169). Such is the sigh of God in the solitude of His unknownness, from which He is delivered by the beings to whom He is revealed and through whom He exists (cf. below, § 3, the mystic meaning of Abraham's hospitality). This brings us back to the beginning: it is not in my power to elicit an answer from Him, but I can answer Him, I can experience in my being a modification "of which He is the reason (*ratio*, in the sense of proportion), and that perhaps is the only way in which we can bear witness for Him, in which we can be in a relation of action and passion with Him" (ibid.). It is this very relationship which we shall analyze further on as a human-divine *sympathism*. —This note is at once too long and too short for what we have to say. The constructive thinking of Étienne Souriau inspires us with gratitude and encouragement in our effort to make the themes of oriental spirituality available to our present-day world.

11. *Man lā ṭajāsaru naḥwahu'l-khawāṭir*, "He whom the boldness of thought cannot attain," the epithet by which He is always alluded to in Ismailian theosophy.

12. Cf. R. Strothmann, *Gnosis-Texte der Ismailiten*, IX, 1, p. 80 of the Arabic text. For indeed the name Al-Lāh refers not to the Super-being, the unknowable Principle, but to the *Deus revelatus*, that is, the First Archangel (*al-Malak al-muqaddas*, First Intelligence, *al-Mubdaʿ al-awwal*, the Protokistos); for *ilāh* = *wilāh*, see also the *Mathnawī* of Jalāluddīn Rūmī, IV, 1169, ed. Nicholson, VIII, 156. Lane (*An Arabic-English Lexicon*, I, 83) also mentions the following derivation as suggested by certain Arab grammarians: *Ilāh* (Hebrew *Eloha*), the deriva-

tion of which is uncertain and of which, according to some authorities, the original form is *wilāh*, "meaning that mankind yearn towards him who is thus called, seeking protection or aid in their wants and humble themselves in their afflictions, like as every infant yearns towards its mother." But Ismailian theosophy does not (or not only) have in mind afflicted humanity yearning for God, but the revealed God Himself (the only God of whom man can speak), thus not only the God for whom men sigh, but the God who is himself a Sigh, the primordial Archangel, nostalgic for knowledge of his Originator, the *Mubdiʿ*, who is unknowable to him except as knowledge of self, since he is precisely that revelation of the *Mubdiʿ* to Himself (*ism al-ilāhīya ushtuqqa lahu mina' l-walah alladhī huwa al-taḥayyur fī idrāk mubdiʿihi*). This etymology is confirmed by another (see the following note) and by one of the *Munājāt* (Confidential Psalms) of Mu' ayyad Shīrāzī.

13. Strothmann, IX, 1, p. 80: *wa* (*ushtuqqa lahu*) *mina' l-hānnīya* (=*al-ḥānnīya*) *allatī hiya al-ishtiyāq ilà' l-idrāk, wa' l-ʿajz yamnaʿ uhu ʿan dhalika li-jalālat mubdiʿ ihi:* "The name of the Godhead (*ilāhīya, ulhānīya*) is derived from *al-hānnīya*), which is nostalgia for knowledge, since his weakness deters him from it in view of the sublimity of his originator." Here it would be necessary to reproduce the Arabic script, which, despite the reservations of philology, provides *ideographic* evidence. Be that as it may, Ismailian theosophy could have found no better way of formulating the notion of the "pathetic God" or of orienting us toward the divine mystery which Ibn ʿArabī designates as *Nafas Raḥmānī.*

14. Ibid.: *ism al-ilāhīya lā yaqaʿ illā ʿalà al-mubdaʿ al-awwal,* "the name of the Godhead applies only to the Protokistos," that is, to the First Intelligence (just as the attributes apply only to the *mubda ʿāt,* that is, to the Cherubinic Intelligences which emanate from that Archangel-Logos).

15. *Fuṣūṣ al-Ḥikam* II, 61 and 245–46. (We refer here to the edition of A. E. Affifi [Abu' l-ʿAlā ʿAffīfī]. *Fuṣūṣ* I = Ibn ʿArabī's text; *Fuṣūṣ* II = the excellent commentary in which Mr. Affifi has combined numerous texts with judicious observations. See also

the *Iṣṭilāḥāt* (Lexicon) of ʿAbd al-Razzāq Kāshānī, s.v. *tajallī*, pp. 174–75.) Three degrees of theophany may be distinguished. The first is a theophany of which it is possible to speak only allusively; that is the epiphany to itself of the Divine Essence as absolute monad in its solitude. In the mystery of its undifferentiated oneness (*aḥadīya*) no description nor qualification can attain it, since it is absolute being, pure and simple, and everything that is other than being is nonbeing, pure and simple (this degree is also called the degree of the "Cloud," cf. Kāshānī, Lexicon, s.v. *ʿamāʾ*, pp. 157–58). The second theophany (*tajallī thānī*) is more precisely the totality of theophanies in which and through which the divine Essence is revealed to itself under the forms of the divine Names (*asmāʾ ilāhīya*), that is to say, in the forms of beings in respect of their existence in the secrecy of the absolute mystery (*fī bāṭin al-ghayb al-muṭlaq*). The third is theophany in the forms of concrete individuals (*tajallī shuhūdī*), which lend concrete and manifest existence to the divine Names. —Here, it goes without saying, we have given only a brief survey of a context requiring a long exposition.

16. Cf. in *3 Enoch; or, the Hebrew Book of Enoch*, ed. Odeberg, 2nd part, Ch. XLVIII, pp. 160–64, the processional of the divine Names and their aspect as angelic hypostases.

17. Cf. A. E. Affifi, *The Mystical Philosophy of Muḥyīd-Dīn Ibn al-ʿArabī*, pp. 35–40; ibid., p. 41 on the divine Names interpreted as *Ḥaḍarāt* (Divine Presences), and pp. 43 ff. on the attribute al-Samīʿ (the Audient) alluded to in the Koran verse of the Night of the Covenant (*a-lastu birabbikum?* Am I not thy Lord?); in this dialogue held in pre-eternity, God is at once the Speaker and the Hearer, the Questioner and the Answerer, addressing the question to Himself, that is, revealing Himself to Himself in the intelligible forms of the Multiple (this became the foundation of the concept of the *aʿyān thābita*, the external hexeities, cf. below).

18. Concerning the eternal archetypal individuations which are the correlata of the divine Names, see Affifi, *Mystical Philosophy*, pp. 47–53. ʿAbd al-Razzāq Kāshānī (Commentary on the *Fuṣūṣ*, p. 181) describes the process in question (commentary on two

lines of the poem occurring in *Fuṣūṣ* I, 143: "We have enabled Him to manifest Himself in us, while He gave us being." In pre-eternity, before He brought us into existence, we were beings in His Essence (His Ipseity), that is, our own essences were individuations of essential states or conditions of the godhead. The Divine Being was then our epiphanic form (*maẓhar, majlà*), the form of our multiple individualities, which means that we appeared in Him. We were His pre-eternal beings; we were not *with* Him, because we were His very own being, the being which He was. We were His organs, His hearing, His vision, His tongue, in short, the virtual individuations of His Names. We were also "times" in Him, by virtue of the anteriority or posteriority of our theophanic condition (*maẓharīya*), that is, of the order in which we were called to be His *maẓāhir* (epiphanic forms). Inversely, in our state of concrete existence, exhaled by the Sigh of His existentiating Compassion (*Nafas Raḥmānī*), we are His apparitional form, and He is our vision, hearing, etc. Creation is not the separation or projection of an extra-divine being, nor emanation in the strictly Neoplatonic sense, but theophany, differentiation by increasing incandescence within being. Far from abrogating the dialogical situation, it is precisely this which guarantees that our dialogue is not an illusion. Just as in pre-eternity our latent existences were the organs of His being, it is this same Divine Being who moves the states of our being. Cf. also below, notes 67–69.

19. *Fuṣūṣ*, I, 112 and II, 128.
20. *Compassio quam Graeci sympatheiam vocant* (Priscian).
21. Hence *mawjūd* (the existent) and *marḥūm* (he who is an object of compassion, *Raḥma*) are interchangeable terms (though of course we should avoid all unfortunate puns on the current use of the term *marḥūm* in reference to the dead, such as the "late" or "dear departed").
22. *Fuṣūṣ* I, 177 ff.; II, 243–44. This divine Compassion takes on two aspects; one is synonymous with the gift of being which the Godhead bestows on beings in accordance with what they are in their eternal individualities; this is the liberating Compassion which acquiesces in their right to existence ("the di-

vine *Nutus*, the Yes which suffices to permit all possibles to take form," Étienne Souriau), which is in the strict sense *Raḥmat al-imtinān;* and there is the Compassion which God grants His worshipers by reason of their acts (the Muʿ tazilite doctrine of divine justice) or in general the dispensation of spiritual perfections to believers; this is called *Raḥmat al-wujūb* (whence the differentiation of the divine Names *al-Raḥmān* and *al-Raḥīm*) cf. *Fuṣūṣ* I, 151 ff. (Solomon was endowed with both), and II, 205–07; Kāshānī, Lexicon, s.v. *Raḥmān, Raḥma, Raḥīm,* pp. 170–71.

23. Here we touch on a conception central to the metaphysics of Ibn ʿArabī (the conciseness of our text makes it necessary to explain certain points which are merely hinted at and which might otherwise provoke misunderstandings). Just as the breath exhaled by man undergoes the formative action of articulate syllables and words, the Breath of the Compassionate One (*Nafas al-Raḥmān*), in exhaling the Words (*Kalimāt*) which are beings, undergoes the form demanded by their pre-eternal essence. What fashions them (active) is likewise that which is fashioned (passive) in them. "God described Himself by the Compassionate Sigh (*Nafas Raḥmānī*). But that which is qualified by a quality necessarily embodies all the implications of that quality. . . . Accordingly the Divine Sigh received (underwent, suffered) all the forms of the world. It is their material substance (*jawhar hayūlānī*); it is nothing other than Nature itself" (*Fuṣūṣ* I, 143–44). "Let him who wishes to know the Divine Sigh know the world, for whoever knows himself knows his Lord who is manifested in it; in other words, the world is made manifest in the Sigh of Compassion by which God (by exhaling them) appeased the sadness of the divine Names. . . ; God counted to Himself through what He existentiated in His Sigh, for the first effect of this Sigh was accomplished in Himself" (*Fuṣūṣ*, I, 145) *Nafs* (ἄνεμος, *anima*) and *nafas* (*animus, suspirium*) come from the same root in Arabic as in Latin. Moreover, *nafs* and *rūḥ* (*anima* and *spiritus*) are both a subtile, diaphanous substance, hence the transmission of the *rūḥ* to the body by means of a blowing (by the Creator Himself in the case of

Adam, by the Angel in the case of Jesus). The Koran, however, says nothing of a universal spiritual substance (*jawhar rūḥānī ʿāmm*). Mr. Affifi regards the notion of πνοή in the *Corpus hermeticum* as equivalent to *Nafas Raḥmānī* (*Fuṣūṣ* II, 192–93). But does the *Corpus hermeticum* know the Divine Sadness (*ishtiyāq, ḥānnīya*)? Dā'ūd Qayṣarī (ibid., II, 194) has the following to say of the notion of Nature as universal Energy: "The relation between universal Nature (*tabī ʿat kullīya*) and the *Nafas Raḥmānī* is similar to the relation between the specific form and the universal form (*jism kullī*), or of the determinate (*mu ʿayyan*) body with the body in general." It should be noted that the concept of Nature here extends far beyond the implications of our *physics*, since it also includes all the beings which are not encompassed in elementary Nature.

"Nature is in reality nothing other than the Sigh of Compassion. . . . The relation of Nature to *Nafas Raḥmānī* is analogous to the relation of specific forms to the thing in which they are manifested. . . . *Nafas Raḥmānī* is the substance in which flower the forms of material and spiritual being. . . . The case of Adam (in whom this Breath was instilled) is the symbol of the creation of the entire cosmos [cf. *Fuṣūṣ* II, 328, the luminous, *nūrānī, spiritus divinus, Nafas ilāhī, Rūḥ ilāhī*]. Physical bodies are manifested in the material cosmos when the Breath penetrates the material substance which is the receptacle of the corporeal forms. Similarly, the Spirits of Light, which are the separate Forms, are manifested by the propagation of the Breath in all spiritual substances. And the accidents are manifested by the propagation of the Breath in accidental Nature, which is the place of theophany (*maẓhar*). Thus there are two kinds of propagation: one in the world of bodies, another in the world of spirits and accidents. The first operates upon a hylic material substance (*jahwar hayūlānī maddī*), the second on an immaterial substance (*jawhar ghayr maddī*)" *Fuṣūṣ* II, 334–35.

Moreover, it may be said that the Compassion (*raḥma*) extends to God Himself. In opposition to the common conception, God is not only Compassionate (*rāḥim*); He is also the object of His own Compassion (*marḥūm*) because since the name is identical to the thing named, the multiple divine Names *are* Himself, and He is One: whereas the Divine Compassion satisfies their sadness aspiring to the essences that manifest them concretely, it is with Himself that God "*com-patit*" (cf. *Fuṣūṣ* I, 119 and II, 142). That is why the concept of a *creatio ex nihilo* vanishes, giving way to the notion of liberation. The existence which God confers upon the eternal Possibles is itself this *Nafas Raḥmānī*; hence the use of the word Compassion (*raḥma, Nafas al-Raḥmān, Nafas Raḥmānī*) in the sense of existence (cf. note 21, above); *fa-kullu mawjūdin marḥūmun*, then every existent is as such an object of this Compassion, but each in its turn becomes a *Rāḥim*, a compassionate subject (cf. below, § 3), and that is the human-divine *sympathesis* (*Fuṣūṣ* II, 20 and n. 26 below). Kāshānī devotes a long article in his Lexicon (p. 182) to this central conception, the feminine, maternal aspect of the Godhead, its creative energy. He points out—and this is of extreme interest—the concordance between this conception and that of the dominant Light (*Nūr qāhir, Lux victorialis*) among the Ishrāqīyūn, the theosophists of Light, the disciples of Suhrawardī (who derived it from the Zoroastrian *Xvarnah*), and shows that there is not even any need to consider acts unaccompanied by consciousness in a separate category, since even a mineral has an occult consciousness (*shu 'ūr fī' l-bāṭin*). Asín Palacios laid the groundwork for a possible investigation of this notion ("Ibn Masarra y su escuela," *Obras escogidas*, I, 148–49), which he relates to the influence in Islam of Pseudo-Empedocles, which extended to others than Ibn ʿArabī (e.g. in Ibn Gabirol). To avoid all "materialist" confusion, we must bear well in mind the descending scale of five meanings implied by the term "matter": (1) The spiritual matter common to the increate and to the creature (*ḥaqīqat al-ḥaqā' iq*). (2) The spiritual matter (*al-ʿunsur al-a ʿẓam*) common to all created beings, both spiritual and corporeal (*Nafas Raḥmānī*). (3) The matter that is common to all bodies, celestial or sublunar. (4) The physical matter—ours—common to all sublunar bodies. (5) The artificial matter common to all accidental figures. Whence we can clearly understand the hierarchy of principles: (1) Spiritual matter. (2) Intelligence. (3) Soul. (4) Celestial matter. (5) Corporeal matter (that of our physics).

24. On this twofold, active and passive, aspect of the Divine Names, cf. Affifi, *Mystical Philosophy*, pp. 46 and 53. (A comparison would be in order with the twofold aspect of the "cosmogonic Eros" in the *Ishrāq* metaphysic of Suhrawardī: *qahr* and *maḥabba*, loving domination and loving submission, homologous to *rubūbīya* and *'ubūdīya*, cf. the preceding note); compare also with the degrees (*ḥudūd*) of the esoteric hierarchy of Ismailism, each of which is simultaneously the limit (*ḥadd*), the guide and awakener of the lower degree, and the limited (*maḥdūd*) in relation to the degree next higher. —Thus the structure of each being is represented as an *unus ambo*, its totality being constituted by its being in its divine creative dimension (*taḥaqquq*) and in its creatural dimension (*takhalluq*); neither the *one* that is *two* nor the *two* that are *one* can be lost, for they exist only insofar as they form an essential interdependent whole (*ta 'alluq*). This is not a "dialectic"; it is the foundation of the *unio mystica* as *unio sympathetica*.

25. Years ago (1938–39) we devoted an entire lecture to the dramatic experience which the discovery of the *significatio passiva* was for the young Luther (still under the influence of Tauler's mysticism). In the presence of the Psalm verse *In justitia tua libera me*, he experienced a movement of revolt and despair: what can there be in common between this attribute of justice and *my* deliverance? And such was his state of mind until the young theologian Martin Luther perceived in a sudden flash (and his entire personal theology was to result from this experience) that this attribute must be understood in its *significatio passiva*, that is to say, *thy* justice whereby we are made into just men, *thy* holiness whereby we are hallowed, etc. (see summary in *Annuaire de l École des Hautes Études, Section des Sciences Religieuses*, 1939, pp. 99–102). Similarly in the mystic theosophy of Ibn 'Arabī, the divine attributes are qualifications that we impute to the Divine Essence not as convention might bid us to postulate it, but as we experience it in ourselves. Here

we wish merely to suggest a parallel which, for lack of space, we cannot discuss in detail.

26. *Fuṣūṣ* I, 178 and II, 250, n. 8 (also Kāshānī's Commentary, pp. 225–26): "There is no point in asking God to give you something. That is the God you have created in your faith, He is you and you are He. You must fulfil (*tataḥaqqaq*) yourself as much as you can *through* the attributes of divine perfection, among them Compassion. This does not mean that you will become God one fine day, for you are *this* God in reality, that is to say, one form among the forms of God, one of His theophanies. When Compassion (*sympatheia*) arises in you and through you, show it to others. You are at once Compassionate (*rāḥim*) and object of Compassion (*marḥūm, significatio passiva*), and that is how your essential unity with God is achieved" (II, 251). "Compassion is in reality a relation originating in the Compassionate One. It postulates its object as soon as it begins to operate (*rāḥima*). But He who existentiates it in its object (*marḥūm*) does not do so in order through it to have compassion for this object; he does so in order that he, in whom and through whom the compassion is brought into being, should through it be Compassionate. . . . The Compassionate One is what he is only because Compassion is brought into being through him. One who is without taste for mysticism or spiritual experience does not dare to say that he is identical to Compassion or to the divine attribute. He says: neither identical nor different" (I, 179). "When God sympathizes with one of His servants, this means that He causes Compassion to exist in him, that is, through him (*significatio passiva!*), so that he becomes capable of sympathizing with other creatures. Thus the passive object of compassion (*marḥūm*) becomes its active subject (*rāḥim*). God does not take him as an object of Compassion, but invests him with this divine attribute, whereby he experiences compassion for others. This is manifestly the case with the Perfect among the gnostics" (II, 252). Cf. the fine commentary of Dā'ūd Qayṣarī (cit. ibid., II, 253): "The vassal is thus qualified by the attribute of his Lord. He becomes the

agent of Compassion (*rāḥim*), whereas he had been its *patiens* (*marḥūm*)." Here we find a relationship of reversibility and simultaneity, *fāʿil-munfaʿil:* and here also we find the seeds of the idea of the creative Feminine (Ch. II, § 3, below). The same will apply to all the divine attributes of activity or operation (*ṣifāt al-afʿāl*). Let us further note that though embracing the totality of the Names, Compassion differs from each one of the many divine Names, which are attributes by which are qualified the existents, the *Ideae* (*maʿānī*) that are epiphanized in them. The meaning assumed by the manifestation (*ẓuhūr*) of Compassion in the forms of the divine Names is the epiphany of these Names in the forms of beings, proportionally to the aptitude and receptivity of these forms, *each* divine Name being an epiphanic form of the total being, that is, of the universal Divine Compassion (cf. II, 253–54, n. 11). Just as each name relates to a distinct essence, so each divine Name is an essence in itself, distinct from the essences of the other Names, and relates to a different state, though all have also a unique reference: the Divine Essence which they name. That is what Abu'l-Qāsim ibn Qasī al-Andalūsī meant when he said that each divine Name taken in itself is named with the *totality* of the Names (II, 254, n. 13); it is in this sense that we here and elsewhere employ the term *kathenotheism.*

27. Cf. *Fuṣūṣ* II, 249 *ad* I, 178. Authentic prayer expresses the praying subject's virtualities of being, that is, what is demanded by the very nature of his being; in other words, its purpose is that the divine Name, whose form (*maẓhar*) it is his mission to be, should be invested in him and fulfilled in him. To take cognizance of this virtuality is to cause it to become prayer (that is the meaning of *duʿā bi'l-ḥāl, bi'l-istiʿdād,* cf. *Fuṣūṣ* II, 21–22 *ad* I, 60). The extreme case is that in which the mystic achieves awareness of his own "eternal individuality" (*ʿayn thābita*), with the infinite succession of his states; then he knows himself as God knows him (cf. Affifi, *Mystical Philosophy,* p. 53), or rather his knowledge of himself becomes identified with God's knowledge of him. In regard to this eternal virtuality of each being and to the idea that the prayer which states it is already

answered (because his prayer is his very being, his being *is* this prayer, the prayer of his divine Name), it would be quite inadequate to formulate the question in terms of determinism. Quite correctly Mr. Affifi esteems it preferable to invoke Leibniz' idea of pre-established harmony (II, 22). Then we shall understand that authentic prayer operates neither as a successful request nor as an effect resulting from a chain of causality, but rather as a *sympatheia* (like the prayer of the heliotrope which "asks" nothing, it *is* this sympathy in being what it is). On pre-established harmony and sympathy, cf. C. G. Jung, "Synchronicity: An Acausal Connecting Principle," pars. 937 ff. See also Ch. V below.

28. *Fuṣūṣ* II, 64, n. 6 *ad* I, 83.
29. Cf. note 27 above, *in fine*.
30. *Al-Ilāh al-makhlūq fī'l-i'tiqādāt.* This is a theme (*khalq al-Ḥaqq fī'l-i'tiqād*, creation of the Divine Being in the faith) which recurs frequently in the *Fuṣūṣ* (cf. II, 65–67 on the line: "In knowing Him, we give Him being," or: "Al-lāh is a designation for him who understands the allusion.") Cf. also below, Ch. III, § 3.
31. *Fuṣūṣ* I, 178 and II, 249–50; Kāshānī's Commentary, p. 225.
32. *Fuṣūṣ* II, 128 (n. 12) to 129, a reference to the *ḥadīth:* "On the Day of Resurrection God will be epiphanized to the creatures in the form they have denied; then He will say to them: I am your Lord. But they will say: We take refuge in God against you. Then he will show Himself to them in the forms corresponding to their respective faiths, and they will worship Him." The case of the Resurrection is a symbolic figure (*tamthīl*); but if this is so, why would He not epiphanize Himself in *this* world in a limited form? (If it were inconceivable that God should limit Himself in His theophanies, the Prophets would not have announced His metamorphoses.) That every servant should worship God in the form of his own faith is the law of God's theophany (if not, how could the Active Imagination ever provide a determinate and concrete inner vision of the Beloved? Ch. II, § 2, below). But that he should deny God in the forms of the other faiths (upon which he casts the anathema, the *takfīr*), that is the Veil. Mystical intuition perceives that God

is manifested in the forms of the other faiths and that these limitations are necessary, for total knowledge is never *in actu.* But it is by being the servant of his own divine Name (cf. n. 26 above, *in fine*) that the mystic is in *devotio sympathetica* with all the Names (cf. § 3 below on the significance of the Perfect Man). An investigation of the mysticism of the divine Names in writings anterior to Ibn ʿArabī would even obtain a certain light from him on certain puzzling points; cf., for example, the ritual described in a short Ismailian romance of initiation, in which it is explained to the novice that he will preserve his Name as long as this Name is his God: "Thy Name is thy Lord, and thou art its serf." Cf. our study "Divine Epiphany and Spiritual Rebirth," p. 143, n. 190.

33. *Fuṣūṣ* I, 113.

34. *Fuṣūṣ* II, 247–49 *ad* I, 177 ff. Never can the *ẓawāhir* (manifest, visible things, phenomena) be the causes of other *ẓawāhir;* an immaterial cause (*ghayr maddīya*) is required (cf. in Suhrawardī the idea that that which is in itself pure shadow, screen, *barzakh*, cannot be the cause of anything). This cause may be the divine Names, or it may be something which has no existence in the outside world and is nevertheless the cause of changes, since the structure of each being is twofold: its apparent (*ẓāhir*) aspect, which is its causalized human dimension (*nāsūt*) and its esoteric (*bāṭin*) aspect, which is its causalizing divine aspect (*lāhūt*) (cf. n. 24, above; thus we return to the notion of *ʿayn thābita*). It is the *lāhūt* which is active (the angelic function, sometimes the Angel Gabriel as Divine Spirit, is designated as this *lāhūt* of each being). "It is a strange science, a rare question; the truth of it is understood only by those who possess the Active Imagination (*aṣḥab al-awhām*); because they are influenced by the things which have no outward existence, they are most capable of understanding the *influences.*" "He in whom the Active Imagination is not at work," says Ibn ʿArabī, "remains far from the question" (cf. Ch. II, § 2, below).

35. Cf. the preceding note; this *lāhūt* can also be assimilated to the Angel Gabriel as Holy Spirit (*Fuṣūṣ* II, 179–80, 187), since Gabriel is the Divine Being Himself epiphanized in this Form,

a Divine Spirit comparable to the Soul of the universe in Plotinus (cf. n. 37, below). But when Ibn ʿArabī declares (I, 66) that when a mystic visionary contemplates a Form which projects in him knowledge he did not previously possess (cf. in Suhrawardī, Hermes and his "Perfect Nature"), "it is from the tree of his soul (*nafs*, Self) that he plucks the fruit of knowledge," we must not make the mistake of interpreting this as an identity which would simply abolish the dimensions of *lāhūt* and *nāsūt*. The identity rests on this dual totality. Here the entire experience of the "Angel" is at stake, both when Ibn ʿArabī compares his own experience with that of the Prophet living familiarly in the presence of the Angel Gabriel (*Futūḥāt* II, 325) and when he likens the Angel's presence to the mental evocation of the Beloved by the Lover and to their real dialogue (*Fuṣūṣ* II, 95). The criterion of objectivity is not that required for outward things, but a criterion proper to the world which is visible only in a relation of sympathetism to the Active Imagination (cf. Ch. II, § 1, below). Here the investigations of analytical psychology can safeguard us against false demands leading to the conclusion that all this is a delusion and a snare. The archetype is visible only through one of its symbols; the symbol is not arbitrary; each of us supplies it with his own being; it is personal with him, the *a priori* law and fact of his being (his *ʿayn thābita*). Each man brings with him the Image of his own Lord, and that is why he recognizes himself in Him; he can know God only through this Lord, this divine Name whom he serves. All this is merely to note the impression made by an archetype upon a being; to ask after its cause is to wish to pass from living symbol to dogmatic crystallization. The form of the Angel, "the tree of his soul from which he plucks the fruit of knowledge," is this Self (*nafs*), his transconscience, his divine or celestial counterpart, of which his conscious ego is only a part, emerging in the visible world. The *lāhūt*, the divine Name, creates my being, and reciprocally my being posits it in the same act in which it posits me; that is our common and reciprocal *passio*, our *com-passio*, and it is this alone that I can grasp as my eternal determination. To wish to know more about it, to go back from this individualized vestige to its cause is to demand the impossible; it is tantamount to inquiring into the specific relations of the eternal archetypal individuals with the Divine Essence.

36. Cf. our study "Divine Epiphany," pp. 79–86, 113–127.
37. This conception of the *unio mystica* follows the connections between Creative Imagination and Creative Prayer outlined in Part Two of the present book; cf. above, nn. 27 and 34 for the role of the Active Imagination in perceiving the efficacy of Prayer. Ibn ʿArabī's comparison of his own experience with the Prophet's experience of the Angel would lead us to group and to analyze the expressions describing the Archangel Gabriel (*Rūḥ Aʿẓam*) as the Principle of Life (*Mabdā' al-Ḥayāt*), reigning in the Lotus of the Limit (*sidrat al-muntahà*, Uppermost Heaven), as Muḥammadic Spirit (*Rūḥ Muḥammadī*), Pure Muḥammadic Essence (*Ḥaqīqat muḥammadīya*), as supreme Epiphany of the Godhead and as the *lāhūt* in each being. This would lead us to understand how the Oriental Avicennans were led from the Active Intelligence to that figure of the Angel of Revelation which is the Holy Spirit, just as the *Fedeli d'amore* who were Dante's companions saw in it the divine Sophia as Madonna Intelligenza (see below Ch. II, nn. 36 and 49). No doubt the figure of Gabriel-Christos in a certain phase of primitive Christology would then appear to us in an entirely new light.
38. *Fuṣūṣ* I, 90 ff.; II, 85, 86.
39. The word *seigneurité* is manifestly impossible; as to *seigneurie*, it might do in a pinch but does not *eo ipso* connote the relationship here implied; it can be a simple title or designate a territory.
40. *Fuṣūṣ* II, 86–87, n. 3 *ad* I, 90. *Inna li'l-rubūbīya sirran, wa huwa anta, law ẓahara la-baṭalat al-rubūbīya.* As the commentators Dā'ūd Qayṣarī and Bālī Effendī, as well as Ibn ʿArabī himself in his *Futūḥāt* (ref. I, 90, n. 8) expressly point out, the verb *ẓahara* must here be understood as *ẓahara ʿan* with the meaning "to disappear," "to perish," "to cease" (equivalent to *zāla ʿan*). To translate here by "to appear, to emerge, to be manifested," would be totally to misinterpret Sahl Tustarī's statement, introduced by Ibn ʿArabī. *Huwa* ("he," the third person) is the pronoun of the absent (*ghayb*, the world of Mystery) whereas

anta ("thou") refers either to the creatural world (*ʿālam al-khalq*) or to the eternal individualities (*aʿyān thābita*). In any case suzerainty (*rubūbīya*) is an attribute which would disappear from God when its effect (its *marbūb*) disappeared. But the divine Names are the Lords epiphanized (*al-arbāb al-mutajallīya*) in beings; consequently, suzerainty is a dignity concerned with divine acts. On the other hand, the *majāllī* in which they are manifested are the effects of these divine Names, and these effects subsist as long as their manifestation, or at least their *aʿyān thābita*, subsist. But by definition these last cannot disappear from being (although their outward, contingent forms can cease to be). Accordingly, though suzerainty is contingent on the existence of the vassal, it cannot disappear from the Divine Being. This leaves us the following situation, which is the foundation of *unio sympathetica:* without the Godhead (*ḥaqq*), which is the cause of being, and equally without the creature (*khalq*), that is, without us who are the cause of God's manifestation, the structure of being would not be what it is, and *ḥaqq* would be neither *ḥaqq* nor *rabb* (the Godhead would be neither divine nor a sovereign lord).

41. *Fuṣūṣ* I, 73 and II, 41–42: That is why Noah says "My Lord!" (*rabbi*) and not "My God" (*ilāhī*), Koran LXXI:20 and 27.

42. *Fuṣūṣ* II, 42 (we have noted above—n. 16—the procession of divine Names as angelic hypostases in *3 Enoch*). Hence the distinction between *ulūhīya* and *rubūbīya.* Whereas the former is in perpetual metamorphosis since *Al-Lāh* is epiphanized in each of His forms, the *rubūbīya* which belongs to each of the divine Names is fixed and does not vary. In prayer, accordingly, we should invoke "*Al-Lāh*" by that of His determinate Names which corresponds to our need and our being.

43. For the definitions that follow, cf. in Kāshānī's Lexicon the important article s.v. *arbāb,* p. 169. Hence the Lord of Lords (*rabb al-arbāb*) is the Godhead in respect of His sublime Name, that of the First Individuation (*taʿayyun*), which is the origin of all the Names, the aim of all aims, toward which all desires converge. One should also bear in mind the word *ilāhīya* as divine Name relative to man, and El-īya (the el-ity) as divine Name

relative to Angel (formed with the suffix *-el:* Micha-el, Azra-el, Seraphi-el, etc.).

44. *Fuṣūṣ* II, 143.

45. In another aspect of this transcendent onomatology, compare the charming cosmogonic myth in which the divine Names of subordinate rank, which may be likened to the Templars (*sadana*) holding the keys to the Heavens and the Earth, are nevertheless deprived of any possibility of exerting their power. They appeal to the Seven Imāms of the divine Names, who themselves are only the guardians of the Temple in respect of the divine Name, but who are able to give being to the Heavens and the Earth. The divine Names then share the roles and establish the cosmos in being with its harmonious relations; cf. "*Inshā'al-Dawā'ir,*" in Nyberg, *Kleinere Schriften des Ibn al-ʿArabī,* pp. 36 ff. of the Arabic text and p. 75 of the Introduction.

46. Thus we must think something on the order of "*al-ma' lūh lahu*" or "*fīhi*" (he for whom and in whom He becomes the Adored, that is, realizes His *significatio passiva;* otherwise, according to the usual meaning given in the dictionaries, *ma' lūh* = *ilāh,* cf. *Fuṣūṣ* I, 81 and II, 60–61; Kāshānī, Commentary, p. 73.

47. *Fa naḥnu bi-ma' lūhīyati-nā qad ja ʿalnāhu ilāhan* (it is our theophany which theomorphoses Him): cf. the significant observations of Dā'ūd Qayṣarī, ed. 1299, p. 173: Here *ma'lūhīya* designates *ʿubūdīya;* the *malūh* is the Worshiper (*ʿabd*), not the Worshiped (*maʿbūd*), "By our condition of worshipers (*ʿubūdīyatuna*) we manifest His condition of Adored One (*maʿbūdīyatuhu*). It is in this sense that we *posit* Him, that we establish Him as God; in all this there is a kind of theophanic locution (*wa fīhī nūʿmina'l-shaṭḥ*)."

48. *Fuṣūṣ* I, 119 and II, 142–43. Either of the two correlates is unthinkable without the other; the divine totality is made up of the increate Godhead (*ḥaqq*) and the created God (*ḥaqq makhlūq*), those two faces of absolute reality (*ḥaqīqat muṭlaqa*) between which duality and dialogue are born eternally. There can be no existence for *īlāh* or *ma'lūh, rabb* or *marbūb,* without its correlate term. And *Ilāh* never ceases to be worshiped, glorified, sanctified, though not necessarily in the dogmatic sense of the

word. For when we say "*al-Ḥaqq* is independent of the universe, He is sufficient unto Himself (*ghānī*)," this refers to the essence in itself (*dhāt*), which as such has no relation to being, and not to the Godhead who is precisely God and Lord in His *ma'lūh* and *marbūb* (that is, in our theopathy, in His passion for Himself which becomes our passion for Him).

49. *Fuṣūṣ* I, 83 and II, 67: "Thus His aim is accomplished in me. Glorification and Worship alternate between God (*Ḥaqq*) and creature (*khalq*). God glorifies the creature and worships him in conferring being upon him; the creature glorifies God and worships Him by manifesting His perfections." No doubt the use here of the word *'ibāda* (worship, divine service) would seem strange or even blasphemous to an orthodox believer. But here precisely we are not on the plane of the usual religious consciousness. *Ḥaqq* and *khalq* are each in the service and obedience of the other; *khidmat* and *ta'at* are the most characteristic attributes of devotion (*'ibāda*), and *Ḥaqq* and *khalq* serve and obey each other reciprocally, for *Ḥaqq* confers being on *khalq*, and *khalq* manifests the perfections of *Ḥaqq*. *Khalq* obeys *Ḥaqq* by carrying out His imperative and *Ḥaqq* obeys *khalq* by giving him the degree of existence to which his eternal virtuality aspires (II, 65–66); cf. below, nn. 67–70 and Ch. V, "Man's Prayer and God's Prayer."

50. *Fuṣūṣ* II, 316, n. 23, *ad* I, 212–13. Thus the reciprocity of this *sympathesis* is such that the Lord is epiphanized for his vassal of love in the object of his Quest (his *maṭlūb*), in order that the vassal may recognize and acknowledge Him, for in another form, alien to the preoccupation that accords with the object of his quest, he would not recognize Him. Thus when Moses was looking for Fire, God appeared to him in the form of Fire, in the Burning Bush, because Fire is the sensuous symbol of the domination of the Beloved (*qahr*) and of the lover's love (*maḥabba*). And Moses was not the only man to whom God has shown Himself in the precise form of his quest; Ibn 'Arabī was also favored with the visions which he relates in his book of the *Futūḥāt;* cf. also *Fuṣūṣ* II, 288, n. 5.

51. Ibid. I, 183 and II, 261, "that is, a word which each man under-

stands according to his aptitude, his knowledge of himself and the world around him, or else it is a symbol for the form of his personal belief. In this sense God is an expression (*ʿibāra*) for the God created in the faith (*al-Ilāh al-makhlūq fī'l-iʿtiqād*), not God as He is in Himself." Compare II, 93 *ad* I, 92: Every servant professes a special belief in his Lord, of whom he asks assistance according to the knowledge he has of himself. Thus the faiths differ with the Lords, just as the Lords differ, although all the faiths are forms of the one faith, just as all the Lords are forms in the mirror of the Lord of Lords. Thus (II, 121 *ad* I, 106) although there is in every creature *lāhūt*, which governs that creature as a divine dimension proportional to the dimension of the creature, it does not follow that the Godhead condescends with equal docility to all determinate beings; God is not limited to the manner in which He is epiphanized for you and makes Himself adequate to your dimension. And that is why other creatures are under no obligation to obey the God who demands your worship, because their theophanies take other forms. The form in which He is epiphanized to you is different from that in which He is epiphanized to others. God as such transcends (*munazzah*) all intelligible, imaginable, or sensible forms, but considered in His Names and Attributes, that is, His theophanies, He is, on the contrary, inseparable from these forms, that is, from a certain figure and a certain *situs* in space and time. This is the legitimate *tashbīh*, as understood by Ibn ʿArabī, an interpretation from which derive somewhat different meanings for the terms *tashbīh* and *tanzīh* from those generally accepted by the theologians and philosophers of Islam. For Ibn ʿArabī *tanzīh* is pure indetermination (*iṭlāq*); *tashbīh* is the necessary delimitation (*taḥdīd*) by those forms in accordance with which each man, in the measure "to which he has made himself capable," represents God. This may be *tanzīh* and it may be *tashbīh*, or it may be a combination of the two: "God is an expression for those who grasp the allusion!" Dā'ūd Qayṣarī (p. 417) regards the word as a reference to the *ḥaqīqa* which is manifested in the form of Messengers, and perhaps this carries us back once again to the fundamental significance of docetism.

52. Cf. Kashānī, Lexicon, s.v., p. 133 and below, Ch. III.
53. *Fuṣūṣ* II, 232 *ad* I, 214; Affifi, *Mystical Philosophy*, p. 70 and 71, n. 2. The *Ḥaqīqat Muḥammadīya* (whether we designate it by this name or prefer one of the eighteen-odd Names for its various aspects, cf. above, n. 37 and below, n. 77) is the primordial index referring to its Lord, because it is the intelligible *Maẓhar* totalizing the essences of the divine Names manifested in the human race or rather in the cosmos. And as each existent is an index referring to *his* Lord (his proper Name being *ʿAbd Rabbihi*, servant of *his* Lord), insofar as he is the outward *Maẓhar* in which the perfections of this Lord are epiphanized, Muḥammad too is the first index referring to his Lord, because He is the Form that synthetizes the epiphanies of each of His perfections.
54. *Fuṣūṣ* I, 83 and II, 66: "It is to this end that He existentiates me: that in knowing Him I give Him being" (cf. above, nn. 40, 47–50), that is, in order that the Name or Names, the Attribute or Attributes that he invests in me may be revealed.
55. Cf. Kāshānī, Commentary, pp. 54–95 (*ad.* I, 91). What the Lord expects of His vassal (*marbūb*) is that he be the form in which His action and His influx are manifested (*maẓhar*). The vassal accomplishes His will (acknowledges his Lord) by the mere fact of his receptivity as a form manifesting His suzerainty, and he is acknowledged by Him thanks to the mere fact that he manifests this suzerainty. He has no *action* outside of his *receptivity* (*qābilīya*) which accomplishes the intention of his Lord. The acknowledged is thus at the same time the acknowledger, since he is also the action which establishes his Lord in the accomplishment of His purpose (which is *you*, the *sirr* of his *rubūbīya*). To the Lord belongs the action (to the *rabb*, for *marbūb* is his action). Of the *marbūb* the *rabb* sees only this assistance by which the being of the *marbūb* fulfils His design. Thus *rabb* and *marbūb* acknowledge each other, are for one another acknowledger and acknowledged (cf. also *Fuṣūṣ* II, 86, n. 47). We can express the same thing by saying that the Lord and His vassal are the guarantors or pledge (*wīqāya*), the one of the other. This Lord of mine is the God in function of whom I live and *for* whom I answer, and He answers *for* me precisely where I answer *for* Him

(cf. Kāshānī, Commentary, p. 134). The vassal is his God's shield, assuming (as *nāsūt* and *ẓāhir*) His negativities (the divine limitations, the limitations of the created God), and God is his shield through being the *lāhūt* in him. A striking aspect of the *unio sympathetica* is that the divine Compassion answers for *your* perfection by *its* divinity, that is, its divinity created in you, which is in your *bāṭin* and your *lāhūt*, your hidden, "esoteric," and divine condition; cf. above, n. 10, the idea of *supra-existence.*

56. In a sense that partakes of theopathic locution (*shaṭḥ*), as Dā'ūd Qaysarī observes (n. 47, above).
57. Cf. n. 17, above.
58. Cf. *Fuṣūṣ* I, 69 and II, 34–35.
59. *Fuṣūṣ* II, 35.
60. That is, of the same nature as the ecstasy of the Cherubim, cf. Kāshānī, Lexicon, pp. 123–24: The ecstatics of love (*al-muhayyamūn*) are the Angels immersed in contemplation of the Divine Beauty; so intense and so total is their absorption in this contemplation that they are unaware that God has created Adam. These are the supreme Angels, to whom the order to bow before Adam is not addressed, because of their absence (*ghayba*) from all that is not divine and because of the nostalgic stupor (*walah*) in which they are transfixed by the splendor of the Divine Beauty. These are the Cherubim (Karūbīyūn); cf. n. 72 below.
61. In particular the two *Futuwwat-Namah* in Persian (still unpublished) of ʿAbd al-Razzāq Kāshānī (the commentator on Ibn ʿArabī, frequently cited here), and of Husayn Kāshifi, the famous Imāmite thinker of the sixteenth century.
62. *Fuṣūṣ* I, 81 and II, 60, that is, the Abstract God of the monotheism alien to the theopathic maxim: "It is by our theopathy that we establish Him as God." True, we may know an eternal Essence (*dhāt*), but we do not know that this essence is God until it is recognized by someone who experiences it as his God (someone who is its *ma'lūh*, for whom and in whom it becomes God, that is, is *theomorphosed*). The Necessary Being whom philosophy isolates with those attributes that give rise to the concept of divinity, is not God. Neither are the *Primus Movens* or

the *Ens Necessarium* (*Wājib al-wujūd*) of the philosophers God in the religious sense. Someone must encounter a God whose *sirr al-rubūbīya* (secret of his divinity) he is, because there alone resides also the *sirr al-khalq* (the secret of the creature).

63. *Fuṣūṣ* I, 81, and II, 60. Kāshānī, Commentary, p. 73.

64. *Fuṣūṣ* II, 62, though we may not speak of an "identity" which would purely and simply annul the secret of the bipolarity *Ḥaqq* and *khalq;* but when (I, 82): "It is in Him that our forms are manifested to you; it is in God that they are manifested to one another. Then they know one another and distinguish one from the other. There are some among us who know that this knowledge of ourselves by ourselves is fulfilled in God (*maʿrifa lanā binā*); and there are some who are unaware of His presence in which this self-knowledge is fulfilled, who do not know that simultaneously we are His gaze and He is our gaze. And in this mystic, simultaneous knowledge, no judgment is pronounced on us except by ourselves. Or better still: it is we ourselves who pronounce the judgment on us, but we do so in Him."

65. *Anā sirr al-Ḥaqq, mā'l Ḥaqq anā;* cf. Affifi, *Mystical Philosophy,* p. 15. An essential difference: Hallāj seems to be *ḥulūlī* (incarnationist, cf. II, 190: God manifesting his divine perfections by incarnating Himself in man), whereas Ibn ʿArabī is *ittiḥādī,* but in the sense of unification such as that implied precisely by the notion of theophany (*tajallī, maẓhar*) not in the sense of an incarnation or hypostatic union—a fact too often forgotten from force of habit. Cf. II, 69: if I am the *maẓhar* of the Divine Being, it is possible only to say that He is epiphanized in me, not that He is I (*lā annahu* anā). It is in this sense that Christ "is God," that is, he is a theophany, but not as if God could say: "I am Christ (*Masīḥ*), son of Maryam." And that is why Ibn ʿArabī accuses the Christians of impiety (*kufr*). Here again there would be occasion to meditate on the meaning of epiphany and docetism and the relations between them.

66. See this unique poem of *unio sympathetica* in *Fuṣūṣ* I, 143 and II, 191.

67. *Fuṣūṣ* II, 190–91; compare Kāshānī's Commentary, p. 180: God is the food of Creation since it is through Him that it subsists,

lives, and persists, comparable to the food through which a man who takes nourishment subsists. Therefore feed all creatures on the Divine Being (*wujūd ḥaqq*), in order that you may therein be His representative (*nā'ib*), and thus you will at the same time feed God on all the determinate forms, all the predicates of being (*aḥkām al-kawn*).

68. Ibid. I, 143 and II, 191: Kāshānī's Commentary, p. 181: Through the being which God gave us whereby to manifest ourselves, we have given Him the possibility of manifesting Himself in us and by us. There is in ourselves a part of *Him* that comes from us and a part of *us* that comes from *Him*.
69. Ibid. II, 191; cf. the text of Kāshānī's Commentary cited in n. 18 above, see also nn. 47 and 49.
70. Angelus Silesius, *The Cherubinic Wanderer*, I, 8 (tr. Trask, p. 13). Cf. also I, 100 (tr. after Plard, p. 77): "I am as important to God as He is to me; I help him to maintain his being, and He helps me to maintain mine." II, 178 (tr. Trask, p. 46): "Naught is, save I and Thou; and if these two were not, / Heaven would fall away, God would no more be God." I, 200 (ibid., p. 28): "God nothing is at all; and if he something be, / Only in me it is, he having chosen me." Cf. Czepko's sestet, cited in Plard, p. 362, n. 35: "God is not God for Himself, He is what He is; only the creature has elected Him God."
71. Cf. the text of Kāshānī's Commentary, n. 67 above.
72. Here we must return to the notion of "wisdom of passionate love" (*ḥikmat muhayyamīya*) related to Abraham (cf. n. 60, above) and observe the following (II, 57–58 *ad* I, 80): the word *muhayyamīya* comes from *hiyām, hayamān* (to love desperately), which is the excess of *'ishq*. This wisdom of ecstatic love is related to Abraham because God chose him as His *Khalīl*. The *Khalīl* is the lover lost in the excess of his love (*al-muḥibb al-mufriṭ fī maḥabbatihi*), totally devoted to his Beloved. But these are all symbols typifying something that transcends them. Indeed, the name of Abraham is used by Ibn 'Arabī not to designate the Prophet as He is known in sacred history, but as a symbol of the Perfect Man, of whom the Prophets and the Saints are regarded as individuations, whereas the "species" Perfect Man is

the complete theophany of the totality of the divine Names and Attributes. If Abraham is here chosen as a symbol by allusion to the fact that he was *khalīl Allāh,* it is not simply because of the idea of *khulla* (sincere friendship, *ṣadāqa*), as is traditionally believed, but because of the idea connoted by the fifth form of the verb (*takhallala*) to mix, mingle, interpenetrate. Through the choice of this etymology he is established as a typification of the Perfect Man, whom God penetrates, mingling with his faculties and organs. This penetration varies in men according to the Name and Divine Attribute they epiphanize. *Ḥaqq* and *khalq* intermingle and mutually nourish one another, yet there is no *ḥulūl* (cf. n. 65 above) for these are symbolic expressions (*'ibārāt majāzīya*). There is indeed nothing material in the representation of *mutakhallil* and *mutakhallal* (that which is mingled *with* and that which incurs the mixture *of,* that which penetrates and that which is penetrated); it is a pure symbol of the relationship between *Ḥaqq* and *khalq,* whose duality is necessary but comports no *alterity,* two aspects of the same absolute *ḥaqīqā,* coexisting the one through the other; the relation between them is that between the color of the water and the color of the vessel that contains it.

73. Cf. Our study "Divine Epiphany," pp. 69–86 (metamorphoses of theophanic visions).
74. Koran XI:72–73: "Our messengers came to Abraham with good news. They said: 'Peace!' 'Peace!' he answered and hastened to bring them a roasted calf. But when he saw that they did not touch it, he mistrusted them and was afraid of them. But they said: 'Do not be alarmed. We are sent forth to the people of Lot.' " Certain commentators (cf. Teheran ed., 1363/1944, p. 164, margin) are not unaware that the messengers were the Angels Gabriel, Michael, and Seraphiel, who appeared as youths of great beauty (see following note).
75. We may say that Ibn 'Arabī gives us the most magnificent mystic exegesis of Andrei Rublev's icon. "To feed the Angel" is to answer for this God who would perish without me, but without whom I should also perish (such is the situation which the mystic Sophia was to point out to the poet on a memorable night in

Mecca, see below, Ch. II, § 1). And if this God is "proof of himself," it is because he is nourished by *my* being, but *my* being is *His* being which precisely He has invested in me. That is why the icon of the three Angels sitting under the oak in Mamre, as we are led by Ibn ʿArabī to meditate upon it, is the perfect image of *devotio sympathetica* (φιλοξενία = Arabic *ḍiyāfa*). Oriental Christianity, in turn, looked upon the three Angels as the most perfect figuration of the three persons of the Trinity. According to the theological and iconographic analysis of Sergei Bulgakov (*Jacob's Ladder*, in Russian, pp. 114–15), each of the three Angels represents a hypostasis of the divine Triad of which he bears the imprint (just as the thrice triple hierarchy of the Angelic degrees in Dionysius corresponds to the three persons of the Triad). This perception is the foundation of the iconographic tradition which made its appearance in the Russian Church toward the end of the fifteenth century with the famous icon of St. Andrei Rublev, painted under the direction of St. Nikon, a disciple of St. Sergei, and it is possible that this icon was the disciple's spiritual testament, the secret of St. Sergei, his secret of the Trinity. Cf. Bulgakov, p. 115, for a nominal identification of the three Archangels similar to one which was not unknown to our Koran commentators (see the preceding note and, on the general significance of the triad in Ibn ʿArabī, Affifi, *Mystical Philosophy*, pp. 87–88). Though this iconographic tradition is not entirely unknown in the West, it is significant at the very least that it appears only in places attached to the Byzantine tradition (San Vitale of Ravenna, St. Mark's of Venice, Santa Maria Maggiore of Rome); cf. Carl Otto Nordström, *Ravennastudien*, pp. 94–95, 103, 115.

76. Cf. *Fuṣūṣ* I, 84 and II, 67: "It is because the rank as 'intimate' (*khalīl*) belongs to the intimate friend in his own right that he offers the repast of hospitality. This degree of 'intimate' is that of mystic gnosis (*ʿirfān*), which is that of the Perfect Man, in whom God is manifested according to the most perfect of His forms. It is He who nourishes the Divine Essence with all the ontic attributes of perfection, that is the meaning of *to offer the repast of hospitality*." Abraham is not the only man to nourish the

Divine Essence by the manifestation of its determinate modes. "When God desires subsistence, all being is food for Him." But Abraham and those perfect men who are like him present this food in the most perfect manner. Ibn ʿArabī himself tells us that for this reason Ibn Masarra associates Abraham with the Archangel Michael. This is an allusion to the motif of the Throne (cf. Asín Palacios, "Ibn Masarra y su escuela," *Obras escogidas* I, pp. 95 ff.) Of the eight bearers of the Throne, Adam and Seraphiel sustain the bodies (the forms), Gabriel and Muḥammad sustain the spirits, Michael and Abraham provide their "sustenance," Malik and Ridwān provide rewards and punishments. Kāshānī comments (p. 79): Ibn Masarra associates Abraham with the Archangel Michael in the sense that Michael is the Angel who provides for the subsistence of the universe of being. God established a bond of brotherhood between the Archangel Michael and Abraham as typification of the Perfect Man.

77. Here we can only suggest the broad outline of this motif. The Perfect Man (*Anthropos teleios, Insān-i-kāmil*) is the perfect theophany (*maẓhar kāmil*) of the totality of the divine Names. He is, at the initial degree, the being who is designated sometimes as Supreme Spirit (*Rūḥ Aʿẓam*), sometimes as Pure Muḥammadic Essence (*Ḥaqīqat Muḥammadīya*), sometimes also as the Angel Gabriel, the First Intelligence sprung from the Breath of Compassion (*Nafas Raḥmānī*), reigning in the "Lotus of the Limit" (cf. *Fuṣūṣ* II, 187 *ad* I, 142). He is the homologue of the *Nous* of the Neoplatonists, of the Obeyed One (*Muṭāʿ*) in Ghazālī, of the sacrosanct Archangel or First Intelligence in Ismailism (*Malak muqaddas, ʿAql Awwal, Protokistos, Deus revelatus*), of the Logos of Christian theology; he is the Holy Spirit (*Rūḥ al-Quds*) as cosmic potency (cf. n. 37 above). We have already noted how his theophanic bond with the concrete person of the Prophet (who, strictly speaking, is alone invested with the name of *ʿAbd Allāh* as prototype of the Perfect Man) is modeled on a Gnostic Christology. The twofold question propounded in our text refers to the situation that arises when a certain class of men among the Spirituals is characterized as

belonging, or aspiring, to the category of Perfect Man; cf. Affifi, *Mystical Philosophy*, pp. 77–85.

78. Cf. Affifi's pertinent remarks (*Fuṣūṣ* II, 88–89, n. 5). The "men of God" (*ahl Allāh*) reject *tajallī* (theophany) in divine unitude (*aḥadīya*). Every existent is a particular form of the absolute Whole; he is not *Ḥaqq*, but *Ḥaqq* is epiphanized in him in his particular form. As for *unitude*, it never involves a *tajallī* for us. It would be contradictory to say: I have contemplated God in His oneness, since contemplation (*mushāhada*) is a relationship between contemplated and contemplant. As long as being endures for me, there is *duality*, not oneness. Ibn ʿArabī rejects all perception of the *waḥdat wujūdīya* in this world (and consequently rejects all "existential" monism). To his mind it is an absurdity to say that the servant, in a state of *fonā'*, has become God (*Ḥaqq*), since "becoming" (*sayrūra*) postulates duality and duality excludes unity. Thus a philosophical postulate, an *a priori* datum of the intellect (*fiṭrat* al-ʿaql), and not a mystical experience or achievement (*dhawq ṣūfī*), is the foundation of the doctrine of *waḥdat al-wujūd.* If Ibn ʿArabī professes that being is one, it is not because this was revealed to him in a mystic state. This unity is a philosophical premise which requires no proof. Even if a man claims to have been united with God or to have died to himself in Him, etc., the event he is relating is inevitably an event in duality. As long as men describe God and speak of themselves, this will be so. But to be aware of the duality of the knower and the known is one thing, to affirm and justify their dualism would be another. In other words, if there is any justification for speaking of monism here, it is in the sense of a philosophical monism formulating the transcendental condition of being, and only because this philosophical monism is precisely the necessary schema in which to meditate *unio mystica* and *unio sympathetica*, that is to say, the fundamentally dialogical situation. For the unity is always a unity of these two; it is not in a third phase which absorbs dualitude, which is the *conditio sine qua non* of the dialogue that fulfils the desire of the "Hidden Treasure yearning to be known." Here philosophical monism is the necessary conceptual instrument with which to describe this

irremissible interdependence of *Ḥaqq* and *khalq* (cf. n. 70 above, the paradoxes of Angelus Silesius compared with those of Ibn ʿArabī), since the unity of the two is savored in a mystic experience which precisely is not and cannot be the experience of a mystic monism or of an "existential" monism. This relationship is too often forgotten, and that is the significance of the substitution of *Anā sirr al-Ḥaqq* (I am the secret of God) for *Anā'l Ḥaqq* (I am God); cf. n. 65 above and nn. 24 and 26 on the meaning of the word *kathenotheism.*

79. Cf. Affifi, *Mystical Philosophy*, pp. 81 and 85, in which the problem is aptly formulated. The two aspects must not be confused even if Ibn ʿArabī, who has both in view, does not always make the distinction between them absolutely clear. There is the metaphysical theory that Man (mankind) is the most perfect revelation of all the Divine Attributes, and there is the mystical theory that certain men, partaking of the category of the Perfect Man, attain to a level of consciousness in which they experience the significance of their unity with the divine reality. On this realization depends the truth of the perfect man as a microcosm *in actu.* But this microcosmic truth (having the form of a καθ' ἕνα) must in turn, when one speaks of the Perfect Man as a cosmic principle, lead us not to confuse the *Ḥaqīqat al-Ḥaqā'iq* (Muḥammadic essence, *Nous*, Holy Spirit) and its concrete manifestations, namely the class of men (prophets and saints) entering into this category of Perfect Man.

80. *Fuṣūṣ* II, 87–88, n. 4 *ad* I, 91: "Each being is approved by his Lord," that is, each being, insofar as he is the *maẓhar* of one of the Names or Lords, is acknowledged by this Lord, since he is the "secret of that Lord's suzerainty." Of course a distinction must be drawn between the fact that the servant is acknowledged by his Lord and the fact that he is acknowledged with regard to the law or ethical system. In the first case it suffices that the servant should be the *maẓhar* of his Lord's action; in the second He must conform to the religious, positive, and moral norms of the moment. But the rebel, the nonconformist, can be acknowledged by his Lord and not by the religious norm, or he may be acknowledged by his own Lord and not by another, because among the

totality of Names each individual takes or receives what corresponds to his nature and capacity. The divine Names make their appearance in men only proportionately to the exigency of their eternal virtualities.

81. The Koran text continues: "Join my servants" (LXXXIX:28), that is, "Join the number of those who have each recognized his Lord and have sought only what poured upon them from him."

82. Cf. I, 92 (Ismāʿīl), and II, 90: this is the paradise of the *ʿārif* (gnostic) and not of the *mu'min* (simple believer), for it is spiritual delight. There is revealed the dual unity, the bi-unity, the *unio sympathetica* of *Ḥaqq* and *khalq*.

83. Ibid. and II, 91, n. 7. "You are the servant, though at the same time the Lord, of him whose servant you are in this respect. And you are the Lord, though at the same time the servant of him whose servant you are according to the language of religion. Whosoever knows you knows me. But if I am not known, you are not known either." There is a twofold *maʿrifa:* (1) to know *Ḥaqq* (the Divine Being) by *khalq* (the creature): that is the *maʿrifa* of the philosophers and of the scholastic theologians (Mutakallimūn). (2) To know *Ḥaqq* by *khalq fī'l-Ḥaqq* (by the creature in the Divine Being). The first meditates on man in himself as a contingent creature. It compares the attributes of man (contingent, perishable, changing, evil, dependent) with those which by contrast it postulates in the necessary Being (eternal, immutable, purely good). Such a science, which is at once exterior to man and inferior to God may satisfy the intellect, but it provides the heart with no appeasement, for it merely unfolds a chain of negative attributes. The second is the more perfect. It is born in an introspective meditation which explores the foundation of the attributes of the soul. The soul understands that it is accomplishing a form of theophany and knows itself insofar as God is epiphanized in it. In the first knowledge, man knows himself as a creature and no more. In the second, the soul knows that its being is at once *Ḥaqq* and *khalq*, increate and created.

84. *Fuṣūṣ* II, 91, n. 8. Thus each being has two aspects: *ʿubūdīya* and *rubūbīya*, vassaldom and suzerainty. He is a servant in the sense

that he is the substrate (*maḥall*) in which is manifested the mode of one of the Lords or divine Names, each man knowing and recognizing his own Lord and contemplating his own essence, his own self and meditating its attributes. This is the first knowledge (homologous to the first described above, n. 83, but with this difference, that here there is the idea of a personal Lord, the divine Name of *my* Lord). In another aspect, each being is the Lord of his Lord (*rabb li rabbihi*). This is the meaning of the second verse cited above: "You are the lord of him whose servant you are in this respect," and this because the mode of the servant is manifested in the Lord, that is, in the divine Name epiphanized in Him.

85. Cf. Ibn 'Arabī's poem cited in Ch. II, n. 1, tr. Nicholson, pp. 66–67; Beirut edn., pp. 38–40.

CHAPTER II
SOPHIOLOGY AND *DEVOTIO SYMPATHETICA*

1. Cf. *The Tarjūmān al-ashwāq, A Collection of Mystical Odes by Muḥyī'ddīn ibn al-'Arabī*, ed. and tr. Nicholson, pp. 10 ff. Cf. *Kitāb Dhakhā'ir al-a'lāq, Sharḥ Tarjūmān al-ashwāq*, p. 3, line 7. The commentary was written by Ibn 'Arabī himself for reasons which have already been noted in the Introduction to the present book (p. 71), and which will be discussed again below (n. 5). Unfortunately, at the end of his invaluable edition, Nicholson translated only extracts from this commentary. In view of its extreme interest to those who wish to follow the operation of Ibn 'Arabī's symbolic thinking, and also of the unusual fact that here a different text is commented upon by its own author, a complete translation would be extremely useful. In *La Escatología musulmana en la Divina Comedia*, pp. 408–10, Asín Palacios gives a Spanish translation of a long passage from the prologue, and in *El Islam cristianizado*, pp. 95–96, he provides a translation of a page of the Futūḥāt referring to the writing of the commentary.

2. In these two lines we have followed Asín's elegant paraphrase. Worth noting is the Koranic term *al-Balad al-Amīn* (xcv:3), "the sacrosanct country"; cf. the symbolic use of the term in Ismailism (the country of the Imām, the place where our Noble Stone is kept, not in the cubic edifice of the material Kaʿaba, but in the celestial Mecca of the Angels), W. Ivanow, *Nāṣir-e Khusraw and Ismailism*, pp. 23–24, and our *Étude préliminaire pour le "Livre réunissant les deux sagesses" de Nāṣir-e Khosraw*, pp. 32–33.
3. Allusion to the title of the commentary: *Dhakhā'ir al-aʿlāq* (Treasures of precious objects).
4. That is, principally, the feminine names celebrated in Arabic chivalric poetry. Outstanding typifications: if Bilqīs, Queen of Saba, and *Salma* (typifying the mystic experience of Solomon) are other names for the maiden Niẓām as a figure of Sophia (*Ḥikmat*), an ideal but significant tie is thus established between this sophiology and the "Solomonian Sophia," that is, the books of wisdom that were the sources of Christian sophiology.
5. *Dhakhā'ir*, p. 4. Ibn ʿArabī had been warned by his two disciples, his two "spiritual sons," Badr the Abyssinian and Ismail ibn Sawdakīn. He arranged for a conference under the arbitration of the Qādi Ibn al-ʿAdīm, who under his direction read a part of his Dīwān in the presence of the moralist doctors. The one who had refused to lend credence to Ibn ʿArabī's statement changed his mind and repented before God. It is not in the least surprising that the supercilious orthodox believer should have found imitators down to our own days, imitators if not of his repentance, at least of his skepticism. No theoretical discussion is possible if one is alien (under the influence of age-old habits of thought) to what was known in Persian as *ham-damī* (σύμπνοια, *conflatio*, the synchronism of the spiritual and the sensory, cf. below), if one persists in setting up an opposition between "mysticism" and "sensuousness" (the antithesis we have posited between these two terms exists only because we have broken the bond between them). Ibn ʿArabī and Jalāluddīn Rūmī made the "conspiration" of the sensible and the spiritual the cornerstone of *their* Islam, that is to say, Islam as they understood it and lived

it. One of the greatest masters of this way was Rūzbehān Baqlī of Shīrāz (d. 1209), who has already been mentioned here: Beauty is perceived as a hierophany only if divine love (*'ishq rabbānī*) is experienced in a human love (*'ishq insānī*) which it transfigures. Ibn 'Arabī went to considerable length in explaining his favorite symbols: ruins, encampments, Magi, gardens, meadows, mansions, flowers, clouds, lightning flashes, zephirs, hills, copses, paths, friends, idols, women who rise like suns (*Dhakhā'ir*, p. 5). "All the things I have just mentioned, or all the things that resemble them, are, if you understand them, mysteries, high and sublime illuminations which the Lord of the heavens sent to my heart, just as He sends them to the heart of anyone who possesses a quality of purity and of elevation analogous to the spiritual preparation that I myself possess. If you bear this in mind, you will prefer to lend faith to my sincerity. Remove from your thought the exterior of words, seek the interior (bāṭin, the esoteric) until you understand." Without contesting the legitimacy or appropriateness of this self-commentary, we must agree however that it suffers from the same drawbacks as those which were added to Avicenna's and Suhrawardī's narratives of spiritual autobiography (cf. our *Avicenna and the Visionary Recital*, pp. 35 ff.). After the author, through the power of his intuition, has penetrated to the innermost secret of his person and of his transconsciousness and succeeded in confirming his personal symbols, he must recede to a level inferior to this intuitive, image-configuring evidence if he wishes to make himself intelligible in rational terms. He is usually obliged to do so if he wishes others to follow him, but he does so at the risk of being misunderstood by all those who are lacking in aptitude. We in turn are obliged to decipher (as we would a musical score) what the author has succeeded in recording of his inner experience. To this end, we must take the same road in the opposite direction and rediscover under the signs of the narrative what the author experienced before setting them down—and so penetrate his secret. But for this precisely his commentary is the first and indispensable guide.

6. Nicholson tr. *ad* XX, 3, p. 87: Beirut edn., p. 78.

7. And that is why Ibn ʿArabī justifies love images as symbols of theosophical mysteries. Actually, he did not "make use" of images as though constructing a system. These figures were immediate inner perceptions. We must bear in mind his whole phenomenology of love (cf. § 2, below), and concurrently the sequence of visionary experiences which run through his entire personal mystical life (which put into play the objectively creative imagination characteristic of the *ʿarīf*, the faculty designated by the term *himma*, Spiritual energy, or power of concentrating the heart, concerning which we shall speak in greater detail below, Ch. IV, § 2). For a long time a being of heavenly beauty favored the *shaikh* with her presence (cf. *Futūḥāt* II, 325; see the translation of this text, Ch. VI, n. 13 below). He compares this vision to the visible and repeated manifestation of the Archangel Gabriel to the Prophet, and also alludes to the *ḥadīth* of the theophany in the form of a royal youth (*Dhakhā'ir, ad* XV, 3, Beirut edn., pp. 55–56; cf. below, Ch. VI, § 1). Rightly Asín draws a comparison with Dante's dream vision (*Vita Nuova*, XII) of a youth clad in a very white tunic, sitting beside him in a pensive attitude and declaring to him: "Ego tamquam centrum circuli, cui simili modo se habent circumferentiae partes; tu autem non sic" (*Escatología*, p. 403). Cf. also the ungraspable youth (*al-fatā al-fā'it*) glimpsed during the ritual circumambulations, whose being encompasses all the secrets that were to be expounded in the great work of the *Futūḥāt* (below, Ch. VI, § 2). On our preferred translation of the title of the *Futūḥāt*, cf. Ch. IV, n. 1 below.
8. Cf. Beirut edn., p. 6; Nicholson tr. *ad* IV, 3, p. 58. The connection between the circumambulations around the *center* and the time of the apparition is significant; cf. the Avicennan narrative of Ḥayy ibn Yaqẓān: "While we were coming and going, turning in a circle, a Sage appeared in the distance." Concerning the night as the time of these visions, cf. Suhrawardī, *Epistle on the Rustling of Gabriel's Wing* and the *Narrative of Occidental Exile*.
9. The transposition effected by visionary perception sets in at once. She is no longer a young Iranian girl in an Arab country. She is a Greek princess, hence a Christian. The secret of this

qualification will be revealed later on in the *Dīwān* (cf. n. 16 below: this Wisdom or *Sophia* is of the race of Jesus, because she too is at once of a human and of an angelic nature; hence the allusions to the "marble statues," the "icons" glimpsed in Christian churches, are all allusions to her person).

10. Cf. Beirut edn., pp. 7 and 170–71; Nicholson tr., p. 148 (and commentary *ad* XLVI, 1, p. 132; "She whose lips are of a dark red color, a sublime *Wisdom* among these contemplated ones," she whose epiphanic figure is the maiden Niẓām. Between the world of mixture and the supreme Contemplated ones, there is a combat of love, because the world needs them and desires them, since for the beings of this world there is no life except through the contemplation of them. The world of Nature obscures the perception of these contemplated Ones to the hearts of the mystics, hence the combat is incessant. The dark red prefigures the mysteries (*umūr ghaybīya*) that are in them.
11. *Tahīmu fīhā al-arwāh,* Nicholson commentary *ad* XLVI, 1, p. 132; cf. above, Ch. I, nn. 60 and 72 on the *muhayyamūn* Angels and Abraham's *ḥikmat muhayyamīya.*
12. Cf. above, Ch. I, § 3, p. 130.
13. Beirut edn., p. 6; Nicholson, text, p. 14.
14. The subtile argument is very beautiful, because it removes all doubt, all suspicion of illusion, from the existence of the spiritual and invisible, once one experiences its action in oneself: to recognize that your heart has been possessed (put into the passive, *mamlūk* = *marbūb*) by these Invisibles is to recognize them as active and predominant subjects; the ego, subject of *cogitor* (and no longer of *cogito*), is immanent in the being who thinks and knows it; hence to know oneself is to know one's lord, because it is this lord who knows himself in you.
15. In that Night of the Spirit in which was uttered the total demand which in itself solves all doubts and on which every Ṣūfī must meditate, there remained only one question for the poet to ask: "O maiden, what then is your name?—*Consolatrix,* she answered [*qurrat al-ʿayn,* "freshness and brilliance to the eye," a familiar metaphor for the beloved]. And as I spoke to myself, she saluted me and went away." He adds: "I saw her again later and came to

know her; I cultivated her company and found in her a knowledge so subtile that no one can describe it." There was no need for the poet to remain in Mecca forever in order that the Image of that "Wisdom" should remain secretly present to him for the rest of his life.

16. The Image of Sophia in Ibn ʿArabī: It would be worthwhile to recompose this image like a mosaic whose pieces have been dispersed (by design) throughout the whole poem. Here we can only attempt the most summary sketch, our prime purpose being to indicate the chain of mental associations produced by the Active Imagination. For our *shaikh*, King Solomon is, if not the traditional author of the Biblical literature of wisdom, at least the prophet in whom is typified the gift of "Compassionate Wisdom" (*ḥikmat raḥmānīya*, cf. *Fuṣūṣ*, ch. XVI), that is, the religion of the *Fedeli d'amore*. Hence the appearance, from the very beginning of the poem with its Koranic reminiscences, of Bilqīs, Queen of Saba (ed. Nicholson, *ad* II, 1, pp. 50–51). But by virtue of her birth (from a *jinn* and a woman) Bilqīs is both angel and earthly woman. Thus she is of the same race as Christ (*ʿīsawīyat al-maḥtid*), not the Christ of conciliar orthodoxy, but that of the Angel Christology of, or related to, docetic Gnosticism and possessing so profound a noetic significance: engendered by the breath which the Angel Gabriel-Holy Spirit breathed into the Virgin his mother, he was in his person the typification (*tamthīl*) of an Angel in human form (cf. *ad* II, 4). By the beauty of her gaze, this Christic wisdom (*ḥikmat ʿīsawīya*) gives death and at the same time restores life, as though she were herself Jesus (*ad* II, 4). She is in person the Light with the fourfold source (Pentateuch, Psalms, Gospel, Koran) described in the famous Koran verse of the Light (xxiv:35). Being of the "race of Christ," this Sophia-Angelos (or Sophia-Christos) belongs to the world of Rūm; she is feminine being not only as *theophany* but also as *theophans* (like Diotima in Plato). And indeed, our poet salutes her as a figure of feminine priesthood, as "a priestess, a daughter of the Greeks, without ornament, in whom you contemplate a radiant source of light" (*ad* II, 6). The ecumenical religious sympathy of the *Fedele d'amore* (cf. above,

Ch. I, § 3, p. 134), has its principle in the priesthood of Sophia, for "if with a gesture she asked for the Gospel, one would think that we are priests, patriarchs and deacons" (*ad* II, 9), that is, we should be as zealous as those dignitaries in confirming the Gospel against what men have falsely imputed to it. "Greek priestess" of a Christianity as understood by Ibn ʿArabī, this *virgo sacerdos* Sophia is said to be "without ornament," that is, when one meditates on her not as adorned with the ornaments of the divine Names and Attributes, but as Pure Essence, the "Pure Good" (*ad* II, 6), though it is through her that the Flaming Splendors (*subuḥāt muḥriqa*) of the Divine Face are manifested. That is why Beauty as the theophany par excellence has a *numinous* character. In her pure numinosity, Sophia is forbidding, she tolerates no familiarity; in her "solitary chamber" rises the mausoleum of those who had died separated from her, and she takes pity on the sadness of the divine Names by giving them being (*ad* II, 7). This is an allusion to the trials attending the mystic's Quest, his waiting punctuated by brief ecstatic encounters. Because she is a guide who always leads him toward the beyond, preserving him from metaphysical idolatry, Sophia appears to him sometimes as compassionate and comforting, sometimes as severe and silent, because only Silence can "speak," can indicate transcendences. The mystic undergoes the trial of Dante hoping that Beatrice will return his greeting, but one does not impose laws "on beautiful marble statues" (*ad* IV, 1–2). Such indeed is the beauty of the Solomonian and Prophetic theophanies, for "they do not answer in articulate speech, because then their discourse would be other than their essence, other than their person; no, their apparition, their coming (*wurūd*) is identical to their discourse; it *is* this discourse itself, and the discourse is their visible presence"; that is what it means to *hear* them, and that is characteristic of this mystic station. Alas! The spiritual must travel by night, that is, through all the activities that are incumbent on a creature of flesh; and when he returns to the sanctuary of his consciousness (*sirr*), this divine Sophia has gone away: "Surrounded in this dark Night by his ardent desires which assail him with swift-flying arrows, he does not know in what direction to turn!" (*ad* IV, 3 and 4). But then "she smiled at me while a flash of lightning appeared, and I did not know which of us two pierced the dark Night." Unity of the apperception: Is it the real feminine being? Or is it the divine reality of which the feminine being is an Image? A false dilemma, for neither would be visible without the other, and thus the earthly Sophia is essentially theophanic (*ḥikmat mutajallīya*), never ceasing to inhabit the heart of the *fedele d'amore* as Angel of Revelation in the company of the Prophet (*ad* IV, 6). To experience human beauty in the feminine being as theophany (cf. § 3 below) is to experience her in the twofold character of Majesty that inspires fear and of grace which inspires ecstasy (*jalāl* and *jamāl*), a simultaneity of the unknowable Godhead and of the manifested Godhead. Consequently the allusions to the extraordinary beauty of the maiden Niẓām and to her astonishing wisdom always combine this aspect of the numinous and the fascinating (e.g. *ad* XX, 16) with the severe hieratic beauty of the pure Essence and the gentle, compassionate beauty of the "feminine lord," whom the *fedele d'amore* nourishes with his devotion, which is in turn nourished by her beauty. "Understand what we are alluding to, it is a sublime thing. We have met no one who had knowledge of it before us in any of the books of theosophy" (*ad* XX, 17). This mistress of wisdom possesses a throne (the divine Names, the degrees of being to be ascended) and an eloquence (her prophetic message). "We have represented all mystic knowledge beneath the veil of Niẓām, the daughter of our Shaikh, the Virgin Most Pure" (ibid. *al'adhrā al-batūl*, the epithet of Maryam and Fāṭima). An Iranian of Ispahān removed to an Arab country, she does not remain enclosed in her place of origin. "She is a queen by reason of her spiritual asceticism, for the Spirituals are the kings of the earth." Finally this exclamation: "By God! I do not fear death, my only fear is to die without seeing her tomorrow" (*ad* XX, 11). Not the fear of an earthly farewell; the exclamation is introduced by a numinous vision of majesty. Death would be to succumb to this vision for not having rendered himself capable of it; for a Spiritual who has acquired this divine faculty there is no point in transcendence to which he cannot follow it.

17. Cf. *Futūḥāt* II, 326; cf. Asín, *El Islam cristianizado*, pp. 462–63.
18. Ibid. Cf. *Futūḥāt* II, 324: "One of the most subtile phenomena of love is that which I experienced in myself. You experience a vehement love, a sympathy, an ardent desire, an emotional agitation so great as to provoke physical weakness, total insomnia, disgust at all food, and yet you do not know *for* whom or *by* whom. You cannot determine the object of your love (*maḥbūb*). It is the most subtile that I have observed in love by personal experience. And then by chance a theophany (*tajallī*) appears to you in an inner vision. Then this love attaches itself (to this mental theophany). Or else you meet a certain person; at the sight the previously experienced emotion attaches itself to that person (as its object); you recognize that this person was the object of your love, though you were unaware of it. Or else you hear a certain person spoken of, and you feel an inclination for the person, determined by the ardent desire that was in you before; you recognize that that person is your companion. This is one of the most secret and subtile presentiments that souls have of things, divining them through veils of Mystery, while knowing nothing of their mode of being, without even knowing whom they are in love with, in whom their love will repose, or even what the love they feel is in reality. This is also experienced sometimes in the anguish of sadness or in the expansiveness of joy, when the cause of it remains unknown. . . . This is due to the *pre*-sentiment that souls have of things even before they materialize in the sphere of the outward senses; this is the premise of their realization."
19. Cf. Ch. I, n. 6 above and n. 24 below.
20. Cf. *Fuṣūṣ* I, 215 and II, 326–27. It should be noted that orientalists usually vocalize Bisṭāmī, whereas the Iranian pronunciation is still Basṭāmī. Basṭām (where the tomb of Abū Yazīd Basṭāmī is preserved and which is still a place of pilgrimage) is a small town a few miles from Shahrūd, a city on the main road from Teheran to Khorāsān.

21. A fundamental maxim for our mystics; cf. in the prologue of Suhrawardī's "Vademecum of the *Fedeli d'amore*" (*Mu'nis al-ʿUshshāq*) the primordial triad: Beauty, Love, Sadness.
22. "And if you love a being for his beauty, you love none other than God, for He is the beautiful being. Thus in all its aspects the object of love is God alone. Moreover, since God knows Himself and he came to know the world [by knowing Himself], He produced it *ad extra* of His image. Thus the world is for Him a mirror in which He sees His own image, and that is why God loves only Himself, so that if He declares: God will love you (III:29), it is in reality Himself that He loves" (*Futūḥāt* II, 326 *in fine*).
23. *Futūḥāt* IX, 327.
24. That precisely is the secret of the *Fedeli d'amore*, which follows from the *sirr al-rubūbīya*. Ibn ʿArabī declares: "It is a difficult question to consider, because it has not been given to every soul to know things as they are in themselves, nor have all been favored with the privilege of faith in the tidings which come to us from God and inform us of what is. That is why God favored His Prophet with a grace of this kind [Koran XLII: 52], and—thanks to God—we are among the number of his servants to whom He has deigned to communicate His inspiration!" (*Futūḥāt* II, 329), a statement flowing from our *shaikh's* profound conviction that he was the seal of Muḥammadan holiness. In short, the mystic's vocation is to recognize that the love he experiences is the very same love with which God loves Himself in him; that consequently he is this divine passion; that his love is literally a *theopathy* and that he must assume its suffering and splendor, because it is, within him, that *com-passion* of God with and for Himself, which through this theopathy calls into existence the beings of His being. Hence it becomes necessary to tear man away from the absurd egotism in which the creature forgets what lives in him, forgets that his passion is *com-passion*, and renders himself guilty of a divine catastrophe when he sets himself up as the goal of his love.
25. *Futūḥāt* II, 329.

26. Cf. also *Futūḥāt* II, 332. "Spiritual love is the love which in the lover conciliates and reunites (*jāmiʿ*) the love of his beloved for his beloved and for himself, just as natural or physical love is the love which loves the beloved only for its own sake."
27. *Fa-tajallà lahu fī ṣūrat tabīʿīya.*
28. *Futūḥāt* II, 331. Cf. II, 333 (in connection with this sign): "Know that when the Spirit assumes a physical form in the apparitional body (*ajsād mutakhayyala,* epiphanic bodies, bodies perceptible by imaginative vision), not in the sensible bodies which present themselves to usual knowledge, these apparitional bodies can nevertheless be the object of a normal perception. Nevertheless those who see them do not all distinguish uniformly between these apparitional bodies and the bodies which, according to them, are real bodies in the strict sense. That is why the Prophet's Companions did not recognize the Angel Gabriel when he descended in the form of an Arab youth. They did not know that he was an apparitional body, so that the Prophet said to them: 'It is Gabriel,' but they did not doubt within themselves that it was a young Arab." (We see how docetism, as a science of the Active Imagination, *'ilm al-khayāt,* becomes a critique of knowledge.) "It was the same with Maryam," Ibn ʿArabī continues, "when the Angel typified himself for her in the form of a beautiful youth. For she did not yet possess the sign that distinguishes Spirits when they take body" (cf. § 3 below, pp. 170 ff., the mystic paraphrase of the Annunciation in Jalāl Rūmī: it is when Maryam recognizes the Angel as her Self that she conceives the Divine Child by him). Similarly on the day of the Resurrection, God will appear to His worshipers; there are some who will not recognize Him and will run from him (as Maryam at first from the Angel, cf. Ch. I, n. 32). Divine Majesty and Angelic Majesty are in the same situation in relation to him to whom they are epiphanized if he is still unaware of them. Thus God must help him by a *sign,* thanks to which he will recognize divine epiphany, angelic epiphany, the epiphany of a *jinn,* and the epiphany of a human soul. "Recognize then *whom* you see, and whereby you see the thing as it is."

29. *Futūḥāt* II, 331. By this sign "God epiphanizes Himself to the soul according to the essence of that soul, which is at once physical and spiritual. Then the soul becomes aware that it sees God, but through Him, not through itself; it loves only Him, not through itself, but in such a way that it is He who loves Himself; it is not the soul which loves Him; it contemplates God in every being, but thanks to a gaze which is the divine gaze itself. It becomes aware that He loves no other than Himself; He is the Lover and the Beloved, He who seeks and He who is sought."
30. The mystic soul assimilates this supreme experience only on condition that it understands the origin and beginning of that love whose active subject appears to the soul in the soul but as something other than the soul, as an event that takes place in it, and whose organ, place, and aim it is. Here the dialectic of love attaches to the mystery of divine pre-eternal life. But since experientially the mystic lover knows the divine Names and Attributes only because he discovers their contents and realities in himself, how could he divine the mystery of divine pre-eternity, the divine nostalgia exhaling its creative sigh (*Nafas Raḥmānī*) if he did not discover and experience it in himself? It is inherent in his creatural condition to "sigh," because this sigh (*tanaffus*) is his release. The Breath exhaled by the Sadness of the Pathetic God (yearning to be known, that is, to realize His *significatio passiva* in His *ma' lūh*, in Him whose God He will become), this Cloud (*'amā'*) is, as we have seen, the creative energy and the "spiritual matter" of the entire universe of beings both spiritual and corporeal, the God through whom and out of whom beings are made (*al-Ḥaqq al-makhlūq bihi*). Since it is this "universal matter," the Cloud is the *patiens* that receives all the forms of being, which are thus the forms assumed by the divine passion to be known and revealed. Such is the beginning of the Creator's love for us. As to the origin of our love for Him, it is not vision but audition, the hearing of the *KuN*, the *Esto*, the imperative of our own being "when we were in the substance of the Cloud." "Thus we are His Words (*Kalimāt*) which are never exhausted. . . . We became Forms in the

Cloud, to which we thus gave being *in actu;* after having been purely ideal existence, it took on concrete existence. Such is the cause that is at the origin of our love for God" (*Futūḥāt* II, 331).

31. Ibid. II, 331–32.
32. Cf. Ch. I, n. 78. The preceding already provides an answer to the question (asked of Ibn ʿArabī by a woman who was a great mystic, p. 150 above) concerning the origin and the end of love. All nominalist conceptions are rejected; love is not a concept added to the essence of the lover, but neither is it simply a relation between lover and Beloved. It is a property inherent in the essence of the lover; the reality of love is nothing other than the lover himself (*Futūḥāt* II, 332). And this must be understood along with this other proposition: that the same Divine Being is the Beloved and the Lover. But precisely this unity is not a unity of undifferentiated identity; it is the unity of a being whom the Compassion essential to his being transforms into a bi-unity (*ḥaqq* and *khalq*), each of whose terms aspires toward the other. On the one hand His aspiration to be manifested and objectified (the *pathos* of the "pathetic God"); on the other hand, in the being who manifests Him, His aspiration to return to Himself; an aspiration which in that being becomes his *theopathy* (*ma' lūhīya*), that is to say, his own passion to be the God known in and by a being whose God He is, and which is thus the passion (the *significatio passiva*) which posits His divinity (*ilāhīya*). Thus we shall say that the aim and end of love is to experience the unity of the Lover and the Beloved in an *unio mystica* which is *unio sympathetica,* for their very unity postulates these two terms: *ilāh* and *ma' lūh,* divine compassion and human theopathy, an ecstatic dialogue between the beloved and the lover. The *unus-ambo* may create difficulties for the schemas of rational logic: the *Anā sirr al-Ḥaqq* cannot be interpreted in terms of Incarnation: "The end or goal of love is the unification (*ittiḥād*) which consists in the beloved's self (*dhāt*) becoming the lover's self and vice versa; it is to this that the Incarnationists (*ḥulūlīya*) refer, but they do not know wherein this unification consists" (*Futūḥāt* II, 334).

33. Thus, as we have already pointed out (n. 7 above), the meaning and perception of theophanies call for an investigation of the function of the Spiritual Energy (*himma*), which is the objectively Creative Imagination. The broad outlines of such an investigation will be found in Part Two of this book.

34. *Futūḥāt* II, 334. "Know that whatever may be the physical form in which the Spirit manifests itself in a sensible body or in an apparitional body, and regardless of the aspect in which we consider it, the following will always be true: the beloved being, who is in every instance something that does not yet exist, is typified in the Imagination, although it has no objective reality; consequently it has, in every case, a certain mode of existence perceptible to imaginative vision, through the "imaginative" power or presence (*ḥaḍrat khayālīya*), thanks to that special eye which is specific to this faculty."

35. Cf. *Futūḥāt* II, 325. Therein consists the "service of love," the divine service which knows neither conquest nor possession; a "sympathetic devotion" which is a passion in harmony with the superhuman virtualities of the beloved being and attempts to accomplish this theophanic virtuality. It is not "positive reality," the effective and material nature of the beloved being, which attaches the lover to that being. Here there is no subtle and confused reasoning (as we are surprised to find Asín maintaining, *El Islam cristianizado*, p. 465, n. 1), but an analysis of the essentially virtual state of that which is the object of love in the beloved being.

36. *Futūḥāt* II, 327; cf. II, 332: "It is certain that the beloved object is something that does not yet exist, and that the love of an already existing object is in no wise possible. The only possibility is the attachment of the lover for a real being in whom there comes to be manifested the realization of the beloved object that does not yet exist." II, 334: "Many sophisms occur in connection with love. The first of all is one we have already mentioned: lovers imagine that the beloved object is a real thing, whereas it is a still unreal thing. The aspiration of love is to see this thing realized in a real person, and when love sees

it realized, it then aspires to the perpetuation of this state, whose realization in the real person it had previously awaited. Thus the real beloved never ceases to be unreal [i.e. always transcendent], although most lovers are unaware of this, unless they have been initiated into the true science of love and its objects." Creative Imagination, creative prayer, creative love are three aspects to be studied conjointly in Ibn ʿArabī (see Part Two). How is it possible that the lover should love what the beloved loves (how can we speak of this total *sympatheia*, this synergy of wills)? And if this is not possible, will the lover not remain in the state of natural love which loves an object only for itself, or treats a beloved person as an object? Ibn ʿArabī further denounces sophism by pointing out that the rule followed by the *fedele d'amore* is that of the invisible Beloved (unreal for sensory evidence) who is manifested to him and can be manifested to him only by a concrete, visible figure. Otherwise, the lover would not be able to make the real object of his love exist concretely and substantially in the real being which manifests it to him (sometimes unbeknownst to him) except by supernatural assistance, through the resurrecting breath which Jesus (through his angelic nature) and other servants of God have had at their disposal. But because the energy of love forces him to give existence to his beloved, the all-powerful Imaginatrix comes to his help. "It is a question that you will find treated in depth in no book as we have done here, for I know of no one who has analyzed it as we have done" (II, 333).

37. Cf. Affifi, *Mystical Philosophy*, pp. 133–36; on the *munāzalāt*, see *Futūḥāt* III, 523 (ch. 384); cf. among other identical statements of fundamental significance for Ismailian Shīʿism, that attributed to the First Imām: "I should never worship a God I did not see"; cf. our study, "Divine Epiphany," p. 138 and see also *Futūḥāt* II, 337, line 5 from bottom of page.
38. *Futūḥāt* II, 337. And here too the answer to the question which "Sophia" asks her *fedele:* "Have you then perished? . . ." (an answer which is an implicit appeal to the capacity to bring forth the more-than-real, to invest the beloved being with his "angelic

function," just as the Divine Compassion in the primordial Cloud calls the latent hexeities of His "most beautiful Names," *al-Asmā' al-ḥusnā*, into existence).

39. Ibid. and II, 338, line 11 ff. The lover "then obeys the illusion of believing that the pleasure he experiences in the sensible encounter with his beloved will be greater than that which he experienced in imagining him. And this happens because this lover is subjugated by the density of material nature and is unaware of the pleasure that accompanies imaginative representation in the dream state. (If he had borne this in mind), he would know that the pleasure conferred by the imagination is greater than that of the sensible external object. That is why such a lover doubts the means he must employ to obtain an objective union (*min khārij*) and questions those whom he knows to have experience in this matter."

40. Ibid. "On this point, we [the mystics] form two groups. There are some who in their Active Imagination contemplate the Image of that real being in whom their Beloved is manifested; they thus contemplate His real existence with their own eyes, and that is union with the Beloved in the Active Imagination; then, in contemplating Him, they are united with Him in a union whose delicacy and sweetness surpass any material, concrete and objective union. It is this [imaginative union] which absorbed the spirit of Qays al-Majnūn, who turned away from his beloved Laylà at the time when she presented herself to him really and objectively, saying: 'Go away from me,' for fear that the density of her material presence should deprive him of that other presence, of his delicate and subtile imaginative contemplation, because the Laylà who was present to his Active Imagination was more suave and beautiful than the real, physical Laylà." Cf. the Breviary of Love of Aḥmad Ghazālī (*Sawāniḥ al-ʿUshshāq*), ed. Ritter, pp. 45–46, 76. "This phenomenon," Ibn ʿArabī adds, "is the most subtile that love can involve. He who experiences it never ceases to be fully satisfied with it, never laments over separation. This gift was imparted to me in large measure among all the *Fedeli d'amore*, but such a gift is

rare among lovers, because in them sensuous density is predominant. In our opinion, if a man has devoted himself exclusively to the love of spiritual things separated from matter, the maximum to which he can attain when he effects a certain condensation is to make them descend to the Imagination, but no lower [that is, not as far as the sensory realm]. Thus if the Imagination represents a spirit's maximum mode of operation, what will be the subtlety of that spirit in respect of immaterial things? The man whose state is such will be the man who can best love God. Indeed, the extreme limit to which he attains in his love of Him, when He does not divest Him of His resemblance to creatures, will be to make Him descend as far as the Imagination, and that is precisely what is ordained in this maxim attributed to the Prophet: 'Love God as though you saw Him' " (*Futūḥāt* II, 337).

41. *Futūḥāt* II, 339: When the mystics finally discover by their experience that God is the same being which previously they had imagined to be their own soul, what happens is similar to a mirage. Nothing has been done away with in being. The mirage remains an object of vision, but one knows what it is; one knows that it is not water.

42. Ibid. II, 361; cf. II, 346–47: "Love is directly proportional to the theophany (that the lover receives of Divine Beauty), and this theophany is proportional to the gnosis he possesses. Those who are liquefied, in whom the effects of love are manifested externally, show thereby that their love is a physical love. The love of the gnostics (*'ārifīn*) exerts no visible outward influence, for the science of gnosis effaces all those effects by virtue of a secret it confers, which is known only to the gnostics. The gnostic *fedele d'amore* (*al-muḥibb al-'ārif*) is a Living Man who never dies; he is a separate Spirit, and the man of physical nature is incapable of experiencing the love of which the gnostic is the subject. His love is something divine; his ardent desire is something pertaining to the lord of love (*rabbānī*); he is assisted by his Name, the *saint* on whom the words of sensible discourse can have no influence."

43. Cf. above, Ch. I, § 3, p. 121.
44. *Futūḥāt* II, 347, in which it is explained why, according to a story of the *Mi'rāj* (the assumption of the Prophet), the Angel Gabriel swoons with love before the Throne (because he knows in whose presence he is, but the substance of his "body," which is supra-elemental, transphysical, is not consumed (cf. the allusion in *Tarjumān al-ashwāq*, II, 2, tr. Nicholson, p. 50).
45. Cf. above, § 2, p. 146, and nn. 37 and 40.
46. Cf. above Ch. I, § 3, p. 130.
47. Cf. *Fuṣūṣ* I, 217.
48. Jalāluddīn Rūmī, *Mathnawī*, Book I, verse 2437 (ed. Nicholson, text, I, 150; commentary, VII, 155–56). On this passage of the *Mathnawī* (which, it should be remembered, is regarded and utilized by the Iranian Ṣūfīs as the Persian Koran, *Qurān-e fārsī*), Nicholson has given a subtle and perceptive commentary in which he refers to the traditional commentaries, the most outstanding among which are the enormous tomes written in Persian in Iran and India, notably that of Walī Muḥammad Akbarābādī (written between 1727 and 1738). It is one of the numerous texts that provide commentators with an opportunity to connect the doctrine of Mawlānā Rūmī with that of Ibn 'Arabī, and it is by reproducing the text of the *Fuṣūṣ* (mentioned below) that they amplify the passage from the *Mathnawī*. "Woman is the highest type of earthly beauty, but earthly beauty is nothing unless it is a manifestation and reflection of the Divine Attributes." (Cf. Najm Dāya Rāzī, in *Mirṣād:* "When Adam contemplated the beauty of Eve, he saw a ray of the divine beauty".) "Putting aside the veil of Form, the poet contemplates in Woman the eternal beauty that is the inspiratrix and the object of all love, and he sees her, in her essential nature, as the *medium* par excellence by which this increate Beauty reveals itself and exerts its creative activity. From this point of view she is the *focus* of theophanies and the giver of life, and can be identified with the power of their radiations. To quote Walī Muḥammad, who joins Ibn 'Arabī in affirming the pre-eminence of Woman (because her being combines the twofold mode of *actio* and *passio*): 'Know that God cannot be contemplated independently of a

concrete being and that He is more perfectly seen in a human being than in any other, and more perfectly in woman than in man.' "

Of course this *creativity* attributed to woman (here implying the creative plurality which our authors justify by verses XXIII:14 and XXIX:16 of the Koran) concerns not the physical functions of the woman but her spiritual and essentially divine qualities, which "create" love in man and make him seek union with the divine Beloved. Here we must think of the feminine human being (cf. in Rilke *der weibliche Mensch*), the Creative Feminine. It is this creative feminine being that is exemplified in the spiritual man who has attained the degree at which he can give birth in himself to the Child of his soul (*walad-e maʿnawī*), the child of his *lāhūt* (his divine dimension, the Angel Gabriel of his Annunciation; cf., below, the passage in which Jalāl Rūmī typifies the situation of the mystic in the situation of Maryam before the Angel). Other commentators, moreover, interpret "Creator" (*khāliq*) as referring to the mediation of Woman in Creation: she is the theophany (*maẓhar*) in which are manifested the most beautiful divine Names: "The Creator, the Originator, the Modeller" (Koran LIX:24 and *passim*). In these Names the Ismailian theosophers typify the supreme archangelical Triad (cf. "Divine Epiphany," p. 101, n. 78), which also bears the traits of the creative Sophia, just as she is recognizable in the creative *Fāṭima* (*Fāṭima-Fāṭir*) of Proto-Ismailism (*Umm al-Kitāb*) and just as in the Iranian name (*Ravānbakhsh*) of the Angel Gabriel or Active Intelligence in Suhrawardī it is possible to recognize the "Virgin of Light of Manichaeism. Here the sources of sophiology are extremely rich and complex; cf. also our article "Soufisme et sophiologie."

49. See the preceding note. It is also essential to note the following: The twofold *pathetic* and *poietic* aspect of the feminine being (that is, of the creative Sophia) enables us to identify the recurrences of the symbol elsewhere. The terms *Noūs poietikos* and *Noūs pathetikos*, which passed from Greek into Arabic, characterize the entire noetics which the Neoplatonists of Islam inherited from Aristotelianism (and the relation between the two

Nous or intellects is rather a *sympathy* than a causal relation). However, what among the Greek Peripatetics was simply a theory of knowledge (with an Active Intelligence not yet separate, not yet an "Angel"), becomes, in the Avicennan disciples of Suhrawardī in Iran, a dialogue of spiritual initiation between the illuminating Active Intelligence (of the Angel) and the human intellect, just as it becomes a dialogue of love among the *Fedeli d'amore* of the Occident and among the mystics who, in Judaism, interpreted the Song of Songs as the supreme version of this dialogue (cf. Georges Vajda, *Juda ben Nissim ibn Malka, philosophe juif marocain*, pp. 21 and 94). Moreover, the *Nous* or Intelligence also has this twofold, passive and active nature, in Plotinus. In turn the Intelligences, archangelical hypostases or Cherubim, which in the cosmology of Avicenna proceed from one another, also present this twofold nature (*fāʿil-munfaʿil*, poietic-pathetic). Hence certain adversaries of the Avicennans criticized their angelology for reintroducing a conception attributed to the old Arabs in the Koran (namely, that "the Angels are the daughters of God," cf. our "Rituel sabéen," p. 189). Once we understand how a sophianic intuition was thus at the source of Avicennan angelology and of the noetics which is an aspect of it, we shall understand how, since the Avicennans were led back from the Active Intelligence to the figure of the Holy Spirit or Angel Gabriel, the *Fedeli d'amore* for their part came to identify Sophia, whom they called Madonna Intelligenza, in that same figure. Without confusing the theophanism of Ibn ʿArabī and the emanationism of the Neoplatonists, we may say that the figure which corresponds to the *Nous* of the Neoplatonists (First Intelligence, supreme Spirit, Muhammadic Spirit, Archangel Gabriel) presents the precise structure which determines the theophanic precedence of the Feminine; see also below, the text corresponding to nn. 59 and 62.

50. *Fuṣūṣ* I, 214–15 and II, 324–25.

51. *Fuṣūṣ* I, 216–17 and II, 329–30, nn. 7 and 8.

52. Cf. n. 48 above, in which the passage invoked for the commentary of the *Mathnawī* (I, 2433–37) corresponds here to *Fuṣūṣ* I, 217 and II, 331–32 (cf. Kāshānī's Commentary, p. 272 and

Futūḥāt IV, 84). In reference to n. 49 above, we suggest that it might be useful to conduct a parallel analysis of the threefold self-contemplation of which Ibn ʿArabī speaks, and, in Avicennan cosmology, of the triple contemplation of each angelic Intelligence by itself, which contemplation, conjointly with its twofold nature (*agens-patiens*) gives rise to a new Intelligence, to a Heaven and to a Soul which moves this Heaven.

53. Cf. *Futūḥāt* I, 136 (ch. X), II, 31, and IV, 24; Qayṣarī's commentary on the *Fuṣūṣ*, p. 127. (This dependence of Jesus on Maryam was also meditated in gnostic circles in the Middle Ages, cf. Alphandéry, "Le Gnosticisme dans les sectes médiévales latines," pp. 55–56). The theosophy of Ibn ʿArabī thus establishes, at the heart of sophiology, a type of *quaternity* which should be analyzed and added to those that have been studied by C. G. Jung in *Aion: Researches into the Phenomenology of the Self*, index s.v.
54. See n. 48 above. The Fire without light, whose will to power set up the Masculine as an absolute agent, dies down and gives way to the clear, gentle light that was its hidden being; see *Fuṣūṣ* I, 216 and II, 328. (Cf. in Jacob Boehme the state of man separated from the heavenly Sophia.)
55. Cf. n. 16 above.
56. *Muṣṭafà āmad ke sāzad ham-damī*, cf. *Mathnawī*, Book I, 1972–74: "There came the elect, who established sympathy. Speak to me, O Ḥumayra, speak to me, O Ḥumayra, put the iron in the fire in order that by that fire which is yours this mountain (made incandescent by love) may change to pure ruby." These obscure allusions call for a long commentary (cf. ed. Nicholson, VII, 134–35). The name Ḥumayra was said to be the diminutive that the Prophet gave his wife ʿĀ'isha. First of all we discern an allusion to a certain practice of *sympathetic magic:* to put the iron in the fire, to provoke a *correspondence* in the heart of the beloved, just as, according to ancient mineralogy, the rubies and other precious stones are transmuted by the subterranean heat which originally emanated from the Sun. As for the transfiguration of the body of the prophet or saint by the divine light (VI, 3058), we find parallels to it in Hellenistic mysticism. The

mysterious appeal has challenged the mystical sagacity of the commentators. Some point out that a feminine name is quite fitting in reference to the Spirit (*Rūḥ*), which admits of the feminine gender in Arabic (and which is regularly feminine in Aramaic). Here then we find an indication that the mystic poet, responding to the Prophet's call, converses with the Divine Spirit as the lover with the Beloved, since the most perfect vision of the Godhead is obtained through contemplation of the Feminine (Kāshānī, Commentary, p. 272). Hence the paraphrase translated above in our text. Further, according to the commentators, we can gather that Mawlānā Rūmī wishes to say that the Prophet descended from the plane of *lāhūt* to the plane of *nāsūt* in order to enter into conjunction with the attributes of sensible human nature, without which he would not have been able to accomplish his mission. He desires then to be fascinated by the beauty of Ḥumayra in order to descend from the transcendent world and to manifest the rubies of gnosis in sensible forms. In this case Ḥumayra represents sensible, phenomenal beauty (*ḥusn*) in contrast to absolute Beauty (*jamāl*), and *ham-damī* proclaims the harmony, the sympathy, established by Muḥammad between the sensible and the spiritual attributes of man, which for our commentators characterizes not only the Prophet but the religion which he established. And accordingly we find no contradiction between this interpretation and the distich in which Ḥumayra clearly designates the Heavenly Spirit. If 'Ā'isha-Ḥumayra (the mother of the Believers (cf. the "Mother of the Living" in Manichaeism) is the theophany (*maẓhar*) of the Divine Spirit, it means that on the earthly plane, that is, on the level of the empirical person of the Prophet, she manifests this Divine Spirit, the Creative Feminine, to which the appeal of an eternal prophetic Logos is addressed. It is in this pre-eternal sphere that the possibility of the reign of the *ham-damī* in the manifest world originates.

57. *Fuṣūṣ* I, 219 and II, 335–36, commentary of Bālī Effendī, p. 430. The text of the *ḥadīth* cannot be analyzed in detail here.

58. Ibid. The principal terms in question are: *dhāt* (Essence, Self), *dhāt ilāhīya* (Divine Essence), origin and source of being; *'illa,*

cause; *qudra*, the power that manifests being; *ṣifa*, divine qualification, the Attribute, that which is manifested. Similarly, Kāshānī observes, the Koran speaks of a "lone soul," to which was given a companion, and from this pair issued the multitude of human beings; but "soul" (*nafs*) is also a feminine term.

59. Cf. Kāshānī's Commentary, pp. 274–75. That is why mystic perception apprehends *agens* and *patiens* as constituting a single concrete whole (*'ayn; Fuṣūṣ* II, 332), for in the state of nuptial union (*nikāḥ*) *agens* and *patiens* form an *essentia unialis* (*ḥaqīqat aḥadīya*), action in passion, passion in action. For the contemplative mystic this mystery of nuptial union concentrates the vision of the Divine Being as *patiens* even where He is *agens* (simultaneity of *esse agentem* and *esse patientem*, Kāshānī, p. 272). This would be the place to insert an entire article on this mystery of nuptial union proper to each degree of being, repeated in each of the descents (*tanazzulāt*) from the One Essence and in each of the individuations of the sensible world (Kāshānī, Lexicon, s.v. *nikaḥ*, pp. 129–30, and the Commentary, p. 272); sexual union is only a reflection of this nuptial union which in the world of the Spirits of pure light takes on the form of that imaginative, projective, and creative Energy connoted by the term *himma* (cf. notes 7 and 33, above, and below, Ch. IV). Cf. in Suhrawardī, the notions of *qahr* and *maḥabba* on the different planes of being.
60. *Fuṣūṣ* I, 219–20 and II, 335.
61. Cf. Kāshānī, Commentary, p. 268.
62. Here there is a twofold allusion: first to the Koran XL:15 (verse of the enthronement of the Prophet, or more precisely, of the *Rūḥ Muḥammadī*, cf. *Fuṣūṣ* I, 220 and II, 336–37, and the commentary of Bālī Effendī, p. 432); second, to the *ḥadīth* which explains it: "When God had created the Intelligence, He said to it: 'Progress,' and so it progressed. Then He said to it: 'Govern,' and so it governed. Then He said to it: 'By My power and My glory! Through you I have received and through you I have given, through you I reward and through you I punish.' " Cf. the commentary of Dā'ūd Qayṣarī (pp. 482–83), who adds: "This Intelligence is the Spirit to which the Prophet refers when he says: 'The first being that God created was *my* light.' " Here

we must make two brief observations: (1) This *Rūḥ* is homologous to the first of the Plotinian Emanations whose twofold, active and passive nature, corresponding to the twofold aspect *'ubūdīya* and *rubūbīya*, has been noted above (n. 49); it goes without saying that the order of the theophanies is not that of the Neoplatonists' successive descending emanations; they are *in every case* epiphanies of the one *ḥaqīqa* of being, contemplated in different ways. Thus the First Intelligence is God Himself epiphanized in a particular form, and the same goes for the universal Soul and all the other theophanies (*Fuṣūṣ* II, 337). (2) Concern for accuracy obliges us to distinguish between allusions to the *Rūḥ Muḥammadī* and allusions to the empirical person of the Prophet. Otherwise we are in danger of distorting the whole theological perspective. The confusions to be avoided are precisely those to which we should be exposed by a confusion of the very different premises presiding on the one hand over the official Christology of the Councils and on the other over primitive Christology (that of the Ebionites) which here finds its extension in prophetology. For this primitive Christology as for this prophetology, we must refer to the motif of the Anthropos or to the enthronement of Metatron in the books of Henoch, in which Rudolf Otto in his day quite accurately discerned a relationship analogous to that which the theology of ancient Iran establishes between the Fravashi-Daīnā and the soul that exemplifies it on earth.

63. Cf. Nicholson, *Studies in Islamic Mysticism*, p. 113. "You are the reality symbolized by Hind and Salmā, 'Azza and Asmā." Cf. Jīlī, *Kitāb al-Insān al-Kāmil*, II, 11–12. These words are part of the revelations on His Names and qualifications, communicated to Jīlī in a vision by the "Angel called Spirit," that is, *Rūḥ*, the feminine gender of which in Aramaic has been noted above (n. 56). But what is said here is by no means a grammatical accident. Cf. the nature of the Holy Spirit as feminine hypostasis in a Syriac writer such as Aphraates, or in the Gospel according to the Hebrews ("my mother the Holy Spirit") or as feminine Aeon in Gnosticism.

64. Quoted in Massignon, *Essai sur les origines du lexique technique de la mystique musulmane*, pp. 237–38. "This word *kūnī* is the feminine of the Koranic word *kun* (be = *fiat*), and refers to the first of the human creatures, the white pearl (*durra bayḍa*) of another *ḥadīth: das ewig Weibliche.* It is of the utmost interest to note that according to the early Qarmate doctrine *kūnī* is the first divine emanation, while a Ṣūfī like Manṣūr Ibn ʿAmmār uses it to personify the perfect Houri of Paradise, to whom the creator of the human race said: *kūnī, fa-kānat* (Be, and she was)."
65. The verse cited above as attributed to al-Ḥallāj figures in Qasīda 10 of the *Dīwān*, tr. Massignon, p. 27 (12th verse); it is also attributed to Badruddīn al-Shahīd (Nicholson, *Studies*, p. 113, n. 1), cf. Jāmī, *Ashiʿʿāt al-Lamaʿāt* (commentary by Fakhr ʿIrāqī), pp. 69–70. We must also consider all the meditations of Shīʿite theosophy on the surname (imputed to the Prophet himself) of *umm abī-hā* ("mother of her father") for Fāṭima (cf. below, n. 70). As to the Fravashi's relation to his soul that has "descended" to earthly existence, we incline to regard it as the prototype (a notion already intimated by Nyberg, *Kleinere Schriften*, p. 125) of the structural bi-unity constituted by the original celestial Self and the earthly self (cf. n. 62 above). From this point of view, it would be worthwhile to undertake a parallel sophiological study of the figures (and implicit features) of Daēnā in Mazdean theosophy and of Fāṭima in Shīʿite theosophy (we are planning to say more of this elsewhere). In such a study a place would be given to the motif of nuptial mysticism (*nikāḥ*), to which we have alluded above (n. 59). For further amplifications of the distich attributed to Ḥallāj and to Badruddīn, see Nicholson, *Studies*, pp. 112–13.
66. Cf. Jāmī, *Ashiʿʿāt al-Lamʿāt*, p. 70. Of course the intentions of Fakhr ʿIrāqī and of Ḥallāj are not contradictory but complementary. As for the verse from the Gospel of St. John (III:3) referred to above, it is a favorite with the theosophical thinkers of Islam, cf. for example, for Ismailism, *Kalāmi Pīr*, ed. Ivanow, p. 114 of the Persian text, where the verse is cited in connection with the idea of spiritual birth (*wilādat-i ruḥānī*), as accom-

plished in the world of *ta'wīl,* while corporeal birth (*wilādat-i jismānī*) is accomplished in the world of *tanzīl.*

67. Cf. our study: "Le Récit d'initiation et l'hermétisme en Iran," pp. 153 ff. Note the expression *Walad ma'nawī* which reappears in the commentators of Mawlānā Rūmī (n. 70, below).

68. The Avicennans came back to this conception. Since they recognized the Angel Gabriel-Holy Spirit in the Active Intelligence (see nn. 48 and 49, above), noetics was for them the beginning of a fundamental mystic experience, as is attested, for example, by the life and work of Mīr Dāmād, one of the most celebrated seventeenth-century masters of theology in Ispahan; cf. our "Confessions extatiques de Mīr Dāmād."

69. *Mathnawī,* Book III, 3706 ff. and 3771–80; cf. commentary *ad* III 3773, ed. Nicholson, VIII, 95: "For the external eye the Angel Gabriel has the appearance (of the beauty) of a new moon, but that is only his apparitional body (*ṣūrat-i mithālī*); his real form consists in the Divine Attributes manifested in him and reflected as an image in the mirror that is the heart of the mystic."

70. Commentary of Ismā'īl of Ankara *ad* I, 1934, cited in Nicholson, VII, 130–31. Here the distichs I, 1934 ff.: "The Call of God whether veiled or not veiled confers what He conferred on Maryam. O you who are corrupted by death inside your skin, At the voice of the Beloved return to nonbeing. This voice is absolute and comes from the king of love, though uttered by the throat of his vassal. He says to him: I am your tongue and your eye: I am your senses, I am your contentment and your anger. Go, for you are he of whom it is said: it is by my ear that He hears, it is through me that He sees: You *are* the Divine consciousness; why say that you *have* that consciousness?" Commentary (pp. 130–31): The first hemistich alludes to Koran verses XLII:50–51: "It is not vouchsafed to any mortal that Allah should speak to him except by inspiration (*waḥy*) or from behind a veil," or through an Angel sent and authorized by Him. The "call of God" (Persian *Bāng-i Ḥaqq* = Arabic *Kalām Allāh*) without articulated words refers to the call from the burning bush heard by Moses (Koran XX:29 ff., XXVII:7–8).

"What He conferred on Maryam" refers to the conception of Jesus through the Holy Spirit, the Angel Gabriel, who breathed his breath into the Virgin Maryam (xx:91, LXVI:12): Jesus is called the Word of God (*Kalimat Allāh*), which was projected into Maryam (IV:169). Hence the paraphrase of Ismāʿīl of Ankara cited above, with which one can compare Suhrawardī's invocation to his Perfect Nature (n. 67, above): "You are the Spirit which engendered me and you are he whom my thought in turn engenders. Like Maryam, like Fāṭima, the mystic soul becomes the "mother of her father" (cf. n. 65, above). See also ed. Nicholson, additional note *ad* I, 1515–21, VII, 371–72, the quotation from Mawlānā Rūmī's great prose work *Fīhī mā fīh* (ed. Furūzānfar, pp. 19–21): "The physical form is of great importance; nothing can be done without the consociation of the form and the essence (*maghz*). However often you may sow a seed stripped of its pod, it will not grow; sow it with the pod, it will become a great tree. From this point of view the body is fundamental and necessary for the realization of the divine intention. [There follows an allusion to the passage from non-being to being, from the mineral to the vegetable state, etc., to the angelic state, and so on *ad infinitum.*] God sowed all that in order that you might recognize that He has numerous abodes of this kind, echeloned the ones above the others, still others that He has not yet shown. . . . It is suffering that leads to success in every instance. As long as Maryam did not feel the pangs of childbirth, she did not go beneath the palm tree (Koran XIX:23–26). This body is like Maryam, and each one of us has a Christ within him (*ta ham-cūn Maryam ast, va har yakī ʿIsa dārīm*); if the suffering of love rises in us, our Christ will be born."

71. Cf. already cited from Nicholson, VIII, 131: "The Father speaks the Word into the soul, and when the *Son* is born, each soul becomes Mary." Cf. also Meister Eckhart, *Telle était Sœur Katrei* (1954), p. 104: "Thus does God: He engenders His only son in the highest region of the soul. In the same act wherein He engenders His Son in me, I engender the Son in the Father. For there is no difference for God (between the fact) of engendering

the angel and (the fact) of being born of the Virgin"; p. 176: ". . . And I say it is a miracle that we should be the mother and brothers of God. . . ."

72. The French translation was established by Mr. ʿOsmān Yaḥià, my pupil and now my co-worker at the École des Hautes Études, who, in addition to the comprehensive work referred to above (Introduction, n. 1), has completed a critical edition of the "Book of Theophanies," now being printed. I have changed only a few words and, to simplify the typography, modified his disposition of the lines.

PART TWO

CREATIVE IMAGINATION AND CREATIVE PRAYER

PROLOGUE

1. Alexandre Koyré, *Mystiques, Spirituels, Alchimistes du XVIème siècle allemand*, p. 60, n. 2; cf. by the same author, *La Philosophie de Jacob Boehme*, p. 218, n. 4.
2. Cf. Koyré, *Mystiques*, pp. 59–60.
3. Cf. Koyré, *La Philosophie de Jacob Boehme*, pp. 349, 376, 505 ff.
4. "Die Fantasey ist nicht *Imaginatio*, sondern ein eckstein der Narren . . ." Paracelsus, *Ein ander Erklärung der Gesammten Astronomey* (ed. K. Sudhoff, X, p. 475, quoted in Koyré, *Mystiques*, p. 59, n. 1.

CHAPTER III
THE CREATION AS THEOPATHY

1. Cf. the aspects already outlined above, Ch. I, §§ 2 and 3. By way of establishing the equivalences of the terminology exemployed in the following paragraphs, let us note the following: *al-Ḥaqq al Makhlūq bihi* = the God by whom and in whom all being is created (the Creator-Creature). *Al-Ḥaqq al-mutakhayyal* = the God manifested by the theophanic Imagination. *Al-Ḥaqq al makhlūq fī'l-i'tiqādāt* = the God created in the faiths. *Tajdīd al-khalq* = the recurrence of creation.
2. Cf. Ibn 'Arabī, *Futūḥāt*, II, 310.
3. Ibid., on the Cloud as essence (*ḥaqīqa*) of the absolute Imagination (*khayāl muṭlaq*), of the Imagination which essentiates

(*khayāl muḥaqqiq*), configures (*muṣawwir*) all the forms or receptacles constituting the exoteric, manifest, epiphanic aspect of the Divine Being (*Ẓāhir Allāh*)

4. Finally, as we have already observed and for reasons that need not be set forth here, the term *eternal hexeity* strikes us as the most direct translation for the term *aʿyān thābita*, employed with such complex connotations in the work of Ibn ʿArabī. *Hexeity* is a characteristic term in the technical vocabulary of Duns Scotus. In employing it here, we do not mean to imply an affinity or homology. Such a question could be raised only in connection with a thorough study of the late Avicennans of Iran, who were themselves permeated by the theosophy of Ibn ʿArabī.
5. *Futūḥāt* II, 313. As the Divine Sigh, the Cloud is a breath inhaled and exhaled *in* the Divine Being (in the *ḥaqīqa* of the *Ḥaqq*); it is the configuration (and the configurability) of the creatural in the Creator. It is the Creator-Creature, that is to say, He in whom are manifested all the forms of the universe, He in whom the infinite diversity of the theophanies successively unfolds (*fa-kāna al-Ḥaqq al makhlūq bihi mā ẓahara min suwar al-ʿālam fīhi wa mā ẓahara min ikhtilāf al-tajallī al-ilāhī fīhi*).
6. *Futūḥāt* II, 311.
7. Quoted in *Futūḥāt* II, 379.
8. Ibid. II, 379.
9. Cf. the five "descending" meanings denoted by the term "matter" in the theosophy of Ibn ʿArabī and in related theosophies; Ch. I, n. 23.
10. Cf. ibid., the remarks of ʿAbd al-Razzāq Kāshānī on *Nafas al-Raḥmān* and *Nūr qāhir* (*lux victorialis*) among Suhrawardī's Ishrāqīyūn, who derive their notion of light from the Zoroastrian *Xvarnah*, "Light of Glory." In general, the entire ontology of the world of Idea-Images (*ʿālam al-mithāl*) is common to the theosophies of Ibn ʿArabī and of Suhrawardī (cf. our edition of the *Ḥikmat al-Ishrāq*, II, index s.v.); compare Mount *Qāf* and its emerald cities with the "Earth created from the surplus clay of Adam" (cf. our study *Terre céleste et Corps de résurrection*, p. 136), or the land of Yūḥ (the fourth heaven, the heaven of the

Sun, or the Nūḥ, Noah), Ibn ʿArabī, *Fuṣūṣ* I, 74: Jīlī, *Kitāb al-Insān al-Kāmil,* II, 27. The ontology of this intermediate world of Archetypal Images more or less fascinated all our theosopher theologians. Muḥsen-e Fā'iz, the great Iranian Imāmite thinker of the seventeenth century, speaks of it as the world which "occupies in the macrocosm the same rank as the Imagination in the microcosm." It is through the organ of the Active Imagination that we penetrate into this world "where spirits are embodied and bodies are spiritualized." Ibn ʿArabī also gave a striking description of the psychic event that marks this penetration: "On that Earth there exist Figures (or Forms) of a marvelous race; they stand at the entrances to the avenues and dominate this world in which we are, its earth and its heaven, its paradise and its hell. When one of us wishes to penetrate this Earth . . . the condition to be fulfilled is the practice of gnosis and solitude outside one's temple of flesh. He encounters the forms that by divine order stand watch at the entrances of the avenues. One of them runs to the new arrival; it clothes him in a dress appropriate to his rank, takes him by the hand, and walks with him through this Earth, and they make of it what they will. He passes near no stone, no tree, no village, nothing whatsoever, without talking to it, if he wishes, as a man speaks with his companion. They have different languages, but this Earth has the characteristic of giving to all who enter it the understanding of all the languages that are spoken on it. When he wishes to return, his companion goes with him to the place where he entered; he removes the dress in which he had clothed him and departs from him" (*Futūḥāt* I, 127). Such Ṣūfī descriptions of this mysterious, transfigured world show a striking correspondence with that of *dharmadhātu* in Mahayāna Buddhism (cf. D. T. Suzuki, *Essays in Zen Buddhism,* Third Series, index, s.v. "dharmadhātu").

11. *Fuṣūṣ* I, 101 and 102; cf. *Ẓill al-nūr* and *Ẓill al-ẓulma,* luminous shadow and dark shadow in ʿAlā'uddawla Semnānī, "Tafsīr."

12. *Fuṣūṣ* I, 103; cf. principally Kāshānī's Commentary, which insists on the fact that though the Imagination effects a differentiation, this does not mean that *mutakhayyal* is equivalent to "illusory"

or "inconsistent," as certain among the profane (*ʿawāmm*) suppose. The essential is to make no mistake about the true nature of this "consistency."

13. And each Name designates in this sense the *Ḥaqq mutakhayyal, Fuṣūṣ* I, 104.
14. Ibid.
15. Cf. below, Ch. V, § 3, "The Secret of the Divine Responses." Here we have an occasion to grasp at its source the contrast between the theophanic idea and the idea of incarnation. The pronoun *huwa* ("He") designates the Hidden, the Absent, (*ʿālam al-ghayb*), it is not employed for the visible present world (*ʿālam al-shahāda*) any more than one can say that any existent in this world is *al-Ḥaqq* (God). This is the crucial reason for the accusation of impiety and infidelity leveled against the Christians by Ibn ʿArabī and after him by all theosopher-theologians, for example, as late as the seventeenth century by Sayyed Aḥmad ʿAlawī, the closest disciple of Mīr Dāmād, in his book *Masqal-e safā*, a straightforward and courteous polemic filled with Bible quotations. Ṣūfī theosophy postulates a primordial theophany (nothing less, but also nothing more), that is to say, an anthropomorphosis on the Angelic plane in metahistory (the divine form of the celestial Adam), whereas the Incarnation on the plane of history, with its sensory, rationally verifiable data, becomes a unique event in a context of irreversible events. (One can speak of *Incarnatio continuata* only in a tropological or metaphorical sense, as the work of the Holy Spirit; there cannot be a repetition of the hypostatic union.) Here we touch on two forms of vision whose irreducibility and consequences do not seem thus far to have been sufficiently considered (cf. below, Ch. VI, pp. 274 ff.). The apparition or reactivation of the theophanic motif in an original form after the definition of Christian dogma by the Councils would require some such conception as the "theology of the history of religions," the idea of which was first put forward by Mircea Eliade; one can only speculate on the question of when the premises for such an enterprise will be available in Christianity and in Islam (especially in Shīʿism).

16. On *marḥūm* = *mawjūd*, cf. Ch. I, n. 21.
17. *Fuṣūṣ* II, 141.
18. Ibid. II, 146.
19. Ibid. II, 147. But of the meaning of theophanic vision, below, Ch. VI, § 2.
20. Ibid. I, 121 and II, 146–47. Cf. Ch. I, nn. 30, 35, 51, above.
21. Ibid. I, 121 and Kāshānī, Commentary, pp. 146–47.
22. See the development of this theme in our study "Divine Epiphany," pp. 69–86.
23. *Fuṣūṣ* I, 124, II, 76 and 150, n. 11; Kāshānī, p. 150, commenting on the Koran verse XXXIX:48: "They will see, coming from God, things they did not imagine." Cf. Ch. I, n. 32.
24. *Fuṣūṣ* II, 150–51; Kāshānī, p. 151.
25. On the irremissible solidarity between *Rabb* and *marbūb*, *Ilāh* and *ma'lūh*, see Ch. I, nn. 47 and 48.
26. Note the connection between the idea of the *knot* (*'uqda*) and the idea of dogma or dogmatic faith (*'aqīda*), which comes from the Arabic root *'qd*, to knot, to conclude. The "dénouement" is resurrection.
27. *Fuṣūṣ* II, 212, n. 12.
28. Ibid. II, 150–52; Kāshānī, Commentary, pp. 152–53.
29. Ibid. I, 155; Koran L:14: the Arabic term translated by "doubt" signifies both confusion, ambiguity (*labs*) and to put on a garment (*lubs*). Thus beneath the exoteric translation of the verse there appears the theosophical meaning of Ibn 'Arabī: "Should we be powerless to *clothe* them in a new creation?"
30. Ibid.; Kāshānī, p. 196; Bālī Effendī, Commentary, p. 288.
31. Kāshānī, p. 195.
32. This point suggests a comparison with the Avicennan ontology of the possible and the necessary.
33. *Fuṣūṣ* I, 156; Kāshānī, pp. 196–97.
34. *Fuṣūṣ* II, 214.
35. Cf. Affifi's excellent analysis in *Fuṣūṣ* II, 151–53 and 213–14; further, his *Mystical Philosophy*, pp. 29, 33–36.
36. *Fuṣūṣ* II, 152; Kāshānī, pp. 154–55.
37. *Fuṣūṣ* I, 125–26; Kāshānī, loc. cit.

38. Kāshānī, p. 151; *Fuṣūṣ* I, 123–24.

39. Kāshānī, pp. 151–52; *Fuṣūṣ* I, 124: "In our Book of Theophanies (*Kitāb al-tajalliyāt*) we have mentioned the form of posthumous ascension in respect of divine teachings, citing those of our brothers with whom we were united in a state of internal revelation (*kashf*), as well as what we taught them and was previously unknown to them in this question. It is a most extraordinary thing that man should be in a state of perpetual ascension (*fī'l-taraqqī dā'iman*), yet unaware of it because of the lightness and subtlety of the veil and the homology of forms." This homology concerns the forms of the *tajalliyāt*, the forms of food, for example: "Every time they take some food from the fruits of these Gardens (of Paradise), they will cry out: 'These are the fruits we ate formerly, but they will only have the appearance of those fruits' " (Koran II:23); *appearance* because, for those who know, the like is precisely *different*.

40. *Fuṣūṣ* I, 24; II, 150–51, n. 12; Kāshānī, p. 152.

41. *Fuṣūṣ* II, 151. Here I should like to mention a conversation, which strikes me as memorable, with D. T. Suzuki, the master of Zen Buddhism (Casa Gabriella, Ascona, August 18, 1954, in the presence of Mrs. Fröbe-Kapteyn and Mircea Eliade). We asked him what his first encounter with Occidental spirituality had been and learned that some fifty years before Suzuki had translated four of Swedenborg's works into Japanese; this had been his first contact with the West. Later on in the conversation we asked him what homologies in structure he found between Mahayāna Buddhism and the cosmology of Swedenborg in respect of the symbolism and correspondences of the worlds (cf. his *Essays in Zen Buddhism*, First Series, p. 54, n.). Of course we expected not a theoretical answer, but a sign attesting the encounter in a concrete person of an experience common to Buddhism and to Swedenborgian spirituality. And I can still see Suzuki suddenly brandishing a spoon and saying with a smile: "This spoon *now* exists in Paradise. . . ." "We are *now* in Heaven," he explained. This was an authentically Zen way of answering the question; Ibn ʿArabī would have relished it. In reference to the establishment of the transfigured world to which

we have alluded above (n. 10), it may not be irrelevant to mention the importance which, in the ensuing conversation, Suzuki attached to the Spirituality of Swedenborg, "your Buddha of the North."

42. *Fuṣūṣ* I, 125; Kāshānī, p. 153; that is, those for whom knowledge results from a divine inner revelation (*kashf ilāhī*), not from simple reflection or theoretical investigation.
43. *Fuṣūṣ* I, 88 and II, 77.
44. Ibid. I, 159; Kāshānī, p. 200, Bālī Effendī, p. 296.
45. Cf. Ch. I, § 3, above.
46. On this theme see above, Ch. I, pp. 116 ff. and nn. 24, 25.
47. Cf. above, Ch. I, pp. 132 ff. and nn. 80 ff. (the entire chapter of the *Fuṣūṣ* dealing with Ismā'īl is of the utmost importance here).
48. *Fuṣūṣ* I, 89 and II, 82. *Furqān* is a designation for the Koran itself or for any other sacred book making it possible to *discriminate* between the truth and error. Thus to be oneself, in person, a "Koran," is to possess (or to *be*) this discrimination.
49. Cf. above, Ch. I, § 3 and below Ch. V, § 3; cf. in *Fuṣūṣ* I, 56, the exegesis of Koran verse IV:1 cited as a commentary on Adamology: the apparent or external form of Adam (*ṣūrat ẓāhira*) and his invisible or inner Form (*Ṣūrat bāṭina*), that is, his Spirit (*Rūḥ*), constituting the total Adamic reality as Creator-creature (*al-Ḥaqq al-khalq, al-Khāliq al-makhlūq*). In consequence the exoteric translation of the verse: "O believers, *fear* your Lord" becomes: "Make of your apparent (visible, exoteric) form the *safeguard* of your Lord, and of what is hidden in you and is your Lord (your invisible, esoteric form) make a safeguard for yourselves."
50. Concerning the vanity of the discrimination effected before the *fanā'* and the authenticity of the discrimination effected once the consciousness is awakened, we might compare this aphorism: "Before a man studies Zen, to him mountains are mountains and waters are waters; after he gets an insight into the truth of Zen through the instruction of a good master, mountains to him are not mountains and waters are not waters; but after this when he really attains to the abode of rest, mountains are once more mountains and waters are waters." Suzuki, *Essays*, First Series,

pp. 22 f. (quoting Seigen Ishin, or Ch'ing-yuan Wei-hsin); cf. also below, the text corresponding to Ch. IV, n. 24, p. 227.

51. Concerning the twofold *Raḥma* (*Raḥmat al-imtinān* and *Raḥmat al-wujūb*), cf. *Fuṣūṣ* I, 151, Bālī Effendī, pp. 278–79. This is the beginning of the chapter on Solomon, introduced by a mention of the letter addressed by him to Bilqīs, queen of Saba. "This is a letter of Solomon, and it is in the Name of God, the Compassionate, the Merciful." Did Solomon then name himself first? Is God the First or the Last? See below (Ch. V, § 3) for how this paradox is resolved by the "method of theophanic prayer."

52. This still seems to be in keeping with the thesis of the Ashʿarite orthodox theologians; but there is a radical difference between it and the ashʿarite idea of *khalq al-afʿāl*. In the doctrine of Ibn ʿArabī, strictly speaking, one can say neither that God *creates* "through the organ" of his servant, nor that He chooses His servant as instrument of the manifestation of this act. We should rather say that when God performs the act which emanates from the "form" of His faithful, it is by being Himself at that moment the form (the *ẓāhir*) of His faithful, since that form manifests Him. And it would obviously have been impossible for the Ashʿarites to accept this view (which is the fundamental theophanic idea); cf. *Fuṣūṣ* II, 207, n. 4, and below, Ch. IV, n. 27.

53. The *speculum* (mirror) remains the fundamental idea employed by this speculative theosophy to explain the idea of theophanies. The commentary of Bālī Effendī (p. 280 *ad Fuṣūṣ* I, 151–52) throws an interesting light on the way in which the disciples of Ibn ʿArabī avoid the trap of an "existential monism" in which we sometimes have the impression of catching them because we neglect to think theophanically ourselves. To say that God (*Ḥaqq*) is "identical" with the creature, that is, to what is manifested in Him, means that the Created is manifested in accordance with one or another Divine Attribute (Life, Knowledge, Power) and cannot be manifested otherwise. To say that He is "different" from the creature means that the creature cannot be manifested except with a deficiency of the Attribute (*imkān, ḥadīth*). In the same sense as we can say: you are iden-

tical with what appears of you in different mirrors, we can say that the Increate-Creator (*Ḥaqq*) is identical with the creature (*'abd*) who manifests one or another of His Attributes, which, however, are in the creature deprived of their essential plenitude. The meaning of identity here is a participation (*ishtirāk*) of two things in one and the same essence (*ḥaqīqa*), just as Zayd, 'Amr, and Khālid participate in common in the same *ḥaqiqa* of being human. There is a common participation of beings and of the Divine Being in being (oneness of being). Their otherness consists in their differentiation through specific qualification. God is identical to what is manifested in regard to the things the two terms have in common, not *omni modo* (Bālī, p. 280).

54. Kāshānī, p. 192: "The ipseity (*huwīya*) of the faithful is the *ḥaqīqa* of God, injected into His Name. The faithful is the Name of God, and his ipseity, invested with this name, is God."
55. Jīlī, *Kitāb al-Insān al-Kāmil,* I, 31.

CHAPTER IV

THEOPHANIC IMAGINATION AND CREATIVITY OF THE HEART

1. Following an indication provided by Jāmī (one of the greatest mystics of Iran, d. A.D. 1495), I incline to translate the title of this immense and celebrated work (*al-Futūḥāt al-Makkīya*) in this way: "The Spiritual Conquests of Mecca." Jāmī points out that *Fatḥ* designates the progress toward God (*sayr ilà'l-Lāh*) culminating in *fanā'* in God, and this *fanā'* is assimilated to the conquest (*fatḥ*) of Mecca by the Prophet, a conquest after which there is no longer separation or flight, "hegira." Jāmī, *Sharḥ Ashi' 'āt al-Lama'āt,* p. 74 (the more usual translation is "Revelations of Mecca." But there are already so many words in Arabic to signify "revelation" that we shall do better to try to define our concepts more closely).
2. *Futūḥāt* II, 309–13.

3. Ibid. II, 312. The science of the Imagination has the characteristic power of giving being to the impossible, since God, the Necessary Being, can have neither form nor figure and the imaginative *Ḥaḍrat*, the *Imaginatrix*, manifests Him precisely in a Form. It is the "place" where the paradox inherent in theophanies, the contradiction between the refusal is resolved: "Thou shalt not see me" and the affirmation: "I have seen God in the most beautiful of His forms." Cf. below, Chs. V and VI.
4. Cf. Ch. III, n. 10 above.
5. *Futūḥāt* II, 312. As Ibn 'Arabī stresses, if in constrast to the situation in the world of sensible objects and forms, which are quantitatively and numerically limited by reason of their physical, objective existence, there is, among the inhabitants of Paradise (cf. Swedenborg's descriptions), simultaneity and identity between desire and its object, it is because both participate in an inexhaustible psychospiritual reality. It is the same as with the pure essences, for example, the whiteness which is present in every white object though whiteness itself is not subdivided. It is in no way diminished through its existence in all white things. The same is true of the animality in every animal, the humanity in every man, etc.
6. Ibid. II, 312–13.
7. Ibid. II, 313. And this is the meaning given to Koran verse L:21: "You were unknowing. We removed the veil that covered your eyes, now your sight is keen." The mode of being preceding death is like that of a sleeper in a state of dream. But when the Imagination has unveiled what it itself is (successive change, Manifestation in every form and the condition of all Manifestation), it is the Imagination itself which permits us to emerge from that state. Salvation does not consist in denying and doing away with the manifest world, but in recognizing it for what it is and esteeming it as such: not a reality beside and in addition to essential divine reality, but precisely a *theophany*, and the world would not be theophany if it were not Imagination. To understand this is to give things and beings their true value, their pure "theophanic function," which is not appre-

hended by dogmatic belief in the material reality of the object. To recognize the Imagination is to be delivered of the fiction of an autonomous datum; it is then alone that the eternal companion of the soul will cease to be the ἀντίμιμον πνευμα (the counterfeiting spirit) bearing witness against it (the mystic sense of the verses L:20 and 22).

8. On *Khayāl muttaṣil* and *Khayāl munfaṣil,* cf. *Futūḥāt* II, 311. Another example: the staff of Moses and the ropes taking the form of crawling snakes (Koran xx:69 ff). Moses thought that these were the effect of the enchantments of magicians operating on the plane of the *Ḥaḍrat khayālīya,* and this was so; but he perceived them as objects of imagination (*mutakhayyal*) without knowing them to be such or what that implied, and that is why he was afraid. It does not seem that this phenomenon should be identified with what is today called optical illusion (Affifi, *Mystical Philosophy,* p. 130, n. 2); Ibn 'Arabī himself argues to the contrary. Cf., rather, the phenomenologically established distinction between "inner voices" and "auditory illusions" in Gerda Walther's fine book, *Die Phänomenologie der Mystik,* pp. 162–68.
9. *Futūḥāt* II, 310–11.
10. Cf. Nicholson, *Studies in Islamic Mysticism,* pp. 117–18, 123, 136; Affifi, *Mystical Philosophy,* pp. 133–36; Jīlī, *al-Insān al-Kāmil,* II, 22–24.
11. Cf. *Fuṣūṣ* II, 139. Certain Koran verses can be invoked in support of the doctrine of the heart as the center of knowledge rather than of love. XLVII:26: "Do they not meditate on the Book, or are their hearts sealed by locks?" LVIII:22: "God has graven the faith in their hearts." III:5: "Those in whose hearts there is doubt cling to what is obscure in the book, out of desire for sedition and striving for its *ta'wīl,* whereas no one knows the *ta'wīl* but God and those who are rooted in science."
12. For the phenomenological point of view, cf. Gerda Walther, *Phänomenologie,* pp. 111–14.
13. Mircea Eliade, *Yoga: Immortality and Freedom,* tr. Trask, pp. 234 ff., 241 ff., and p. 410, in which he speaks of the Hesychastic

tradition distinguishing four "centers" of concentration and prayer. Cf. Ch. V, n. 20, below, on the four subtile centers and the angelology of the microcosm in Iranian Ṣūfism.

14. Affifi, *Mystical Philosophy*, p. 119.
15. Cf. *Futūḥāt* II, 526 ff.; Affifi, *Mystical Philosophy*, p. 133, n. 2; *Fuṣūṣ* II, 79: Ibn ʿArabī declares that the creative organ, or energy, which the Gnostics call *himma*, corresponds to what the *Mutakallimūn* designate as *ikhlāṣ* and the Ṣūfīs as *Ḥuḍūr;* he himself prefers to call it *ʿināyat ilāhīya* (divine premeditation). Regardless of the name we give it, this faculty can be understood only by those upon whom the gift has been conferred and who have experienced it; but these are few.
16. *Fuṣūṣ* I, 88 and II, 78 ff.
17. Here *wahm* and *himma* appear in different aspects according to the way in which they affect the Imagination. Cf. Jīlī: *wahm* is the most powerful of the human faculties (on the macrocosmic plane of the Celestial Man, Azrael, the Angel of Death, issues from its light); *himma* is the most noble of these faculties, for it has no other object than God (from its light issues the Archangel Michael); Nicholson, *Studies*, pp. 116–18.
18. Cf. *Fuṣūṣ* II, 107 (the quotation comes from the *Shadharāt al-dhahāb* of Ibn al-ʿImād, V, 196) and Affifi, *Mystical Philosophy*, p. 133.
19. Kāshānī, p. 272. Thus we have: (1) The world of Ideas (*maʿānī*). (2) The world of Spirits separate from all matter (*arwāḥ mujarrada*). (3) The world of thinking Souls (*nufūs nāṭiqa*). (4) The world of archetype-images, having figure and form but of an immaterial body (*ʿālam al-mithāl*). (5) The visible and sensible world. Or (Kāshānī, p. 110) as hierarchy of the Presences of the Divine Being in His theophanies, we have: (1) *Ḥaḍrat al-Dhāt* (Presence of the Essence, of the Self). (2) *Ḥaḍrat al-Ṣifāt wa'l-Asmā'* (Presence of the Attributes and Names, or *Ḥaḍrat al-Ulūhīya*, Presence of the Godhead). (3) *Ḥaḍrat al-Afʿāl* (Presence of the Divine Acts, operations or "Energies," or *Ḥaḍrat al-Rubūbīya* (Presence of the Suzerainty). (4) *Ḥaḍrat al-Mithāl wa'l Khayāl* (Presence of the Image and the Active Imagination). (5) *Ḥaḍrat al-Ḥiss wa'l-Mushāhada* (Presence of

the sensible and visible). The four first degrees constitute the world of Mystery. Here Dā'ūd Qayṣarī, another classical commentator on the *Fuṣūṣ* of Ibn ʿArabī, has a highly interesting development (pp. 27–28): like every individual, each "monad" (*fard;* the entire passage suggests presentiments of Leibnizian monadology) among the individuals of the universe is the emblem of a divine Name. Since each divine Name comprehends the Essence (*dhāt*)—which itself comprehends the totality of the Names—it also comprehends the other Names, and thus every individual (each monad) is itself a world in which and through which this individual knows the totality of the Names. In this sense it is true to say that the universes are infinite. However, since the universal (that is, comprehensive, inclusive) divine presences are five in number, the universal worlds encompassing all the others are likewise five in number. Two poles: (a) The Presence of the absolute Mystery (*Ḥaḍrat al-ghayb al-Muṭlaq;* (b) the Presence of the absolute Manifestation (*Ḥaḍrat al-Shahādat al-muṭlaqa*). This gives us the following hierarchy: (1) The Presence of absolute Mystery: this encompasses the eternal hexeities of the *Ḥaḍrat* of Knowledge. Next comes the Presence of relative Mystery (*Ḥaḍrat al-ghayb al-muḍāf*) comprising two modes, namely: (2) The world of the Intelligence (world of the *Jabarūt* or of the *Arwāḥ jabarūtīya* corresponding to the world of *Rubūbīya,* of the Lords; in Suhrawardī, the world of the Angel-Archetypes, Lords of the Species), the world that is closest to the absolute Mystery, and (3) The world of immaterial Souls (world of the *Malakūt,* or of the *Arwāḥ malakūtīya*), closest to the absolute *Shahāda.* (4) *ʿĀlam al-Mithāl,* closest to the sensible world. (5) *ʿĀlam al-Mulk,* which is the human world, integrating all the worlds, since it is the epiphany (*maẓhar*) of the *ʿĀlam al-Mithāl,* just as the latter is the epiphany of *Malakūt,* which in turn is the theophany of *Jabarūt,* which is the epiphany of the world of eternal hexeities, which is the Epiphany of the Divine Names of the *Ḥaḍrat ilāhīya* and of the *Ḥaḍrat wāḥidīya* (Presence of plural Unity), which, finally, is the epiphany of the Presence of absolute Unity (*Ḥaḍrat aḥadīya*). Asín Palacios tried to establish analogies between the *Ḥaḍarāt* of Ibn ʿArabī and the *Dignitates* of Ramon Lull; cf. *Obras escogidas*, I, 204 ff.

20. Kāshānī, p. 272: The One Essence passes by way of five descending stages (*tanazzulāt*) to the world of *Shahāda,* or sensible world, the limit of the universes. Each of these "Descents" comprises *action* and *passion:* they are also called the "five nuptial unions" (*nikāh*). One and the same Essence (*ḥaqīqa*) is polarized into action and passion; its Apparent Exoteric (*ẓāhir*) aspect is the world, whereas its Hidden, Esoteric (*bāṭin*) aspect is the Divine Being (*Ḥaqq*), and it is this Esoteric aspect which governs the Manifest aspect. *Fuṣūṣ* I, 218: "The same *res divina* (*amr ilāhī*) is nuptial union in the world formed by the Elements, *himma* in the world of the Spirits of light, and coordination (*tartīb*) of premises in the world of concepts in view of the actualization of the logical conclusion." *Fuṣūṣ* II, 332–33: The world and man are at once *Ḥaqq* and *Khalq.* The Divine Being (*Ḥaqq*) is in each form the Spirit (*Rūḥ*) which governs that form: the creatural (*Khalq*) is the form governed by that Spirit. The integral reality (*ḥaqīqa*) is the Creator-creature (*al-Ḥaqq al-khalq, al-Khāliq al-makhlūq,* I, 78), the Hidden-Manifest (*Bāṭin-Ẓāhir*). So it is at every stage of the Descents: each is a nuptial union, a syzygia (*izdiwāj*) of two things with a view to the production of a third. The union of the masculine and the feminine is only the aspect, in the sensible world, of a structure repeated on every plane of being. (Modeled on this same type: the union of the *fedele d'amore* and his Lord. The "appeased" soul does not return to God in general, but to *its* Lord of love. To this context we should also relate Ibn ʿArabī's extraordinary dream, in which a nuptial union is concluded with each of the cosmic powers, the stars of the Sky, the "letters" that typify them; Nyberg, *Kleinere Schriften*, pp. 87–88.)
21. Kāshānī, pp. 110–11.
22. *Fuṣūṣ* I, 88–89 and II, 81–82; Affifi, *Mystical Philosophy*, pp. 134–35. It is by concentrating his *himma* on the form of a thing in one of the *Ḥaḍarāt* that the gnostic is enabled to produce it immediately in the field of extramental existence, that is, in a sensible form. By preserving the form of that thing in one of

the higher *Ḥaḍarāt*, he preserves it in the lower *Ḥaḍarāt*. Conversely, when by the energy of his *himma* he preserves this thing in one of the lower *Ḥaḍarāt*, the form of the thing is preserved in a higher *Ḥaḍra*, for the persistence of the *following* postulates the persistence of the *preceding*. This is known as implicit guarantee, preservation in being by implication (*bi'l-taḍammun*); this is eminently the case with the fruit of the gnostic's contemplations. A gnostic may be distracted from one or more *Ḥaḍarāt* while he preserves the form of a thing in the *Ḥaḍra* that he is contemplating; but all the forms are preserved through the fact that he preserves this one form in the *Ḥaḍra* from which he is not distracted. Ibn ʿArabī explains the *divine creativity* in the same manner, but he stresses the difference: inevitably a man is distracted from one or several of the *Ḥaḍarāt*, whereas God never ceases to contemplate the forms of the things He has "created" in each of the five *Ḥaḍarāt*. And here Ibn ʿArabī is aware that he is explaining a secret which mystics have always guarded jealously, because this theosopher, who has been termed a "monist," is well aware of the limitation (corrective) which this brings to their theopathic locution, *Anā'l-Ḥaqq*. "This question I have just expounded has never up until now been treated in any book, neither by myself nor by anyone else, except in the present book. Hence it is something unique, without precedent. Take care not to neglect this" (*Fuṣūṣ* I, 89).

23. Ibid. Hence the meaning of the Koran verse: "We have neglected nothing in the Book" (VI:38), for it contains at once that which is happening, that which has happened, and that which has not yet happened.
24. Cf. on another plane the three states of discrimination mentioned above, Ch. III, n. 50.
25. In his treatise *Mawāqiʿ al-nujūm*, quoted in Affifi, *Mystical Philosophy*, p. 133, n. 2.
26. Ibid., p. 137, n. 2.
27. Cf. Ch. III, n. 52, in which we have discussed the meaning which should be given here to the notion of the intermediary and which distinguishes it from any conception of the Ashʿarite type. It

is fitting to speak of an intermediary which is the organ of theophany, but in the sense that the organ, as an organ, *is* precisely the theophany.

28. Affifi, p. 136; *Fuṣūṣ* II, 79–80.
29. Thus we are not dealing with the simple verification of a general law, expressed or not in occasionalist terms as applying to all beings, for the human creativity we are here speaking of presupposes and demands a concentration of the heart (an *enthymesis*), a gathering (*jamʿīya*) of all a human being's spiritual energies (*quwwāt rūḥānīya*) on their supreme object and their elevation to their maximum purity with a view to the projected creation; but this is possible only for the gnostic as Perfect Man. Consequently Ibn ʿArabī interprets the episode of the clay birds modeled by the child Christ and animated by his breath as narrated in the Gospels of Childhood and the Koran ("Gospel of Thomas," IV, 2; "Arabic Gospel of Childhood," 36: M. R. James, *Apocryphal New Testament*, pp. 59 and 82; Koran III:43; *Fuṣūṣ* I, 140; Affifi, *Mystical Philosophy*, p. 136). He further says: "One can understand this question only through a personal mystical sense (*dhawq*), as Abū Yazīd Bastāmī restored breath to an ant he had killed, for even there he knew through whom he exhaled this breath" (*Fuṣūṣ* I, 142). Finally: "We have said all this because we know that the material bodies of the universe undergo the *himma* of souls when they maintain themselves in a state of mystic concentration" (*Fuṣūṣ* I, 158). Here we should consider the Avicennan theory of the celestial Souls which, unlike human souls, possess Imagination in the pure state, since they are free from the senses and from sensory perception and move the Spheres precisely thanks to this Imagination.
30. On this control, see especially *Fuṣūṣ* I, 126–37, the whole of Ch. XIII (on Lot), in which the question is treated at length.
31. *Fuṣūṣ* I, 122 and II, 148, n. 9; Kāshānī, p. 148.
32. *Fuṣūṣ* I, 89 and II, 148; Kāshānī, p. 149; Bālī Effendī, p. 217. To possess a heart, to have the science of the heart (*qalb*) is to know the *taqlīb* (metamorphosis, permutation, transmutation) of the Divine Being metamorphosing Himself into forms and

theophanic figures. Thus the gnostic, through himself, knows the Divine Self (Bālī Effendī here finds an application of the maxim: "He who knows himself [that is, his soul] knows his Lord"). Through the metamorphoses that take place in his soul the gnostic knows the metamorphoses of the Divine Self (*dhāt al-Ḥaqq*) in their epiphanic forms. That is why the heart alone is the foundation of divine science, for every other subtile organ or center (*rūḥ* or otherwise) has a determinate *maqām* (e.g. the intellect cannot know that an Image corresponds to the whole, to the five *Ḥaḍarāt;* it discriminates. The validity of the Image must be grounded on the *himma,* for the heart perceives the unity of the multiple). The gnostic's self (*nafs*) is not heterogeneous to *Ḥaqq,* since it *is* the divine Name invested in this eternal hexeity. To be a gnostic is to recognize these forms in their metamorphoses. To be an a-gnostic is to deny and reject them. It is herein that the science of the heart differs radically from the argumentative dialectic of the dogmatists. It is the privilege of those who know *Ḥaqq* by *tajallī* and *shuhūd* (intuitive vision), in the state of concentration (of "Koran"); it is to know *Ḥaqq* by *Ḥaqq;* this science of the heart is specified according to its theophanies; its form or mode varies with the receptacle.

33. *Fuṣūṣ* I, 122; Kāshānī, p. 148.
34. *Fuṣūṣ* II, 148–49; Kāshānī, p. 150.
35. Why, then, is the "darkening" represented by these dogmatisms, which bring with them the radical evil of endless and futile controversies and disputes, necessary? Assuredly the question cannot be avoided. But the answer, which is equally radical, will here consist essentially in the lived doctrine which delivers the disciple of Ibn ʿArabī from these limits, for then the question and the evil it denounces are without foundation. The science of the heart (of the *qalb* and of the *taqlīb*) is then the answer and the practical solution. Such an answer does not quibble about the reason for a state of fact, but transcends it.
36. Kāshānī, p. 149.
37. Kāshānī, p. 150.

38. Ibid. The rational dogmatists have no need of such an appeal because they have no need of vision, whereas the simple believer begins with imaginative vision and typification (*takhayyul* and *tamaththul*) and rises by way of personal visualization and verification (*rū'ya* and *taḥqīq*) to *walāya* in *tawḥīd*. The appeal of the Prophets summons us to this Divine Being (*Ḥaqq*) corresponding to mental vision. The rational dogmatist, on the other hand, is utterly incapable of producing a "prophetic theology," since he is concerned only with arriving at a dogmatic definition (*taqyīd*). Though rightly perceiving that this question takes on the most serious importance for the divine sciences and their mysteries, Bālī Effendī (pp. 221 and 222) seems to be gravely mistaken about what is at stake. In this connection he sketches a kind of apology of Sunnism and seems to believe that it would be most desirable to "achieve" an increasing indetermination of the Divine Being (that is, a universalization void of all particular determination). In taking this path one incurs a hopeless confusion between what is *lā bi-sharṭ* (absolutely unconditioned in respect both of the universal and of the particular) and what is *bi-sharṭi-lā* (subject to a negative condition, that is, the universal conditioned by the absence of all particular determination). This is a crucial distinction already grounded in Avicennan metaphysics. But obviously, theophanic figure, function and vision cannot go hand in hand with an increasing negativity which abolishes all determinations and tends toward a conceptual void or a totally emptied concept. On the contrary all theophany and all visionary experience imply a form that is well determined in the mind, because they are in essence a perception of the *unconditional* (*lā bi-sharṭ*) as manifested precisely not in a negatively conditioned universal but in the conditioned pure and simple (*bi-sharṭ*), as presupposed by the correlation between *rabb* (Lord) and *marbūb* (vassal, servant), between the form *which* is manifested (*mutajallī*) and the form of him *to whom* it is manifested (*mutajallā lahu*). From this point of view it would be of particular interest to study how in Shī'ism Imāmology (in so far as it permits a mental vision of the Holy

Imāms) and the theosophy of Ibn ʿArabī mutually fecundated one another. We hope to discuss this more fully in a future work. Cf. also Ch. V, n. 17 below and Ch. VI (*coincidentia oppositorum*).

39. In connection with the end of the preceding note we recall this category which we propose, here and elsewhere, to call "mystic kathenotheism" and which we should like to add, because it does not seem to be considered there, to the fine analyses provided by Gerda Walther in her book *Die Phänomenologie der Mystik*, pp. 160–61 and 180–81.
40. Cf. above, p. 121, and Ch. I, n.26 *in fine*.
41. Cf. Mircea Eliade, *Yoga*, pp. 241 ff.
42. *Futūḥāt* II, 449. Affifi (*Mystical Philosophy*, p. 114) thinks that the four Spheres are the four Elements; there is also some reason to believe that they might be the four *Ḥaḍarāt* following the *Ḥaḍra* of absolute Mystery (n. 19, above).
43. *Futūḥāt* II, 581.
44. As can be noted when the mystic Youth appears just as the spiritual pilgrim is passing the Black Stone (Ch. VI, § 2, below), the symbolism of the Black Stone makes possible a series of allusions leading to the final identification. The column that juts out of the Temple is the *Rūḥ* of Muḥammad, that is, his Holy Spirit, Gabriel, Angel of Revelation, who assumes the same role toward the Prophet as toward Maryam (Affifi, *Mystical Philosophy*, p. 75, n. 3). The Youth's point of emergence situates him as the homologue of the Angel in respect of the mystic; he is the mystic's Self, his divine Alter Ego, who projects revelation into him (cf. ibid., p. 118, n. 3, and above, Ch. I, n. 35).As for the designation of any manifestation of the *Quṭb* (Pole) as Black Stone, it is a usage anterior to Ibn ʿArabī. Thus when Abū Madyan (d. 594/1197) was asked if the Black Stone felt any effect produced upon it by the people who touched it and kissed it, he replied: "I am the Black Stone" (ibid., p. 76, n. 1).
45. "This," says Ibn ʿArabī, "is what Ibn Masarra alluded to in his *Kitāb al-Ḥurūf*" (Book of Letters, that is, of the philosophical alphabet); cf. Asín Palacios, "Ibn Masarra y su escuela," *Obras escogidas*, I, 91). Without wishing to minimize the connection

established by Asín, we tend to agree with Affifi (*Mystical Philosophy*, p. 76, n. 1) that it would be well to distinguish here between the symbolic theme introduced by Ibn Masarra and its amplification by Ibn ʿArabī.

46. With this term (for the exercise of the *himma*) cf. what has been stated above about Ibn ʿArabī's interpretation of the injunction "to be oneself, in person, a 'Koran.'"
47. *Fuṣūṣ* I, 155–56; Bālī Effendī, pp. 287–88; Kāshānī, p. 195.
48. Ibid. I, 157; Bālī Effendī, p. 292.
49. Ibid. I, 158 and II, 218–19; Bālī Effendī, p. 294; Kāshānī, p. 199. This "magic power" implies *taskhīr* (submission of the thing to a power outside it and acting upon it) and *taṣarruf* (the faculty of disposing of, and utilizing, that power to arrive at a change in the thing). *Taskhīr* is of two kinds: one is exerted by the *himma* and implies the spiritual degree of mental concentration which enables this *himma* to attain the things of our world or the things of the celestial universes (certain Ṣūfīs exercise this faculty while others for high spiritual reasons abstain from it). The other consists solely in the enunciation of the imperative without previous exercise or need of *himma*, and the only case of this has been Solomon commanding the Jinns as forces of Nature. In those to whom it is imparted this exceptional gift raises the divine dimension (*lāhūtīya*) to its supreme limit, to the point where it totally dominates the human dimension (*nāsūtīya*). Our authors stress that Solomon was ordered by his Lord to ask for a power that would belong to no one else after him and that his prayer consequently was not inspired by a personal "will to power."
50. *Fuṣūṣ* I, 100–01. This was a "manifestation" not premeditated by those who were thus manifested in the form of stars; consequently a perception which occurred only for Joseph in the treasure of his imagination. Otherwise his brothers would have known that they saw him, just as the Angel Gabriel knew that the Prophet saw him (Bālī Effendī, p. 153).
51. For this comparison of the mistake made by Joseph with that made by ʿĀ'isha, cf. *Fuṣūṣ* I, 99–101, II, 107, n. 3; Bālī Effendī, p. 152; Kāshānī, p. 110.

52. Cf. n. 49, above; it was also in response to a divine injunction that Solomon asked for a power that would belong to him alone.
53. Kāshānī, p. 200; Bālī Effendī, p. 296. This is an archetypal image. A similar indication is found in the *Book of Zoroaster* (a Persian poem of 1581 double verses by a Zoroastrian of the thirteenth century). On the subject of Peshōtan, immortal son of King Gushtasp (Zoroaster's protector) and one of the future companions of Saoshyant, who are now sleeping while waiting for the coming of the Savior, we are told that Zoroaster, after having celebrated the liturgy, gave him milk: "He drank of it and forgot death." Certain Zoroastrian doctors comment: the meaning of "eternal life" is "knowledge of self," that is, knowledge of the imperishable essence; just as milk is the food of infants, this knowledge is the food of the spirit. Cf. *Le Livre de Zoroastre* (*Zarātusht-Nāma*) *de Zartusht-i Bahrām ibn Pajdū*, tr. Rosenberg, p. 59.
54. *Fuṣūṣ* I, 100 and 158; Bālī Effendī, pp. 153 and 296; Kāshānī, p. 200.
55. It is thus that Abraham made a mistake at the outset, because, not having accomplished the *ta'wīl*, he did not understand that the child in his dream symbolized his own soul, *Fuṣūṣ* I, 78 and 85 ff.; Taqī ibn Mukhallad, ibid., pp. 86–87. Our allusion to alchemy in the text refers to this same conception, according to which, in the *Tetralogies of Plato*, the alchemical operation is defined as consisting in *extrahere cogitationem*. Practitioners wishing to subject "alchemical gold" to the test of the stylus would be making a demand similar to that of Taqī ibn Mukhallad, and their efforts would achieve comparable success.
56. Cf. Koyré, *La Philosophie de Jacob Boehme*, pp. 119 ff.
57. Precisely: *taḥawwul al-Ḥaqq fi'l-ṣuwar fī tajalliyātihi* (metamorphosis of God into the forms of His theophanies), cf. our study, "Divine Epiphany," pp. 69 ff.
58. Grammatically, both can invoke the ambiguity of the Arabic suffix (*illā wajhu-hu*); on the theosophical meaning of this verse, cf. Kāshānī, p. 111; *Futūḥāt* II, 313; and n. 60, below.
59. It is this Angel that is meant when it is said that God has an Angel who is in charge of the gift of visions and is called Spirit

(*al-Rūḥ*); he is below the lowest Heaven; he commands the forms and figures in which a man who has a dream perceives himself and other beings (cf. II Baruch, 55, 3, in which the Angel who presides over authentic visions bears the name of Ramiel). Thus when man takes leave of his sensory faculties, the objects which normally besiege his waking consciousness cease to veil his perception of the forms that are in the power ("in the hand") of this Angel. He is then able, even in a waking state, to perceive what a sleeper perceives in his sleep. The subtile element in the man is transferred, with its energies, from the *Ḥaḍrat maḥsūsa* (sensory sphere) to the *Ḥaḍrat al-khayāl al-muttaṣil*(the imaginative faculty having its basis in the frontal part of the brain). Then this Angel-Spirit, guardian of the forms and figures having an existence of their own in the world of the autonomous Imagination (cf. n. 19 above, *ʿālam al-mithāl*) gives the visionary vision of the spiritual things which are "embodied" in this intermediate world; cf. *Fuṣūṣ* II, 377. This process should be borne in mind when we consider the further visionary experiences mentioned by Ibn ʿArabī; cf. also below, Ch. VI, n. 13.

60. Cf. *al-Insān al-Kāmil,* II, 4 and 8–10 (Jīlī refers to his *Kitāb al-kahf wa'l-raqīm;* cf. also Nicholson, *Studies,* pp. 110–11. This is a central "arcanum"; the undivided relationship, or individualization of the relationship, between the *increate* Holy Spirit and the *created* Angel-Spirit (in the sense of this word as employed in the school of Ibn ʿArabī) as mystery of the pre-eternal individuation. Cf. also the vision mentioned further on (Ch. VI): the allusion of the mystic Youth (eternal companion, imperishable "Face" of the mystic visionary) to his enthronement and to his pre-eternal investiture with the science of the supreme Calamus (*Qalam aʿlà* = *ʿAql awwal,* the First Intelligence). "Functionally," it is not impossible to establish an analogy between the relationship of the *Rūḥ al-Quds* to the Angel *Rūḥ* on the one hand and on the other hand that of the *Spiritus principalis* to the *Spiritus sanctus,* the Angel of each believer, among the Cathari (Cf. Söderberg, *La Religion des Cathares,* pp. 174 ff., 215).

CHAPTER V
MAN'S PRAYER AND GOD'S PRAYER

1. Cf. above, pp. 129–30, and Ch. I, n. 70.
2. Cf. above, pp. 130–31 and Ch. I, n. 75, the motif of the hospitality of Abraham in the iconography of Oriental Christianity; cf. the lesson of the mystic "Sophia" to her disciple, pp. 143 ff. and above, Ch. II, n. 38.
3. Cf. Mircea Eliade, *Yoga*, pp. 216 ff. Thus the spiritual exercise here proposed involves neither Yogic postures (cf. ibid., p. 217, Ibn ʿIyāḍ), nor the phenomena which occur in the séances of *dhikr*, whether collective or not (ibid., pp. 390–91 and 408). Here we are dealing with personal prayer, the meditation and practice, in private, of ritual Prayer (*Ṣalāt*), a method and practice which make it precisely a *Munājāt*.
4. *Fuṣūṣ* I, 222–23.
5. Quoted ibid. II, 342.
6. Cf. Sayyed Kāẓem Reshtī (successor of Shaikh Aḥmad Ahsā'ī as head of the Shaikhī school of Iran in the last century), *Sharḥ Āyat al-Kursī*, p. 2.
7. This aspect of the Prayer which *eo ipso* attains its object "objectively" can be considered phenomenologically in still another way (as beneficial effect on another person who is unaware of its source, or as telepathy, cf. Gerda Walther, *Phänomenologie*, p. 125).
8. *Fuṣūṣ* I, 222–23 and II, 341–42.
9. Cf. above, p. 132 and Ch. I, nn. 55 and 80–81.
10. *Fuṣūṣ* I, 92. This whole chapter on Ismāʿīl throws particular light on the All in the Each, the individuation and singularity of the undivided relationship between the Lord and his vassal, a constant of the spiritual experience for which we have suggested the term "mystic kathenotheism."
11. The Lord who is the *Knower* (active) exists as such only if He has an object *known* to Him; reciprocally, because He is *known*

to him in whom He reveals Himself by knowing him, He too is in this sense put into the passive (He is known) whereas that which, in the first meaning, was the *object* of His knowledge, then becomes the active *subject*, the Knower. These are the two aspects here assumed by the two existential modalities polarizing the one *ḥaqīqa*, each becoming inverted into the other.

12. *Fuṣūṣ* I, 83. The commentary given in parentheses is our own.
13. Cf. Ch. I, § 3, p. 121, above, the words of Sahl Tustarī ("divine suzerainty has a secret, and it is *thou* . . .; if this *thou* should disappear, the suzerainty would also cease to be") and Ch. I, n. 40, above: a warning against the trap into which translators have fallen for lack of attention to the pertinent lessons of the commentators. *Ẓahara ʿan* must be taken as *zāla ʿan* (to cease, to disappear). On the bearing of these words, see the texts mentioned in Ch. I, n. 40.
14. Ch. I, n. 49 above.
15. Cf. *Fuṣūṣ* I, 106 ff. and II, 342: *ṣirāṭ*, the *path* of being that every being follows, the path he takes by reason of what he is.
16. See our Study "Divine Epiphany," chiefly pp. 113–40.
17. Along with the practice of spiritual pilgrimages, mental visitations, observing an elaborate liturgical calendar for private devotions, based principally on the anniversary dates of the Fourteen Most-Pure (Muḥammad, Fāṭima and the Twelve Imāms). Each day of the week, each hour of the day, and each hour of the night has its Imām. Here we shall allude chiefly to a euchology that is today in current use in Iran, *Mafātiḥ al-Jannān* (The Keys of Paradise) by Shaikh ʿAbbās Qummī, a veritable treasure trove for religious psychology. We have noted above (Ch. IV, n. 38, *in fine*) the coalescence between Shīʿite Imāmology and the theosophy of Ibn ʿArabī (the figures of the Imāms taking their place in the theophanies, still a frequent theme of meditation among the Zahabī dervishes of Iran). This raises in turn the question of the origins of the vocabulary and theosophical schemas of Ibn ʿArabī and his school.
18. *Fuṣūṣ* I, 223. Here we are reminded of Swedenborg's thesis: "Each Angel is the entire Church," *De Coelo et Inferno*, pars. 52 and 57; Cf. our "Divine Epiphany," p. 124.

19. Kāshānī, p. 278; for this homology, cf. also Jīlī, *al-Insān al-Kāmil*, II, 10 (Ch. 51).
20. Countless references might be cited; we shall limit them here to the commentary on the *Nahj al-Balāgha* by Mīrzā Ibrahīm Khū'ī (*al-Durrat al-Najafīya*), pp. 29–31, and one of the numerous (unpublished) epistles of Shāh Ni'matullāh Walī Kermānī, one of the most celebrated masters of Iranian Ṣūfism of the fifteenth century (d. 834/1431), from which we extract the following passage: "There are four degrees (or planes) to which the four letters ALLH (Allāh) refer, namely, the heart (*qalb*), the intelligence (*'aql*), the spirit (*rūḥ*) and the soul (*nafs*). And there are four angels that are the vehicles of these four degrees. The heart is the side of Gabriel, for the heart is the abode of Knowledge and Gabriel is its mediator. . . . The two names *Gabriel* and *heart* have the same meaning. The *intelligence* is the side of Michael, for Michael is the meditator of the subsistence of the creatures, just as the intelligence is the mediator of essential subsistence, namely, knowledge and wisdom. The *spirit* is the side of Seraphiel, for in him are the divine forms which are the divine attributes hidden in the spirit of which it is said: 'I breathed of my Spirit into him.' The attribute of Seraphiel is this breathing of spirit. . . . The *soul* is the side of Azrael, who is the form of the divine supremacy. . . . Azrael is he who gathers in the spirit at the time of death, and the essence of each being is his spirit. According to the same homology, in the world of natural Qualities (or Elements), Water is the form of Gabriel, Earth is the form of Michael, Air is the form of Seraphiel, and Fire is the form of Azrael" (Epistle on the *riwāyat* of Khwārizmī: "I [the Prophet] and 'Alī [the First Imām] are a single tree, human beings are many trees"). On the macrocosmic plane, of which microcosmic angelology is the internalization, a recent Zahabī book, *'Athār Aḥmadīya*, gives a diagram of the following schema: *Seraphiel*, supreme divine Spirit (*Ḥaḍrat wāḥidīya*), uppermost column to the right of the Throne (*'arsh*), uppermost summit of *Jabarūt*, *yellow* light. *Gabriel*, universal divine Intelligence, uppermost column to the left of the Throne, lesser summit of *Jabarūt*, *white* light. *Michael*,

universal divine soul, lesser column at the right of the Throne, major summit of *Malakūt, red* light. *Azrael,* universal divine Nature, lesser column to the left of the Throne, minor summit of *Malakūt, green* light. Here we have simple examples showing the extreme complexity of these schemas and their variants. On the "Supports of the Throne," cf. above, Ch. I, n. 76.

21. Cf. Festugière, *La Révélation d Hermès Trismégiste,* IV, 248 ff.
22. Cf. the fourteenth thesis of the Sālimīya (disciples of Ibn Sālim of Basra), quoted in L. Massignon, *Essai sur les origines du lexique technique de la mystique musulmane,* p. 299: "God speaks, and it is He Himself who is heard to speak through the tongue of every reader of the Koran" (but the direction of the analysis here pursued makes it impossible for us to identify this proposition with a "monist degenerescence of the rule of meditation," though we should also not attempt to reduce it to Islamic orthodoxy).
23. For this parallelism, see *Fuṣūṣ* I, 224; Kāshānī, p. 279.
24. Compare the two maxims cited in "Divine Epiphany," p. 138: "I would never worship a God I did not see." And "He who does not know his Imām does not know God."
25. Cf. above, Ch. II, nn. 37 and 40.
26. *Fuṣūṣ* I, 225.
27. *Praesens* (from *prae-sum*); we might say with Schelling *consens* (from *con-sum, Introduction à la philosophie de la mythologie,* tr. Jankelevitch, II, 48) to express the idea of mutual requirement, the *taʿalluq* of the *rabb* and the *marbūb.* The orant who is not *present with* his Lord and does not succeed in "seeing" Him mentally is one who does not "feed" his Lord on the substance of his own being (cf. n. 2, above, recalling the mystical meaning given to Abraham's hospitality).
28. Cf. Bālī Effendī, p. 436. Among other effects, there is the fructification of the Koran verse XXIX:44: "Prayer preserves from wickedness, because," says Ibn ʿArabī, "it is a law imposed on the orant not to concern himself with anything else than his prayer as long as he applies himself to it and is called a *muṣallī*" (*Fuṣūṣ* I, 224). In *Fuṣūṣ* II, 343 attention is drawn to the *ta'wīl* of the verse cited above as typifying the *maqām* in which no

immoral action can emanate from the mystic, because he is in a mystic station (*maqām*) in which the obligations implied by discrimination between obedience to the Law and revolt against it are suspended.

29. *Fuṣūṣ*, I, 224, ambivalence of the Arabic root *qrr*, "to be refreshed or consoled" and "to remain, to rest, to establish oneself in a place (*istiqrār*)." The eyes "rest" (are refreshed, *qurrat al-ʿayn*) in the contemplation of the Beloved, so that the lover can no longer consider anything else, nor conceive of anything other than the Beloved, whether in a concrete thing or in a sensory phenomenon (a theophany of the divine attributes in the outside world) or in a mental vision. The usual sense of the word *qurrat* is thus interpreted by Ibn ʿArabī as equivalent to that of *istiqrār*.
30. *Fuṣūṣ* I, 225.
31. Bālī Effendī, p. 436.
32. Bālī Effendī, pp. 437–38.
33. *Fuṣūṣ* I, 225 and II, 344; Bālī Effendī, p. 439.
34. In the sense that Prayer of God is the revelation, the epiphany of the human being as His mirror. Reciprocally, the Prayer of man is the "creation," that is, the reflection and manifestation of God, whom man contemplates in the mirror of his self, because he him-*self* is that mirror.
35. Cf. pp. 109–10 above, the application of this verse to the heliopathy of the heliotrope. Compare the exegesis here analyzed with what has been said above about the verse: "all things perish except His face." Cf. Ch. IV, nn. 58 ff. above.
36. *Fuṣūṣ* I, 226.
37. Ibid. and II, 345–46; cf. I, 68 ff.; above, pp. 112 ff.; and our study "De la Gnose antique à la Gnose ismaélienne."
38. Cf. Ch. III, n. 49 and Ch. V, n. 9, above.
39. Dā'ūd Qayṣarī, Commentary, p. 492.
40. *Fuṣūṣ* I, 60–62, 65.
41. Cf. his "Invocation to Perfect Nature" (i.e. the "angel of the philosopher") in our *Motifs zoroastriens dans la philosophie de Sohrawardī*, p. 49.

CHAPTER VI
THE "FORM OF GOD"

1. Cf. principally Hellmut Ritter (*Das Meer der Seele,* pp. 445 ff.), who has carefully assembled the sources of this *ḥadīth,* the variants and the various *isnād* (chains of transmission). It will be noted that the traditionist who transmitted it (Ḥammād ibn Salama (d. 157/774) taught it only after a stay in Iran, in a Ṣūfī establishment of ʿUbaddān on the shore of the Persian Gulf. According to Ibn al-Dayba (d. 944/1537) this *ḥadīth* was often told in the popular Ṣūfī circles of his time. It would be a mistake, however, to restrict its observance to these circles. Apart from what is said of it here, it suffices to refer to the work of a profound mystic such as Rūzbehān Baqlī of Shīrāz (d. 605/1209), for example, his *ʿAbhar al-ʿĀshiqīn* (The Jasmin of the *Fedeli d'amore*) to note the speculative importance of this *ḥadīth* in his system of theophanic thought as well as its experiential value, which is borne out by the dreams and visions related in the same mystic's *Diarium spirituale.* Ibn ʿArabī has also made an extremely subtle allusion to this *ḥadīth* in the commentary that he himself wrote in the margin of his "Sophianic poem" (*Kitāb Dhakhā'ir al-aʿlāq,* a commentary on the *Tarjūmān al-ashwāq,* pp. 55–56), beside the passage where the whiteness of the dawn and the purple of the sunset are spoken of as the signs of a divine modesty, an idea that could have come only to a mystic experiencing theophany in this childlike form.
2. Cf. C. G. Jung, "The Psychology of the Child Archetype," pars. 271–300.
3. Cf. in particular the text of the theologian Ghazālī quoted in Ritter, *Das Meer der Seele,* pp. 448–49. The crucial question is not whether or not Images have a value "on the basis of" which we can speculate on the Divine Essence and conclude that they tell us nothing of the "form" of God, who has no form, any more than the form in which the Angel Gabriel appeared to the

Prophet tells us anything about the Angel's real form. For to uphold this piously agnostic thesis is obviously to know nothing of the theosophy of the *Ḥaḍarāt* (above, Ch. IV, nn. 19–22). However, once this is understood, it is evident that the gnostic method does not consist in concluding, by rational inference, from a visible form to an absence of form, a pure formlessness which would supposedly be the pure metaphysical essence. The "form of God" is the form that shows itself in the theophanic Image and none other, and God can be known by us only in this form (cf. Ch. IV, n. 38 above). One must be guilty of a deplorable confusion between the unconditioned, *lā bi-sharṭ*, and the negatively conditioned, *bi-sharṭi-lā*, which is the universal, to make the latter the supreme metaphysical essence: related to the "universal," the Image ceases to be anything more than an *allegory;* related to the absolute unconditioned, that is to say, *absolved* equally from the universal and the particular, the Image becomes a theophanic *symbol*). Indeed, it presupposes the ideas of the *ʿālam al-mithāl* and of the theophanic Imagination which we have here attempted to analyze: *anthropomorphosis* occurs not at the terminal level of the sensory (physical, historical) world, but at the level of the Angel and the angelic world (cf., for example, the Angel Gabriel as *Anthropos,* in Mandeism, in the book of Daniel; W. Bousset, *Hauptprobleme der Gnosis,* pp. 176–77). Accordingly, the very status of the Image as well as the validity of the homologations of the Image, are here at stake. The significance of theophanies is to be found neither in literalism (the anthropomorphism that attributes human predicates to the Godhead) nor in allegorism (which does away with the Image by "explaining" it), any more than it is to be found in *tashbīh* or *taʿṭīl,* idolatry or iconoclasm. All our mystics repeated this over and over again, and by their dialectic of the double negativity of the *tawḥīd* the Ismailians maintained themselves on a ridge dominating the two abysses. In short, this significance of theophanies differs equally from a nominalist and gratuitous conception of art and from an Incarnation implying a "consubstantiality" of the Image of the invisible imagined with its help. This meaning is rather to be found in a *coincidentia oppositorum,* the dual structure of the one *ḥaqīqa*, at once singular and plural eternal and transient, infinite in its finitude, for its infinitude does not signify a quantitative illimitation of the number of its theophanies, but the infinitude of this Essence, which, because it is in itself the simultaneity of opposites, implies the multiplicity of its Apparitions, that is, His typifications, each of which is *true* according to the Divine Face pertaining to each of the beings to which it shows itself.

4. Cf. Jīlī, *al-Insān al-Kāmil,* II, 3–4. It is advisable to follow these pages in meditating on the *visio smaragdina* (in which the gold and the green are predominant), for they make possible a penetration of it. Jīlī does not effect a *tafsīr*, that is, a literal exegesis, nor even a *ta'wīl,* if by this we insist on understanding an allegorical exegesis, but a *tafḥīm,* that is, in the strict sense of the word, a *hermeneutics,* an Understanding, which is here a truly existential hermeneutics, since the vision of the Divine Face epiphanizes the Face which the Godhead has in each being and which is the Holy Spirit of that being. This vision conforms to the Spirit of this being, because this being's Spirit is in correspondence with a certain sensible, corporeal form (*Ḥaḍarāt*). For this reason, this Face of the vision cannot be defined as a certain relationship or point of view (the compromise solution of the rational theologians); it is essential to the Divine Being; in other words, it is essential to the infinite Godhead to manifest itself in this or that finite form. The Godhead *is* this Form, and this Form is all this and nothing more: apparition. The theophanic event is twofold: there is the determinate form (this hair, this dress, these sandals) and there is the hidden *meaning* (*ma'nà*) which is not to be sought within the context of general abstract truths or in human truths sublimated and applied to God, but in the irremissible connection between the Form seen and the being to whom God shows Himself in this form. In this hidden meaning there is precisely the *coincidentia oppositorum* which governs the twofold status of the Divine Being: a twofold status here typified precisely by the two golden sandals, which, however, are not an *allegory.*

5. He who is in essence forever inaccessible to vision is the Divine Being in His absoluteness, the Utterly Other; He can be *seen* only in the co-determination which binds the determinate Lord to his vassal (the divine *alter ego* to his (terrestrial self) and individualizes their relationship. But the Utterly Other remains beyond the "seignorial" figure (the *rabb*) who epiphanizes Him individually. These words mentally apprehended by Ibn ʿArabī at the beginning of his quest are decisive: "I have epiphanized myself in no other form of perfection than your hidden being (*maʿnà-kum*). Recognize the high nobility that I have given you. I am the Sublime, the Most-High, whom no limit limits. Neither the Lord nor His vassal knows me. Sacrosanct is the Godhead (*ulūhīya*) and such is its rank that nothing can be associated with it (whereas *rubūbīya* is precisely the individualized divine relationship of which *you*, the servant, are the secret). You are a determinate self (*al-anā*); I am myself (unconditioned, conditioning the form of each self). Do not look for me in yourself, you would be going to futile pains. But do not seek me either outside of you, you would not succeed. Do not renounce looking for me, you would be unhappy. Rather, look for me until you find me, you will not cease to rise. But observe well the rules in the course of your quest. Take the road with your eyes open. Discriminate between me and thee. For you will not see me, you will see only your own hexeity (*ʿaynaka*, your essential individuality, your 'source' or 'Angel,' or your own 'eye'). Rest therefore in the mode of being of companionship (association with your divine Partner, the mystic Youth who appeared before the Black Stone)" (*Futūḥāt* I, 50).
6. Cf. Ritter, *Das Meer der Seele*, p. 438, who has assembled a number of very fine texts.
7. Cf. the analysis of a few passages of Ibn ʿArabī given above, Ch. II, § 2, "The Dialectic of Love"; cf. also Rūzbehān Baqlī of Shīrāz, *ʿAbhar al-ʿĀshiqīn* (n. 1 above). Here, of course, the name of Plato may be mentioned, provided we do not forget that in all probability our Ṣūfīs knew only fragments or quotations from his work. Platonism as such should rather be con-

sidered merely as an example, the most eminent if you will, of the phenomenon under consideration. Above all, we should think of the popular preachers who carried their pious audience away by designating the Godhead by the feminine names of the heroines of Arabic chivalry poetry (Sa'dà, Lubnà, Layla) and celebrating a love addressed to God as to a feminine being. A particularly striking case is that of the Persian preacher who sent his audience into a trance by interrupting his sermon to order the Koran reader to intone verse VI:52, XVIII:27: "They desire to see my face" (cf. Ritter, *Das Meer*, pp. 441–42). All this was quite scandalous in the eyes of official Islam and its orthodox theology. But it must be pointed out that these attempts at theophanic experiences present us with a very different problem from the "anthropomorphoses" of the Koran, in the presence of which the rational theologians resorted in perplexity to allegorical exegesis, cf. n. 3, above.

8. "For the same reason," Jāḥiẓ writes, "those among us [Muslims] who represent God in a human form are more ardent in their divine service than those who deny this resemblance. Indeed, I have often observed how a man in this case sighed and sobbed with yearning for God if one spoke of divine visitation; wept if one spoke of the vision of God; fell into a faint if one spoke of the elimination of the partitions separating him from God. How much greater still must be the yearning of one who hopes to sit down alone with his God and converse with his Creator" (*Ḥujjat al-nubuwwa*, quoted from Ritter, *Das Meer*, p. 441).
9. Cf. Herzog, *Realencyclopädie*, IV, art. "Christusbilder," esp. pp. 73–81. Cf. also our study "Divine Epiphany," p. 156, in which we have already pointed out the close connection between Christology and anthropology: the image of Christ as emblem of the inner image and of the ideal form in which the human being appears to himself.
10. We are thinking principally of the mosaics in the top row on the north wall of the basilica of San Apollinaro Nuovo, built in the year 500 by King Theodoric who was of the Arian faith. Here, in the thirteen mosaics commemorating his life and miracles,

Christ is represented as a beardless youth of exquisite beauty, accompanied by a person whose precise function has never been explained. Contrastingly, in the mosaics of the south wall representing the scenes of the Passion, Christ presents the virile, bearded type that has become classical. In all probability the contrast reflects the contrasting implications of Arian and orthodox Christology. If we bear in mind that other Arian compositions in the basilica were replaced by orthodox representations and that the iconographies of the baptistery of the Arians and of the baptistery of the orthodox show the same contrast, we shall come close to holding the key to the two iconographic systems. In any case, we have before us no simple question of art history (a question of workshops and techniques) but a mutation in consciousness revealed in the mutation of iconographic symbols: the change from the type of *Christus juvenis* (the young shepherd, the young patrician) to the virile type postulated both by the ideology of the imperial Church and by a theology based on the reality of the divine sufferings in the flesh, on the reality of physiology and history. Before this could happen, men had to lose their sense of theophanic events occurring "in a celestial place"; henceforth "docetism," in its beginnings the first theological critique of historical knowledge, became a mere caricature of itself.

11. The differentiation between lived psychic time and objective physical time made up of continuous, homogeneous moments, was clearly raised by the great mystic ʿAlā'uddawla Semnānī (14th century); cf. our study, "L'Intériorisation du sens en herméneutique soufie iranienne."
12. Cf. the two maxims quoted in Ch. V, n. 24 above. Unlike the rest of Islam, Shīʿism possesses a highly developed religious iconography. Among the circle of the Sixth Imām, Jaʿfar Ṣādiq (d. 148/765), it will be worth our while to mention the curious and endearing figure of Hishām ibn Sālim Jawālīqī (Shahrastānī, *Milal*, pp. 87–88). He seems to have been one of those who drew all the implications from their Imāmism, clashing head-on with the prudish dialectic to which the first theologians of orthodox Islam constrained themselves. He taught that

God has a human form and a body, but a subtile body consisting neither of flesh nor blood. He is a brilliant, radiant light; He has five senses like a man and the same organs. Abū ʿIsà al-Warrāq (d. 247/861) notes in the doctrine of our Imāmite a trait which shows a remarkable sense of the *coincidentia oppositorum:* God possesses abundant black hair, which is black light (*nūr aswad*). One wonders whether a Stoic terminology is concealed beneath the statement that God is a "body" (an immaterial body, to be sure, since it is in the subtile state). Essentially it is a presentiment of this kind that is revealed in an Iranian Shīʿite of the seventeenth century, Muḥsen-e Fā'iẓ, a disciple of Mullā Ṣadrā and of Ṣūfī inspiration, when he points out that in speaking of a "body" Hishām meant to say a substance or "essence subsisting in itself" (*Biḥār al-Anwār*, II, 89).

13. It would be worthwhile to reconstitute the sequence of visionary experiences in the life of Ibn ʿArabī (cf. Ch. IV, n. 59, above), his own personal and experiential verification of his maxim: "He in whom the Active Imagination is not at work will never penetrate to the heart of the question" (*Futūḥāt* II, 248). For, as he himself bore witness, Ibn ʿArabī had received an ample measure of this gift of visualizing or visionary Imagination. "This power of Active Imagination," he confesses, "attains in me such a degree that it has visually represented to me my mystic Beloved in a corporeal, objective, and extramental form, just as the Angel Gabriel appeared to the eyes of the Prophet. And at first I did not feel capable of looking toward that Form. It spoke to me. I listened and understood. These apparitions left me in such a state that for whole days I could take no food. Every time I started toward the table, the apparition was standing at one end, looking at me and saying to me in a language that I heard with my ears 'Will you eat while you are engaged in contemplating me?' And it was impossible for me to eat, but I felt no hunger; and I was so full of my vision that I sated myself and became drunk with contemplating it, so much so that this contemplation took the place of all food for me. My friends and relatives were astonished to see how well I looked, knowing my total absti-

nence, for the fact is that I remained for whole days without touching any food or feeling hunger or thirst. But that Form never ceased to be the object of my gaze, regardless of whether I was standing or seated, in movement or at rest" (*Futūḥāt* II, 325). This life of intimacy with the celestial Beloved may be compared with that revealed to us by the *Diarium spirituale* of Rūzebehān Baqlī of Shīrāz, an uninterrupted sequence of dreams and visions that ran through his entire life, both in the sleeping and in the waking state (cf. Ch. II, n. 71 above).

14. Cf. Ch. I, n. 40 above. When Ibn ʿArabī compares his own visionary experiences with that of the Prophet experiencing the familiar presence of the Angel Gabriel, this comparison suggests certain parallelisms that are of crucial importance in connection with this primordial Image. It is the Holy Spirit in each of its individuations (cf. Ch. IV, nn. 59 and 60 above), here then the Spirit of his Spirit, the Form of his Form, his Eternal Face, his Self, which gives him his origin and contains him, individuates itself in him at the level of the Divine Name whose object and correlate he is; it is in this sense that the Angel Gabriel is the apparition of his own Self. Cf. Ch. IV, n. 44 above, the series of homologations: *Rūḥ Muḥammadī*, Holy Spirit, Angel Gabriel, the Youth, the Black Stone, the Pole. These homologations enable us to decipher the meaning of the great theophany accorded to Ibn ʿArabī, which was at the origin of his book of the *Futūḥāt*.
15. Cf. above pp. 138–39 and Ch. II, n. 7. The mystic episode that is here the "key" to the *Futūḥāt* has been the subject of an excellent interpretation by Fritz Meier in "The Mystery of the Kaʿba."
16. Compare this admonition ("before it escapes," *qabla'l-fawt*) with the allusive term that serves to designate the Youth (ungraspable, unfixable, evanescent, escaping like time, *al-fatà'l-fā'it*). He is the secret of the Temple: to grasp the secret, which once grasped will never escape again, is to penetrate the Temple with him.
17. *Futūḥāt* I, 47 ff. We may roughly distinguish four moments in this prelude. The *first* moment is constituted by the processional and the encounter before the Black Stone; it culminates in the

declaration in which the Youth states *who* he is. The recognition of the mystic meaning of the Kaʿaba, emerging through its stone walls, goes hand in hand with the mystic's encounter with his own celestial pleroma in the person of the Youth. The Youth commands him: "Behold the secret of the Temple before it escapes; you will see what pride it derives from those who revolve in processional around its stones, looking at them from beneath its veils and coverings." And indeed the mystic sees it take on life. Gaining awareness of the Youth's rank, of his position dominating the where and the when, of the meaning of his "descent," he addresses him in the world of Apparitions (of Idea-Images, *ʿālam al-mithāl*): "I kissed his right hand and wiped the sweat of Revelation from his forehead. I said to him: 'Look at him who aspires to live in your company and desires ardently to enjoy your friendship.' For all answer he gave me to understand by a sign and an enigma that such was his fundamental nature that he conversed with no one except in symbols. 'When you have learned, experienced, and understood my discourse in symbols, you will know that one does not apprehend or learn it as one apprehends and learns the eloquence of orators. . . .' I said to him: 'O messenger of good tidings! That is an immense benefit. Teach me your vocabulary, initiate me into the movements one must give to the key that opens your secrets, for I should like to converse by night with you, I should like to make a pact with you.' " Again, he who is thus introduced as the eternal Companion, the celestial *paredros*, answers only by a sign. But "then I understood. The reality of his beauty was unveiled to me, and I was overwhelmed with love. I fainted and he took hold of me. When I recovered from my faint, still trembling with fear, he knew that I had understood who he was. He threw away his traveler's staff and halted (that is, ceased to be the evanescent one, he who escapes). . . . I said to him: 'Impart to me some of your secrets that I may be among the number of your doctors.' He said to me: 'Note well the articulations of my nature, the ordering of my structure. What you ask me you will find etched in myself, for I am not someone who speaks words or to whom words are spoken. My knowledge extends only to myself, and my essence (my person) is no other than my Names. I am Knowledge, the Known and the Knower. I am Wisdom, the work of wisdom and the Sage (or: I am *Sophia*, *philosophy* and the *philosopher*).' " As Fritz Meier has aptly noted ("The Mystery of the Kaʿba," p. 156), these last sentences, which derive from the Theology of Aristotle, leave us no doubt as to the identity of the Youth. In Aristotle they are spoken by the mystic isolating himself from his body and penetrating his spiritual being; here they are spoken by the spiritual being, manifesting himself to his earthly *self* in the confrontation of a vision and dialogue. The mysterious Youth is the divine *Alter Ego*, the Self in transcendence, that is, the person who is the celestial pole of a bi-unity whose total being has as its other pole the earthly self: an invisible *thou* of celestial essence and an *I* manifested on the earthly plane (cf. Semnānī, who in his *Tafsīr* bases the sevenfold meaning that he finds in the Koran on the seven subtile organs, *laṭā'if*, of man: theophany, *tajallī*, emerges in the absolutely secret subtile inwardness (*laṭīfa khafīya*), in the subtile organ which is the seat of the I, *anā'īya*). Here we must also mention the fundamental representation of Zoroastrian anthropology: the Daēnā-Fravashi, angel-archetype of the terrestrial individual (Meier, pp. 125–26, and our book *Terre céleste et Corps de résurrection*, pp. 67 ff.). The Youth reveals in his person the being of what had been suggested by the symbol of the column jutting from the mystic Temple, the hermeneut of the Divine Secrets. He is the mystic's *Rūḥ*, Holy Spirit, Angel Gabriel, the Black Stone emerging from the Kaʿaba (the "White Stone" as soon as he is recognized); he is the mystic's divine Name, his eternal hexeity (n. 14, above). As Jīlī (*al-Insān al-Kāmil*, II, 89, 2) observes, the Kaʿaba typifies the Divine Essence; the Black Stone is man's subtile or spiritual being (*laṭīfa*, *Geistwesen*, "Angel"). Without the divine Self typified by the Kaʿaba, the world as totality of phenomena could not be, any more than the individual man could exist without the Idea, the "Angel," of his person.

18. *Futūḥāt* I, 50.
19. Now come the *second* and *third* moments of this "dialogue with the Angel" of which mystical literature offers few comparable examples. We must pay the closest attention to this encounter with the Angel and the initiatic pedagogy based upon it if we are not to lose the thread of this dialogue between two beings who are *each other.* The two terms converge, yet are not confounded, when the *Alter Ego* asks his human self to recount his *itinerarium spirituale.* For this Quest could lead the human self to a goal that had been known since pre-eternity to his divine *Alter Ego,* who in answer makes this known to the human self through the story of his pre-eternal enthronement. The event in Heaven and the event in Earth combine into a single drama. The *second* moment is represented by the injunction: "Perform your circumambulations following in my footsteps. Contemplate me in the light of my Moon, in such a way as to find in my nature what you will write in your book and dictate to your copyists" (that is, the book of the *Futūḥāt,* cf. n. 14 above). Real dualitude in real unity is signified by this imperative: "Tell me what realities of the subtile world the Divine Being has shown you in the course of your circumambulations, those things that not every pilgrim is permitted to contemplate, in order that I may know your *himma* and your hidden depths (*maʿnāka*). Then I shall have you present to myself on high, in accordance with what I shall have learned of you (as I shall have known you)" (*Futūḥāt* I, 48). The visionary's answer is the *third* moment: "You who are the contemplator and the contemplated, yes, I shall tell you those of the secret realities that have been shown me, those which walk with pride in trains of light, those which are one in essence beneath the veils." This answer is the narrative of the spiritual phases through which Ibn ʿArabī has passed and through which the realization of his theophany causes his disciple to pass in turn. Here we have a mental confrontation with the undifferentiated Divine Being, opposing itself as an object; the passage from the dogmatic religion of the "God created in the faiths" to the religion of the gnostic, the *ʿārif,* the initiate, whose *heart* has rendered itself capable of receiving all theophanies because

it has penetrated their *meaning*. The "Form of God" is for him no longer the form of this or that faith exclusive of all others, but his own eternal Form, which he encounters at the end of his circumambulations (the "Prayer of God" which is his own being), in whose company he enters the Temple which is the invisible Divine Essence of which this Form is the visible form alone visible to him. To attain this end he must first consent to the great renunciation, he must annul the pretentions of objective and objectivizing dogmatism (n. 5, above). In order that the mystic may attain to his divine companion, become present to his divine *Alter Ego* with a presence corresponding to the capacity of his *himma*, he must pass through three phases, three inward discoveries: first, he must discover how the condition of the servant who discriminates before having experienced *fanā'* (Ch. III, n. 50, above) prevents the joining of the pact between the Lord and his vassal of love, between the Lord and the man *for whom* and *in whom* he manifests himself. Secondly, the vision of the Angel-Anthropos, the Adam whose son he is, that is, who is his archetype in the world of Mystery—turning with him around the *Ka'aba*, and whom he has seen mounting his throne, that is, enthroned as the divine Khalīfa homologue of the Throne among beings. Thirdly, the revelation of the Throne: the Throne is the heart of being (*qalb al-wujūd*), "the Temple which contains me is your heart." The secret of the Temple is the mystery of the heart. And we have shown *who* the column jutting from this Temple is: the Black Stone transfigured into a person now endowed with movement, the initiating Youth who enjoins the mystic to follow in his footsteps.

20. Cf. also Meier, "The Mystery of the Ka'ba," p. 164. The sevenfold circumambulation of the Ka'aba—which delimits our innermost essence; cf. in Semnānī (above, n. 11) the seven *laṭā'if*, the subtile organs or centers of the total human being—typifies the appropriation of the seven Divine Attributes in the course of an ascent which successively attains the different spheres of the Self. As for Jīlī, the mystic through circumambulation attains to his ipseity, his origin, his pre-eternal root; he becomes the partner of this amazing dialogue pressed to the limits of

transconscience, in which the dualization of his being reveals his mystery to him, and in which, in his divine *Alter Ego*, his total individuality becomes fully visible to him.

21. This is the *fourth* moment of the great initiatic prelude of the *Futūḥāt* (I, 51). The divine *Alter Ego* to whom the mystic relates his long Quest has already gathered the fruit of this quest in pre-eternity: "My faithful confidant (that is, the mystic Youth) said to me: 'O, my most noble friend, you have told me nothing that I did not already know, and that I do not bear engraved and subsisting in my being.' I said to him: 'You have inspired in me the desire to learn with you, by you, and in you, in order that I may teach according to your teaching.' He said to me: 'Assuredly, O Expatriate returning home! O resolute seeker! Enter with me into the Ka'aba of the Ḥijr, for that is the Temple that rises above all veils and coverings. It is the entrance of the Gnostics; there is the repose of the pilgrims engaged in the processional.' And immediately I entered the Ka'aba of the Ḥijr in his company." (It should be noted that the enclosure designated as the Ka'aba of the Ḥijr is said to contain the tomb of Ismā'īl; one of my Ismailian friends finds in this fact a subtle allusion on the part of Ibn 'Arabī.) Then, after the Youth has revealed to him *who* he is ("I am the seventh. . . ."), he reveals the mystery of his—or, one should rather say, "their" —pre-eternal existentiation and enthronement; the Angel who is the supreme Calamus (*al-Qalam al-a'là*) descending on him from his lofty dwelling places, breathing into him the knowledge of self and of the other. "My heaven and my earth split asunder; he taught me the totality of my Names." Then, after the Angel, the supreme Calamus, had invested him with the dignity of the Angel (that is, the royal dignity, *haḍrat al-malak*, cf. n. 22 below on *malak-malik*) and left him, he prepared to *descend*, to be sent out as a divine Envoy, while the angels of his microcosm approached him and kissed his right hand. But what is this *descent?* Is it reality? If it were possible to indicate it otherwise than by a sign and an enigma, the whole mystery of the polarization between the human Ego and the divine Ego would be negated. " 'I am the Garden of ripe fruit, I am the fruit of the totality.

Raise now my veils and read everything that is disclosed in the lines graven on my being. Put what you will have learned from me and in me in your book, preach it to all your friends.' Then I raised his veils and considered everything that was in him. The light that was placed in him enabled my eyes to see the secret science [*'ilm maknūn*] that he conceals and contains. The first line I read and the first secret I learned from this writing are what I shall now relate in Chapter II of this book [the *Futūḥāt*]." The reappearance and the role of the mystic Youth in the *Kitāb al-Isrā'* confirm what we have attempted to analyze here (above, Ch. IV, n. 44, and, in this chapter, nn. 14, 17, 19). This is the book in which Ibn 'Arabī relates a personal experience reproducing the nocturnal assumption (*isrā'*) of the Prophet.

22. Let us briefly recall that by this term (angelophany) we mean divine anthropomorphosis on the plane of the spiritual universe, the human Form or divine humanity of the angelic world (the *Adam rūḥānī* of Ismailism) in contrast to the idea of the divine Incarnation on the plane of earthly, historical and physical humanity. On the former depends that "theophanic function" of beings, for which the terms of angel and angelophany seem the most appropriate. It goes without saying that this theophanic idea of the ἄγγελος is far more than a delegation which make him a simple "messenger." It corresponds to the Iranian term *Izad* (divinity) which, since the coming of Islam, has often overlapped with the term *fereshta*, the Persian equivalent of the Greek ἄγγελος. To give the same force to the Arabic term *malak*, it suffices to bear in mind the notion of *rabb al-nū'* (angel-lord, or archetype of a species) among the Ishrāqīyūn. Actually the Arabic word (imported from the Syriac) is derived from the root *l'k* of the verb *al'aka*, to send, to entrust with a mission, whence *mal'ak*, messenger, angel. But in current usage the weak sign *hamza* ceases to be written and the word passes as a derivative of the root *mlk*, to possess, to reign, and in unvocalized writing *malak* (angel) and *malik* (king) are identical. However, this phenomenon of induction involves no danger of misunderstanding. Meditating on the ideographic aspect of the

matter, our authors pass from one meaning to the other: every angel is a king (though the proposition cannot be reversed!) as is signified in this fine definition by the ultra-Shīʿite Shalmagānī: "The Angel (*malak*) is the being who possesses himself (*alladhī malaka nafsahu*, reigns over his own soul)." We find the same allusion in the *Shaṭḥīyāt* of Rūzbehān Baqlī of Shīrāz (Shahīd Alī 1342, fol. 14a); cf. Rūzbehān Baqlī, *Commentaire sur les paradoxes des Soufis*.

EPILOGUE

1. Étienne Souriau, *Avoir une âme*, p. 141.

LIST OF WORKS CITED

LIST OF WORKS CITED

ʿAbbās Qummī. *Safīnat Biḥār al-Anwār*. 2 vols. Teheran, 1352–54/1934–37.

Affifi, A. E. (Abu'l-ʿAlā ʿAffīfī), ed. *Fuṣūṣ al-Ḥikam*. 2 vols. Cairo, 1365/1946. (*Fuṣūṣ* I = Ibn ʿArabī's text; *Fuṣūṣ* II = Affifi's commentary.)

———. *The Mystical Philosophy of Muḥyīd-Dīn Ibn al-ʿArabī*. Cambridge, Eng., 1939.

Aḥmad (Sayyed) ʿAlawī. *Masqal-e ṣafā*. Institut Franco-Iranien, MS 5.

Aḥmad Shīrāzī (Shaikh). *Āthār-e Aḥmadīya*. Shīrāz, 1374/1955.

Alphandéry, Paul. "Le Gnosticisme dans les sectes médiévales latines." In: *Congrès d'Histoire du Christianisme*, vol. III. Paris, 1928.

Angelus Silesius (Johannes Scheffler). *The Cherubinic Wanderer*. Selections tr. Willard R. Trask. New York, 1953. *Pélerin chérubinique*, tr. Henri Plard. Paris, 1946.

Asín Palacios, Miguel. *El Islam cristianizado, estudio del sufismo a través de las obras de Abenarabi de Murcia*. Madrid, 1931.

———. "El Místico Abu'l-ʿAbbas ibn al-ʿArīf de Almería." In: *Obras escogidas*, 3 vols. Madrid, 1946. I, 217–42.

———. "Ibn Masarra y su escuela: origines de la filosofía hispano-musulmana." In: *Obras escogidas*, I, 1–216.

———. *La Escatología musulmana en la Divina Comedia, seguida de la Historia y Crítica de una polémica*. 2nd edn., Madrid, 1943.

Bālī Effendī. Commentary on the *Fuṣūṣ*. Constantinople, 1309/1892.

Bousset, Wilhelm. *Hauptprobleme der Gnosis*. Göttingen, 1907.

Bulgakov, Sergei. *Jacob's Ladder* (in Russian). Paris, 1929.

Cerulli, Enrico. *Il "Libro della Scala" e la questione delle fonti arabo-spagnole della Divina Commedia*. Vatican City, 1949.

CORBIN, HENRY. "Recherches sur l'herméneutique luthérienne." In: *Annuaire de l'École des Hautes Études, Section des Sciences Religieuses.* Paris, 1939. Pages 99–102.

———. *Avicenna and the Visionary Recital,* tr. Willard R. Trask. New York (Bollingen Series LXVI) and London, 1960. (Orig.: *Avicenne et le récit visionnaire.* 2 vols. Teheran and Paris, 1952, 1954. Bibliothèque iranienne 4–5.)

———. "Confessions extatiques de Mīr Dāmād." In: *Mélanges Louis Massignon,* I, 331–78. Institut français de Damas, 1956.

———. "Imagination créatrice et prière créatrice dans le Soufisme d'Ibn 'Arabī," *Eranos Jahrbuch,* XXV (1956), 122–240. (The original version of Part One of the present volume.)

———. "De la Gnose antique à la Gnose ismaélienne," *Atti del XII⁰ Congresso Volta,* Accad. Naz. dei Lincei. Rome, 1956.

———. "Divine Epiphany and Spiritual Rebirth in Ismailian Gnosis." In: *Man and Transformation* (Papers from the Eranos Yearbooks 5), pp. 69–160. New York (Bollingen Series XXX) and London, 1964.

———. *Étude préliminaire pour le "Livre réunissant les deux sagesses" de Nāṣir-e Khosraw.* Teheran and Paris, 1953. (Bibliothèque iranienne 3a.)

———. *Histoire de la philosophie islamique. I. Des origines jusqu'à la mort d'Averroës (1198).* Paris, 1964.

———. "L'Intériorisation du sens en herméneutique soufie iranienne," *Eranos Jahrbuch,* XXVI (1957), 57–187.

———. "L'Ismaélisme et le symbole de la Croix," *La Table Ronde* (Paris), December 1957, pp. 122–34.

———. *Les Motifs zoroastriens dans la philosophie de Sohrawardī.* Teheran, 1946.

———. *Œuvres philosophiques et mystiques de Sohrawardī* (= *Opera metaphysica et mystica,* II). Teheran and Paris, 1952.

———. "Le Récit d'initiation et l'hermétisme en Iran," *Eranos Jahrbuch,* XVII (1949), 121–87.

———. "Rituel sabéen et exégèse ismaélienne du rituel," *Eranos Jahrbuch,* XIX (1950), 181–246.

———. "Soufisme et sophiologie," *La Table Ronde* (Paris), January 1956, pp. 34–44.

———. "Sympathie et théopathie chez les 'Fidèles d'Amour' en Islam," *Eranos Jahrbuch,* XXIV (1955), 199–301. (The original version of Part Two of the present volume.)

———. *Terre céleste et Corps de résurrection: de l'Iran mazdéen à l'Iran Shī'ite.* Paris, 1961.

———. See also HESCHEL, ABRAHAM; RŪZBEHĀN BAQLĪ SHĪRĀZĪ; SUHRAWARDĪ, SHIHĀBADDĪN YAḤYĀ.

DĀ'ŪD QAYṢARĪ. Commentary on the *Fuṣūṣ*. Lith. Teheran, 1299/1882.

ECKHART, MEISTER. *Telle était Sœur Katrei,* tr. A. Mayrisch Saint-Hubert. Paris, 1954. (Documents spirituels 9.)

ELIADE, MIRCEA. *Yoga: Immortality and Freedom,* tr. Willard R. Trask. New York (Bollingen Series LVI) and London, 1958; 2nd edn., 1969.

FESTUGIÈRE, A. J. *La Révélation d'Hermès Trismégiste.* 4 vols. Paris, 1949–54.

GHAZĀLĪ (AL-), AḤMAD IBN MUḤAMMAD. *Sawāniḥ al-'Ushshāq.* Persian text ed. Hellmut Ritter. Istanbul, 1942. (Bibliotheca Islamica 15.)

HERZOG, JOHANN JAKOB. *Realencyklopädie für protestantische Theologie und Kirche.* 24 vols. Leipzig, 1896–1913.

HESCHEL, ABRAHAM. *Die Prophetie.* Cracow, 1936. (Tr. in part by Henry Corbin, *Hermès,* 3ème série, No. 3, Brussels, 1939, pp. 78–110. English: *The Prophets.* New York, 1962.)

IBN 'ARABĪ, MUḤYIDDĪN. *Fuṣūṣ al-Ḥikam,* ed. A. E. Affifi. 2 vols. Cairo, 1365/1946. (*Fuṣūṣ I* = Ibn 'Arabī's text; *Fuṣūṣ* II = Affifi's commentary.)

———. *Kitāb al-Isrā'.* Hyderabad, 1948.

———. *Kitāb Dhakhā'ir al-a'lāq, Sharḥ Tarjūmān al-ashwāq.* Beirut, 1312/1895.

———. *Kitāb al-Futūḥāt al-Makkīya fī ma'rifat al-asrār al-malikīya wa'l-mulkīya.* 4 vols. Cairo, 1329/1911.

———. *The Tarjūmān al-ashwāq, A Collection of Mystical Odes by Muḥyī'ddīn ibn al-'Arabī,* ed. and tr. R. A. Nicholson. London, 1911. (Oriental Translation Fund, New Series, XX.)

IVANOW, W., ed. and tr. *Kalāmi Pīr. A Treatise on Ismaili Doctrine, also Called (wrongly) Haft-Bābi Shāh Sayyid Nāṣir.* Bombay, 1935. (Islamic Research Association 4.)

———. *Nāṣir-e Khusraw and Ismailism.* Bombay, 1948. (The Ismaili Society, Series B, No. 5.)

JA'FAR IBN MANSŪRI AL-YAMAN. *Kitābu'l Kashf,* ed. R. Strothmann. Oxford, 1952.

JALĀLUDDĪN RŪMĪ. *Fīhi ma fīh,* ed. Badī' Ozzamān Forūzānfar. Teheran, 1330/1912.

———. *Mathnawī*, ed. and tr. R. A. Nicholson. 8 vols. Leiden and London, 1925–40.

JAMES, MONTAGUE RHODES. *The Apocryphal New Testament*. Oxford, 1960.

JĀMĪ, ʿABD AL-RAḤMĀN. *Nafaḥāt al-Uns*. Lucknow, 1915.

———. *Sharḥ Ashīʿʿ āt al-Lamaʿāt* (Persian). Commentary by Fakhr al-Dīn ʿIrāqī. Teheran, 1303/1886.

JĪLĪ, ʿABD AL-KARĪM. *Kitāb al-Insān al-Kāmil*. Cairo, 1304/1886–87.

JUNG, C. G. *Aion: Researches into the Phenomenology of the Self*, tr. R. F. C. Hull. The Collected Works of C. G. Jung, 9, ii. New York (Bollingen Series XX) and London, 1959; 2nd edn., 1969.

———. "The Psychology of the Child Archetype." In: *The Archetypes and the Collective Unconscious*, tr. R. F. C. Hull. Collected Works, 9, i. New York (Bollingen Series XX) and London, 1959; 2nd edn., 1969.

———. "Sychronicity: An Acausal Connecting Principle." In: *The Structure and Dynamics of the Psyche*, tr. R. F. C. Hull. Collected Works, 8. New York (Bollingen Series XX) and London, 1960; 2nd edn., 1969.

KĀSHĀNĪ, ʿABD AL-RAZZĀQ. Commentary on the *Fuṣūṣ*. Cairo, 1321/1903.

———. *Iṣṭilāḥāt al-Ṣūfīya* (Lexicon). Printed in the margin of Kāshānī's commentary on the *Manāzil al-Sā'irīn*. Teheran, 1315/1898.

KĀSHĀNĪ, ʿIZZUDDĪN. *Misbāḥ al-Hidāya*, ed. Jalāluddīn Homāyī. Teheran, 1947.

KĀẒEM (SAYYED) RESHTĪ. *Sharḥ Āyat al-Kursī*. Tabriz, 1271/1855.

KHŪ'Ī, MĪRZĀ IBRĀHĪM. *al-Durrat al-Najafīya* (commentary on the *Nahj al-Balāgha*). Tabriz, 1292/1875.

KOYRÉ, ALEXANDRE. *Mystiques, Spirituels, Alchimistes du XVIᵉ siècle allemand*. Paris, 1955.

———. *La Philosophie de Jacob Boehme*. Paris, 1929.

MAJLISĪ, MUḤAMMAD BĀQIR. *Biḥār al-Anwār*. 14 vols. Teheran, 1305/1887–88.

MASSIGNON, LOUIS. "Élie et son rôle transhistorique, *Khadirīya*, en Islam." In: *Études carmélitaines: Élie le prophète*, II, 269–90. Paris, 1956.

———. *Essai sur les origines du lexique technique de la mystique musulmane*. 2nd edn., Paris, 1954.

———, ed. and tr. al-Ḥallāj, *Dīwān*. Paris, 1955. (Documents spirituels 10.)

MEIER, FRITZ. "The Mystery of the Kaʿba: Symbol and Reality in Islamic Mysticism." In: *The Mysteries* (Papers from the Eranos Yearbooks 2), pp. 149–68. New York (Bollingen Series XXX) and London, 1955.

MUḤYĪ LĀRĪ. "Futūḥ al-Ḥaramayn" (poem). Bibliothèque nationale, MS supplément persan 1389.

NICHOLSON, REYNOLD A. *Studies in Islamic Mysticism.* Cambridge, Eng., 1921.

———. See also IBN ʿARABĪ; JALĀLUDDĪN RŪMĪ.

NORDSTRÖM, CARL OTTO. *Ravennastudien.* Stockholm, 1953.

NYBERG, HENRIK SAMUEL. *Kleinere Schriften des Ibn al-ʿArabī.* Leiden, 1919.

ODEBERG, HUGO, ed. and tr. *3 Enoch or, The Hebrew Book of Enoch.* Cambridge, Eng., 1928.

PROCLUS. Πρόκλου περὶ τῆς καθ' Ἕλληνας ἱερατικῆς τέχνης (Treatise on the Hieratic Art of the Greeks). French tr. in *Recherches de science religieuse,* 1933, pp. 102–06.

RENAN, ERNEST. *Averroës et l'Averroïsme.* 8th edn., Paris, 1925.

RINGBOM, L. I. *Graltempel und Paradies.* Stockholm, 1951.

RITTER, HELLMUT. *Das Meer der Seele.* Leiden, 1956.

———. "Philologika VII," *Der Islam* (Strasbourg), XXI (1933), 84–89.

———. See also GHAZĀLĪ (AL-), AḤMAD.

ROSENBERG, FRÉDÉRIC, ed. and tr. *Le Livre de Zoroastre (Zarātusht-Nāma) de Zartusht-i Bahrām ibn Pajdū.* St. Petersburg, 1914.

RŪZBEHĀN BAQLĪ SHĪRĀZĪ. *Commentaire sur les paradoxes des Soufis (Sharḥ-e Shaṭḥīyāt),* ed. and tr. Henry Corbin. Teheran and Paris, 1966. (Bibliothèque Iranienne 12.)

———. *Le Jasmin des Fidèles d'Amours (K. ʿAbhar al-ʿĀshiqīn). Traité de soufisme en persan,* ed. and tr. Henry Corbin and M. Moʿīn. Teheran and Paris, 1958. (Bibliothèque Iranienne 8.)

SCHELER, MAX. *The Nature of Sympathy,* tr. Peter Heath. New Haven, 1954.

SCHELLING, FRIEDRICH VON. *Introduction à la philosophie de la mythologie,* tr. S. Jankelevitch.

SEMNĀNĪ, ʿALĀ'UDDAWLA. "Tafsīr." MS in possession of the author.

SHAʿRĀNĪ (AL-), ʿABDU'L-WAHHĀB. *Kitāb al-Yawāqīt.* 2 vols. Cairo, 1305/1888.

SHAHRASTĀNĪ, ABU'L-FATḤ MUḤAMMAD. *Kitāb al-Milal wa'l-Niḥal.* Lith. Teheran, n.d.

SÖDERBERG, HANS. *La Religion des Cathares.* Uppsala, 1949.

SOURIAU, ÉTIENNE. *Avoir une âme, essai sur les existences virtuelles.* Paris, 1938.
———. *Les différents modes d'existence.* Paris, 1943.
———. *L'Ombre de Dieu.* Paris, 1955.
STROTHMANN, RUDOLF. *Gnosis-Texte der Ismailiten; arabische Handschrift Ambrosiana H 75.* Göttingen, 1943. (Abhandlungen der Göttinger Akademie der Wissenschaften, Phil.-Hist. Kl., 3. Folge, No. 28.)
———. See also JA'FAR IBN MANSŪRI AL-YAMAN.
SUHRAWARDĪ, SHIHĀBADDĪN YAḤYĀ. *Ḥikmat al-Ishrāq.* In: CORBIN, HENRY, ed., *Œuvres philosophiques et mystiques de Sohrawardī* (= *Opera metaphysica et mystica,* II). Teheran and Paris, 1952.
SUZUKI, DAISETZ TEITARO. *Essays in Zen Buddhism.* First and Third Series. 2nd edn., London, 1949 and 1953.
VAJDA, GEORGES. *L'Amour de Dieu dans la théologie juive du Moyen Age.* Paris, 1957.
———. *Juda ben Nissim ibn Malka, philosophe juif marocain.* Paris, 1954.
VALLI, LUIGI. *Il Linguaggio segreto di Dante e dei "Fedeli d'amore."* Rome, 1928. (Biblioteca di filosofia e scienza 10.)
WALTHER, GERDA. *Die Phänomenologie der Mystik.* Olten, 1955.
YAḤIÀ, 'OSMĀN. *L'Histoire et la classification des œuvres d'Ibn 'Arabī.* Damascus, 1964.

INDEX

INDEX

Index

Index

Index

Index